INSTITUTE FOR PUBLIC POLICY RESEARCH

Understanding Local Needs

by
Janie Percy-Smith
and Ian Sanderson

AUTHORS' ACKNOWLEDGEMENTS

The authors would like to thank all those who have assisted in the various stages of the Knowing About Needs project. In particular, we would like to thank the Institute for Public Policy Research (and especially Anna Coote) for commissioning the original research; Leeds City Council for funding it; the project steering group for overseeing the research; the interviewers, research assistants and data technicians who were involved in the fieldwork; all the residents of Kirkstall who participated in the project; the professionals and front-line service providers who agreed to be interviewed; and colleagues at the Policy Research Unit who assisted with various parts of the work; and Paul Wetherly who has been involved in the project from the beginning and who read and commented on more than one draft of Part One.

CONTENTS

Section II: INTERMEDIATE NEEDS

INTRODUCTION

Anyone concerned with reshaping Britain's welfare state for the 21st century must address the question of need. Whatever else a welfare system is about - and this is a subject of deepening controversy - it is surely about the collective provision of services and facilities to meet individual needs. Broadly speaking, decisions are taken to pool resources where it is thought to be impossible, inefficient or unfair for individuals to meet their own needs, and yet to be in the general interest for their needs to be met.

But this is not a simple matter. Half a century has passed since William Beveridge published his report, upon which the modern welfare state was founded. Beveridge had a clear idea about people's needs, which was more or less appropriate for his time. The mass of the population in a nation emerging from years of slump and war was afflicted by urgent and basic problems (in Beveridge's words, the "five giants": Want, Disease, Ignorance, Squalor and Idleness). They needed, first and foremost, jobs, then homes, education, health care and a basic level of financial security.

Fifty years later, society has changed considerably - and in no small part as a consequence of welfare state policies. While society used to be shaped like a pyramid, with a small proportion of well-off people at the top and everyone else at the mercy of the "five giants", it now looks more like a rugby ball: there's a band of privilege at the top, and a small but significant proportion at the bottom who are still sorely disadvantaged. But the large middle section is full of individuals who are reasonably healthy, well off and well educated, and who can rely in temporary periods of sickness or unemployment on a national health service and a social security system.

As this new configuration has emerged, people have developed new and diverse expectations and desires. Increasingly, they are distrustful of politicians, suspicious of large government and reluctant to pay taxes. They do not want to be told what is good for them. At the same time, the costs of running the welfare state have risen alarmingly, due to changes in the age profile of the population, and to expensive new technologies, especially in health care.

Conventional ideas about meeting needs are thus being undermined from two directions. On the one hand, individuals who have grown up under a welfare state are casting doubts upon the competence of politicians and "experts" to decide, behind closed doors, what everyone needs. On the other, those who want to contain costs and achieve better value for money are challenging old certainties about *which* needs should be met collectively, and by what means. All of this lends a special urgency to the question: *How are needs defined and measured for the purpose of planning, delivering and evaluating public services and facilities?*

The project described in the following pages attempts to address this question. It is a pilot study of a Needs Audit, the first of its kind in Britain, commissioned by the Institute for Public Policy Research, as a key component of its programme to develop strategies for a modern welfare system. The study has been funded by Leeds City Council and carried out by a team at the Policy Research Unit of Leeds Metropolitan University.

The auditing team, led by Janie Percy-Smith and Ian Sanderson, has been able to draw upon a wealth of practical experience in conducting social audits. A strong conceptual framework has been provided by the work of Len Doyal and Ian Gough, whose book, *A Theory of Human Need*, was published in 1992 by Macmillan. Ian Gough provides a brief introduction to their work in the opening chapter of this report.

We set out to discover how far a needs audit such as this one could help in building a more open, responsive and effective welfare system. The audit was designed with three basic objectives: to identify individuals' perceptions of how far their needs were being met; to involve service users, community groups, front-line workers and professionals in assessing services and facilities, and to empower communities by providing information which could help them monitor services and facilities and hold policy-makers accountable. More specifically, the aims of the study were as follows:

- To apply the conceptual framework derived from the work of Doyal and Gough to provide the basis for a coherent analysis of needs.

- To examine people's own perceptions of their needs in relation to health and welfare, and to compare these with the views of policy makers, community representatives and service-providers.

- To examine how far needs are currently being satisfied by public service provision in the area of health and welfare.

- To articulate people's experience of existing services and facilities, and their views about how these could be improved or changed.

- To attempt to reconcile differing perspectives on health and welfare needs and to achieve a consensus on what the priorities for action ought to be.

- To identify strengths and weaknesses in the needs auditing model used.

The report falls into two parts. The first evaluates the auditing methods adopted for the study. The second presents the detailed findings of the Audit, which was conducted in the Kirkstall ward of Leeds. If we appear to have put the cart before the horse, that is because the main purpose of the project has been to test the potential of the needs auditing process, so that the methods we have used in Leeds can be adapted in the light of our experience and applied in other neighbourhoods, as an integral part of local policy-making. For enabling us to do this, we are especially grateful to the people of Kirkstall, who participated in the project knowing that it was only a pilot study and bore no immediate promise of change in their own conditions. They would doubtless agree that the usefulness of a needs audit, however faultless its design and execution, must be judged by the policies and practices to which it contributes.

Anna Coote
Series Editor.

PART 1

1:1: WHAT ARE HUMAN NEEDS?
Ian Gough

What are human needs? We all use the term: 'We need to fix this roof' ... 'That family really needs some financial assistance' ... 'My mother needs a home help'. Yet the idea of common human needs has been criticised and denounced in recent years. From the New Right, needs are viewed as the impositions of professionals and other do gooders. To gear social policy to common human needs, it is argued, is to risk paternalism at best and dictatorship at worst; far better to listen to and meet people's wants or demands via the market. This hostility finds an echo on the left and among social movements and community groups. Needs are defined by those with power, whether experts, men, whites, the able bodied, and are imposed on the powerless - women, blacks, people with disabilities, the poor. A needs based strategy, far from being a path to liberation, is all too often a source of oppression.

The result of all this has been either scepticism that human needs exist, or a belief that all needs are relative. Most researchers in Britain and other developed countries accept that deprivation is relative to place and time, that the meanings of food and shelter, for example, are defined by the roles and expectations which membership of a social group entails. Representatives of social movements argue that particular groups have needs, but that they can only be truly known by members of those groups, whether elderly, black, people with disabiltities, single mothers and so on. Clearly, if this is so, any common yardstick of welfare is unattainable, and a comprehensive audit of needs such as that which we have attempted cannot succeed.

Yet despite all this, the idea of common or universal human needs won't go away. And for good reason: the notion that all people have basic human needs and that we can chart how far they are met or not met is central to any coherent idea of social policy and social progress. This study uses a theory developed by Len Doyal and myself which attempts to overcome these limitations (Doyal and Gough, 1991). It is summarised in Figure 1.

The meanings of 'need'

To begin with, some conceptual clarification is necessary, since need is such an ubiquitous word in the English language. Let us distinguish three common usages of the noun and verb 'need'. First, it can refer to a 'drive' or motivational force, such as the need to sleep or eat. Maslow (1943) interprets the term thus in his famous hierarchy of needs. This meaning draws our attention to the biological aspects of human behaviour over which we have no choice. For example, ultimately we all have to sleep. But over a far broader spectrum of behaviour biology constrains rather than determines human choice, hence we are only indirectly concerned with needs interpreted in these terms.

Secondly, 'need' is universally used to refer to any necessary means to a given end. For example, to say 'I need a new hi fi' implies that I have the goal of a better quality of reproduced music. It is this protean use of the word (and its equivalents in other languages) that in part explains the widespread view that needs are essentially relative. The truth behind this is that all needs statements conform to the relational structure 'A needs X in order to Y'. We will refer at times to the means necessary to attain specific ends, but when doing so we will qualify the word need in some way, or use the term 'need satisfier'.

Thirdly, the question is, therefore, whether or not there is some Y which can be said to be in the interest of everyone to achieve, whatever their culture. Generally speaking the answer is clearly

FIGURE 1
The theory in outline

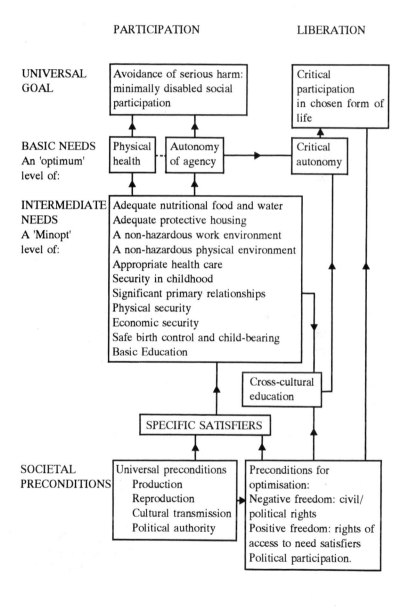

PARTICIPATION   LIBERATION

UNIVERSAL GOAL — Avoidance of serious harm: minimally disabled social participation | Critical participation in chosen form of life

BASIC NEEDS An 'optimum' level of: — Physical health | Autonomy of agency | Critical autonomy

INTERMEDIATE NEEDS A 'Minopt' level of: — Adequate nutritional food and water / Adequate protective housing / A non-hazardous work environment / A non-hazardous physical environment / Appropriate health care / Security in childhood / Significant primary relationships / Physical security / Economic security / Safe birth control and child-bearing / Basic Education

Cross-cultural education

SPECIFIC SATISFIERS

SOCIETAL PRECONDITIONS — Universal preconditions / Production / Reproduction / Cultural transmission / Political authority | Preconditions for optimisation: / Negative freedom: civil/ political rights / Positive freedom: rights of access to need satisfiers / Political participation.

yes. All persons have an objective interest in avoiding serious *harm* which in turn prevents them from pursuing their vision of the good, whatever that is. This pursuit of the good entails, as others have argued, an ability to *participate* in the form of life in which they find themselves.

If there are preconditions for social participation which apply to everyone in the same way then universal needs can be said to exist. Needs can thus be distinguished from wants. To repeat a hackneyed example, a diabetic may want sugar, but she needs insulin. She even needs insulin if she does not know of its existence. She needs it ultimately because without it her social participation will become more and more impaired. This is an objective situation and is not necessarily reflected in subjective feelings such as unhappiness. Nor is it an 'individualist' concept. We all live our lives in groups and build our conceptions of ourselves through participating with others in social life. Nor, lastly, is it a static concept: we may wish to participate in a social form of life other than that which we grew up in.

If human needs are the universal preconditions for participation in social life, we contend that all people have a strong right to need satisfaction. This follows because membership of all social groups entails corresponding duties, yet without adequate levels of need satisfaction a person will be unable to act in accordance with those duties. It is contradictory to ask of someone that they fulfil their social duties, yet to deny them the pre-requisite need satisfaction which will enable them to do so. This is why social rights of citizenship follow from an unambiguous concept of human need.

Basic Needs

Basic human needs, then, are the universal pre-requisites for successful and, if necessary, critical participation in a social form of life. We identify these universal pre-requisites as *physical health* and *autonomy* (see Figure 1).

The bottom line, so to speak, of physical health is survival: to act and to participate we need to be at least alive, so survival chances are an important indicator here. However, much more than this is required if social participation is not to be seriously impaired. We must also enjoy a modicum of good physical health. Health can be conceptualised in negative terms as the absence of specific diseases, where disease is defined according to the biomedical model. This is best operationalised via measures of disease patterns and disability. 'Disability', according to the WHO, is any restriction on a person's ability to perform an activity in the manner or within the range considered normal for a human being. It is distinguished from 'handicap' which is an explicitly social notion referring to limits on a person's ability to fulfil a social role.

Yet physical health alone is insufficient to tap impairments to successful social participation, as the broader WHO definition of positive health acknowledges. Autonomy of agency - *the capacity to make informed choices about what should be done and how to go about doing it* - is the definitive attribute of human beings. We contend that autonomy is impaired when there is a deficit of three attributes: mental health, cognitive skills and opportunities to engage in social participation.

The concept, even the very existence, of mental health has, of course, aroused fierce debate and relativist criticism. Yet mental illness, defined as an 'extreme and prolonged inability to deal in a rational way with one's environment', undermines a person's confidence and competence to participate in social life in all cultures.

The second component of autonomy of agency comprises the cognitive skills necessary for social participation. These include a person's understanding of the rules of her culture and her ability to reason about them and interpret them. These require both culturally specific skills and universal skills, such as language use and literacy. The opportunity to participate in significant social roles

constitutes the third component of autonomy of agency. We identify
four social roles common to all human societies which we label
production, reproduction, cultural transmission and political
authority. To be deprived of the opportunity to participate in any of
these, let alone all of them, is a serious restriction of personal
autonomy. This restriction can of course stem from many different
factors, including cultural rules (eg. the exclusion of women from
certain roles), economic circumstances (eg. unemployment or
poverty) or role stress stemming from conflicting demands (eg. the
'dual burden' of many women).

We have specified the general preconditions for successful
participation in any social form of life. But some forms of life are
extremely oppressive to their members, and all harm some of their
members. Successful participation in a cruel or exploitative system
is hardly a recipe for welfare. Beyond the goal of successful
participation lies the goal of critical participation in a social life
form which is, as far as possible, of one's own choosing (Figure 1).
Beyond autonomy of agency lies critical autonomy - the ability to
situate, criticise and, if necessary, challenge the rules and practices
of the culture one is born into, or presently lives in. Critical
autonomy entails the same levels of physical and mental health as
autonomy of agency but wider cognitive skills and social
opportunities.

Intermediate Needs

So a needs audit should try to assess the levels of physical health
and critical autonomy of different individuals and groups. But this
does not get us very far. These basic needs can be met in numerous
different ways. Common needs do not imply uniform satisfiers - far
from it. There is an almost infinite variety of goods, services,
activities and relationships which, to a greater or lesser extent, meet
basic needs. It is this openendedness which has led many
researchers who accept the theoretical possibility of universal needs
to argue that their objective assessment is beyond our reach. How

is relativism of this second sort to be rebutted? There are two levels at which this problem can be handled.

The first level involves the identification of those characteristics of need satisfiers which everywhere contribute to improved physical health and autonomy. Let us call these intermediate needs. For example, provision of energy and/or protein is (or should be) a common property of foodstuffs, protection from the elements is (or should be) a common property of dwellings, and so on. These intermediate needs are grouped into 11 categories in Figure 1. Nine of these apply to all people, one refers to the specific needs of children, and another to the specific needs of women for safe birth control and child bearing. All eleven are essential to protect the health and autonomy of people, and thus to enable them to participate to the maximum extent in their social form of life, whatever that is. So a needs audit should try to measure the levels at which all these intermediate needs are satisfied.

But even this is insufficiently detailed if we want to get at the level of welfare of small scale communities, and if we want an audit to inform social policies in the community. We need, secondly, to identify those specific satisfiers which best meet local needs, and to monitor people's access to these. Here the focus is on more specific goods, services and policies which do, or could, improve human welfare in particular social situations such as in a particular area of a city.

It is this task which the Leeds audit set itself. The ambit of the study is very broad - and necessarily so. Human needs are a complex set of pre-requisites for effective human action and social interaction. If any one of them is absent, people suffer and their health and autonomy is impaired. So auditing human needs cannot simply mimic market research, which can quite reasonably enquire into people's views about a particular brand of cigarette or soap powder. Assessing needs means gaining some overview about all aspects of life vital to people's capacity to participate in society.

How Should Needs be Audited?

If this much is agreed, we still face the question of how to assess
need satisfaction in practice. Further awkward problems are then
posed. What indicators of basic and intermediate needs should be
used? What standards of need satisfaction should be set in order to
calculate shortfalls in welfare? Above all, who should decide the
answer to these and other thorny questions? Two extreme
approaches have traditionally been adopted in answer to these
questions, each suffering from different deficiencies and entailing
different dangers.

On the one hand, there is the 'expert knows best' approach. If
objective needs are not necessarily the same as subjective wants,
then you cannot simply ask people what they need. You must
instead rely on the knowledge of experts, professionals, researchers
and so on. For example, a doctor has specialised knowledge which
enables her, given the appropriate information, to judge people's
state of health in a more informed way than can people themselves.
Similarly, nutritionists can specify objective criteria with which to
evaluate diets whatever our own views about what is good for us.
Yet this 'top down' approach to determining and auditing needs has
drawbacks and dangers which are only too well known. Experts
and professionals can put their own interests before the well being
of their clients or research subjects. Often too they will be so
ignorant of the reality of life for ordinary people that their
proposals can be counter-productive or just plain stupid.

A general revulsion against professional and bureaucratic dictat has
fuelled support for the opposite approach. This stresses the right
and ability of different communities and groups to decide on their
own needs and to do their own need audits. The detailed knowledge
we have of our own communities can be tapped and the
participation and empowerment of ordinary people encouraged.
Many of the progressive community initiatives of recent years have
advocated and practised this 'bottom up' approach to needs

auditing. Yet this too has its drawbacks and dangers. For one thing it can advantage the already privileged in a group, or those groups with more resources. For another, it can simply endorse prejudice and ignorance, whatever the evidence against them. Lastly, it offers no way of reconciling different notions of need and cannot establish common criteria of welfare other than the lowest common denominator of whatever the separate groups will endorse.

A needs audit, we would argue, must accept and seek to overcome this profound antinomy between top down and bottom up approaches. Related to this, it must also try to situate the 'codified knowledge' of researchers in all the fields of basic and intermediate needs listed above alongside the 'experientially grounded' knowledge of ordinary people in their everyday lives. More than this, it must enable them to confront each other and try to reconcile any differences which emerge.

This is the methodology adopted in this study. First, it has used whatever codified knowledge is available in official data sources to chart local patterns of health, economic security and other indicators of need satisfaction. Second, a range of local representatives, service providers and professionals have been questioned to get their views on detailed needs and need shortfalls in the study area. On the other hand, the audit has attempted to tap the experientially grounded knowledge of people in the study area via a postal questionnaire and follow up interviews of a smaller sample. Last, and perhaps most innovative, public meetings were arranged at which these two perspectives on needs in Leeds could be summarised, conflicts of opinion identified and a start made in agreeing on the needs which should be given priority for satisfaction. In this way the study can feed into the next stage which is actually improving the environment and services so that well being can be improved.

This methodology is open-ended but cumulative. Though basic and intermediate needs are universal, the forms in which they can be met, and the levels at which they can be satisfied, are continually open to improvement. Yet this does not endorse a relativist position of 'anything goes'. The test of what to include, of what measures to use, of what policies to back, is always the idea of universal human need outlined above, and an acceptance that we can learn about, and judge between, better and worse methods of meeting needs. New insights gleaned from a study such as this should be incorporated into the evolving stock of codified knowledge about needs - unless and until they are in turn overthrown by superior ways of understanding and improving human welfare.

1:2. THEORY INTO PRACTICE

The development of a methodology for community needs auditing was founded upon two bases. Firstly, Doyal and Gough's theoretical work outlined in the previous chapter produces a framework for defining and assessing the main dimensions of need to provide the foundation for the development of social welfare policies. Secondly, the objective of 'empowerment' produces a requirement for a methodology which enables and encourages communities to participate actively and fully in the articulation of their own needs. These two bases address, respectively, substantive and procedural aspects of the rights of citizenship which should be embodied in a modern welfare system (Coote, 1990).

The purpose of this chapter is two-fold. First, it outlines the rationale for the formulation of an auditing methodology and describes the 'Needs in Leeds' methodology in detail. The second purpose is to evaluate our success in implementing this methodology and the extent to which it fulfils the substantive and procedural requirements outlined above, and to draw out lessons for future development.

Rationale for the Needs Auditing Methodology

The substantive and procedural dimensions of the theoretical framework discussed in part 1:1 embody a critique of traditional approaches to needs assessment in which experts and professionals play a predominant role. In particular, an emphasis on professionally-defined need satisfiers can obscure the essentially political nature of the task of assessing need satisfaction. If we accept that there exists a variety of interests and values among different, often conflicting, groups we must be wary of consensual assumptions implied in the dominance of any one approach to defining how needs should be met, which should be the subject of open debate and participation by all interested parties.

To promote such open debate and full participation the process of needs auditing must seek to overcome the dichotomy between 'top-down' and 'bottom-up' approaches (part 1:1). The core of the needs auditing methodology involves a combination of top-down and bottom-up approaches to go beyond the bare sketch provided by available data sources. There are several components to the methodology. Firstly, the audit attempts to tap experientially grounded knowledge in a systematic way to obtain a reliable quantitative picture of what Bradshaw (1972) terms 'felt' needs through a questionnaire survey of a sample of individuals in the community. Secondly, in-depth interviews are conducted with a number of respondents to obtain qualitative information which provides a fuller understanding of the 'meaning' of the quantitative picture.

The third component involves conducting in-depth interviews with local community groups and politicians who represent the people and provide a 'collective' perspective on needs. The fourth element in the core of the methodology comprises interviews with professionals involved in delivering services to the community in order to obtain the 'top-down' picture of needs. The emphasis here is placed on 'front-line' workers who work most closely with clients and their needs.

Having obtained information on needs and their satisfiers from this broad range of perspectives there arises the issue of how to accommodate the 'political' process of negotiation of a reconciliation between the different perspectives. An initial attempt is made at this through public meetings held in the community, at which the different perspectives are summarised, areas of conflict identified, and a start is made in negotiating a consensus on needs and on priorities for their satisfaction.

The outputs from such a community needs audit feed into the next stage of the policy-making process where appropriate policies and action are formulated taking into account availability of resources and competing calls on those resources from other communities and programmes. The relationship between needs auditing and the broader policy-making process is discussed more fully in part 1:4.

Having outlined the rationale for the formulation of an approach to community needs auditing and the components of our methodology, we can now describe in more detail how the methodology was implemented in this Leeds audit study.

Needs Auditing in Practice: Needs in Leeds

The main stages in the implementation of needs auditing in the Leeds study are summarised below and discussed in more detail in this section:

(i)   Select a study area in Leeds for implementation of the audit

(ii)   Collect existing available data relating to the study area to provide 'codified knowledge' of needs

(iii)   Undertake pre-survey 'ground work' in the study area to publicise the audit and establish contacts with the relevant statutory services, voluntary organisations and community groups

(iv)   Undertake a 10 per cent sample postal survey of adult residents in the study area to obtain information on residents' perceptions of their 'felt' needs and the extent to which these are being met by existing services

(v)   Conduct in-depth interviews with a sub-sample of respondents from selected groups to obtain more qualitative information on individual felt needs

(vi)   Undertake structured discussions with a range of community groups and representatives and voluntary organisations in the area to obtain a more 'collective' view of needs

(vii)   Undertake structured discussions with a range of professionals and front-line local workers involved in service delivery in the area to obtain information on their perspective on the levels of need satisfaction in the area

(viii)   Integrate findings from study of codified knowledge, 'bottom-up' and 'top-down' approaches and highlight areas of consensus and disagreement

(ix)   Organise public meetings to bring together individuals, groups, voluntary workers and professionals to discuss the issues and determine the potential for consensus on needs and priorities.

For this pilot project a study area was required which provided a variety of socio-economic conditions within an area convenient for analysis. On the basis of an examination of available data from the 1981 Census, supplemented by local knowledge, the Kirkstall electoral ward was selected as satisfying the criteria. The ward, situated in west Leeds, is long and narrow and stretches nearly three miles from the inner city Burley Lodges area along the north slope of the Aire Valley through suburban areas of Burley and Kirkstall to Hawksworth Wood, a large 'peripheral' council estate, and the 'Vespers' an area of private housing including a significant modern development. For the purpose of this study, the ward was sub-divided into the four areas of the Vespers, Hawksworth Wood, Kirkstall and Burley.

There is a broad mix of housing types and tenures in the ward including 'back-to-back' terraces (Burley area), private detached and semi-detached (Burley, Kirkstall and Vespers), council houses

(Hawksworth Wood) and some council flats and maisonettes. The total population of the ward is around 20,000 with above average proportions of younger people up to 29 years and elderly people aged 65 and over compared with the city as a whole. The proportion of the ward's 'non-white' population is above the average for Leeds as a whole with groups of Asian origin predominating, the proportion of Afro-Caribbean and other groups being below average. The majority of the ethnic minority groups live in the Burley area of the ward.

The proportion of people in employment in the ward is below the average for Leeds as a whole. This is due to above average levels of unemployment but also a relatively low activity rate due to the high proportions of younger people in further education and of elderly, retired people, consistent with the age structure discussed above. Kirkstall ward ranks relatively high on various indicators of deprivation from the 1981 census as reflected in its ranking of ninth in Leeds on the Jarman Index which is used to identify 'under privileged' areas for the purpose of planning GP services.

Having defined the study area, the next stage involved the collection of available sources of data which could provide codified knowledge on indicators of need. The aim was to attempt to build a picture of needs from such sources which could be compared with that emerging from our primary research. Sources of data examined included the 1981 Census, information from the local authority housing and social services departments, and from the local health authority, crime statistics, and so on.

An important aspect of the study which required considerable time and effort involved 'ground work ' in the study area to inform relevant people about the audit and enlist their co-operation and to establish contact with statutory services, voluntary organisations and community groups in the areas. This involved letters, phone calls and meetings, the distribution of publicity material explaining the exercise and a press release to local press and radio. A pre-survey leaflet was prepared and sent in advance to all individuals sampled for the questionnaire survey and this contained a summary in the relevant ethnic minority languages.

The postal questionnaire survey was designed to tap the opinions of individuals about needs and need shortfall in their household and community. The target response sample was 10 per cent of the adult population (ie 1,500-1,600 individuals) and a systematic random sample of some 4,600 adults was taken from the electoral register, employing an assumed response rate of about one third. A questionnaire was designed to obtain information on the level of satisfaction of the basic and intermediate needs derived from the theoretical framework outlined in part 1:1 (see Figure 1). A set of needs indicators was derived as follows:

Basic Needs Indicators

- A good standard of general health
- Freedom from stress, worries and depression
- Having spare time for personal and leisure activities

Intermediate Needs Indicators

- A good standard of education
- A healthy diet and safe drinking water
- A decent standard of housing
- A job with safe and healthy working conditions
- A satisfying job
- Living in a pleasant, clean and peaceful area
- Access to health care services
- Access to social services
- Having close friends and relatives who can be relied upon
- Having enough money and insurance to feel reasonably secure
- Being safe from acts of crime and violence
- Having an influence on decisions of organisations

- Feeling confident in one's children's future.

In broad terms, the questionnaire was designed to obtain both factual and judgemental information from respondents in relation to these indicators, although not all were covered in the same degree of detail. The questionnaire was divided into a number of sections with the following headings:

- About You and Your Household
- About Your Quality of Life
- About Your Home and Environment
- About Work and Money
- About Your General Health
- About Health and Welfare Services
- About Social and Community Contacts
- About Your Children

Questions were designed to determine the perceived importance of the various indicators, the respondent's current status, perceived problems, satisfaction with current services and views on desired changes. The questionnaire was quite lengthy but considerable attention was given to the framing of questions and response categories, structure and routing to ensure ease of completion. Maximum possible use was made of pre-coded responses with 'tick-boxes', and the number of 'open-ended' questions was minimised. A number of health and social service workers were consulted on the design and content of the questionnaire and piloting exercises were conducted with students, with elderly people at a local day centre and with parents and workers at a local day nursery.

The questionnaire was posted to specific identified individuals and, in order to encourage response to the survey, all people who completed and returned a questionnaire were offered the chance to enter a 'Prize Draw' with three prizes of £100, £60 and £30. In the event a total of 1,529 valid responses was received which represents 33.4 per cent of the original sample and achieved the target of 10 per cent of the adult population. These responses were coded and input for computer analysis using SPSSX Data Entry II. Data analysis was undertaken using the SPSSX statistical package.

The response sample provided a reasonably good representation of the population of the study area although there were certain specific deficiencies. Thus, younger people were rather under-represented, especially younger men, whereas the elderly were over-represented, especially older men. As regards ethnicity, members of the Asian community were under-represented and this was a cause for concern which will be discussed later. In terms of economic activity status, the response from the unemployed was somewhat below average whereas retired people, those looking after home and family and the long term sick and disabled were rather over-represented.

Respondents were asked to indicate on their completed questionnaires whether or not they would be prepared to be interviewed in greater depth in the next stage of the audit to follow up their responses to the postal survey. The aim of this stage of the exercise was to obtain more detailed qualitative information in face-to-face interviews to allow a better understanding of the 'meaning' of responses to the postal questionnaire.

It was decided to focus in this stage on selected sub-groups of the sample defined in life-cycle and socio-economic terms. The elderly and women with young children (aged under 11 years) were selected because they tend to be particularly heavy users of health and welfare services and to require specific need satisfiers. It was also decided to target ethnic minority respondents in view of the relatively low response amongst this group to the questionnaire survey.

An interview schedule was prepared and a team of four experienced interviewers was recruited, one of whom was of Asian origin to undertake the interviews with ethnic minority respondents. People were contacted and those willing to be interviewed were visited in their homes. A total of 75 interviews was completed, 32 and 33 respectively with the elderly and women with young children spread across the ward, and 10 with ethnic minority respondents, mainly in the Burley area.

As indicated earlier, extensive ground work was undertaken prior to the questionnaire survey to establish contact with statutory service providers, voluntary organisations and community groups. This was seen as important in terms of generating interest in, and commitment to the audit. Contacts made at that stage were kept informed of progress as a basis for arranging subsequent interviews to obtain their perspectives on the problems and needs of people in the area.

A semi-structured interview schedule was prepared taking the form of a broad frame-work of issues for discussion with individuals or groups of people. The topics covered were housing, access to local facilities, problems and risks in the local area, financial problems, health and welfare services, informal caring, community and voluntary activity and children. However, not all these topics were covered in every interview due to time constraints on interviewees. Two experienced workers were recruited to assist with these interviews with a wide range of individuals and groups (Appendix).

Following completion of the postal survey and interviewing stages of the audit, all the information collected was analysed and a short summary report was produced outlining some of the main findings and highlighting key issues for discussion. This report was circulated to all the professionals and community and voluntary organisations who had been interviewed and also distributed in local libraries, health centres and community centres to form the basis for discussion at public meetings.

Three public meetings were organised in different parts of the study area. Publicity leaflets were printed, circulated widely and displayed in local shops, pubs, community centres and public places. In addition, a press release was sent to local media resulting in several articles in the local press and radio interviews.

This publicity was intended to encourage local people to attend the meetings. Specific invitations were extended to all the local professionals and community and voluntary organisations who had been contacted during the course of the study and to local councillors and the MP. At each meeting a presentation of the main findings of the study was made and followed by a chaired discussion of key issues focussing on trying to reach consensus on the issues requiring action and on priorities.

The three meetings were attended by a total of 42 people, mostly local residents and representatives of local community groups although some professional workers also attended, drawn from health and social services, education and police. The majority of those attending were women, all were white and there were no younger people (under 25) present.

Examples of Findings

Residents, community representatives and local workers were asked to indicate what factors contributed to quality of life and well-being. Overall factors relating to health were seen as most important: 92 per cent of residents considered that 'having a good standard of general health' was very important. On the other hand, only 57 per cent of residents thought that having access to social services was very important and only 54 per cent considered it very important to have an influence on organisations whose decisions affect their lives.

There were differences between age groups. The elderly gave relatively higher value to being safe from crime, living in a pleasant, clean and peaceful area, having financial security and access to social services. Younger people tended to attach lower value to most factors, especially being free from stress, worries and depression, living in a pleasant area and having a satisfying job. On the other hand they valued spare time more highly than older people.

Differences also emerged between the values and priorities of the various groups of local professionals, particularly between police and probation workers and health and social service workers. The former tended to place less value on all factors, especially having a safe and satisfying job, having access to social services and support from friends, and having an influence on organisations.

These differences indicate potential difficulties in gaining a consensus between different groups but they also strengthen the case for ensuring that a wide range of views is obtained in needs auditing exercises.

Some 22 per cent of residents reported poor or very poor health increasing to 27 per cent in the Hawksworth Wood area where a third of people also reported a long-standing illness, disability or infirmity. Our findings highlighted the inter-relationship between poor health and a range of external factors such as poor housing and environment, unemployment and financial hardship.

These factors also clearly contribute to reported problems of mental health particularly stress, worry and depression. For example, over a third of the unemployed reported a serious problem with worry and anxiety and about a quarter with stress and depression. Worry and anxiety is also a problem for a significant number of women with young children. These findings are important because such problems will not be reflected fully in demand for primary health care.

We found a relatively high level of awareness of the harmful effects of smoking, drinking, poor diet and lack of exercise. For example, 60 per cent of smokers thought that they smoked too much for the good of their health. A half of those aged 18-34 thought that they did not get enough exercise for good health, and a quarter of this age group thought that their diet was not good for their health. Such awareness was higher among younger than among older age groups. Our findings suggest that the problem is not lack of awareness but rather circumstances which prevent people from changing their habits - related, for example, to time, money and motivation. This has implications for health promotion policy.

Our interviews with front-line workers highlighted the relationship between poor housing conditions and health and social problems. Of the respondents themselves, nearly a quarter indicated that they had a serious problem with poor heating in their homes and a fifth with dampness and condensation. These problems were suffered disproportionately by young people, ethnic minorities and the unemployed.

Over a third of residents indicated that they felt financially insecure or very insecure and significant proportions reported serious difficulties in paying household bills. For example, over half of all respondents reported serious difficulties with their poll tax and nearly a quarter with their fuel bills. Elderly people expressed most concern about poll tax, fuel and phone bills whereas younger people reported greatest difficulty with clothes, furniture and housing costs. Those experiencing financial difficulties were more likely to report 'mental health' problems, especially those who had difficulty paying for food.

We produced a detailed picture of the implications of financial hardship for lifestyle and health - people going without 'luxuries' like holidays, days out, 'treats for the kids', Christmas presents, new clothes, books and toys; people getting into debt, often with 'loan sharks', especially at Christmas.

One in ten of all residents was involved in caring for a sick, elderly or disabled person and the audit indicated the scale of such informal caring in terms of the tasks taken on by carers and the relief provided by the statutory health and welfare services. Carers indicated their main needs as better financial support and better advice and information, ie. more support from the state to enable them to undertake their caring responsibilities better. Our findings indicated a need for a more detailed study of the problems and needs of carers.

A range of problems faced by children was revealed. In certain areas long-standing and repeated illness was related to the complex of problems of poor housing, financial hardship, poor environment etc. Lack of space and safe facilities for young children to play was particularly problematical in the Burley area. Many parents were concerned about lack of creche and pre-school facilities and also about the safety of their children in the street and local parks. There was also concern about the lack of facilities and activities for older children which was widely seen as contributing to them "getting into trouble". One aspect of this was the high cost of using sports facilities.

The audit produced valuable detailed information about specific problems and needs in relation to local facilities and amenities. Examples were the poor choice and high cost of local shopping facilities, accessibility and mobility problems in certain groups and areas, the need for pedestrian crossings, the need for community facilities, particularly for the Asian community, the lack of safe play facilities for younger children and activities for older children, problems with dumping of rubbish and with dogs. Such information is particularly valuable because improvements in local facilities and amenities which address problems and needs identified by local people and workers can make a significant impact on people's perceived quality of life often at relatively limited cost.

The audit revealed a relatively low level of community participation; for example, only seven per cent of residents were members of a community, tenants' or residents' association. In interviews a degree of cynicism about politicians was expressed and a majority of people felt that they had no influence over central government (81 per cent) or the local authority (68 per cent). The audit revealed a strong sense of powerlessness in the community but also a desire amongst some for more power to control their own lives.

We found interviews with front-line community health workers to be valuable in highlighting the scale of health problems and understanding their causes. Health visitors, school nurses, community psychiatric nurses etc are clearly very close to the problems which people face and their detailed, first-hand knowledge is of great potential value in the policy-making process. However, such front-line workers have been a neglected resource. Our findings reinforce the case for ensuring full involvement of, and participation by, such front-line workers in the policy process.

Problems, Issues and Lessons

There are several aspects to the evaluation of the Knowing About Needs study. How successful was the methodology in terms of application of the theory of need outlined in part 1:1? How successful was the methodology in auditing needs in a community? What were the main problems and how should they be addressed? What are the main lessons for the further development of needs auditing practice?

As regards application of the theoretical framework there are, as indicated in the introduction to this chapter, both substantive and procedural aspects to consider. Substantively, we can ask how well the methodology performs in terms of collecting appropriate information about people's needs. We would argue that the methodology succeeds in collecting a wide range of different types of information consistent with the theoretical specification. A picture of need is obtained in terms of a broad range of indicators relating to health and well-being. A rich mixture of both quantitative and qualitative information is obtained which can provide a more comprehensive picture and understanding of people's problems and needs. A wide range of different perspectives is tapped combining professionals' views on needs with both collective and individual experientially grounded perspectives on needs.

However, one aspect of the theoretical framework which is rather more problematical concerns the prospects for generating a consensus on the nature of needs and priorities. There are two main problems here. The first concerns the process by which the information on needs from all the different sources and perspectives is synthesised and key differences and issues are highlighted. A 'value free' stance is implied here but there is clearly a danger in practice that a particular set of values will condition this process. The second problem concerns the actual forum which is generated for the discussion and resolution of differences. We would conclude that the public meetings which we convened for this purpose were not very successful and we will return to this problem below.

This raises the procedural dimension of the framework: how successful was the methodology in encouraging the community to participate actively and fully in the articulation of their own needs? The study generated a lot of interest and involvement amongst local groups but since it was essentially a 'pilot research exercise' it was not able to guarantee a 'pay off' in the form of improvements to services to meet identified needs. Clearly, this influenced the commitment of local people, community groups and professionals to the audit. However, on the basis of our experience we are confident that this approach to needs auditing could make a significant contribution to encouraging community participation if it were undertaken as part of the actual process of service planning and development and facilitated by the agencies concerned.

What is required is an approach to needs auditing undertaken in genuine partnership with local communities rather than imposed from outside by professionals working in the relevant agencies. In this context the model of community practice propounded by Bayley et al (1989) is relevant. They identify three stages in the development of community-oriented work. The first stage involves working 'outside the community', the traditional approach of large-scale centralised organisations focussing on people as 'clients' and making little reference to other workers or resources in the locality. The second stage sees the development of working 'alongside the community' which involves decentralisation to localities and the development of community-based inter-agency working as an adjunct to mainstream activities. In the third stage, activity 'within the community' develops where community-based multi-agency working becomes integrated into the community, harnessing resources from all agencies and from the voluntary sector, community groups and individuals (ibid, p51-55).

Given the context of our work it was difficult to generate the degree of local commitment to, and involvement in, needs auditing to achieve working fully 'within the community' and this must to some degree qualify conclusions on the effectiveness of the methodology. However, we did make considerable efforts to contact and consult with locally-based workers in statutory services and voluntary organisations and also local community groups and representatives. This was very important to the credibility of the study and its effectiveness in obtaining information on needs and need satisfaction from a broad range of interests and perspectives.

The results of the study are discussed at length in Part 2 and indicate the limitations of any one source of information on needs and levels of need satisfaction and the importance of obtaining a broad range of information and perspectives. Needs indicators based on secondary data provide a partial and aggregate picture of what Bradshaw (1972) calls 'comparative need' and the limitations of such data are discussed in more detail in the next chapter. A sample questionnaire survey can provide statistically valid, systematic information on people's opinions and experience if the response sample is broadly representative of the population of the study area. However, there are various potential limitations to this means of obtaining information; these are illustrated by our study.

Issues of representativeness of the sample arise in a postal survey which is subject to a differential response from different sectors of the population. Thus, in our response sample younger males and people of Asian origin were rather under-represented, while middle-aged women looking after home and family and retired males were rather over-represented. This pattern is consistent with experience in other postal surveys. An additional interesting indicator of representativeness can be obtained from the comparison of the Kirkstall Ward turnout in the 1990 local elections of 36 per cent with the 63 per cent of our response sample who said they had voted in local elections. It would seem that those who vote are also more inclined to return questionnaires.

Notwithstanding the practical measures we took to encourage response from potentially under-represented groups, the relatively low response to the questionnaire survey from ethnic minority groups, and particularly from people of Asian origin, remains a cause for concern and is discussed in more detail below. More generally, it is clear that in large scale questionnaire surveys there is a trade-off between the amount of information and depth of detail obtainable on the one hand, and response rate on the other. Lengthy and detailed questionnaires deter respondents. Consequently, questionnaire design is a compromise - detail which helps in understanding the 'meaning' of responses is sacrificed.

This is why in-depth, follow-up interviews with a sub-sample of respondents are important to put flesh on the bones of the questionnaire survey findings. These interviewees provided valuable information about people's felt needs, largely of a qualitative nature, although care must be exercised in the interpretation and use of such information. Such interviews are time-consuming and expensive which limits the number which can realistically be undertaken. It is appropriate, therefore, to target interviews on the basis of analysis of the questionnaire survey results, to investigate in greater depth the problems and issues of particular groups in the community.

The issue of representativeness arises again in relation to the interviews with community representatives and professional workers. Problems arise here due to the 'committed' nature of the views of different groups arising from values, motivation and interests partly conditioned, in the case of local workers, by professional background and training. Community groups may have particular pre-occupations which emphasise the interests of their sections of the community. The perspective of local workers will be conditioned by the users of services with whom they come into contact and may not reflect fully the needs of those who do not use services. Indeed, the study revealed certain differences between various professional groupings and community representatives in terms of the perceived importance of the various indicators of needs and quality of life which suggests differences in values and priorities (2.1).

This emphasises the need for a wide range of community representatives and professional workers to be interviewed. We made considerable efforts to obtain interviews with a wide range of people but encountered a recurrent problem of time constraints. In particular, front-line workers in the statutory services are experiencing serious pressures of work which produced difficulties in arranging interviews and limited time to undertake them. However, there was a widespread recognition amongst such professionals of the importance of the study and it is clear that they felt that they had an important contribution to make to needs assessment.

As indicated earlier, front-line workers are traditionally neglected in the assessment of need and our research has highlighted very strongly the crucial importance of their knowledge and experience. Thus, in relation to housing and health problems, and the problems facing children, for example, the knowledge of community health workers mirrored very closely the findings from the questionnaire survey indicating the value of their 'closeness to the client/customer'.

Given the time constraint, interviews with professionals must be carefully planned and conducted in an organised and incisive way by experienced interviewers with an understanding of the issues involved. Busy people must be left with the feeling that their time has been well spent; this also raises the issue of the 'pay off' from the exercise since the prospect of action to improve services to meet needs will help to generate commitment. Here, again, problems arose from the 'research' nature of our study. These could be overcome if the needs auditing exercise was an integral part of the service planning and development process.

The attempt to discuss and negotiate issues and priorities in a series of public meetings proved, in the event, to be the most problematical aspect of the exercise. Despite extensive publicity the meetings were relatively poorly attended particularly by members of the general public. Moreover, the majority of those who did attend were community representatives and activists. Attendance by professionals was poor, despite personal invitations to them, and those who were present seemed reluctant to intervene in the discussion to any great extent. Consequently, the dialogue between professionals, community representatives and local people which we hoped to generate did not really materialise.

To a large degree these problems were not unexpected due to the well-documented tradition of poorly-attended public meetings in situations where there is no single 'burning issue' or threat perceived by the community. In general, the majority of people adopt a rather passive stance in relation to the public policy-making process and this was doubtless reinforced in this case by a scepticism about the prospect of any concrete 'pay off' from our study. So, once again our evaluation of the potential contribution of the auditing methodology in a 'real' policy-making context must be qualified.

It may be that such public meetings are not the best forum for the political process of negotiation between different interest groups over local needs and priorities. The fundamental requirement is to develop a 'culture of participation' whereby local communities are more fully involved on an on-going basis in the process of service planning and development. A needs auditing exercise would then not be a 'one off' exercise in consultation but rather part of a continuing exercise in participation. One way of moving towards this might be through the establishment of 'panels' of local people who can give voice to the concerns and aspirations of the community.

Let us return to the problem of the relatively low degree of involvement in the auditing process on the part of ethnic minority groups, especially those of Asian origin, and highlight some broader implications. Again, there is widespread experience of this in the public policy-making process. We made specific attempts to promote the involvement of ethnic minority groups. We attempted to establish contacts with organisations representing such groups; we provided explanations of the exercise, offering assistance if needed, in the main languages in the pre-survey publicity and accompanying the questionnaire; interviews were undertaken by representatives of these communities.

Nevertheless, we were not very successful in involving these groups in the exercise. Response to the questionnaire survey was relatively low; we had difficulties obtaining follow up interviews with respondents and interviews with community representatives; and these communities were not represented at the public meetings.

In our view, this problem highlights the limitations of needs auditing from 'outside the community', to use again Bayley et al's (1989) model.

This problem strengthens our conviction that needs auditing should focus on specific 'communities' and that members of these communities should be empowered to undertake auditing themselves with appropriate advice, support and resources. This raises the question 'what is a local community'? The audit highlighted a considerable degree of variation within the study area in housing, social and economic conditions and in perceived problems and concerns. There are clearly several 'communities' within the ward but it is not easy to define them precisely. Perhaps the clearest examples are Hawksworth Wood, based on a distinctive council estate, and the Burley Lodges area; other examples might be the old 'village' areas of Burley and Kirkstall. As indicated earlier, 'ethnic minority communities' can be delineated on racial, cultural and religious grounds.

In our view, the definition of communities should be a matter for residents, and this supports the argument for empowering them to undertake their own needs audits in relation to areas which are understood locally to constitute communities. This conviction would apply particularly to Asian communities with their distinctive culture and language and, perhaps, reservations about the extent to which mainstream statutory services recognise and meet their problems and needs. We found evidence of a strong desire amongst Asian communities for resources and support for facilities which would enable them to strengthen their communities and the support which they are able to provide to their members. This would underpin the argument for empowering these communities to undertake audits of their problems and needs within the context of broader measures to increase their voice in local service planning and delivery.

This raises the general problem of the link between community-based needs auditing and the power given to local communities in the policy-making process. Thus, the generation of commitment in local communities to the process of needs auditing will require an understanding that this will lead to action to address the problems and needs which are articulated, and to improve local services. This could apply particularly to ethnic minority communities and emphasises the link between needs auditing and the broader issue of community participation in decision making. In our view, the success of community-based needs auditing is contingent upon the decentralisation of power within and from the statutory agencies.

Given a commitment to such a devolution of power needs auditing exercises should, in our view, be focused on local communities as part of broader community development initiatives. They should not be undertaken by professionals or researchers from 'outside the community'. Rather, communities themselves should be encouraged and empowered to take the initiative, with appropriate advice, support and resources.

1:3 WHAT IS DISTINCTIVE ABOUT NEEDS AUDITING?

Traditionally, approaches to needs assessment have been dominated by the 'expert knows best' thinking referred to earlier. Assessment of health and welfare needs has tended to be conducted at a distance by research and information officers and planning officers in health and local authorities mainly on the basis of available information about, for example, the demography of a particular area, its socio-economic structure and other similar indicators. What has generally not been included is any attempt to involve service users or the community more generally in the identification of what is required to meet their needs or in decision-making processes about priorities and forms of service-delivery.

Recent developments in health and welfare policy have laid a far more explicit duty on health authorities and local authorities to identify needs in their area as a result of the Children Act 1989, NHS and Community Care Act 1990. However while there is a greater emphasis on the need for consultation in this legislation there are, as yet, no guidelines on how to carry out a needs assessment nor how local people should be involved in the process. In addition there appears to be little agreement about what constitutes need nor on how to reconcile differences between people involved in the process of needs assessment (Walker, 1991).

The model of needs auditing described here goes some way towards overcoming these difficulties. Firstly, it is grounded in a coherent theory of need; second, it brings together both top-down and bottom-up perspectives on need and provides a model for involving local people in the process of needs assessment; and finally it at least addresses the issue of how one might go about confronting differences in perspective between groups within the community.

It is interesting that a similar approach and methodology has been used in relation to other areas and policy arenas. A notable example of a similar study is the Walker Riverside Study on Newcastle (University of Newcastle-upon-Tyne, 1991) which also involved pre-survey consultations, a survey of local residents and public meetings focusing on the problems of a run-down council estate.

In this chapter we first discuss the difficulties associated with using existing sources of information for the purpose of assessing health and welfare needs before looking at how the information generated through the needs auditing process overcomes some of the limitations identified. Finally, we consider how needs auditing can contribute to the democratisation of the health and welfare system.

Existing Sources of Information and their Limitations

Agencies involved in the planning and delivery of health and welfare services already generate a considerable amount of information. However, much of this information has serious limitations in terms of its contribution to the process of needs assessment. In evaluating the use of existing information we need to ask the following questions:

- Is the information *valid*? Does it measure what we want to measure?

- Is the information *reliable*? Does it give an accurate picture of what we want to measure?

- Is the information *comprehensive*? Does it give us a full picture?

- Does the information relate to the relevant area or population?

- Is the information up-to-date?

It is worth considering each of these questions in turn in relation to data on health and welfare needs.

The *validity* of an indicator relates to whether or not it measures what you want to measure. For example, adequate protective housing is one of the intermediate needs identified by Doyal and Gough that we examined in the Leeds project. However, although some information on housing conditions already exists (for example in local authorities' housing investment programme applications) it may not be a good measure of real housing need. For example, do 'official' measures of overcrowding or of unfit housing give us information that allows us to determine whether or not certain people have their needs for adequate, protective housing met?

A particular problem arises in this regard where proxies are used for what we actually want to measure. For example, years of attendance at school may be substituted for the level of educational attainment, or the ratio of GPs to numbers of people in the population may be susbstituted for the level of primary health care available in a given area. Here inputs are being used as substitutes for outputs or outcomes.

The *reliability* of data relates to its accuracy: does the level of need revealed by a certain indicator correspond to that which really exists? This is a particular problem associated with routinely collected information. The extent to which certain conditions or circumstances are reported, detected or recorded depends on administrative procedures and rules. So, for example, official figures for unemployment are well-known to be an unreliable and inaccurate indicator of the numbers of people not in paid work. Similarly, when figures for the numbers of people who are disabled are derived from the register of disability they are likely to underestimate the true number of people with disability.

A further problem arises in relation to the *comprehensiveness* of the information available. Most agencies routinely collect only information that they are statutorily required to collect and in a form that is appropriate to that purpose, or else gather information as a 'by-product' of other activities. Given that the assessment of need has tended traditionally to play only a limited role in the planning and delivery of services, most information that is already collected is incomplete and gives only a partial picture of need if it gives one at all. So, for example, homelessness statistics may tell us something about some people who are experiencing certain types of housing need. However, they do not give us a complete picture of either housing need or homelessness nor do they tell us anything about the type of housing that is required, at what price, or how their housing problems contribute to other difficulties such as unemployment or poor health.

A major problem encountered when using existing information collected by other agencies is the fact that it may relate to different geographical areas or populations other than those in which we are interested. This arises from the multiplicity of different administrative boundaries that exist within a given area. So, for example, in some areas one may find that all of the following boundaries exist and the relevant agencies only collect information that relates to the populations within those boundaries:

- the area covered by the local authority which can then be sub-divided into electoral wards

- district health authority areas which are generally not the same as local authority areas

- local authority housing management areas (which do not generally relate to wards)

- areas covered by social services area offices

- school catchment areas

- census enumeration districts

- postal districts.

The absence of common administrative boundaries makes it very difficult, if not impossible, to bring together all the relevant information on a particular population. If we incorporate, in addition, people's own subjective identification with a particular community which may also not relate to any of the above boundaries, a further complication is added.

Much of the information which is routinely used as a basis for strategic planning of services is derived from the Census. At the time of writing, information from the 1991 Census was not yet available and so decisions were made on the basis of indicators derived from the last Census. Given the rapidly shifting patterns of need and changing socio-economic structure, this is clearly inadequate information on which to make detailed decisions about the allocation of resources and forms of service delivery. Nowhere is this more apparent than in relation to the structure of families and households. Many health and welfare agencies still seem to be working on the assumption that the typical household consists of a breadwinning male head of household, non-working wife and children, thereby failing to take sufficient account of the rise in single person households, female labour market participation rates and single parent families.

The Use of Existing Information

These shortcomings in existing data should not be taken to indicate that such information has no role to play in the assessment of needs. Existing sources of information may be useful at the following points in the needs auditing process:

- At the preliminary stage of a needs audit, existing data may be used to identify the population(s) which are to be the focus of the initial needs audit; for example the use of 'standard' indicators of social deprivation to identify more or less disadvantaged areas which then become the focus for more intensive study using the needs audit methodology. A good example of how existing information can be collected and presented in a useful, accessible way as the first stage in a more participative process is the consultation document produced in Sheffield as part of the city's 'Health for All' initiative (Halliday, 1991)

● Existing data may be used to complement the findings of the needs audit. For example where valid social indicators already exist relating to specific aspects of need, the collection of new data may be avoided and the assessment of need may be undertaken by combining old and new data as appropriate

● Existing data, especially where it is highly aggregated, may be useful for the purposes of comparison or to provide a context in which to situate the findings of a needs audit. The comparative or contextual use of secondary data might also include the analysis of historical trends (to examine for example, whether the level of need satisfaction has improved or deteriorated in a population over a specific period) and the comparison between populations (for example, one area of a city with a larger, more inclusive population).

The Contribution of Needs Auditing

Needs auditing offers the potential to provide information about needs that is reliable, valid, relevant to the population or area being researched, comprehensive and up-to-date. In addition, if a standard model is adopted it will enable meaningful comparisons to be made between populations or areas thus facilitating judgements about the equity of service provision. And, given that the needs auditing model which we are advocating involves people in the identification and articulation of needs and need satisfaction, it can also contribute to their empowerment.

If we are to institute a system of welfare that is needs-based, it is vital that we have a coherent theory of needs which informs the process from the initial identification of needs, through policy formulation and planning, to service delivery and the monitoring and evaluation of need satisfaction. We can then devise instruments for the collection of information which relates directly to our categories of need. In the pilot study in Leeds, a postal questionnaire was drawn up with questions that related directly to the set of intermediate needs which we have identified. Also, a similar checklist of questions informed our interviews with policy makers and front-line service providers.

There are two main issues concerning the reliability of information. The first concerns the reliability of the data collected in relation to what it is supposed to measure that is, the views of people on needs indicators and levels of need satisfaction. This is a matter of pursuing best practice in survey methodology - survey design, sampling and interviewing. We discussed potential problem areas in the previous chapter but with adequate resources, expertise and a commitment to 'objectivity', a needs audit can produce reliable information representative of the population under study.

The second issue concerns the reliability of subjective views of various parties in relation to levels of need satisfaction. The point here is that there is no 'objective truth' in this regard but rather different perspectives based on different value-laden 'world views'. A needs audit seeks to identify and highlight these differences, to attempt to reconcile them where possible, and to negotiate a consensus about problems and priorities. Again, assuming that this process is 'brokered' in an honest and impartial way, we regard it as producing the most reliable assessment of need which can be achieved.

The idea of comprehensiveness - incorporating all aspects of that which one is attempting to assess - is incorporated into needs auditing in a number of ways. First, we asked some questions about all the basic and intermediate needs specified in the theoretical framework with the exception of the cognitive aspects of autonomy. Second, a basic assumption of the needs auditing model is the idea that needs do not conform to agency or departmental boundaries but are interconnected. For example, needs related to income, housing and health should be seen as closely interrelated. In this sense a comprehensive view of needs was built into our methodology. Third, we asked questions not only about needs but also about need satisfiers and levels of need satisfaction - about experiences of existing services and ideas on how they might be changed or improved.

The information generated by the needs audit was analysed within six months of its being collected. To that extent it was far more up to date than many other sources of data, notably the Census, and therefore constitutes a better basis on which to make policy decisions.

The proposition that people have basic and intermediate needs that ought to be met to a decent standard by the health and welfare system implies a notion of equity. Thus, it is far more difficult to justify differences in levels of need satisfaction than differences in want satisfaction. It is therefore important that we should be able to monitor inputs, outputs and outcomes in terms of the principle of equity. A particular problem of much existing data is that they relate to such large populations (eg. regions) that inequalities between groups become invisible. Highly aggregated information, as a rule, tells us very little about whether or not resources are allocated equitably or whether the outcomes of policies and programmes are equitable between individuals, groups or areas. Needs auditing provides the information required for the assessment of equity in resource allocation and outcomes both within and between communities.

Social Auditing and Democratisation

A health and welfare system must be an open system if it is to be responsive. In other words it should be clear on what basis decisions are being made and resources allocated or withdrawn. This implies the democratisation of the system. Social auditing can contribute to the democratisation of the health and welfare system in a number of ways.

First, democratisation requires that citizens become active participants rather than passive recipients in the health and welfare system. Needs auditing promotes active participation by involving people in the identification and articulation of needs and in decision-making and service planning. It should be noted however that encouraging participation is difficult. We do not have a participative political culture and people are generally unwilling or perceive themselves to lack the skills to participate in a more active form of citizenship.

Needs auditing can also contribute to the opening up of the process of health and welfare policy-making by increasing the flow of information and understanding between citizens and professionals and thereby demystifying some of the processes involved. Moreover, by giving citizens a voice and an active role in the health and welfare system, needs auditing can contribute to their empowerment. Shifting some power away from experts, professionals and policy-makers is not necessarily an end in itself but may be a means of delivering health and welfare services that are more effective because they are more in tune with the communities they are intended to serve. The needs auditing methodology recognises that there is likely to be a plurality of groups and interests within a given area and suggests a means by which agreement on priorities might be achieved through discussion and negotiation. Finally, needs auditing can contribute to a higher level of accountability at all levels of the system. This issue will be discussed in greater detail in the next chapter.

1:4   NEEDS AUDITING, EFFECTIVENESS AND QUALITY IN WELFARE PROVISION

In this chapter we consider some issues which relate to the role of needs auditing in helping to create an effective system of health and welfare provision. Firstly, we discuss briefly the concepts of effectiveness and quality in the public sector and the extent to which these must be based upon the assessment of need. We then discuss the contribution which needs auditing can make to the achievement of a definition of need which can be widely accepted as 'legitimate'. We then consider more specifically the role needs auditing can play in management processes so as to contribute to the production of more effective health and welfare outcomes. Finally, we discuss the potential role of needs auditing in promoting accountability.

Needs, Effectiveness and Quality

What constitutes 'quality' in the public sector? Traditionally, discussions of performance of public sector organisations have been dominated by the three Es - economy, efficiency and effectiveness (Cave, 1990). Economy (the cost of acquiring resources) and efficiency (the relationship between resources and outputs) are important components of performance. Nevertheless the concept of effectiveness is the most important since it addresses the extent to which an organisation is securing outcomes which achieve its defined objectives. It can be defined in a broad way in terms of the achievement of defined purpose at minimum overall cost in resources. Put another way, effectiveness is about ensuring maximum 'added value', where value is defined in terms of the purpose of the organisation.

However, the definition of what constitutes 'value' in the context of health and welfare services is a contentious matter. Essentially, public services exist to meet the needs of the population in relation to certain aspects of quality of life and well-being which the market cannot be relied upon to provide. Therefore, priorites are established through the political process in which objectives referring to desired standards of provision in relation to need, and to considerations of equity in access to services and in service outcomes, must be set against those referring to efficiency considerations. In the determination of priorities a number of different perspectives exist, associated with different 'interests'. What, then, should public services produce?

- What people want or expect as individual customers?
- What people want or expect as groups or communities?
- What people need as determined by professionals?
- What people should have in the view of politicians?

Traditionally, the determination of priorities in public sector organisations has been dominated by the last two of the above perspectives in a context of essentially bureaucratic organisation conditioned both by the ideologies of professional interest groups and by the values deriving from the prevailing political control. This corresponds to the top-down approach to the assessment of need satisfaction (see part 1:1). However, the mode of bureaucratic organisation is being undermined by various economic and social trends reinforced by the legislative programme of successive Conservative governments. A new 'post-bureaucratic' form of organisation can be seen to emerge involving a devolved approach to management, the replacement of 'control by hierarchy' with 'control by contract' and the 'empowerment of the customer' (Hoggett, 1991).

With these developments has come a new emphasis on the 'quality' of public services (Pfeffer and Coote, 1991; Gaster, 1991; Walsh 1991). Discussion of quality emphasises the importance of giving the customers of services a greater say in what is provided and how. Services should be responsive to customers' wishes and expectations and they should be provided in a caring and 'customer-friendly' way. A quality service is an effective service in the sense that it produces outcomes which achieve the defined objectives and purpose of the organisation. However, quality goes beyond effectiveness by highlighting certain attributes which actually affect the definition of purpose. In this sense it is a more normative concept.

Three distinctive features of quality can be identified. The first is the emphasis on satisfying the requirements of customer or service user. This entails a new emphasis on 'listening to customers' - finding out their views, involving people in decisions and ensuring high levels of satisfaction. It is argued that senior managers, professionals and politicians can no longer be the sole arbiters of decisions on priorities and judgements on effectiveness. Public sector organisations should be 'opened up' to those they are intended to serve. People should be 'empowered' either as users/customers of specific services or as citizens, playing a more active role in the political process. Moreover, people should be entitled to receive certain minimum standards of service and these should be specified in 'charters' with rights of redress.

The second feature is a focus on the nature of the interaction between service providers and recipients - the 'service relationship' (Walsh, 1991). For many public services performance cannot be defined solely in terms of <u>what</u> is provided (as in the case of a product) but must refer also to <u>how</u> it is provided - to the experience of the interchange between provider and receiver. This applies particularly in the case of health, education and social services where human interaction is a key component of the service. It involves consideration of psychological and social aspects of the interaction and also of the context in which the interaction takes place. It leads to a focus on practices and conditions at the point of service delivery or 'at the front line' (Gaster, 1991).

The third distinctive feature of quality is an emphasis on 'cultural change' in public sector organisations, to create organisations dedicated to achieving quality services. One component of this is the reform of organisational structures to break down the traditional model of hierarchical control and departmentalism and to create devolved structures, more responsive to those who use or need public services. However, changes in values and ways of working are also needed to create a commitment on the part of all employees to achieving quality.

These attributes of quality imply a re-distribution of power in favour of the users of public services and also in favour of the front-line workers who actually deal with 'service relationships'. Consequently, the achievement of quality involves radical organisational change. However, the approach to quality embodied in the Conservative Government's Citizen's Charter (HMSO, 1991) portrays the empowerment of customers as an essentially neutral, technical phenomenon designed to introduce a 'pseudo-market' discipline into the public sector.

The promotion of such a consumerist model in the public sector can be criticised as imposing a particular implied purpose and role which is restricted to the delivery of specific services and neglects broader political objectives. Its 'transactional' view of relations between public sector organisations and their 'customers' neglects the role of the public sector in addressing 'market failures'. This means that conditions of social efficiency and equity will not be achieved by basing service provision on the manifest wishes and expectations of customers. In particular, it devalues the concept of 'externalities' which, by definition, need to be addressed on a collective level in order that external benefits can be maximised and the impact of external costs minimised in relation to groups and communities. It implies the empowerment of those 'customers' with access to resources who can readily register their wishes and expectations at the expense of those less able to articulate their problems and needs. In addition, it implies an empowerment of those who have an interest in services and activities which address externalities identified at the collective level (Sanderson, 1992).

Indeed, it is possible to question the appropriateness of the concept of the 'customer' to the public sector context. A central justification of the consumerist model derives from the assumption that consumers are empowered through choice in the market. However, even in private sector markets choice is constrained and conditioned by imperfect information, by advertising and persuasion, and by inequitable distribution of income. The implications of inequities in the power to articulate requirements are more serious when social welfare provision is at stake. Moreover, the relationship between public sector organisations and the actual and potential beneficiaries of their services and activities cannot be conceived simply in terms of choice, as Stewart and Clarke (1987) emphasise: 'The customer of a public service is not the same as the customer of a service in the market. The customer does not necessarily buy the service; the customer may have a right to receive the service; the customer may be compelled to receive the service; customers may be refused a service because their needs may not meet the criteria laid down'.

The determination of the pattern of desiderata, rights, compulsions, refusals and priorities in relation to services requires an assessment of needs on both an individual and collective level. The crucial issue is the relative power accorded to individuals and groups, professionals and politicians in this process. The danger of the consumerist model is that it implies a re-distribution of power, under an allegedly neutral banner of 'choice and efficiency', which has implications for what is perceived as the 'legitimate' purpose, role and activities of the public sector. Specifically, legitimacy is seen increasingly to reside more in the delivery of specific services than in the pursuit of a broader role in building 'citizenship' through active participation in the political process, or in enhancing a collective conception of 'quality of life'.

This process is strengthened by the trend towards 'government by contract' which is embodied in the 'enabling model' of the New Right. In this model the role of the public sector is reduced essentially to one of securing the provision of specific services through contracts with a range of agencies in the private and voluntary sectors, or in the public sector operating along commercial lines. Government by contract places the focus on service outputs which can be specified and measured as a basis for control and performance assessment through the contractual relationship (Hoggett, 1991). There is a danger that less tangible 'outcomes', especially those relating to collectively defined needs, will be neglected and devalued thus reinforcing the *de facto* restriction of the perceived legitimate role of the public sector.

This critique of the consumerist model of public services emphasises the dangers inherent in the devaluation of the relevance and importance of the concept of need which is implied in the re-structuring of the public sector. This re-structuring can be seen as involving a re-distribution of power away from those interests structured around the provision of welfare outcomes for the most 'needy' and which address collectively-defined needs (Cochrane, 1991; Berry, 1988). We see the consumerist model of quality as playing a role in this restructuring process. However, from this point of view there is a danger of throwing out the baby of need with the bathwater of professional power. The concept of need is fundamental to effectiveness in welfare provision even if we accept (as we do) the importance of redressing the balance of power in favour of those who use services. The assessment of need must extend beyond individuals' perceptions and address collective interests in order to provide the basis for the achievement of conditions of social efficiency and equity which the market manifestly fails to do.

Needs Auditing and Legitimacy

On the basis of the above discussion, we can highlight the importance of recognising the *plurality* of interests involved in decisions on the purpose, role and legitimate activities of the public sector and on the distribution of benefits from those activities. A balance is desirable which avoids undue domination by particular interests, whether those of individuals as 'customers', specific groups of people, or professional groups. The implication is that the assessment of need satisfaction should be recognised explicitly as a *political* process open to influence by a variety of interests. Attention then focuses on the balance of power achieved between these interests and the ways in which that power is exercised in the process.

We would argue that the needs auditing model which we have elaborated and evaluated provides a framework within which progress can be made towards such a pluralistic approach. Thus, it can accommodate the perspectives of individuals as 'customers', of groups and communities with collective interests, of different groups of professionals, and of elected politicians. The role of these various interests can be made explicit, visible and open to scrutiny. In a practical context, focused on specific communities, it can provide a means to promote active participation and the empowerment of people as 'citizens' and to achieve a balance of interests, individual and collective, 'customer' and 'provider', professional and political. Thus, it makes an important contribution to the achievement of quality in public services, moving beyond the consumerist model to a 'democratic approach' which emphasises the empowerment of people as 'citizens' through participation and a system of rights, and ensures that the collective dimensions of welfare are addressed effectively (Pfeffer and Coote, 1991).

However, we would also argue that the realisation of such progress does depend upon certain important political preconditions. Thus, the achievement of a pluralistic approach can be seen to require an 'open' political process in which particular interests are not able to exert a dominating influence. It assumes that existing 'dominant interests' are prepared, or are forced, to relinquish some of their power to traditionally 'subordinate interests'. Unless these political implications are addressed there is a danger that the needs auditing model will constitute merely a 'rationalistic veneer' which serves to legitimise the existing structure of power.

Indeed, this argument applies more broadly to initiatives in the public sector to decentralise organisations in order to achieve a closer relationship between service providers and users (Hambleton, 1988). Community-based needs auditing can be seen as an important component of a commitment to achieve real local participation in the process of service planning and delivery. As part of a broader commitment to 'community development' it can play a role in the empowerment of disadvantaged groups and those whose interests failed to gain adequate representation in traditional centralised bureaucratic structures. However, there is a danger that decentralisation can represent merely a superficial change in managerial and organisational structures which fails to challenge the power of established dominant interests.

Without the necessary political preconditions, needs auditing is open to being usurped by these dominant interests and used as a legitimising facade to mask a continuity of traditional patterns of power and domination. This would be reflected in control over the needs auditing process being vested in groups of senior managers and professionals rather than in front-line workers in partnership with representatives from local communities. It would be reflected in an approach to needs auditing which proceeded 'outside' or 'alongside' the community rather than one which developed 'within' the community involving true partnership (Bayley et al, 1989).

What are the prospects for achieving the political conditions necessary to support the pluralistic approach implied in the needs auditing model? Achievement of the ideal conditions of freedom from domination of any particular interest is undoubtedly unrealistic. Doyal and Gough (1991) rely on Habermas' (1970) conception of the 'ideal speech situation'..."where communication is undistorted by the particularity of ideology and where generalisable interests can be collectively conceptualised and pursued in an efficient and rational fashion" (Doyal and Gough *op cit.* p121). The achievement of this goal requires that participants have an understanding of the issues of concern and methodological and communication skills to resolve disputes. Moreover, fully democratic debate must be possible, free from the domination of particular interests. Three attributes of 'democracy' are identified: political structures, opportunities for citizen participation and the responsiveness of the state to such participation. Doyal and Gough (*op cit.* p230) argue that:

> 'The greater the enfranchised citizenry and its level of electoral participation, the greater the state's tolerance of diverse political parties, the more responsive the system of government to public opinion, the more extensive the domain of economic and social life subject to effective democratic influence by citizens, the more citizens are mobilised within a wide variety of autonomous movements - the more rational will be the ongoing process of resolving disputes.'

It is possible to criticise this view of rational debate as unrealistic on the grounds that processes of discussion and debate about public policy issues will, in any circumstances, be 'structured' by the influence of ideological factors and by inequalities in the distribution of power and resources. Doyal and Gough follow Habermas in seeing the state of 'communicative competence' as a goal to be striven for by liberating people from structures of political and ideological domination as supported, for example, by the power of 'experts' and professionals to shape people's perceptions of society and their place in it. However, this leaves unresolved the crucial question of just how far it is feasible to go along this path of 'liberation'. In this regard, Doyal and Gough advocate a 'dual strategy' embracing both radical centralisation via codified welfare rights and a radical decentralisation.

In practical terms, it is possible to detect some progress towards the Habermasian ideal in the decentralisation initiatives which have been implemented, in particular in local government and health services. There have been genuine moves to strengthen the process of democratic debate by promoting participation and empowering people as users and citizens through funding, support and community development initiatives (Hambleton and Hoggett 1987, Hambleton 1988). However, it is by no means clear that such moves have had a major impact upon traditional structures of power and domination; as Hambleton (1988) says, '...a new kind of participatory democracy is not just around the corner.' Nevertheless, it would appear that progress towards a more open, pluralistic, participatory democracy can be promoted by decentralisation and we would see the needs auditing process as playing a potentially significant role in this context.

However, there is a dilemma which must be addressed in the development of a health and welfare system which seeks to secure certain rights to need satisfaction. A participatory and community-oriented approach in health and welfare provision can be usurped by sectional interests and can result in major inequities in need satisfaction outcomes. If everyone is to have the right to a certain level of need satisfaction, such a right must be guaranteed by a central authority and this implies a strong role both for the central state and for a central executive in sub-national units of government. Indeed, the simultaneous decentralisation of power for operational matters and the centralisation of power for strategic policy matters (including the issue of equity in service provision) can be observed in organisational changes which are being implemented widely in local government and the health service (Hoggett, 1991; Barrett and McMahon, 1990).

We now discuss briefly the way in which needs auditing fits into the policy-making process so as to contribute to the production of more effective outcomes as a contribution to the achievement of quality in public service provision.

Needs Auditing and Effective Outcomes

We argued earlier that the process of needs assessment is about deriving a set of desiderata, rights, compulsions and refusals in relation to the problems which people face. The first stage in the process involves an analysis of relevant problems and needs and of the impact of current services and activities. It is this stage which is the main focus of the methodology which we have described and evaluated above. However, the process must extend beyond this stage to develop guidelines for addressing the perceived problems and shortfalls in need satisfaction. This involves two elements. Thus, shortfalls must be assessed firstly in relation to the relevant legislative framework, particularly with a view to identifying specific 'statutory responsibilities' and, secondly, in relation to the objectives of the organisation. On this basis guidelines for addressing needs can be derived specifying the following conditions:

- where it is seen as *desirable* to address a shortfall in need satisfaction
- where people have a *right* to have a shortfall addressed
- where a shortfall must be addressed through *compulsion*
- where a shortfall *cannot or will not* be addressed.

This stage of the process will produce a specific set of requirements for need satisfaction assessed on both individual and collective levels. In this sense, such requirements are seen as closely related to objectives and this has two important implications. First, it means that such objectives provide an important basis for assessing the performance of the organisation since effectiveness will require progress towards meeting them. Second, it means that the process of deriving the above guidelines must be explicitly political. Consequently, it is important that an open participatory approach to decision making is achieved at this stage involving the pluralistic balance between different interests which we discussed earlier.

The next stage of the policy process involves moving from defined requirements for need satisfaction to specific policies and programmes and this requires the consideration of available resources. Policies will then represent guidelines for the allocation of resources to address shortfalls in need satisfaction, standards and targets can be specified indicating the degree to which needs can be met, and appropriate programmes of action specified. Again, this process of deriving priorities for the use of available resources is explicitly political and, in our framework, requires the extension of participatory forms of decision making.

The implementation of programmes of action by public sector organisations has been radically affected by the introduction of compulsory competitive tendering and the split between purchaser and provider. As a result, implementation increasingly takes place through 'third party' agencies, with control achieved through the contract, rather than through direct provision with control achieved through internal management structures. For example, the new planning regime in the National Health Service has been developed to accommodate the purchasing role of district health authorities (DHAs). DHAs must specify their purchasing intentions in 'service specifications' based on the purchasing plans which indicate how health needs will be addressed with available resources. Contracts are then negotiated with providers on the basis of the service specifications (Dept of Health, 1991).

The separation between purchaser and provider, which is also being increasingly introduced in local government, has certain implications for our model of needs auditing and its role in promoting effectiveness and quality. Two questions arise. Firstly, can all relevant needs be met adequately through 'government by contract'? Secondly, can the participation of 'front-line' workers in the process of needs assessment be secured adequately if service provision is separated organisationally from service planning and needs assessment?

As we argued above there may be a risk of neglect of less tangible outcomes due to a focus in contracts on service outputs which can be specified and measured as a basis for control and performance assessment. This could affect the ability of local authorities in particular to address perceived needs relating to a role in promoting citizenship and achieving broader political objectives.

The separation of purchaser and provider roles means that the involvement of front-line workers in the process of needs assessment and the development of the purchasing plan changes from an issue of the distribution of power within the organisation to an issue of inter-organisational relations. The importance of involving professional staff in provider units in the process of needs assessment is emphasised in advice from the NHS Management Executive to DHAs (Dept of Health, 1991). However, the history of inter-organisational relations does not provide a basis for optimism in a context of increasing fragmentation in the public sector (Webb, 1991). On the other hand, it may be that accommodating these inter-organisational relations is no less problematical than handling the intra-organisational devolution of power to front-line workers which itself clearly represents a considerable challenge to public sector organisations.

These potential concerns about the 'government by contract' model lead us to emphasise the importance of appropriate systems for monitoring and reviewing performance. We have defined effectiveness in terms of the ability of the organisation to achieve outcomes which meet identified needs and we have argued that the needs auditing model can help to produce an assessment of requirements which has a legitimacy founded upon efforts to promote fully democratic participation (not, it should be emphasised, on a claim to achieve this). Effective management requires that managers know on a continuous basis how 'successful' the organisation is in securing outcomes which achieve required levels of need satisfaction and this should be the purpose of performance review systems.

As discussed earlier, performance is conventionally defined in terms of the three concepts of 'economy', 'efficiency' and 'effectiveness'. There has been a tendency for economy and efficiency to dominate the assessment of performance because measures of resource use and service outputs are inherently easier to define and quantify than measures of outcomes which are required for the assessment of effectiveness. However, economy and efficiency provide a very narrow definition of performance in the public sector context, neglecting the crucial issue of the extent to which service and activity outputs achieve adequate levels of need satisfaction.

From this perspective, then, it is not possible to assess performance adequately with reference to outputs of services and activities. It is important that systems for monitoring and evaluating performance go beyond measuring the extent to which output standards and targets are achieved and incorporate an assessment of the broader outcomes and the extent to which these meet defined needs. We have discussed extensively the potential role of needs auditing in helping to produce an assessment of requirements for need satisfaction which can be widely supported as legitimate. In addition, if undertaken on a continuous, periodic basis it can play an important role in monitoring the impact of services and activities as perceived by individuals, groups, professionals and politicians which provides the basis for assessing how well needs are being met.

We have emphasised the importance of addressing the broader political dimension of the purpose of public sector organisations in the definition of need, particularly the extent to which such purpose includes an attempt to promote the development of citizenship through active participation in the public policy-making process. The assessment of performance in this respect is by no means easy and straightforward but we consider that needs auditing can potentially play an important role in helping to build citizenship by promoting more active democratic participation in the devolution and decentralisation of power.

It can help public sector organisations move up the 'ladder of participation', to progress beyond 'passive' strategies of informing and consulting to more 'active' strategies which involve and empower people as 'citizens' (Burns 1991). However, we have emphasised that progress 'up the ladder' requires a commitment to the re-distribution of power to achieve a more pluralistic context and that there is a danger of 'empowerment initiatives' being developed as superficial phenomena which fail to address the distribution of power and merely provide a facade which serves to legitimise the status quo.

Needs Auditing and Accountability

The promotion of citizenship also has important implications for the accountability of public sector organisations. Such organisations exercise power through the raising and use of public funds and through activities, some coercive, which affect everyone's lives. Accountablity to 'the public' for the exercise of such power is essential. Accountability is achieved primarily through the electoral process but this is an imperfect means. Consequently, there is a need to supplement this process with other means of accountablity. This is achieved through the scrutiny and auditing procedures exercised by the National Audit Office in the case of central government, and the Audit Commission in the case of local government.

Current means of accountability are primarily 'passive' in nature, corresponding to the predominance of essentially passive approaches to participation at the 'bottom end' of the ladder of participation. On the other hand, while moves up the ladder towards more genuine and active forms of participation help to develop citizenship, so too can the promotion of active citizenship be seen as enhancing accountability. Two crucial dimensions in the task of enhancing accountability are information and participation. In our view, needs auditing can play an important role in this task (Percy-Smith, 1992).

This can be elaborated with reference to Stewart's (1984) 'ladder of accountablity' which includes the following rungs:

(i)   *Accountability for probity and legality*: to ensure that monies are used properly and in the manner intended and that legal powers are not exceeded;

(ii)   *Process accountability*: to ensure that there is no maladministration and that the principles of procedural justice are adhered to;

(iii)   *Performance accountability*: to ensure that performance reaches the required standards;

(iv)   *Programme accountability*: to ensure that a particular agency or department or policy team is meeting its defined objectives;

(v)   *Policy accountability*: to ensure that agencies are held accountable for the totality of activities and non-activities, ie. agencies should be held accountable not only for those programmes which they introduce but also for areas for which they have responsibility in which they fail to take action;

(vi)   *Political accountability*: to ensure accountability for the overall direction of policy, the attribution of praise or blame and, where appropriate, the renewal or withdrawal of a mandate.

In many areas of the health and welfare system it is not currently possible to go beyond performance accountability since objectives are often not clearly stated (if they are stated at all), areas of responsibility are not clearly specified and, crucially, information is not available on the outcomes of policies and programmes. Ultimately, how far up that ladder of accountability it is possible to go, will depend on clear specification of aims and objectives and the availability of appropriate information. The latter point is especially relevant to the idea of political accountability.

At present both policy accountability and political accountability for outcomes of the health and welfare system are almost impossible. MPs do not have access to information that would enable them to hold the government effectively to account; and citizens do not have the information they need to hold either service-providers or politicians accountable.

Needs auditing can provide relevant information that will contribute to accountability. Firstly, an initial needs audit can provide 'baseline' information about local needs against which to assess future programmes. Secondly, follow-up audits will generate information about the level of needs fulfilment. At a national level, publication of information derived from local needs audits will enable governments to be held accountable for the direction of health and welfare policies and for policy failures in terms of unmet needs or gross inequities in needs fulfilment.

If such accountability is to be a real possibility, it is imperative that the process of carrying out our needs audits conforms to a number of criteria. First, needs audits should conform to a model that allows for comparisons to be made between groups and areas. Second, as discussed earlier, it is important that needs audits are carried out 'within' the community, and that communities should be 'enabled' to carry out their audits in an effective manner. Finally, the information that is generated through the needs auditing process should be collated and written in an accessible form and made widely available. Similarly there should be an obligation on the part of whatever agency is responsible for collating information at a regional or national level to make that information public.

1:5 CONCLUSION

The basic premise underpinning this study is that a modern welfare system should be organised around the needs and interests of ordinary citizens who use its services and should empower those citizens (Coote, 1990). Such a system should help to promote a fair society in which every individual is treated with equal respect and has an equal chance in life. It should therefore recognise and respond to differences between individuals and groups who have different experiences and different needs by virtue of gender, race, age, disability etc.

Consequently, we see both substantive and procedural aspects to the satisfaction of 'rights to welfare'. As regards the substantive aspect, we have argued, using Doyal and Gough's theoretical framework, that basic human needs are the universal pre-requisites for successful participation in any social form of life. These universal pre-requisites are physical health - the absence of disease and disability - and autonomy - the capacity to make informed choices about action. Certain 'need satisfiers' can be identified which everywhere contribute to improved physical health and autonomy and these are termed 'intermediate needs', for example, adequate nutritious food and water, protective housing, appropriate health care, physical and economic security etc. These are essential to protect people's health and autonomy and enable them to participate to the maximum extent in their social form of life. As such, it can be argued that people have a strong right to the satisfaction of these needs.

The assessment of need should attempt to measure levels of satisfaction of intermediate needs. However, if we wish to inform the development of welfare policies at the community level, it is also necessary to identify specific satisfiers relevant to the problems and needs of particular communities. The 'community needs audit' aims to achieve an overview of all aspects of life essential to people's capacity to participate fully in society.

In applying such a needs audit an important question arises: what kind of information should be obtained and from whom in order to formulate a reliable picture of people's needs? We refer to the procedural aspect of 'empowerment' which requires that citizens participate actively and fully in the articulation of their own needs. This implies a rejection of the traditional domination of needs assessment by professionals and experts and asserts the right and ability of individuals, groups and communities to have their say, and even to undertake their own needs audits.

The needs audit attempts to integrate the 'codified knowledge' of professionals with the 'experiential knowledge' of ordinary people; to overcome the dichotomy between 'top down' and 'bottom up' approaches; to reconcile different perspectives. It embodies a process whereby such a reconciliation can be negotiated recognising differences in interests and values between the parties involved. It focuses on communities as the context in which people can articulate their needs as individuals and as members of groups, and in which professionals perceive the need for services which they are involved in administering.

We have discussed the implementation of the pilot needs audit in the Kirkstall area of Leeds which sought to obtain information on a range of indicators of basic and intermediate needs from secondary sources, from individuals living in the area, from community and voluntary groups, from professionals and from political representatives. Both quantitative and qualitative data were obtained and local meetings were used to promote discussion of the issues. This pilot study has provided a good indication of the potential of the methodology. It provided a comprehensive picture of needs in the context of a coherent theoretical specification and in terms of quantitative and qualitative information, combining professionals' views with both individual and collective experientially-grounded perspectives on needs. Moreover, it has indicated the potential for encouraging community participation if an audit is undertaken as an integral part of the actual process of service planning and facilitated by the agencies concerned.

However, there are several problem areas relating to the representativeness of sampling, the involvement of ethnic minorities, the representativeness of the views of community groups and professionals, the achievement of a 'value free' stance in the integration of different perspectives and the process of reconciling such differences. Many of these problems point to the need for local communities to be empowered to undertake the auditing process themselves with appropriate advice, support and resources as part of a broader commitment to community development and to the promotion of a 'culture of participation'.

Contemporary discussions of 'quality' in public services emphasise the empowerment of 'customers' or 'citizens', in effect at the expense of the traditional dominance of professionals and politicians in the processes of defining need and deciding priorities for resource allocation. Recent developments in health and welfare policy place a more explicit duty upon health and local authorities to identify the needs of their areas. Community needs auditing can make an important contribution to satisfying these requirements, providing a potentially robust assessment of needs through an empowering process.

Needs auditing can provide information about needs which is reliable, valid, comprehensive, relevant to the population or area concerned and up-to-date. It overcomes many of the deficiencies of existing sources of information. Moreover, if a standard approach were adopted it would facilitate comparisons between different areas and enable judgements to be made about the equality of service provision. Needs auditing can contribute to the democratisation of health and welfare services by promoting citizen participation, opening up policy-making processes, encouraging discussion of priorities and promoting accountability.

We have argued that needs auditing can make an important contribution to increasing the effectiveness and quality of health and services. Effectiveness is essentially about achieving outcomes that meet people's needs while quality emphasises 'getting close to the customer', the nature of the 'service encounter' and cultural change in public sector organisations. We have emphasised the importance of redressing the balance of power in needs assessment in favour of those who use services, but we would also stress the dangers inherent in the consumerist model of reducing needs assessment to individual wants and expectations. It is necessary to recognise the plurality of interests involved in decisions about health and welfare issues and the need for a participative approach within which a balance can be achieved between different interests. We argue that the needs auditing model provides a framework within which progress can be made towards such a *pluralistic* approach.

More specifically, we argue that needs auditing can accommodate the perspectives of individuals as 'customers', of groups and communities with collective interests, of different groups of professionals, and of elected politicians. The role of these various interests can be made explicit, visible and open to scrutiny. In a practical context, focused on specific communities, it can provide the means to promote active participation and the empowerment of people as 'citizens' and to achieve a balance of interests, individual and collective, 'customer' and 'provider', professional and political. We would see this process being enhanced by moves to decentralise power by statutory agencies. However, we would also emphasise a danger of 'superficial' measures which fail to achieve real decentralisation and devolution of power but rather serve to legitimise the existing structure of power.

Therefore, needs auditing can help to produce an assessment of need satisfaction and requirements which has a legitimacy founded upon efforts to promote and encourage democratic participation. This provides the foundation for promoting effectiveness and quality in health and welfare services. Moreover, if undertaken on a continuous, periodic basis needs auditing can play an important role in monitoring the impact of services and activities as perceived by individuals, groups, professionals and politicians which provides the basis for assessing how well needs are being met.

We have highlighted the role which needs auditing can play in promoting accountability of public sector organisations to 'the public'. It provides a basis for transcending passive means of accountability based on measures of performance and promoting full political accountability for outcomes in relation to needs. Moreover, the promotion of active citizenship can be seen as enhancing accountability.

This pilot needs audit has indicated the potential role that needs auditing can play in promoting effectiveness, quality and democratisation in our health and welfare services. As a 'research' exercise it had limitations in terms of generating real participation and we feel that more needs audits are now required in the context of service planning by statutory agencies. However, we would emphasise our conclusion that the success of community-based needs auditing is contingent upon the decentralisation of power within and from such agencies, with communities themselves encouraged and empowered to take the initiative with appropriate advice, support and resources.

Therefore, needs audits should be generated and conducted 'within the community', with local people retaining ownership of the auditing process yet working in partnership with professionals in the statutory services and voluntary organisations. This should be part of a broader process to encourage the development of a 'culture of participation' in relation to the planning and delivery of local services. Indeed, local community-based needs auditing would itself play an important role in promoting the development of such a culture.

What is needed, then, is the incorporation of needs auditing into the local policy-making and political process. It should not be seen merely as a 'technical' exercise. It should involve the devolution of power and the promotion of real participation in the process by local communities. It would redress the 'balance of power' in the process of assessing need satisfaction away from 'experts' and professionals towards citizens in their local communities.

At the same time, it is important to ensure that simple 'wants' of consumers and the self-defined interests of groups of citizens do not dominate the process of needs assessment. It should be emphasised that a balanced approach is required whereby citizens' and professionals' perspectives are confronted with each other and reconciled with available 'codified knowledge'. Optimistically, we can see community needs auditing as promoting the development of a more open, pluralistic, participatory democracy and more effective health and welfare services which satisfy defined rights to welfare.

However, needs auditing should not be seen as a universal panacea for the ills of the welfare state. Rather it should be seen as a useful tool that can contribute to the creation of a more effective, more responsive, more open and more integrated, needs-based health and welfare system. Neither should needs auditing be thought to offer ready-made answers to the difficult questions of who gets what, how and when. Choices will still have to be made and priorities set. Those decisions are necessarily and properly political choices and should be made through a process open to fully democratic participation. We argue that needs auditing increases the likelihood that those choices will be made on the basis of comprehensive and detailed information about needs, that the decision-making process will be more open and will have involved citizens in discussion about possible priorities, and that the outcome will be a more equitable and effective health and welfare system. Moreover, if this is not the case then citizens will know about it and will be in a position to hold politicians and agencies accountable.

Finally, if new social rights are to be developed along lines proposed elswhere by the Institute for Public Policy Research (Coote 1992), it will of course be necessary to specify the substance of those rights. This requires a coherent theory of needs and a means of assessing them, if we are to avoid the danger of entitlements being drawn up in a traditional 'top-down' or arbitrary manner. For the new rights to be genuinely useful, they must reflect the day-to-day experience of the citizens whose access to health and welfare services they are designed to protect.

PART 2

THE FINDINGS

This report attempts to incorporate the findings from all the various elements of the study - codified knowledge, postal questionnaire, follow-up interviews, interviews with community representatives and professional workers and public meetings.

It is structured as follows.

Section I examines perceptions of the importance to well-being and quality of life of the various indicators. We then go on to look at data relating to basic needs - physical health and autonomy - drawn from all sources. Section II uses the same data sources to assess intermediate needs: food, drink and lifestyle; housing; physical environment; health and welfare services; work and economic security; social contacts and community participation and children's needs. The key issues are then summarised and priorities identified. The Appendix lists the professionals, 'front-line' workers and community representatives interviewed as part of the study.

SECTION I: BASIC NEEDS

2.1 FACTORS INFLUENCING WELL-BEING AND QUALITY OF LIFE

Before asking residents and professionals in the study area about their perceptions of basic and intermediate needs, we wanted to find out the relative importance attached to factors that could be assumed to affect well-being and quality of life and whether or not there was general agreement that those factors identified were important.

To that end we developed a list of factors based on the basic and intermediate needs discussed in 1:1. We then asked respondents to the postal survey to indicate the degree of importance they attached to each of these factors. The same exercise was also repeated with the professional workers and community representatives interviewed.

Residents' Perceptions

It can be seen from the pattern of responses shown in Table 1 that the vast majority of respondents consider most factors to be 'fairly' or 'very important'. In order to differentiate opinions we can examine the proportion of respondents considering each factor to be 'very important', and Figure 2 (p77-80) displays this for all respondents and by sex and age grouping.

Looked at in this way health-related attributes can be seen to have a high perceived importance, as do 'being safe from acts of crime and violence', 'having a decent standard of housing' and 'living in a pleasant, clean and peaceful area'. The lowest rankings overall go to 'having an influence on organisations which affect your life', 'having spare time for personal and leisure activities' and 'having access to social services'.

In general women tend to attach greater importance to all factors than men. Moreover, women attach significantly greater importance than men to 'feeling confident about children's future', 'having access to health care and social services', 'having a decent standard of housing', 'living in a pleasant, clean and peaceful area' and 'having close friends and relatives

Table 1: Perceived Importance of Factors Contributing to Quality of Life and Well-being. All Residents (%)

	Not at all important	Of little importance	Fairly important	Very important	Don't know
A good standard of general health	1.1	0.3	6.0	92.4	0.2
Being free from stress, worries and depression	1.1	1.3	6.8	80.2	0.6
Spare time for personal & leisure activities	1.9	3.3	39.1	55.2	0.4
A good standard of education	1.7	3.6	29.2	64.5	1.0
A healthy diet & safe drinking water	0.9	0.5	12.3	86.0	0.3
A decent standard of housing	0.5	0.2	14.8	84.3	0.3
A job with safe & healthy working conditions	1.4	1.0	17.4	79.6	0.5
A satisfying job	1.7	1.2	29.2	67.3	0.6
Living in a pleasant, clean & peaceful area	0.9	0.8	24.2	73.8	0.3
Access to health care	0.9	0.3	11.1	87.5	0.2
Access to social services	4.3	7.7	29.1	57.2	1.7

Close friends & relatives who can be relied on	1.9	2.5	31.6	63.8	0.2
Enough money & insurance to feel reasonably secure	0.7	1.0	24.6	73.5	0.3
Safe from acts of crime & violence	0.6	0.3	8.3	90.6	0.3
An influence on decisions of organsations which affect your life	1.6	5.5	36.8	53.8	2.3
Confidence about your children's future	4.2	1.8	13.1	76.6	4.4

who can be relied on'. Conversely, men attach more importance than women to 'having spare time for personal and leisure activities' and tend to place relatively high value on 'having a good standard of health', 'being free from stress, worries and depression' and 'having a job with safe and healthy working conditions'.

Looking at the pattern across age groupings, in general the perceived importance of factors increases with age: the elderly have a greater tendency to see all factors as very important. However there are some significant differences between age groupings in terms of specific factors. Younger people (18-34) tend to place less importance than other age groups on housing and the local area, freedom from stress, worry and depression, financial security and access to social services, but place relatively high value on being in good health, feeling confident about children's future, having a good standard of education and having spare time. The middle age grouping (35-64) tends to attach relatively high importance to more material considerations - housing, financial security and a satisfying job. The elderly tend to place more value on security and support - safety from crime, financial security and the support of friends and social services - and place less importance on being in good health, having a safe job, feeling confident about children's future, influencing organisations and having spare time.

The pattern for ethnic minorities shown in Figure 2 should be treated with some caution because of the limited response from this group. Nevertheless, it would appear that ethnic minority respondents tend to attach rather less importance to all factors than white respondents. However, they attach relatively more importance to 'having a good standard of education' and 'having a satisfying job' whereas housing, freedom from stress, worry and depression and having spare time are given relatively low importance.

For people in paid work, above average importance is attached to being in good general health, having a safe and satisfying job, having a good standard of education and spare time, that is, factors which could be seen to relate to work, prospects and fitting in leisure with work. On the other hand, below average importance is given to crime and the local area, financial security and support of friends and social services.

Analysed in terms of level of educational attainment, the main discernible difference is between those with no qualifications and those with degrees and postgraduate qualifications. The former tend to think all factors are important and place relatively high value on freedom from crime, housing and the local area, having a safe job, financial security and support from friends and social services. (There are similarities here with the priorities of the elderly of whom a high proportion have no formal qualifications.) Those with degree-level education attach relatively high importance to health and diet, a satisfying job and spare time while much lower priority is given to crime, housing, the local area, financial security and support of friends and social services. The other groups have intermediate positions on most factors.

From these results, it is possible to discern certain differences in the priorities and values of different groups of respondents. Although there are strong similarities in the overall rankings of factors, differences in relative priorities are evident. First, women tend to feel more strongly about the importance of all these factors than men, and older age groups tend to feel more strongly than younger people. Men attach above average importance to factors relating to work, freedom from stress and having spare time;

women tend to value care and support, children's prospects and the quality of housing and the local area. Younger people attach relatively high importance to feeling confident about children's future, education and spare time; middle-age groups emphasise more material considerations - housing, work, financial security. The elderly tend to value security and support - safety from crime, financial security, support of friends and access to health and social services.

Those in work place relatively high values on factors relating to work, prospects and fitting in leisure time. The unemployed place above average importance on having a healthy diet and safe job, financial security and an influence on organisations. Those looking after home and children place relatively high value on factors relating to health, children's future, housing and the local area and support of friends and social services. Ethnic minorities tend to value good education and a satisfying job. The importance given to crime, housing and local area, a safe job, financial security and the support of friends and social services tends to diminish with increasing level of educational attainment.

If we examine the responses by area, it is more difficult to discern clear patterns and it would appear that variations relate to the age, sex and economic activity characteristics of each area. Thus, in Hawksworth Wood it is possible to identify the values of the elderly (crime, health care, housing financial security and support from social services) and of those looking after home and children (health, children's future, housing, local area and social services). In the Vespers, the values of middle age groups and 'carers' are in evidence (health, freedom from stress etc, education). Kirkstall also has a relatively high proportion of elderly people whereas the Burley area is more mixed and a clear pattern here is difficult to identify.

Residents. Perceived importance of factors contributing to well-being and quality of life: All, sex, age, race, economic status. (Percentage of respondents indicating 'very important').

%

Figure 2:1

Figure 2:2

Good general health

Free from stress, worry, depression

Time for personal & leisure activities

Good standard of education

Residents. Perceived importance of factors contributing to well-being and quality of life: All, sex, age, race, economic status. (Percentage of respondents indicating 'very important').

% *Figure 2:3*

% *Figure 2:4*

 Healthy diet, safe water   ▦ Decent housing

▦ Safe, healthy
work conditions   ◩ Good standard of education

Residents. Perceived importance of factors contributing to well-being and quality of life: All, sex, age, race, economic status. (Percentage of respondents indicating 'very important').

Figure 2:5

Figure 2:6

Peaceful, clean, pleasant area

Access to Social Services

Access to health care

Close, reliable friends & relatives

Residents. Perceived importance of factors contributing to well-being and quality of life: All, sex, age, race, economic status. (Percentage of respondents indicating 'very important').

% **Figure 2:7**

% **Figure 2:8**

◹ Financial security	▨ Safe from crime & violence
▨ Influence over important decisions	◹ Confident of children's future

Perceptions of professionals and community representatives

In our interviews with local professionals, front-line workers and community representatives, interviewees were asked to indicate their perceptions of the importance of the various factors affecting quality of life for the local community. Their responses are illustrated in Figure 3 (p82-83), again showing the percentage responding 'very important' for each factor.

This pattern of priorities can be compared with the results for the respondents to the postal survey discussed above. In aggregate, local professionals and community representatives are less inclined to regard these factors as 'very important'. However, they tend to attach relatively greater importance than the general population to having access to health and social services, feeling confident about children's future, having a good standard of education and having an influence on organisations. On the other hand, more 'material' considerations, such as having a safe and satisfying job, financial security and living in a pleasant, clean and peaceful area are given rather less importance.

Figure 3 also disaggregates the priorities of various sub-groups of local professionals and community representatives. Thus, it can be seen that workers in the social services tend to place more value on the 'material' considerations of having a safe job and financial security and also on having the support of social services and friends and having spare time. Health workers emphasise the importance of having good health and diet and attach relatively high importance to feeling confident about children's future, having an influence on organisations and having a satisfying job. They attach less importance than social service workers to having the support of social services and friends.

Police and probation officers are significantly less likely than other professionals to regard these factors as "very important" for quality of life and well-being. They attach relatively low importance to having a safe and satisfying job, having the support of social services and friends, having a good diet and having an influence on organisations. On the other hand, they attach relatively high importance to freedom from stress, worry and depression and having a good education.

Professionals and community representatives. Perceived importance of factors contributing to well-being and quality of life: All, community representatives, social service & social careworkers, health service workers, police & probation. (Percentage of respondents indicating 'very important').

Figure 3:1

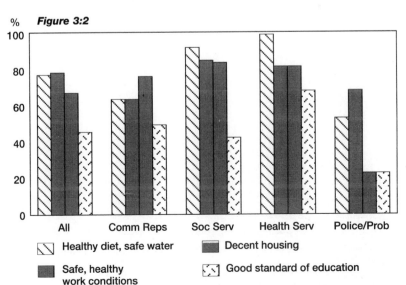

Figure 3:2

Professionals and community representatives. Perceived importance of factors contributing to well-being and quality of life: All, community representatives, social service & social careworkers, health service workers, police & probation. (Percentage of respondents indicating 'very important').

Figure 3:3

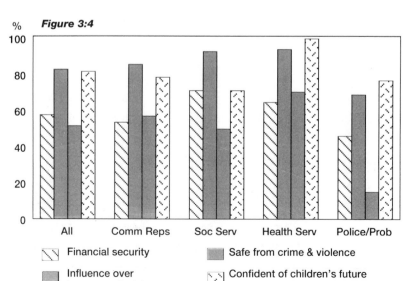

Figure 3:4

Therefore, it would seem that there are certain differences in the priorities of the different groups of professionals, particularly between police and probation and other groups (especially social services), but also between social services and health workers. The main differences relate to the perceived importance of having a safe and satisfactory job, having access to social services, having a good education, feeling confident about children's future and having an influence on organisations.

The ranking for community representatives (eg. community groups and politicians) again shows notable differences compared to the groups of professionals (Figure 3). Relatively high importance is attached to having a good standard of education, having access to social services and having a safe job. On the other hand, lower importance is given to having a good standard of health, a healthy diet, freedom from stress and worry and a decent standard of housing. This pattern of priorities is rather distinctive in relation to both the various groups of professionals and the general public.

Conclusions

This analysis of perceptions of the relative importance of factors influencing well-being and quality of life, suggests that the list of basic and intermediate needs developed by Doyal and Gough which informs this study (see 1:1) is one that is broadly agreed to by local residents, professional workers and community representatives alike. The majority of people we spoke to or who completed the postal questionnaire identified these factors to be 'fairly important' or 'very important' to well-being and quality of life.

It is only when one analyses the factors in terms of which are more likely to attract 'very important' responses that some differences begin to emerge between groups. For example, among local residents there are some differences in the relative importance attached to certain factors between respondents from different age groups, between men and women and on the basis of educational attainment and employment status.

Amongst the professionals interviewed it is possible to find some differences between different groups and between professionals and local residents although such differences should not be over-emphasised. Again there are certain differences in the perceived importance of the factors listed, between community representatives and local residents and the degree of difference is generally larger than that between professionals and residents.

While one should not over-emphasise such differences as exist it is important to recognise that they may have implications for the assessment of need since the degree of importance attached to different factors may affect perceptions of the severity of problems and approaches to solving them.

The existence of such differences in the values and perceptions of various groups - professionals, community representatives and residents - strengthens the case for obtaining a wide range of views about needs both in terms of integrating bottom-up and top-down approaches and in terms of ensuring that all the relevant front-line professional groupings are covered.

2:2 THE PHYSICAL HEALTH AND AUTONOMY OF PEOPLE IN KIRKSTALL

As indicated in Part 1, we have identified the two basic human needs as physical health (ie the absence of death, disability and disease) and personal autonomy (comprising mental health, cognitive skills and opportunities to engage in social participation). In general, residents in the study area, local professional workers and community representatives agree that physical health and (to a slightly lesser extent) autonomy (or proxies for autonomy) are important for well-being and quality of life.

In this chapter we look at both objective and subjective indicators of physical health and autonomy. Since the particular focus of our study was health and welfare needs, we gave certain aspects of autonomy (eg. cognitive skills) relatively less attention than physical health. However, in practice it is very difficult to separate out physical health and autonomy and, as our research shows, impaired autonomy (as a result, for example, of stress) is positively correlated with poor general health.

Physical Health: Codified Knowledge

As a first step in assessing the extent to which basic needs for physical health are being met in the study area and at what level compared with other parts of the city or other parts of the country, we collected together a considerable amount of existing 'codified' knowledge.

One indicator of the physical health of a population is mortality rates. Mortality data alone provide only a partial measure of health since they omit serious non-fatal illnesses such as chronic arthritis. Therefore it is important to examine both mortality and morbidity data in so far as they are available.

It is clear that the *absence* of death, disease and disability is an unattainable state (though the absence of specific *causes* of death, ill-health or disability may be attainable). However, defining health in this way implies that lower rates of mortality and morbidity signify an improved health status for the population as a whole. This general principle does not provide guidance on trade-offs in situations where, for example, mortality rates are rising for some causes of death and falling for others or where the health status of the population as a whole is improving but inequalities in health are widening.

In this section mortality and morbidity data is reported for Kirkstall Ward or, in most cases, the closest approximation to the ward for which data is held. To make sense of much of this data it will be compared with that for Leeds as a whole and/or England and Wales. In most cases, the most recent available data is given to provide a 'snap-shot' and no data on trends is reported. The aim is the more limited one of charting what the health status of the population is rather than whether, or how far, it has improved. Similarly, no data is given relating to inequalities in health within the population except in so far as the health experience of Kirkstall or Leeds West is compared to that of Leeds as a whole or England and Wales.

In assessing the health status of the population of Kirkstall and comparing it to other areas a significant problem concerns the relative weight to be assigned to specific indicators such as various causes of death. This problem can be addressed through the construction of a composite index combining a number of indicators or variables. An example of this approach with relevance to health is the Jarman index already referred to in Part 1.

The Jarman Index is intended to identify underprivileged areas, these being areas where the General Practitioner workload is likely to be heavier. The index is calculated on the basis of the following socio-economic indicators:

Socio-Economic Indicators: Descriptive list of variables used to calculate the Jarman Index

*Over 65   People aged 65 or more as a percentage of all residents in private households.

Pensioner alone   Pensioners (females over 60, males over 65) living alone as a percentage of all residents in private households.

One parent   People in households consisting of one person over 16 and one or more children under 16 as a percentage of all residents in private households.

Unskilled   People in households headed by a person in socio-economic group 11 as percentage of all residents in private households.

Unemployed   People aged 16 or more seeking work or temporarily sick as a percentage of the total economically active population.

*Lacks amenity People in households lacking exclusive use of a bath and inside WC as a percentage of all residents in private households.

Overcrowded   People in households living at more than one person per room as a percentage of all residents in private households.

Changed address People aged 1 or over with a usual address one year before the census different from present usual address as a percentage of total residents.

Ethnic minority People in households headed by a person born in New Commonwealth or Pakistan as a percentage of all residents in private households.

UPA8 Score   An index based on eight of the ten variables which are listed above from OVER 65 to ETHNIC MINORITY excluding those marked*. This is also known as the Jarman Index.

Source: Wain and Moore (1989)

Using 1981 Census data the Jarman score has been calculated for each electoral ward in Leeds. Of the 32 wards, Kirkstall is ranked ninth with a score of 26.1. This compares with a score of 47.9 for University, the most deprived ward, and -16.4 for Halton, the least deprived. Thus Kirkstall is one of the more deprived wards in Leeds.

The Jarman Index has the advantage of facilitating the ranking of populations as more or less deprived. This is a controversial procedure since it not only involves selecting a small number from the wide range of possible indicators and variables but also weighting these in order to calculate a score. In any case since the index does not include a health variable, the health status of a population can only be indicated indirectly in so far as more deprived populations are likely to have greater health needs and put a heavier demand on health services.

An alternative approach is to select a range of indicators each of which provides a direct measure of health but without using the data to calculate a composite index or score.

The Faculty of Public Health Medicine of the Royal Colleges of Physicians of London has identified 13 key public health indicators as follows:

- Percentage of births under 2500g
- Abortion rate by maternal age
- Abortions by maternal age
- Standardised Mortality Ratios (SMR) for selected causes of death
- Death rates by sex for selected causes
- Deaths by sex for selected causes
- SMRs for 'avoidable' causes of death
- Years of life lost: selected causes of death: rates
- Years of life lost: selected causes of death: totals
- Perinatal mortality rates
- Infant mortality rates
- Childhood mortality rates

Source: Moore (1989)

Mortality

Ten of the thirteen indicators relate to mortality and the remainder concern ill-health and morbidity. Health in Leeds (Moore, 1990) presents the key public health indicators for the two former district health authorities in Leeds, West and East. In this section selective data relating to the key indicators is reported and supplemented with mortality data from other sources.

Low birthweight is associated with increased rates of morbidity and mortality in childhood. In 1989, 661 births under 2500g occurred in Leeds representing 7.0 per cent of total live and still births. Although the percentage figure has fluctuated in recent years it has varied little from that for England and Wales and was equal to it in 1989.

The four major causes of death of men and women in Leeds West (in terms of numbers) are malignant neoplasms (cancers), ischaemic heart disease (IHD), cerebrovascular disease (strokes), and disease of the respiratory system. In the period 1985-89 two in three (66.7 per cent) male deaths and just over three in five (62.9 per cent) female deaths were attributed to the first three of these causes. In 1987, 75 per cent of all deaths of Leeds West residents was due to these four causes. For both men and women in Leeds West ischaemic heart disease is the single most important cause of death and for both sexes the standardised mortality ratio is statistically significantly raised for this cause.

The category 'all malignant neoplasms' is broken down into the three major types: lung cancer and, in women, breast cancer and cancer of the cervix. Lung cancer is a more significant cause of death in men than women: one in ten male deaths in the years 1985-89 was due to lung cancer as against one in twenty five female deaths. However for both men and women the standardised mortality ratio for lung cancer is statistically significantly raised in Leeds. In women breast cancer is as significant a cause of death as lung cancer. The number of deaths from cancer of the cervix is not large. The annual number of deaths (expressed as a four-year moving average) of women aged 15-64 in Leeds West has declined in the period 1981-88 along with the standardised mortality ratio. During this period an annual average of nine women aged 15-64 died from cancer of the cervix in Leeds West.

Heart disease, cancer and cerebrovascular disease are all preventable or potentially reducible causes of death. Out of a total of 8,465 deaths of Leeds residents in 1985, 5,011 (59 per cent) were classified as preventable. Ischaemic heart disease was the cause of 2580 preventable deaths, that is over half of all preventable deaths, and heart attacks were responsible for two in three of these IHD deaths. Lung cancer was the cause of 12 per cent of all preventable deaths.

The standardised mortality ratios (though not numbers of deaths) for 'all causes' of death for Kirkstall ward are somewhat lower than for Leeds, and the overall death rate in Kirkstall almost exactly matches that for England and Wales (ie. there is no discrepancy between the death rate for 'all causes' in Kirkstall and the rate we would 'expect' given its age and sex structure). Of the specific causes of death listed, the Kirkstall SMR compared to Leeds as a whole is notably lower only for diseases of the circulatory system, heart attacks and strokes.

A significant proportion of deaths due to heart disease and lung cancer is attributable to smoking. Of total deaths due to these causes in Leeds in 1987, 22.7 per cent and 87 per cent respectively were attributed to smoking. Deaths from smoking (ie. deaths from illnesses - heart disease, lung cancer, bronchitis and emphysema - attributed to smoking) accounted for 13.3 per cent of all deaths in Leeds in that year.

As well as number of deaths, heart disease and cancer are also the two major causes of years of life lost. The majority of deaths due to heart disease and cancer occurs in the elderly population so that the average years of life lost for each individual dying of these causes is relatively low. However, the high incidence of these causes means that the annual years of life lost in the population as a whole is high. Conversely the number of deaths due to, for example, motor vehicle traffic accidents and suicide is relatively low. In the years 1985-89, traffic accidents and suicides caused 285 male deaths out of a total of 10,405 (2.7 per cent) and 131 female deaths out of a total of 10,882 (1.2 per cent). However, the majority of such deaths occurs in younger age groups so that the average years of life lost for each individual is relatively high. Therefore, these causes of death look more significant relative to heart disease and cancer when considered in terms of years of life lost in the population as a whole rather than number of deaths. Thus, for example, the ratio of traffic accidents to heart disease is 3.7 per cent in terms of number of male deaths but 19.2 per cent in terms of male years of life lost.

During the period 1985-89 the average annual number of deaths (male and female) in Leeds West due to motor vehicle traffic accidents was 36. This can be compared to a total of 141 deaths due to accidents and violence in Leeds West in 1988. Thus traffic accidents account for a significant proportion of all deaths due to accidents. Of 112 deaths due to accidents in Leeds West in 1986-87, 24 (21 per cent) were due to road traffic accidents, 11 (10 per cent) to accidents at home, one to work accident, and 76 to 'other causes' (Moore, 1989). On the other hand, only a small proportion of road traffic accident casualties is fatal. In 1988 there were 2,959 reported personal injury road accidents in Leeds involving 3,828 casualties. Of these 82 (2.1 per cent) were fatal, 634 (16.6 per cent) serious, and 3,112 (81.3 per cent) slight.

Analysis of perinatal, postneonatal, infant and childhood mortality rates for Leeds shows that in 1989 there were 91 deaths of infants under one year old giving an infant mortality rate of 9.4, higher than that for England and Wales at 8.4. However the perinatal mortality rate (ie. still births and deaths under one week per 1,000 total births) for Leeds is 7.6, lower than that for England and Wales (8.3). In each year in the period 1984-89 (except 1988), the rate is higher for Leeds than England and Wales. The reasons for this difference are not clear although infant mortality is 'closely associated with socio-economic factors, rising from social class I to social class V' (Wain and Moore, 1990).

Nearly half (47 per cent) of all infant deaths occur before the 28th day and nearly a third (31 per cent) before the seventh. Thus risk of death diminishes rapidly during the first year of life. The risk of death in childhood (1-14 years) is low. In Leeds in 1989 there were nine deaths of children aged 1-4 years (0.24 per 1000) two of which were in Kirkstall ward, and 16 deaths of children aged 5-14 years (0.19 per thousand) three of which were in the Kirkstall ward. The risk of death at age 1-4 years is approximately one fiftieth of that under one year. The major cause of childhood deaths is injury. Of the 25 deaths of Leeds children aged 1-14 in 1989, 7 (28 per cent) were due to motor vehicle traffic accidents (Wain and Moore, 1990).

Morbidity

Mortality provides the standard approach to measuring health, as signified by the Key Public Health Indicators. However,

'It is important to realise that for conditions which rarely lead to death, such as chronic arthritis, mortality data give a poor reflection of the true burden of ill-health in the community. Information about ill-health or morbidity is scarce at present, but would be particularly helpful for the accurate assessment of the health needs of the population.' (Wain and Moore, 1990).

In this section a limited range of indicators of morbidity is presented relating to accidents, communicable disease and dental health.

Information on accidents is in the form of record of attendance for accident at the Leeds General Infirmary Accident and Emergency Department. Eighty per cent of attenders are residents of Leeds West (Wain and Moore, 1990). Between 1986-88 there was a sharp rise in the number of new attendances for accidents in each age group, particularly among the elderly. The risk of accident declines with age: approximately one in 10 young people attend for accidents each year, three times the rate for the elderly.

Overall, accidents at home are the most common, accounting for 27.8 per cent of all accidents, and being the most frequent type of accident among the young (35.6 per cent) and the elderly (51.9 per cent). Accidents in public places are second most important in terms of frequency, accounting for 23.8 per cent of all accidents and being the second most common type of accident in each age group. Among the population of working age, accidents at work are the most common.

The most common types of injury sustained, accounting for half of the total, are lacerations and contusions/abrasions (cuts and bruises/grazes). However the frequency data for types of accident and injury do not indicate the seriousness of the accident or injury. So although the frequency of head injury is low relative to that of contusions/abrasions, such injuries may be generally more serious so that the overall burden of ill health is greater.

Attendances for accidents are classified by the postal districts in which they happen and in which the person lives. Kirkstall (Leeds 4 and Leeds 5) does not figure in the five districts in which the majority of accidents occurred. On the other hand Leeds 5 is one of the six postal districts with the highest rates of attendance in terms of the place of residence of the accident victim (Wain and Moore, 1990). The six districts are all in close proximity to the Leeds General Infirmary so the higher attendance rates 'may reflect the use of the department rather than be a true reflection of the pattern of accidents across the city' (ibid).

A proportion of attenders for accidents is admitted to the wards for a variety of treatments ranging from observation to surgery. In 1986 there were 5,510 admissions for the effects of accidents (but also including a proportion of cases due to violence and poisoning), representing almost 25 per cent of attendances for accident in that year (ibid).

Numbers of road traffic accidents and resultant casualties in Leeds increased during the period 1983-88. Car drivers and passengers account for about half and pedestrians a quarter of all road traffic accident casualties.

The number of cases of communicable disease is based on notifications to the Medical Officer for Environmental Health by doctors in accordance with the Public Health (Control of Disease) Act 1984. There may be some degree of underestimation due to lack of notification, although in Leeds there is a good tradition of notification. The incidence of the listed communicable diseases in Leeds is low, the most frequently occurring in 1987 being rubella, measles and food poisoning. The incidence of all the listed diseases is low in postal districts 4 and 5, except hepatitis of which there were five cases in Leeds, four in 1987, compared to the highest incidence of eight cases in Leeds 14 and a total in Leeds of 53 cases.

There are significant differences in the standard of dental health between postal districts in Leeds. Children are classified according to the postal district of the school attended (not home address, which may be different) and by clinic catchment area (which may not correspond closely with postal district and ward boundaries). The mean number of decayed, missing and filled teeth (DMF) was 3.74 for Leeds as a whole and 3.72 for Leeds West. The mean number DMF is somewhat lower for Kirkstall clinic but markedly higher for Leeds 5 at 4.11 and, especially, Leeds 4 at 5.88 (postcodes of schools). In fact Leeds 4 has the highest mean number DMF of all postal districts, more than three times that recorded for Leeds 23 with the lowest number at 1.87. Leeds 5 is ranked nineteenth out of 26 postal districts for which data are recorded (ie. only seven districts have a higher mean number DMF). These findings are mirrored by those from a survey of a random sample of 762 five year old children in Leeds West in 1987-8 (Moore, 1989). Leeds 4 and 5 are two of the four postal districts in Leeds West with the highest DMF rates. The mean number DMF in Leeds 5 is more than four and a half times that in Leeds 21 (Otley): 3.10 compared to 0.67. More specifically, Kirkstall children have 30 times as many extracted teeth as children in Otley.

In addition to this 'objective' data on health, there is also some information available on people's own perceptions of their health status. In 1986 Leeds Western Health Authority carried out a survey as part of the Yorkshire Healthy Life survey. In addition the number of people with a disability is reported from the 1987 Population Survey undertaken by Leeds City Council.

In the Yorkshire Healthy Life Survey a large majority of respondents (80 per cent) say they are 'very' (25 per cent) or 'reasonably' (55 per cent) healthy as against a small minority (8 per cent) who say they are 'not very healthy' or 'definitely ill, in poor health'. On the other hand, nearly a third (31 per cent) say they have a long-term illness or disability (the most frequently cited being arthritis at three per cent) while 58 per cent have no such long-term illness or disability. On the face of it, it is surprising that four times as many people report long-term illness/disability as consider themselves not very healthy or in poor health. However it may be that a large proportion of respondents with long-term illness or disability perceive their health as reasonable in terms of their expectations of health and/or the seriousness of their illness/disability.

The 1987 Population Survey carried out by Leeds City Council asked whether citizens have a disability that affects them in terms of work or mobility or generally looking after themselves. The finding that 2.6 per cent of the total population have a disability defined in this way contrasts markedly with the 31 per cent of respondents who report a long-term illness or disability in the Yorkshire Healthy Life Survey. As might be expected the risk of disability increases steadily with age.

Physical Health: Experiential Knowledge

The above information tells us something about the health status of people in Leeds but not a lot about the health of people in the study area. It has been added to considerably as a result of the postal survey undertaken in the first phase of the project. In the postal questionnaire we asked a number of questions about physical health. First, we asked people to rank their general health over the previous 12 months. Seventy-eight per cent of respondents said that they were in good health and of these 23 per cent said they were in very good health. A slightly larger proportion of men (81 per cent) than women (76 per cent) said that their general health was good with significantly more men (27 per cent) than women (20 per cent) saying they were in very good health.

Not surprisingly the proportion of respondents who report good or very good health declines with age and, conversely, the proportion of respondents reporting very poor health rises with age. Thus, 13 per cent of the 18-34 age group report poor or very poor health compared with 35 per cent of those 65 years and over (see Figure 4).

Some groups suffer worse general health than others. Approximately twice as many Asian respondents (seven per cent) report very poor health as do whites (three per cent). Unemployed and retired people report poorer health than those in paid work, with 89 per cent of those in paid work saying that they were in good or very good general health compared with 78 per cent of unemployed people and 53 per cent of retired people (see Figure 5).

By far the smallest proportion of respondents reporting very good health (14 per cent) live in the Hawksworth Wood area compared to over 23 per cent for all other areas. Twenty-seven per cent of residents in Hawksworth

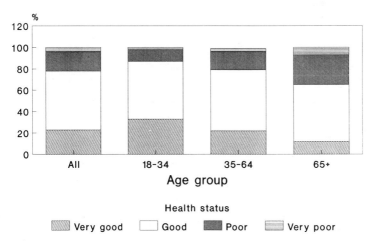

Figure 4
Health status by age

Wood report bad or very bad health compared with only 15 per cent of
those in the Vespers.

Those with poor health are disproportionately represented among those
living in flats: 29 per cent compared with 18 per cent for the sample
as a whole (this is because of the relatively high proportion of the elderly
living in flats). Fifty per cent of those people who describe their housing
as damp report poor or very poor health as do one third of those who
describe their home as being in a state of disrepair.

Secondly, we asked whether respondents had experienced any major
illness or injury over the past year. Twenty per cent of all respondents
said this was the case. This proportion increases with age; 33 per cent of
those aged 65 or over reported a major illness or injury compared with 14
per cent of the 18-34 age group. A markedly higher proportion of Asian
respondents (34 per cent) reported a major illness or injury than white (20
per cent) or Afro-Caribbean respondents.

The third question we asked about physical health was whether or not

Figure 5
Health status by labour market status

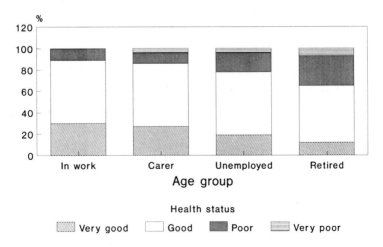

respondents had a long-standing illness, disability or infirmity. Twenty-seven per cent of all respondents say they have a long-standing illness, disability or infirmity. Again, not surprisingly, this proportion increases with age; nine per cent of those aged 18-34 responded positively compared with 44 per cent of those aged 65 and over. In contrast to the responses for general health and illness during the previous year, a lower proportion of non-white respondents (19 per cent) than white respondents (27 per cent) report a long-standing illness, disability or infirmity.

A significantly higher proportion of unemployed respondents than those in paid work, or at home caring report a long-standing illness, disability or infirmity. However the proportion is still lower than the overall average. Retired respondents report a rate more than three times that of those in paid work and almost twice that of the unemployed.

As with general health people living in the Hawksworth Wood area are more likely than people in other areas to report that they suffer a long-standing illness, disability or infirmity.

We asked people whether their life-style was affected by their state of health. Twenty per cent of respondents replied that their state of health did place a major limitation on the way they lived their life. More women than men said this was the case (21 per cent as compared to 19 per cent). Slightly fewer members of ethnic minority groups said this was the case than did white respondents. As one would expect those who describe their health as poor or very poor are far more likely to say that their way of life is constrained by their health (51 per cent and 83 per cent respectively).

When we asked people to describe the kinds of limitations caused by ill-health by far the most common related to mobility. People said they were generally 'less active' as a result of their illness or, more specifically, had difficulty walking or climbing stairs. Others were unable to engage in sports or leisure activitites such as gardening, or had difficulty carrying out routine household chores like shopping or cleaning. A significant number of respondents mentioned that their illness caused them to feel depressed or to lack confidence and for some, depression impaired their ability to engage in social activities.

These kinds of limitations were underlined in the follow up interviews where, again, lack of mobility emerged as a particular problem especially among the elderly. Several other elderly people mentioned that poor eyesight (due, in the main, to glaucoma or cataracts) prevented them from undertaking leisure or social activities such as reading and playing cards.

Professionals' Perceptions of General Health

During our interviews with professional workers we asked them to comment on the main health problems of residents in the Kirkstall ward. Local GPs whom we interviewed thought that the main health problems among adults in the area were coronary heart disease among both the white and Asian communities, and also lung cancer and circulatory problems caused by smoking. In addition, a community worker mentioned chest complaints, perpetual colds and 'low level infectious diseases' which were related to damp housing. This view was echoed by health promotion workers who were also concerned about the relationship between stress, heavy smoking and heart disease. One GP mentioned the especially high incidence of heart disease and diabetes among Asian residents. No clear reason could be given for this although it was thought that it might possibly relate to the high levels of animal fat in the diet (caused by cooking with ghee), stress and lack of exercise, especially among women.

Clear differences were thought to exist, between different sub-areas within the ward: residents in Hawksworth Wood and to a lesser extent, Burley, were thought to have worse general health than those living in other areas.

Community health workers whom we interviewed thought that the main health problems in Hawksworth Wood and Burley were gastro-enteritis and chest infections among children. Head lice was also thought to be a problem. This view was echoed by the officer-in-charge of a local family nursery centre who said that children in Hawksworth Wood suffered from sickness and diarrhoea, sometimes from birth, resulting in frequent hospital admissions among infants. She also spoke of the problem of upper respiratory infection resulting in ear, nose and throat operations, the most common being the insertion of grommets. One GP felt that Asian babies were particularly prone to diarrhoea and enteritis because they are more likely to be bottle fed than babies in other ethnic groups.

By contrast, in Kirkstall, the main health problems were thought to be those associated with old age, eg. dementia, rheumatoid arthritis and heart problems, according to local community health workers. However, it was also felt by the officer-in-charge of an elderly person's day centre, that physical health problems among the elderly are exacerbated by such things as loneliness and depression. The manager of another day centre for elderly Asians also mentioned failing eyesight, loss of teeth, lack of mobility and breathlessness as particular problems encountered by the elderly.

A number of health problems were thought to affect women in particular. Many of these relate to mental health which will be considered in the next section. In addition, it was felt by some that women (especially in Hawksworth Wood) experienced a high level of gynaecological problems (eg. cervical cancer and ovarian problems) due to the commencement of sexual activity at an early age.

Poor dental health among all groups was felt to be a particular problem by a number of professionals interviewed. Community dental officers thought that the problem was caused by the diet of the 'white working class', which included a high level of sugared drinks, sweets and chocolate, exacerbated by poor oral hygiene and smoking. Moreover, a particular problem was identified among Asian children because of the practice of sweetening babies' milk and high consumption of sweets.

Autonomy: Experiential Knowledge

The scope of our needs audit was drawn in such a way as to focus more on physical health than autonomy. Nevertheless given the lack of 'objective' information on people's level of autonomy, we included a question in the postal survey asking people to indicate whether they had a serious problem with stress, depression, anxiety/worry or sleeplessness, all of which might be assumed to impair autonomy, although caution must, of course, be used in interpreting 'self-diagnosis' responses in this area.

Forty-eight per cent of respondents indicated that they had no serious problem with any of these conditions while 25 per cent indicated that they suffered from more than one of the problems mentioned. More men (55.5 per cent) than women (44 per cent) said they did not suffer from any of these problems, while 52 per cent of those aged 18-34 reported no problem compared to 43 per cent of those aged 65 and over. However, the greatest differences occur if we look at the economic activity of respondents. Fifty-six per cent of those in paid work reported no problems compared to 44 per cent of those engaged in caring activity, 43 per cent of retired respondents and 34 per cent of the unemployed. Significant differences also occur between residents in the different sub-areas: sixty-three per cent of residents in the Vespers reported none of these problems compared to 39 per cent of those living in Hawksworth Wood.

Eighteen and a half per cent of all respondents reported that they suffered from stress (20 per cent of women compared to 16.5 per cent of men). Also, as shown in Figure 6, the incidence of stress appears to decrease with age with 23 per cent in the 18-34 age group saying they are sufferers compared to 19 per cent in the 35-64 age group and 13 per cent among those aged 65 or over. (However as was pointed out to us at one of the public meetings this might be because 'stress' is a term more widely used by younger people.)

Figure 6
Autonomy by age

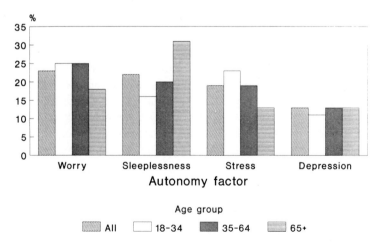

Figure 7
Autonomy by labour market status

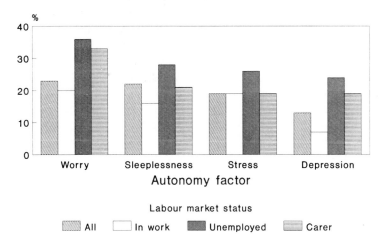

Stress was reported more often by non-white respondents (28 per cent) than white respondents (18 per cent) and by the unemployed (26 per cent) than those in paid work or caring for home and family (both 19 per cent) and retired people (14 per cent) (Figure 7). People living in Burley were more likely to suffer from stress (22 per cent) compared to the other sub-areas.

A higher proportion of respondents said that they suffer from anxiety (23 per cent) than from stress. A pattern emerges similar to that of the responses for stress with a higher proportion of women (25 per cent) than men (21 per cent) experiencing anxiety and with the elderly reporting a lower incidence of anxiety. Those in the middle-age group, however, report a similar incidence of anxiety to those in the youngest age group (25 per cent in both cases, Figure 6). However, whereas stress is most prevalent in Burley, anxiety is most prevalent among residents in Hawksworth Wood, 29 per cent of whom say they have a serious problem with anxiety.

Of the elderly people we interviewed who mentioned anxiety or worry as a serious problem, a number mentioned their own or a dependant's health as a cause of anxiety. Anxiety about others was also mentioned by some of the women with young children who we interviewed - in this case the anxiety related to children. One women in Burley said that anxiety meant she 'doesn't allow [her] son to play out,' adding that, 'He hasn't played out for three years.' Ethnic minority interviewees spoke of 'general anxiety' or anxiety about specifics such as paying the poll tax.

Thirteen per cent of the sample reported that they suffer from sleeplessness with significantly more women (25 per cent) than men (17 per cent) affected. Sleeplessness, unlike stress and anxiety, increases with age with 16 per cent of those aged 18-34 reporting a problem and 31.5 per cent of those aged 65 and over (Figure 6). Sleeplesness is less common among ethnic minority respondents than it is among white respondents (22 per cent) and more common among unemployed and retired respondents than other groups (Figure 7). This view was confirmed by the follow-up interviews with elderly people in all three sub-areas who made comments such as 'I'm tired all day' or 'I sleep through the day rather than through the night.' Another elderly respondent said that she had been given sleeping tablets but was worried about addiction. While elderly interviewees complained of insomnia, women with young children were more likely to complain of tiredness. Sleeplessness is most likely to be found among the residents of Hawksworth Wood (29 per cent) compared to only 13 per cent of those living in the Vespers.

Depression is the least reported of this set of problems with 13 per cent of respondents saying they have a serious problem. More women (14 per cent) than men (10.5 per cent) report depression with no differences emerging when examining the results by age or ethnicity. Significant differences do occur, however, if we take account of the economic activity of those suffering from depression (Figure 7). Twenty-four per cent of those who are unemployed and 19 per cent of those caring for home and family report a serious problem with depression compared to 14 per cent of retired people and 7.5 per cent of those in paid work. Women with young children spoke a lot about depression or 'moods'. One woman living in Hawksworth Wood described a 'feeling of helplessness'.

Professionals' Perceptions of Autonomy

When interviewing professionals about the general health problems of residents in the area many mentioned mental health problems as giving serious cause for concern in relation to a number of different groups. Some, but not all of their concerns mirrored those of the population as a whole. So, for example, a community worker in Burley spoke in general terms about 'a problem of fragile mental health' due to the pressures of living in the area and financial difficulties; one manifestation of this was behavioural problems among children. A community health worker was also concerned about the problems of stress and lack of stimulation for children. Similarly, GPs, community health workers and a local clergyman all mentioned stress-related complaints such as headaches and insomnia as problems for many people. The same local clergyman was also concerned that people had psychological problems due to abuse.

Physical Health: Key Issues

The theory of needs that informs our research identified physical health and personal autonomy as the two basic human needs. Our study confirms the salience of physical health and, to a lesser extent, autonomy for the majority of people.

In order to assess the extent to which these two basic needs are being met among residents in the area we examined some existing data sources, asked local people for their own perceptions and invited professionals working in the area and community representatives to comment.

The codified knowledge on general physical health is mostly collected by the health authority and relates to mortality and morbidity. This information tells us *something* about the health of the population but leaves many questions unanswered. One particular problem is that much of the information is only available by health authority area which covers too many people to permit a deep understanding at a community level. A second problem relates to the fact that, in the case of morbidity, the information relates only to illnesses serious enough to require hospital treatment thereby excluding the myriad health problems that cause people to go to their GP or, indeed, the health problems that people for whatever reason 'learn to live with'.

Finally, the codified knowledge tells us nothing about what a particular disease or disability means to the sufferer or their family. Nevertheless, 'objective' measures of physical health are important for comparative purposes.

Given the main focus of our study on health and welfare needs we were less concerned to bring together 'codified knowledge' on the autonomy status of individuals living in the study area. But, in any case, to do so would have been difficult since there are few 'objective' measures of autonomy or lack of autonomy. The latter, in particular, manifests itself in a variety of different ways. The most extreme - severe mental breakdown - are perhaps amenable to being measured (eg. admissions to mental hospital etc), but the less extreme, but more common, instances (eg. depression and anxiety) are much less amenable to measurement since help, if sought at all, may come from a variety of formal and informal sources.

Our survey of local residents and follow-up interviews makes clear the extent to which a significant proportion of the population are not having their basic needs for physical health and personal autonomy met. It also makes clear the extent to which the two are inter-related with people reporting poor general health often also reporting problems with stress, depression, worry or sleeplessness. Our findings also reinforce the view that physical health and autonomy are conditioned (if not determined) by external factors such as housing, the local environment, economic status and so on. There is now a considerable body of research that demonstrates the extent to which such things as poverty, unemployment and poor housing are positively correlated with poor general health. This study adds to that body of research.

In general our interviews with professional workers in the area simply added to the picture that had already been drawn by studying the codified knowledge on physical health and the residents' own perceptions as revealed in the postal survey and follow-up interviews. However, they were particularly useful in terms of elaborating (often using medical terminology to name specific diseases) on the health problems of particular groups within the overall population eg. women, children or ethnic minorities.

Surprisingly, given the salience of health as an issue, it was not raised for direct discussion either at the public meetings or in the interviews with community representatives. Instead the discussion focused on intermediate needs and how these impinged on physical health.

SECTION II: INTERMEDIATE NEEDS

2:3.   DIET AND LIFESTYLE

A basic pre-requisite for good health is adequate, nourishing food and clean water. In this chapter we look at the extent to which these intermediate needs are being met among residents in the study area. Another pre-requisite for good health is a lifestyle that is, at least, not damaging to physicial health. To that end we also include information on certain aspects of lifestyle known to affect health namely, smoking, alcohol consumption and exercise.

Diet and Lifestyle: Codified Knowledge

There is an assumption that people living in western, developed countries do have access to clean water and, with a very few exceptions, to adequate nutritious food. Very little information is readily available, however, on the extent to which people's needs in this respect are being met in the study area.

Aggregate information for the West Yorkshire area indicate that about two per cent of samples reveal choloforms in the water. As regards food quality, data is available on the incidence of notified food poisoning in Leeds by postal district. During 1990 there were 965 formally notified cases of food poisoning in Leeds (plus an additional 507 ascertained cases). In total, therefore, this represents approximately one case for every 480 people in Leeds. In the postal districts LS4 and LS5 (the nearest approximation to the Kirkstall ward) there were 37 notified and ascertained cases, representing a broadly similar ratio to total population as in Leeds as a whole.

Diet and Lifestyle: Experiential Knowledge

To enlarge our understanding of the extent to which the need for nutritious food, clean water and non-harmful lifestyle were being met we asked local residents for their views on a range of topics related to these issues. We asked respondents to say whether they thought that their usual diet was good for their health, that food in the shops is generally safe to eat, and that their drinking water is generally safe; also, whether they smoke or drink too much for the good of their health and whether they thought they got sufficient exercise.

Seventeen per cent of respondents thought that their usual diet was not good for their health (18 per cent of men and 16 per cent of women). Younger respondents and unemployed respondents were more likely than the average to take this view with 25 per cent and 27 per cent responding in this way. This compares to nine per cent of elderly respondents and 12 per cent of those aged 35 to 64. Those people who think their diet is unhealthy are distributed evenly between the four sub-areas of the ward.

The proportion of those stating that their usual diet is not good for them increases as the (self-reported) standard of general health declines. Thus, 12 per cent of those in very good health think that their diet is not good for their health compared with a quarter of those in very poor health. Thirteen per cent of respondents thought that food bought in the shops is generally not safe to eat and 25.5 per cent that water is generally not safe to drink. A further 18.5 per cent and 21 per cent respectively responded that they didn't know.

Ethnic minority groups were more likely than white respondents to think that shop-bought food is unsafe with 22 per cent of non-whites expressing concern compared to 12 per cent of white respondents. Those reporting a poor standard of health were also more likely to be concerned about the safety of food and water. Of those in good health 10 per cent thought that food was unsafe and 23 per cent water, whereas of those in poor health 17 per cent thought food unsafe and 33 per cent water. Residents in the Vespers (the 'better-off' part of the ward) were far more likely than residents in other areas to be satisfied with the safety of food and water. 95 per cent of Vespers residents think that food is safe and 74 per cent that water is safe compared to 87 per cent and 70 per cent respectively for the other areas.

We asked people whether or not they smoked and drank too much for the good of their health. Sixty-four per cent of the sample do not smoke, and non-smokers are more likely than smokers to report a very good standard of general health. Seventy-three per cent of those who say they are in very good health do not smoke compared to 56 per cent of those in very poor health. Sixty per cent of smokers (21 per cent of the total sample) think

Figure 8
Smokers reporting excessive smoking

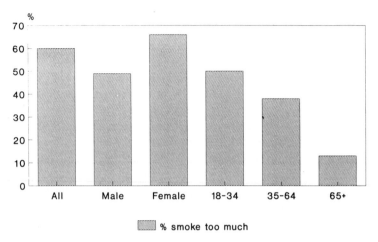

% smoke too much

they smoke too much for the good of their health (Figure 8). Women are more likely than men to think they smoke too much with 65 per cent of women smokers and 50 per cent of male smokers expressing concern. The group most likely to smoke are those aged 35-44, with 53 per cent of this group saying they are smokers. Concern about damage to health decreases with age. Sixty-five per cent of smokers aged 18-34 thought they smoke too much for the good of their health compared to 37 per cent of smokers aged over 65.

Ethnic minority respondents are less likely to smoke than white respondents (72 per cent are non-smokers compared to 64 per cent of the white population), but ethnic minority smokers are less likely to think they smoke too much for the good of their health. Only 40 per cent of non-white smokers expressed concern compared to 60 per cent of white smokers.

Residents in Hawksworth Wood are more likely to be smokers than residents of other parts of the ward: only 53 per cent of Hawksworth

Wood residents are non-smokers compared to 64 per cent in the ward as a whole.

Thirty per cent of respondents do not drink alcohol with more than twice as many women as men being non-drinkers (37 per cent compared to 18 per cent). Young people are more likely to drink than older people: 21 per cent of those aged 18-34, 34 per cent of those aged 35-64 and 45 per cent of those aged 65 and over are non-drinkers. Only seven per cent of the sample (10 per cent of drinkers) think they drink too much for the good of their health. Ethnic minority respondents are less likely than whites to drink (40 per cent compared to 29 per cent) and are slightly more concerned about the damage to their health, with 14 per cent expressing concern compared to 11 per cent of white drinkers. Residents in Hawksworth Wood are least likely to drink with 40 per cent saying they are non-drinkers.

The impression that people are concerned about the quality of food and water, the healthiness of their diet and smoking came through quite strongly in the follow-up interviews. All the groups that we interviewed and in all areas expressed concern about the quality of drinking water. Elderly people in Hawksworth Wood expressed concern that the water is 'polluted'. Another commented that the 'water smells of chlorine and tastes funny'. In Kirkstall and Burley elderly residents were concerned that the water was 'dirty and discoloured' and one commented that 'water just doesn't taste the same as it did 30 years ago'.

A number of women with young children were concerned about water being conducted through lead piping. One woman commented that the water 'tastes awful', complained of 'bits floating in it' and said there were frequent outbreaks of diarrhoea and sickness. Similarly, a woman in Burley thought that poor quality drinking water caused stomach upsets and, as a consequence, she had changed to drinking bottled water.

Concern about the safety of food bought in shops covered a range of issues including additives, the selling of food after the 'sell by' dates in local shops and food irradiation. A fairly typical comment (by an ethnic minority interviewee) was 'I don't know what is in foods.'

Many of the people we interviewed were concerned that their diet was not healthy enough. Their reasons for not eating more healthily centred around three issues: lack of access to shops selling good quality food, lack of motivation and lack of money. For example, an elderly resident in Burley commented that she only got fresh vegetables at the weekends when her family was able to shop for her. Concern over the cost of a healthy diet was mentioned by very many of the women with young children, especially those living in Hawksworth Wood and Kirkstall. This was also a concern of a pensioner who commented that she 'had to live within my means'.

Concern about smoking was more common than concern about drinking (reinforcing the postal questionnaire results) and was especially prevalent among women with young children who expressed fears about cancer, bronchitis, heart disease and chest problems. A number of interviewees wanted help to stop smoking. One commented that she thought such assistance ought to be available from the GP, another that she would like to try hypnotherapy and another that she was already going to a self-help group. One woman said that she hadn't the willpower to stop while another said she would stop smoking if she had 'better housing, more money and a husband'. Someone else (who was especially aware of the health risks) said she 'didn't want to stop'.

In the postal survey we asked people to say whether or not they thought they get enough exercise for the good of their health. Fifty-one per cent of respondents think that they do get enough exercise with 40 per cent saying they do not and nine per cent responding that they didn't know. Men are more likely than women to think they get enough exercise (52 per cent compared to 49.5 per cent) and older people more likely than younger people (44 per cent of 18-34 year olds; 52 per cent of 35-64 year olds; and 54 per cent of those aged over 65 think they get enough exercise).

Asian people are more likely to think that they do not get enough exercise (63 per cent compared to 40 per cent for the sample as a whole). This is also the case for those who are retired (58 per cent of whom said they get insufficient exercise) and those looking after home and family (52 per cent).

Of those reporting good or very good health, 56 per cent think they get enough exercise compared to only 45 per cent of those in poor or very poor health. A further 14 per cent of the latter group 'don't know' whether they get enough exercise. In the follow-up interviews it became clear that many of those who say they do not get enough exercise are unable to take exercise because of ill-health. This was especially the case among elderly people. Among women with young children a different set of reasons emerged for not getting enough exercise - lack of motivation/laziness, lack of time and lack of money. Many of the women interviewed said they would like to engage in activities such as keep fit, swimming, aerobics and weight-training, but were prevented from doing so because of child care responsibilities and/or paid employment. Some mentioned the need for creche facilities at sports and leisure centres, but for many this would make little difference since the major obstacle was lack of time.

Diet and Lifestyle: Professional Workers' Perceptions

The professional workers were concerned about the consequences for health of poor diet and related factors such as smoking and drinking, but did not demonstrate the same fears as residents about the safety of drinking water or food bought in shops. One GP thought that high levels of smoking and drinking were contributory factors in what was seen as the high incidence of coronary heart disease. He was also concerned about the risks of passive smoking and the problems for babies caused by mothers who smoke. Concern was expressed about both the health and social effects of heavy drinking. For example it was thought that alcohol-related problems were often a factor in family break-up.

Inadequate diet and high levels of consumption of convenience foods was mentioned in connection with high cholesterol levels, obesity and heart disease. However one GP thought that poor diet was due to lack of awareness and education rather than lack of money (although he conceded that local shops did not provide a good range of fresh food at affordable prices). This was not borne out by the evidence of our survey and interviews with residents who showed considerable awareness about the importance of a healthy diet.

Diet and Lifestyle: Public Meetings

The issue of diet and lifestyle was raised at two of the public meetings (Burley and Hawksworth Wood). In Burley the discussion focused on how to get peole with unhealthy lifestyles to change. The view was expressed that since people often did not face the consequences of their lifestyle (in terms of damage to health) until some years afterwards, their behaviour was unlikely to change. This view was reinforced by a community health worker who argued that current methods of health education had clearly failed and this was because they put the onus on individuals to change their lifestyle without taking account of the way a number of factors were inter-related. For example, people might smoke or drink too much to alleviate the stress caused by unemployment or lack of money and 'scare tactics' simply resulted in more stress, guilt or depression.

In Hawksworth Wood, participants seemed to agree that issues relating to diet and exercise were personal choices and that individuals had to take responsibility for their own actions. However it was accepted that people might become 'apathetic' as a result of factors beyond their control such as unemployment and this might undermine personal motivation. Some people present thought that children were increasingly being fed on expensive 'junk-food' rather than healthy food suggesting that poverty was not the cause of poor diet. Some older people in particular, were quite judgemental about what they saw as the inadequacies of young parents.

Diet and Lifestyle: Key Issues

In general it can be argued that people in the study area are having their needs for adequate, nutritious food and clean water met. However, it should be a matter for concern that such high proportions of residents do not believe that their drinking water or shop-bought food is safe.

While in general people in the area are not (as far as we know) undernourished it is clear that people are not eating as healthily as they might and this view is shared by residents and professionals alike. The reasons this are varied but include lack of access to shops selling good quality food, lack of motivation and lack of money. Lack of knowledge of what constitutes a healthy diet is seen as an issue by some professionals.

Awareness of the dangers to health of smoking, drinking and lack of exercise also seems to be quite high among residents. Again the reasons why people do not adopt healthier life-styles seems to relate to their circumstances. For example, the fact that smokers are more likely to be found in the poorer parts of the study area seems to reinforce the view expressed at one of the public meetings that health education needs to take account of such factors.

Another issue to emerge is the extent to which culture affects lifestyle. On most of the issues that we asked questions about, different responses were forthcoming from ethnic minority respondents than from the population as a whole. In other words the way in which intermediate needs are met must take account of cultural differences.

2:4.   HOUSING

One of the intermediate needs that we identified was for adequate, protective housing. In assessing the extent to which people's need for housing has been met in the study area we look first at the available data relating to housing in Leeds and Kirkstall Ward. In the second section of this chapter we report the findings of the survey of residents in which we asked people to comment on the adequacy of their home for their needs and the changes that, in their view, were necessary to improve it. The consequences of poor housing for health and well-being were explored in greater depth with interviewees, with professionals workers and with community representatives.

Housing: Codified Knowledge

This section presents data relating to the housing stock in Leeds and, so far as is possible, Kirkstall, and the need for housing.

Figure 9 shows the dwelling stock in Leeds at 1 April 1990 by forms of tenure. Sixty-eight per cent of the housing stock is private (rented and owner occupied).

A breakdown of the local authority housing stock in Leeds by age, by size and type shows that the bulk of the housing stock (72 per cent) is post-war and over half (60 per cent) consists of houses (56 per cent) and bungalows (4 per cent). Over half of the housing stock (62 per cent) consists of one and two bedroom units: this is a result of a relative shift towards small units in the post-war period.

Housing in the study area comes within the Kirkstall and Burley Housing Management offices (HMOs) but their boundaries do not coincide with the ward. The Kirkstall stock is slightly older than Leeds as a whole: 35 per cent of dwellings are pre-war, as compared to 28 per cent for the city as a whole, and there is a lower proportion of small units. The Burley stock includes a large number of older and smaller back-to-back houses and a smaller than average proportion of dwellings with four bedrooms or more.

Information relating to numbers, age, size and type of dwellings, and form of tenure, does not provide an indication of how far housing need is

Figure 9
Household tenure: sample and Leeds

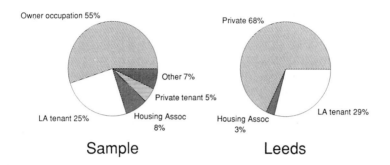

Source of Leeds data: Leeds CC

satisfied. Information is also required relating to the condition of the housing stock (numbers unfit and in need of renovation), suitability (eg. the match between size of household and dwelling, numbers of dwellings in need of adaptation for use by the elderly or disabled, numbers of dwellings lacking basic amenities), and the amount of pent-up housing need (numbers of homeless and concealed households).

There is a significant problem of unfit dwellings in Leeds in both the private and public sectors. A total of 35,762 dwellings is estimated to be unfit, representing 12 per cent of the total housing stock. The bulk (80 per cent) of these unfit dwellings is in the private sector, and 14 per cent of all private dwellings is estimated to be unfit (including private rented and owner occupied dwellings). A somewhat lower proportion of local authority dwellings (nine per cent) is estimated to be unfit.

A large proportion of the housing stock (37 per cent) is estimated to be in need of renovation. The majority of these dwellings is in the private sector but the problem is relatively more important in the local authority sector: the proportion of local authority housing in need of renovation (56 per cent) is considerably larger than that of private housing (30 per cent). The categories 'unfit' and 'in need of renovation' may both cover a range of particular housing problems so the figures presented here do not give a precise indication of the burden of poor quality housing.

There is a total of 25,226 dwellings in Leeds specially designed or adapted and intended for use by the elderly and disabled, that is one in eight dwellings. The figure includes 6,872 sheltered dwellings for the elderly. However an estimated additional 20,000 elderly households in Leeds need specially adapted or designed accommodation, which suggests significant unmet need. In addition, 2,400 households are estimated to need accommodation specially adapted/designed for the disabled.

Overcrowding is not a major problem in Leeds: 8,800 households are estimated to be living at a density greater than one person per room. This estimate accords with 1981 Census data which shows 8,737 overcrowded households (more than one person per room) in Leeds, 3.3 per cent of all households.

The 1981 Census also provides data on numbers of households lacking basic amenities. Under one per cent of households in Leeds were without a bath and one per cent were without an inside toilet.

'Pent-up' housing need consists of households lacking separate accommodation, that is, primarily sharing and homeless households. An estimated 47,600 households fall into this category in Leeds at 1 April 1990. However there are reasons for thinking these estimates may be unreliable. A downward revision is suggested by the possibility that not all of these are 'potential' households since not all sharing households desire separate accommodation. For example 'a follow-up survey of 'sharers' discovered in the 1977 NDHS [National Dwellings and Household Survey] suggested that only 41 per cent of married couple and 33 per cent of single parent concealed households actually wanted separate accommodation' (National Housing Forum, 1989), although other research carried out by the London Research Centre suggests 79 per cent of married couple and 71 per cent of lone parent concealed households constitute potential households (ibid).

The number of concealed and sharing households registered on the council waiting list gives an indication of the number of potential households since registration effectively expresses the desire for separate accommodation. Of single persons sharing accommodation 4,118 are currently registered on the waiting list. This is little more than ten per cent of the estimated total of single persons sharing households. No figure is given for the number of concealed households registered on the waiting list. However the waiting list may not be a good indicator of the true number of potential households because, even if it is up to date, it is not likely that all concealed or sharing households desiring separate accommodation will register. This is particularly the case for households with little prospect of being rehoused, especially single people.

The number of waiting list and transfer applications held can also be analysed by Housing Management Office (HMO). At 31 December 1990 the total number of applications held for Kirkstall HMO was 1,284: 828 waiting list applications and 456 transfer applications.

The waiting list registers the 'stock' of households at a particular time expressing a need or desire for local authority housing (though it will not include all households in need of accommodation). However in order to assess the opportunity to obtain a council house or move within the council's stock this has to be set against the 'flow' of lettings. Analysis of Leeds City Council lettings between 1988 and 1990 shows a reduction in the flow of new tenants over the period indicating, in conjunction with the increased waiting list, a reduced opportunity to obtain a council house or move within the council stock.

Not all households on the waiting list are considered to be in need. Of 19,666 households on the waiting list at 1 April 1990 (excluding transfer applications) 12,433 were estimated to be in special need and over half of these were households with or expecting child(ren).

During the year 1 April 1989 to 31 March 1990 Leeds City Council accepted responsibility for securing accommodation for 1,290 homeless households, representing an annual increase of over six per cent. This represents an average monthly rate of acceptance of over 100 homeless households. Almost all of these households were assessed as being a priority need.

The number of households accepted as homeless during a quarter or year does not indicate the 'stock' of homeless households resident in temporary accommodation at any particular time. This will depend on the average period of time between a household being accepted as homeless and being rehoused or otherwise leaving temporary accommodation. An examination of the throughput of households into and out of temporary accommodation, their destinations, and the stock of households resident in temporary accommodation at any one date shows that more than 100 homeless households were resident in hostel accommodation at the start and finish of the final quarter of 1990 and during the intervening three months 282 families had been admitted and 284 families had left. These figures suggest that homeless households spend, on average, about one month in hostel accommodation, though care must be taken in interpreting data for just one quarter in this way. Three in five families leaving hostel accommodation during the quarter were rehoused, found their own accommodation or returned home. However no indication is given of what proportion of these households found satisfactory and secure accommodation. The other two in five households were either transferred to other hostels (28 per cent) or their destination was not known (12 per cent).

A central issue in access to housing is affordability. In November 1990 some 50,000 council tenants in Leeds (about 62 per cent of the total) were in receipt of partial or full rent rebates. In all, nearly 100,000 people were in receipt of poll tax benefit and this represents about 14 per cent of the total population.

Housing: Experiential Knowledge

This information gives us some understanding of the extent to which housing needs are being met in Leeds as a whole but it tells us very little about residents in the study area. Neither does it tell us very much about the suitability of people's housing to their circumstances. We sought to ascertain people's own perceptions of the level to which their housing needs are being met through the postal survey and follow-up interviews in which we asked about the kind of housing people occupied, the form of tenure, size of the home, adequacy of facilities within the home, problems with the building occupied and improvements people would like to see.

Some 81 per cent of respondents live in houses and 10 per cent in flats. The highest proportion of flats is in Hawksworth Wood (16 per cent) and Kirkstall (13 per cent). There is a relatively high proportion of bungalows in the Vespers area. A relatively high proportion of the elderly live in flats - 20 per cent of those 65 and over compared with 6 per cent of those under 65.

In Figure 9 the household tenure of respondents is compared with the pattern of tenure in Leeds as a whole. Some 55 per cent of respondents own, or are buying, their homes - a rather lower proportion than Leeds as a whole. The proportion of homeowners is highest (at about two thirds) in the 35-64 age grouping and in the Vespers area (92 per cent), it is lowest amongst the elderly (46 per cent) and in the Hawksworth Wood area (29 per cent). A quarter of respondents overall are council tenants but one third of the elderly are in this category. Hawksworth Wood has the highest proportion of council tenants (54 per cent) while there are only 1.5 per cent in the Vespers area. The Burley and Kirkstall areas are closer to the average in terms of pattern of tenure but Burley has a relatively high proportion of private tenants (11.3 per cent). The proportion of housing association tenants is highest in Hawksworth Wood (10.4 per cent) and amongst the elderly, particularly women.

Burley has the highest proportion of respondents in smaller (1-2 bedrooms) properties at nearly 47 per cent; conversely, nearly three quarters of those in the Vespers and two thirds of respondents in Hawksworth Wood live in properties with three or more bedrooms.

Only three per cent of all respondents share facilities, mainly outside space, cooking, bathroom and laundry facilities. About a half of all sharers are in the 18-34 age group and 43 per cent live in the Burley area. The highest incidence of sharing is amongst lodgers (18 per cent) and private tenants (11 per cent).

The main perceived deficiencies are outside space and laundry facilities with 19 per cent and 14 per cent respectively not having these or stating that they are not adequate for their needs. Some seven per cent responded that their bedrooms are not adequate. These deficiencies are experienced most by the younger age grouping, followed by the elderly for laundry and outside space; also the perceived deficiencies are greater amongst non-whites and the unemployed.

Burley has the highest proportion of respondents reporting deficiencies (29 per cent outside space; 20 per cent laundry; nine per cent bedrooms) but a fifth of respondents in Kirkstall identified outside space and 15 per cent of those in Hawksworth Wood have inadequate, or no, laundry facilities. Private tenants fare worst for these facilities followed by lodgers and housing association tenants, then council tenants.

The worst problems reported by respondents in their homes are poor heating (some 24 per cent indicating a 'serious problem'), damp/condensation (20 per cent) and lack of space and noise (both 14 per cent). These problems tend to be experienced most by younger age groups, especially poor heating, dampness and lack of space, followed by the elderly for heating and dampness. These problems are also suffered disproportionately by non-whites, the unemployed and those looking after home and children. Moreover, relatively high proportions of the unemployed also indicate problems with noise and general disrepair.

The Burley and Hawksworth Wood areas have the highest proportion of respondents indicating these problems, especially dampness, poor heating, noise and lack of space (Figure 10). Poor heating and dampness are the main problems in Hawksworth Wood, reported respectively by 44 per cent

Figure 10
Problems in home by area

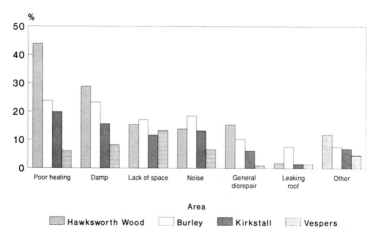

Figure 11
Problems in home by autonomy

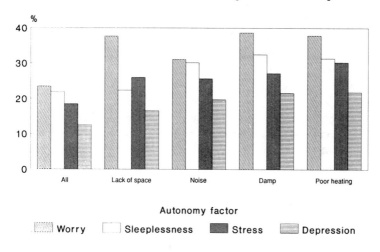

and 29 per cent of respondents. Burley is above average in respect of dampness, noise and lack of space. General disrepair is also of above average concern in Hawksworth Wood.

Within these areas an analysis of the incidence of these problems by sub-group shows that problems of dampness and poor heating particularly affect the young and unemployed in Hawksworth Wood and Burley and those looking after home and family in Hawksworth Wood. Noise is a particular problem for the young and unemployed in Burley and Kirkstall and for the elderly in Hawksworth Wood. Problems with lack of space are reported particularly by the young, non-whites, unemployed and 'carers' in Burley, and also by young and middle-aged people in the Vespers area.

The highest incidence of these problems is amongst private, housing association and council tenants, and the pattern across tenures reflects the pattern by area. Poor heating and dampness are the worst problems for council and housing association tenants (cf. Hawksworth Wood). These problems are also indicated by a relatively high proportion of private tenants, a quarter of whom also report problems of lack of space and noise, the latter also figuring prominently for housing association and council tenants (cf. Burley area). All classes of tenant report above average problems with general disrepair.

This pattern of incidence of housing problems can be compared with the perceived importance of 'having a decent standard of housing' analysed in part 2:1. There we found that younger people tend to attach rather less importance to housing than older groups, especially the 65+ group, although there is a higher incidence of reported problems amongst the young.

Relatively high priority to housing is given, then, by the elderly, by those looking after home and children and by residents of Hawksworth Wood and these priorities tend to match the incidence of problems of, in particular, poor heating, dampness and condensation on the Hawksworth Wood estate.

Respondents experiencing problems of poor heating and dampness in particular are rather more likely to indicate that their general health has been poor or very poor over the past year. For example, around 30 per cent of those reporting problems with heating and dampness also report poor or very poor health compared with 22 per cent of all respondents. Moreover, Figure 11 shows that people experiencing housing problems also have above average propensity to report various 'mental health' problems, particularly, again, those with dampness and poor heating for which the reported incidence of worry, sleeplessness, stress and depression is well above average. Noise is also associated particularly with sleeplessness, stress and depression, and lack of space with worry/anxiety.

Respondents were asked what single major change they would wish to make to their home. The pattern is consistent with the incidence of major problems discussed above. Thus, in Hawksworth Wood the main desired changes involve improvements to heating systems, windows and structural repairs. These are also stated frequently by respondents in Burley, where extension of space is also a concern, involving kitchens, living areas, bedrooms and outside space. Improved heating, replacement windows or double glazing and improved kitchens are the main desired changes in Kirkstall, while extension of living space figures prominently in the Vespers.

The picture of housing problems emerging from the questionnaire survey was reinforced by comments made during interviews. There was an overwhelming concern about damp and condensation, cold, draughty houses and inadequate heating. This was particularly prevalent among residents on the Hawksworth Wood Estate. Typical comments include: 'There is no heating in the bathroom; it's always damp; we can't keep paper on walls' and 'There is poor ventilation and condensation in the bathroom so we need to open the window making it cold.'

Residents in Burley were also concerned (although to a lesser extent) about damp, draughts and poor heating. Other comments on this issue included the need for financial help with heating (from an elderly Hawksworth Wood resident) and double-glazing and better insulation.

Inadequate facilities mostly related to bedrooms, play space, storage space and laundry facilities and comments of this nature were particularly prevalent among women with young children in Kirkstall and Burley. In Burley a number of women commented that there was nowhere to dry clothes, in Kirkstall that there was not enough storage space especially for baby equipment. In all areas comments were made about the lack of space for children to play, both inside, and outside where the problem was not just lack of space but lack of safe space. A number of interviewees mentioned the hazards to children playing outside from the traffic (see also part 2:9).

Lack of general space in the home was a particular problem for ethnic minority interviews. Typical comments included reference to problems of overcrowding when 'family or friends come to visit'. However lack of space was also a problem for residents in Burley who were concerned about the small size of rooms especially kitchens and bedrooms. Other inadequacies related to housing disrepair and lack of money to effect improvements. In particular rotting window frames were a concern as was the lack of electrical sockets. Other issues raised include the need to have a downstairs toilet installed because the interviewee was disabled, and noise (especially in Kirkstall) from aircraft and traffic.

Housing: Perceptions of Professionals and Community Representatives

In interviewing professional workers in the area we asked them to comment on the main housing problems, the impact of those problems on residents' health, the main housing needs, the shortcomings of existing services and what was required in order to address residents' housing needs.

Main Housing Problems

Professional workers' perceptions of the housing problems in the Kirkstall ward focus on quantity, quality, management, cost and social factors. These will be discussed in turn.

The issue of quantity relates in particular to local authority housing for which there is a long wait (apart from the most urgent cases) especially in the more popular areas like Burley and for larger houses appropriate to the needs of extended families. In particular there is a shortage of good quality family housing especially larger houses with four bedrooms; housing for young single people; housing for young couples; housing for mentally ill and mentally handicapped people. Only limited council properties are available in the Kirkstall area. Shortages in the local authority sector were due, in the view of one housing manager, to sales of council houses and controls on councils preventing them from building new homes.

Housing associations were thought to provide good quality housing at higher rents which is okay if the tenant was on benefit but created difficulties for the low paid. However there are also long waiting lists for housing association accommodation.

In Burley it was felt that there is a mixture of good and bad housing. However there is a significant problem of overcrowding due to extended families living in inadequate accommodation. Also there is a lack of accommodation for young single people and this exacerbates overcrowding as young people continue to live in their parents' home. Some people would like to move to houses with gardens. Home care workers identified a lack of suitable accommodation for elderly people and people unable to climb stairs which is a particular problem in Burley because of the large number of back-to-backs with steep stairs.

Damp, mould and condensation are widely regarded to be major problems in all areas and are exacerbated by inadequate heating. As a result of unfit bedrooms, families have to sleep together in the living room to keep warm and dry during winter, according to social workers interviewed. Underfloor heating in maisonettes was singled out as a particular problem since it is expensive to run; those in Argie Avenue were specifically identified. Cold and damp is made worse in local authority homes by broken windows which are not replaced. According to social workers this is seen by the council to be a tenant responsibility, but many tenants cannot afford to replace them.

Houses on Hawksworth Wood estate were frequently described as being inadequate despite some repairs and improvements to some of the houses in recent years eg re-roofing, wall ties and new electrics. There are still many improvements needed: some houses only have one electric socket upstairs so that people run wires from room to room. There are still houses with bare brick walls with wires and pipes exposed. In addition there is a problem of flooding on the estate due to the need for a new drainage system.

In the local authority sector, it is claimed, the problem of housing disrepair is exacerbated by the slow response to requests for repairs, identified as a problem by many of those interviewed. This was seen to be particularly bad on Hawksworth Wood where the standard of repairs was described as 'abysmal' both in terms of response time and standards of work. In Burley there is a widespread view that uncertainty about whether or not some houses are going to be demolished means that repairs are not being carried out. The poor state of repair of maisonettes on Argie Avenue was also mentioned frequently.

Concern was voiced about the lack of improvement grants available to owner-occupiers to repair poor standard housing and it was felt that Asian families in particular do not have money to pay for improvements themselves. In the private rented sector there is a problem of inadequate maintenance of properties by landlords. This was felt to particularly affect parts of Burley such as the Stanmores, Knowles and Grahams where there is a danger of deterioration due to the high proportion of houses owned by private landlords and let to students. A local councillor argued that there was a need for an urban renewal initiative here.

There has been a growth in the importance of the private rented sector especially in Burley and Kirkstall because of the lack of local authority housing. Private rents are high and are not always met by housing benefit. Mentally ill and mentally handicapped people are thought by social workers to have a particular problem with private landlords who may charge for rent and board but do not in fact supply adequate food, heating or hot water. Because of the under-supply of rented property, people take what they can get. There is little protection for tenants against landlords who know how to exploit loopholes in the law. Changes in benefit rules have lead to an increase in evictions for non-payment of water rates and poll tax.

A particular problem that was mentioned by social workers was the lack of insurance of some low-income households who could not, as a result, afford to repair damage to their properties.

Hawksworth Wood was seen as being an area with major social problems arising in part from the council's allocations policy. The estate has a bad reputation although it is attractive, well laid out, spacious and with a large and settled population, many families having lived there since it was built. But, according to a local councillor, it now has a large number of tenants who have financial difficulties (especially unemployed and single parents) leading to a concentration of social problems. Furthermore, these problems are exacerbated by incompatibility between neighbours and family conflicts between 'clans'. It is claimed that 'decent' people are unwilling to come and live there and, consequently, there are usually 18 empty houses at any one time. It is policy to use these empty properties for homeless and 'anti-social' people evicted from elsewhere who, it is claimed, get priority over those who would like to stay on the estate to be near their families (because of Leeds City Council's policy of not using bed and breakfast accommodation for the homeless). Many people want to move out but feel trapped and hopeless, and there is a feeling of social isolation according to one health worker interviewed.

Concern was expressed by a local clergyman about the policy of placing young people next door to old people in flats; a practice which was described as 'irresponsible'. The problem of generation mix in multi-storey blocks was also highlighted: the elderly feel trapped when lifts break down; noisy young people, 'drop-outs' and alcoholics being housed in blocks leads to misuse of communal facilities such as lifts according to one home care manager. People are afraid to go out a night; kids 'knock on doors and put things through letter boxes' claimed representatives of a local community association.

Similar problems were also identified in Argie Avenue where the multi-storey flats were criticised by a local GP as a 'complete disaster'. He described a situation of 'unhappy people imprisoned in high-rise blocks' and argued that 'they should be demolished and replaced with ordinary housing'. Such housing was seen as especially unsuitable for families with children by the head teacher of a local school. Part of the problem in places like Hawksworth Wood was seen as a 'cycle of deterioration' with a bad reputation deterring all but 'desperate' families, resulting in the concentration of social problems.

Impact on Health

All those interviewed about housing thought that poor standard housing did have a significant impact on the health of both children and adults causing problems such as asthma and bronchitis, coughs and colds and respiratory illness. Some social workers also thought that poor housing can lead to people being inappropriately admitted to hospital.

A number of children's health problems were linked to poor housing. For example, the local councillor claimed that there had been an outbreak of dysentery in Hawksworth Wood at schools and nursery and problems of flea infestation were indicated by the local environmental health officer. Social workers referred to problems of conjunctivitis among children resulting in exclusion from school because it is contagious; skin problems such as impetigo and ring worm; poor hygiene leading to stigmatisation of children at school; and lack of sleep due to children having to sleep in bedrooms with parents because of unfit bedrooms.

The officer-in-charge of a day nursery in Burley described the problem of lack of play space for children living in flats and bed-sits. This had a negative impact on children's physical, emotional and social development and also resulted in parents feeling unable to cope with children.

Poor housing was also identified as a factor in health problems among the elderly. Social workers interviewed thought that fear of hypothermia leads some elderly people to stay in bed to keep warm resulting in depression and a decrease in mobility and coping skills. More generally, it was felt that some elderly people's well-being was adversely affected by the fact that the areas in which they live have changed and there is no longer the same community spirit that there used to be. The manager of an elderly person's day centre thought that older people don't always get suitable housing or the kind of housing they want and that they should be consulted before new housing for the elderly was built.

This view was reinforced by comments made by the manager of a day centre for elderly Asian people. He thought the main issue was the availability of housing in particular areas where the Asian community lives and the type of housing available in those areas. In particular there was a need for houses large enough to accommodate extended families with downstairs bathrooms and good heating. He also thought that elderly Asians suffered in particular from isolation and loneliness if they were in areas away from family and friends.

Poor housing was considered to have an adverse effect on people's mental health. In particular lack of space and overcrowding were mentioned as factors leading to stress and other problems such as marital tension and domestic violence. Overcrowding means youngsters leave home early and have to fend for themselves according to the local MP. One social worker spoke of 'the general apathy that results from a continual struggle against overwhelming odds'.

On Hawksworth Wood it was suggested, people are under a lot of pressure just to survive. It was also suggested by a number of those interviewed that frustration because of inability to get repairs done and the consequent poor state of repair of properties led to stress and depression.

Main Housing Needs

The following groups were thought by an area housing manager to be in particular housing need: families with young children who are homeless, elderly people with health problems requiring specialist dwellings, large, extended Asian families; and young single homeless people (this is a major problem: the housing manager sees three or four such young people each day). However there is high demand and few vacancies in the local authority sector. In particular there is a lack of vacancies for houses for families with children, although in Hawksworth there are more vacancies but little demand. Only people who have grown up there or have family there are willing to move to that area, it was claimed.

Social workers expressed concern at the lack of housing for mentally ill and mentally handicapped people. The elderly were also thought to have particular housing needs summed up as follows by a home care team leader: 'spacious ground floor accommodation with green spaces situated near to facilities such as shops, post office, bank; a gardening and re-decoration service and fast response to requests for repairs'. It was also suggested that housing allocations policy should consider both social and housing needs and not place elderly and young people too close together.

Other housing needs related to repairs and improvements to existing properties. In Burley it was argued that people generally want to stay in the area but that the houses need considerable improvements. However some people currently living in back-to-backs wanted houses with gardens.

Housing needs of people living in the Hawksworth Wood estate were thought to vary between those residents who wanted to move off the estate and others who wanted to stay. For the latter group it was felt that there is insufficient accommodation for single people and young couples.

Shortcomings of existing services

In general the main shortcoming of the existing housing service was identified as being caused by the shrinking of the housing stock. An environmental health officer argued that because of the government's aim to reduce the public housing stock and the limits on the ability of local councils to spend profits from sales of council houses on new-build there is not enough housing stock. Within the stock that exists many tenants are in unsuitable accommodation eg. older people in three bedroom houses with stairs and families with young children in maisonettes and flats.

On the Hawksworth Wood estate houses were built between the wars and are basically of a good structure and built to a better standard than the maisonettes and high rise blocks built in the 1960s, but they are unmodernised and poorly heated. Recent work has been done on insulation but they need a lot of money to be spent on them to bring them up to standard. In the view of the environmental health officer this would be worthwhile expenditure whereas refurbishment of maisonettes is of doubtful value: the costs are so high that rents would become prohibitively expensive.

In Burley where there has been new build - a mix of two and three bedrooms and some flats and sheltered housing - there has been high satisfaction and low vacancy rates. However where there is new property on offer there is likely to be around 40 people applying for each unit according to the housing manager.

Another shortcoming of existing housing services was felt to be the inadequacy of the local authority repairs service. Complaints included the length of time taken to get repairs done, the overly bureaucratic system for reporting repairs and the fact that users of local authority services are not dealt with sympathetically. It was felt that this is partly because users are not confident or articulate but also because they are not listened to. Assistance in getting house repairs done is the most common problem brought to the Advice Centre in Hawksworth Wood. There are also problems of lack of communication between Housing Office and tenants eg. about the status of repairs. Some people experience difficulty in getting to Kirkstall Housing Office to pay rent or notify problems. It was generally felt that the Burley housing office is good and prompt in responding to needs.

A problem of backlog in the whole house improvement programme has developed due to cuts in the capital programme; Burley and Hawksworth Wood have been particularly affected. As a result, the City Council is 'patching up' out of the revenue budget according to the local MP. He also referred to the problem of cross-subsidisation of housing benefit from rents which takes resources away from repairs and improvements. Education welfare officers questioned the priorities being used to assess need for maintenance of properties by the local authority throughout the city.

According to probation officers, housing associations are now less helpful than private landlords when accommodation is being sought for clients of probation service. They were also critical of a lack of imagination on the part of the local authority and housing associations about how they provide accommodation.

Other problems referred to were cuts in improvement grants to owner-occupiers, which is a particular problem in Burley, and the lack of a coordinated policy between all agencies.

What is to be done

There was considerable concern expressed about the need to expand the housing stock and refurbish existing properties. Many people interviewed thought that the local authority needs to be allowed to borrow the money required for improvements and new-build. In particular there is a need for a greater variety of stock to cater for different needs. Thus, larger houses are needed for extended families; locally-based sheltered housing schemes are needed for the elderly which should be built by the local authority since Housing Trusts and Associations are charging 'bonds' for new tenants which the elderly cannot afford; and adequate housing and support are needed for people discharged from mental hospitals and prison. On the other hand, certain properties should be demolished, for example, concrete slab flats and maisonettes in the 'Argies' and houses in the 'Carberrys' and 'Burley Lodges' according to home care managers.

Many people referred to the need to review allocation policies. And there is a need for better communication with tenants and information about how the allocation system works according to a local councillor. A local health worker thought there should be someone to listen to residents' problems and liaise with the housing manager since he has very little time to listen to individuals so people leave even more angry after having seen him. The policy on re-housing in relation to flats should be reviewed and allocations policy should ensure the separation of elderly and young in maisonettes and flats in the view of social workers. In general it was felt that allocations should consider social as well as housing needs.

Improvements and repairs to public sector housing attracted considerable comment. In particular people wanted to see a more 'holistic' approach to improvements. For example the local MP suggested that problems of both damp and cold could be solved by the installation of new heating systems and energy-saving measures. In general it was felt (by social workers interviewed) that standards of housing in the public sector should be equivalent to those of housing association properties. This was summed up by the environmental health officer as 'housing in a reasonable state of repair with functional rooms adequately designed for health and safety with sufficient bedrooms and living rooms offering adequate space and natural light.'

It was felt by several of the professionals interviewed that there is a need for comprehensive rehabilitation and improvement programmes in the old Burley Village area and in the Burley Lodges area. More improvement grants are also needed to help people who lack the resources to upgrade their homes.

The local MP advocated more locally based housing management and greater tenant involvement in estate management as part of a broader approach to community development. A local vicar also emphasised 'community': 'people not only need better housing they also need assistance in living together and looking after their housing'. In addition the needs of particular groups should be addressed: home care and support services should enable elderly and people with disabilities to stay in their own homes according to home care managers; and private landlords should be monitored and action taken against them especially in relation to vulnerable groups.

In specific terms, the following needs in relation to housing were identified:

- More housing for single people through, for example, the conversion of older and larger properties into small units.

- More sheltered housing for older people which would also release under-occupied housing for families with children.

- New developments and management and services should be small and locally-based to avoid the problems associated with large estates and impersonal management.

- Better advice and information and education on how to avoid the health problems associated with poor housing.

- Better utilisation of private sector stock. Long term vacancies should result in compulsory purchase.

- Housing suitable to the particular needs of elderly Asian people in areas where there is already an Asian community and associated services such as interpreters.

- Setting up of a 'care and repair' scheme to provide help to elderly people and single parents to improve and maintain their properties.

Housing: Key Issues

Housing itself emerged as a key issue in our research generating considerable comment especially among professionals and community representatives. In particular the links between poor housing and ill-health and impaired autonomy were clearly set out. The salience of housing as an issue is especially pronounced among residents of the Hawksworth Wood estate as is shown by the amount of often angry comment it provoked at the public meeting there.

Our review of existing data shows that while there is considerable information available about housing in Leeds there are a number of difficulties associated with it. The first problem is that most of the information that exists is collected by the City Council's Department of Housing for their own purposes. Consequently, it refers, in the main, to local authority housing thus excluding other tenures notably owner-occupation (now the largest tenure group) for all practical purposes other than 'fitness'. Secondly, it can usually only be disaggregated to housing management areas which are not coterminous with ward boundaries. Thirdly, the measurements of housing need that are used for the purpose of allocations reflect statutory definitions (eg. of homelessness, of vulnerability etc) which may not encompass the totality of housing needs. Finally, again, the information imparts little insight into the meaning of housing need for particular groups of people.

Our study demonstrates the extent to which poor or inadequate housing can pervade all aspects of people's lives thereby having a significant negative impact on health and autonomy. The most commonly reported housing problems are poor heating and dampness/condensation which affect people living in the rented sector (public and private), especially in Hawksworth Wood and, to a lesser degree, Burley. People experiencing such problems tend to have worse than average states of general health and above average incidence of problems like stress, anxiety, depression and sleeplessness. This pattern of housing problems was corroborated during the follow-up interviews with particular concern being expressed about the effects on children's health.

The professional workers and community representatives interviewed identified a similar set of housing needs to those identified by residents themselves. They were particularly concerned about the effects of poor housing on mental health. Professionals and community representatives also echoed local authority tenants' criticisms of the housing services, especially repairs, and the authority's allocations policy. Professional workers however, were more likely than residents to emphasise the shortage of housing, especially local authority housing.

From all the elements of our study it is possible to identify a set of housing needs and measures to address them that command widespread agreement. These include: new housing for rent to meet the need of particular groups such as large Asian families in the Burley area, sheltered housing for the elderly and suitable accommodation for the mentally ill discharged into the community; a systematic programme of improvements in the Hawksworth Wood area to eradicate problems of damp, condensation and poor heating; an urban renewal initiative in the Burley area that recognises that some residents want to keep the existing back-to-backs while others would prefer that they are demolished to make way for houses with better amenities and gardens; the need for more effective management by the local authority especially with regards the repairs service and allocations policy.

2:5.   ENVIRONMENT: ACCESS AND SECURITY

People's health and autonomy are likely to be impaired if their physical or work environment are hazardous to them or where there are barriers to their accessing facilities that might enhance health and autonomy.

In this chapter we look at the following issues:

- the characteristics of the local environment
- perceived problems in the local area
- access to facilities such as play-grounds, shops, community centres and open spaces
- risks from crime and occupational injury

Environment: Codified Knowledge

In considering the physical environment we were particularly interested in access to facilities; people's likes and dislikes about the area in which they live and environmental problems and risks. As a result very little codified knowledge is available or relevant besides figures for road traffic accidents and local crime statistics.

Figures for road traffic accidents were available from West Yorkshire Highways, Engineering and Technical Services on a ward basis. These figures were extremely detailed and comprehensive. They show that there were a total of 96 road traffic accidents in the study area during 1990. None of these resulted in fatalities but 15 (16 per cent) were described as resulting in 'serious' injury and a further 81 (84 per cent) in 'slight' injury. Twenty-eight per cent of these accidents involved pedestrians.

Local crime statistics available from West Yorkshire Metropolitan Police were more problematic in that they relate to local 'beat' areas not exactly coterminous with our areas. The breakdown of the total into burglaries, thefts of/from motor vehicles and criminal damage is shown in Figure 12.

However, on their own these figures tell us really very little about the level of risk in the study area. Comparison with the figures for other beat areas would tell us a bit more about the relative risks but to make real comparisons possible we would need to know the population of each

Figure 12
Crime by area and offence

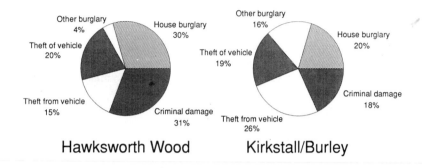

Hawksworth Wood   **Kirkstall/Burley**

Source: W.Yorks Metropolitan Police

beat area in order to compute the number of criminal offences per head of population. (This, of course, takes no account of differential rates of reporting crimes.)

Environment: Experiential Knowledge

From the postal questionnaire we were able to gain a more detailed picture of the problems and risks associated with the environment. We asked local residents about how long they had lived in the area, what they liked and disliked about it, how easy did they find it to get to certain facilities and what they saw as the problems and risks in their local community.

The different sub-areas of the ward differ in terms of the length of residence of respondents. Burley and the Vespers area have the highest proportions of people resident for ten years or less. In the Vespers area this is due, in part at least, to the construction of new private housing during this period whereas in Burley much can be attributed to 'turnover' of young people, given the significant private rented sector and cheap back-to-back housing. Hawksworth Wood and Kirkstall are more 'settled' areas, the former having a significant proportion of respondents (over a fifth) resident for over 30 years.

Respondents were asked if their home is conveniently situated for a range of facilities or if they consider that the facilities are 'not relevant'. Less than two per cent of respondents consider shops, public transport and GP/Health Centre to be not relevant but the proportions for sports and leisure facilities and a community centre are 12 per cent and 24 per cent respectively. As regards the former, the proportion increases with age but for the latter it decreases with age. Thus, nearly a third of those aged 18-34 considered a community centre to be not relevant, compared to 18 per cent of the elderly.

A fifth of all respondents consider their homes not to be conveniently situated for a dentist with above average proportions in the younger age groups and amongst those living in the Vespers and Hawksworth Wood areas (39 per cent of respondents in the Vespers and 26 per cent in Hawksworth Wood) (Figure 13). Nearly 15 per cent of respondents considered themselves to be not conveniently situated for work, shops and a community centre. Access to work is particularly problematical in Hawksworth Wood and Vespers (17 per cent); shops in Vespers (29 per cent); and community centre in Vespers (30 per cent) and Burley and Kirkstall (both 21 per cent). Nearly a fifth of respondents in Burley and Hawksworth Wood consider their homes not to be conveniently located for sports and leisure facilities.

These views were elaborated on in the follow-up interviews. Elderly people were concerned about access to shops. Several people mentioned that not having a car made shopping difficult. Either they were forced to rely on local shops which they felt were expensive and had a poor range of goods or they had to use public transport to get to the larger shops. A number of people commented on the usefulness of the Access bus but others said they couldn't get out without a taxi or lift as the bus service was infrequent. Typical comments were: 'We need cheap public transport and a cheap taxi service for the elderly and the disabled' and 'We need a little bus to come round the estate to pick up the old folk'. Elderly people in Kirkstall and Burley were more likely to think that their areas were quite convenient for both shops and public transport though some people commented that they found walking difficult because of the hills.

Women with young children were on the whole less concerned about access to shops except in Kirkstall. In Burley a number of women commented positively on the proximity to shops.

The other facility that was a matter of comment in <u>all</u> areas was a community centre. An elderly resident of Hawksworth Wood commented that 'there's nowhere here to meet people - for all age groups, not just the elderly' and in Burley it was observed that 'Burley doesn't have a real centre or community centre'. Similar concerns were voiced by women with young children who we interviewed. One woman in Hawksworth Wood commented that the existing community centre was too far away.

Other facilities which presented access problems for women with children included dentists in both Burley and Kirkstall; banks (in Kirkstall); sports and leisure centres (in Burley). The general issue of access was raised eg. the difficulty of getting about with pushchairs.

Respondents were asked to indicate the main likes and dislikes about the

Figure 13
Access to local facilities by area

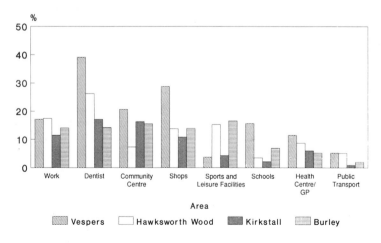

% with no convenient access to facility

area in which they live. The main factors which people like are indicated in Table 2. It can be seen that open 'green' space and access to woods

and parkland is the main positive factor in the Vespers, Hawksworth Wood and Kirkstall, its prominence increasing with distance from the city centre. Conversely, convenience for facilities and amenities becomes increasingly important nearer to the city centre, figuring most prominently in Burley. Friendly neighbours and local community is also seen as important, particularly in Hawksworth Wood and Burley.

As regards dislikes, Table 3 indicates the prominence of traffic/busy roads and litter/refuse dumping in the Vespers, Kirkstall and Burley. There is some unease in the Vespers about proximity to the Hawksworth Wood Estate. Concern about crime and vandalism and dogs is also in evidence in these areas. The pattern of dislikes for residents of Hawksworth Wood is rather different. Here, the main negative factors relate to problems with neighbours, neglect of the area and disrepair of housing. Crime, vandalism and dogs are also concerns, as is the problem of 'misbehaving' youths and children with nothing to occupy them.

This picture is supported by responses to specific stated problems. The main problems perceived by people in their local area are traffic and busy roads (51 per cent of respondents overall), litter (46 per cent), dogs (41 per cent), vandalism (35 per cent) and poor facilities for children (30 per cent). For most problems concern is greatest amongst younger age groups; this is particularly so where the problems affect children eg. poor facilities for children, traffic and busy roads, lack of open space. Poor facilities for children is also more likely to be mentioned by women than by men. Perceptions of different age groups are closer on litter, dogs and vandalism; for litter, concern increases with age. Concern about problems tends to be greater amongst the unemployed and those looking after home and family particularly in relation to lack of open space and facilities for children, and dogs, and the unemployed have a particularly high concern about noise.

Perception of problems tends to be higher in Hawksworth Wood and Burley than in the Kirkstall and Vespers areas (Figure 14). Particular concerns in Hawksworth Wood are dogs, litter, vandalism and poor facilities for children; in the Burley area these are also significant perceived problems but with rather lower levels of concern, with the

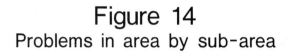

Figure 14
Problems in area by sub-area

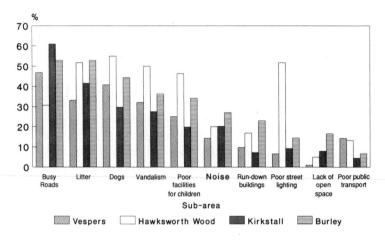

exception of litter. Noise, run-down buildings and lack of open space figure more prominently in Burley than in other areas. Busy roads are also seen as a problem in Burley and this is by far the most commonly

mentioned problem among residents in the Kirkstall area, mentioned by 61 per cent. Litter is the other main concern in Kirkstall, as it is in the Vespers where busy roads and dogs also figure prominently. Figure 15 indicates that respondents who perceive the problems of, in particular, poor facilities for children, noise and vandalism are rather more likely than average to indicate that they suffer from 'mental health' problems, especially worry, sleeplessness and stress and, in the case of facilities for children, depression.

The follow-up interviews showed that perceptions of problems (other than crime) in the three areas fall into three broad categories: traffic, lack of facilities for children and a dirty environment caused by litter, dogs etc. In Hawksworth Wood concern was expressed about both busy main roads and people using the estate as a short cut. A suggestion was made that 'sleeping policemen' ought to be installed. In Kirkstall, concern focused on the difficulty in crossing main roads. In particular it was suggested that pelican crossings were needed over Abbey Road by the Vesper estate. In Burley concern over heavy traffic and lack of pedestrian crossings was coupled with concern over car parking in the area by non-residents.

Lack of facilities for children and young people was seen as problematic in itself but also because it was felt that this led to anti-social behaviour. For example a number of people made comments about 'youths hanging around', 'young kids in gangs' and 'kids harassing people' especially in Hawksworth Wood. Others commented on the lack of open space for children (in Burley and Hawksworth Wood), the lack of safe space (in Kirkstall) and the lack of clubs and play groups for children (Burley and Hawksworth Wood).

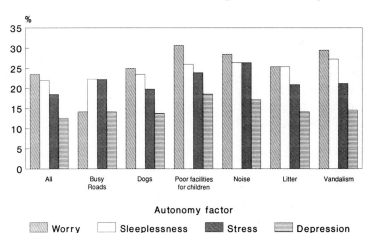

Figure 15
Problems in area by autonomy

Table 2 : <u>Factors which Respondents Like about their Area</u>

	per cent of Responses
A <u>Vespers</u>	**(n=159)**
Open space/woodland/parkland/nice outlook	39.6
Quiet and peaceful	17.6
Convenient for both city and countryside	12.6
Convenient for local facilities/amenities	10.1
Friendly neighbours/community	8.8
Good public transport	5.0
B <u>Hawksworth Wood</u>	**(n=166)**
Open space/woodland/parkland/nice outlook	30.1
Friendly neighbours/community	27.1
Quiet and peaceful	13.9
Convenient for local facilities/amenities	12.0
Generally like the area	8.4
C <u>Kirkstall</u>	**(n=395)**
Open space/woodland/parkland/nice outlook	29.1
Convenient for local facilities/amenities	25.8
Friendly neighbours/community	11.4
Quiet and peaceful	10.6
Good public transport	7.6
Generally like the area	7.3
D <u>Burley</u>	**(n=430)**
Convenient for local facilities/amenities	24.2
Friendly neighbours/community	19.8
Convenient for city centre	12.6
Open space/woodland/parkland	11.6
Quiet and peaceful	11.2
Good public transport	7.0

Table 3: <u>Factors which Respondents Dislike about their Area</u>

	per cent of Responses
A <u>Vespers</u>	**(n=133)**
Traffic/busy roads/lack of crossing facilities	16.5
Proximity of Hawksworth Wood Estate	12.8
Litter/refuse dumping/dirt	10.5
Crime and vandalism	9.8
Misbehaving youths and children/lack of facilities	9.0
Roaming dogs/excrement	8.3
Lack of local shops/facilities	8.3
B <u>Hawksworth Wood</u>	**(n=210)**
Troublesome and neglectful neighbours	13.8
Run-down, neglected area/disrepair of housing	12.9
Roaming dogs/excrement	10.9
Misbehaving youths/children/lack of facilities	10.4
Crime and vandalism	9.0
Traffic/busy roads/lack of crossing facilities	8.6
Litter/refuse dumping/dirt	6.7
Lack of local shops/facilities	5.7
Too many hills/restricts mobility	5.2
C <u>Kirkstall</u>	**(n=306)**
Traffic/busy roads/lack of crossing facilities	23.5
Litter/refuse dumping/dirt	11.4
Crime and vandalism	8.8
Too much noise/aircraft noise	7.5
Roaming dogs/excrement	5.2
Lack of local shops/facilities	5.2
Disrepair of roads/footpaths	5.2

D Burley   **(n=437)**

Litter/refuse dumping/dirt   16.2
Traffic/busy roads/lack of crossing facilities   10.8
Roaming dogs/excrement   9.8
Crime and vandalism   9.2
Run-down, neglected area/disrepair of housing   7.3
Troublesome and neglectful neighbours   7.1
Misbehaving youths/children/lack of facilities   6.8
Too much noise   6.4

Concern about the dirty environment focussed on dogs and litter and the dumping of rubbish. In Hawksworth Wood interviewees complained about 'dogs roaming in packs' and 'dog mess in gardens' and similar comments were made in relation to Burley. A number of suggestions were put forward to control dogs such as a registration scheme, fines for untethered dogs, higher fines for fouling and exclusion of dogs from parks.

Concerns about litter focussed on the dumping of household rubbish in Hawksworth Wood and Burley and litter in the area around Kirkstall Abbey. Additional problems identified by interviewees included badly maintained footpaths (Hawksworth Wood and Burley) and rundown buildings in Kirkstall and noise in Burley.

The main perceived risks relate to crime against property- burglary (62 per cent of respondents overall) and theft of or from vehicles (39 per cent). The risks of crime against the person cause much less concern overall, but are of significantly more concern to women than to men. Again, there is a tendency for younger age groups to show a greater degree of concern about the risks of both property and person-related crime, but this pattern is much less marked in the case of burglary than car theft (and rape and assault). Non-white respondents show significantly above average concern about racial harassment. Those looking after home and children tend to feel more at risk than other groups, except in the case of car theft which is of most concern to those in work.

Concern about burglary, though high throughout the ward (62 per cent), is greatest in the Hawksworth Wood (69 per cent) and Vespers (66 per

Figure 16
Risks in area by autonomy

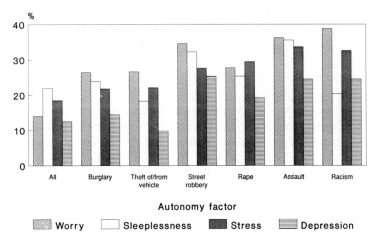

Autonomy factor

| Worry | Sleeplessness | Stress | Depression |

cent) areas, while the perceived risk of car theft is highest in Vespers and Burley. Concern about assault, robbery and rape is greatest in Burley and the perceived risk of the latter is above average in Vespers. From Figure 16 it can be seen that respondents who indicate that they feel at risk from crimes against the person and racism are more likely than average to report problems with indicators of autonomy.

This pattern of concerns was reflected in the comments made by interviewees. Burglary was a concern in all areas and suggested solutions included more police on the streets, police patrols and neighbourhood watch schemes and harsher penalties. Vehicle theft was also mentioned quite often especially by interviewees from Hawksworth Wood. Vandalism was a widespread concern again especially in Hawksworth Wood including things like 'damaging cars, smashing lights and interfering with people's gardens' and was explicitly linked by many to lack of facilities for young people. Violent assault and rape was mentioned by residents in Burley and racial harassment by ethnic minority interviewees.

Overall, burglary is stated as the single main concern by a third of all respondents; busy roads is next with 12 per cent. This order of priorities is consistent across groups and areas although the concern about burglary is above average amongst the elderly and in Hawksworth Wood, while concern about busy roads is above average in Kirkstall.

In summary, in terms of convenience of location for various facilities, the main problem is access to dentists, particularly in the Vespers and Hawksworth Wood; also to workplace in these areas, to shops in the Vespers, to community centres in Vespers, Burley and Kirkstall, and to sport and leisure facilities in Burley and Hawksworth Wood.

As regards problems in the local area, the main perceived problems are traffic and busy roads, litter, dogs, crime and vandalism and concern about the behaviour of children and facilities available for them. Roads, litter, crime and vandalism tend to be the most prominent concerns in the Vespers, Kirkstall and Burley. Hawksworth Wood is rather different with concern about litter, crime and vandalism supplemented by concern about dogs, behaviour of, and facilities for, children, problems with neighbours and neglect of housing.

On the other hand, people like the green open space and access to parks and countryside, particularly in Vespers, Hawksworth Wood and Kirkstall, and the convenience of facilities and amenities, particularly in Burley and Kirkstall. Another positive factor is friendly neighbours and community, and this is important in Hawksworth Wood notwithstanding the negative feelings of some residents about troublesome and neglectful neighbours.

These patterns of perceived problems can be compared with the importance attached by various groups to the two attributes of quality of life - 'living in a pleasant, clean and peaceful area' and 'being safe from acts of crime and violence' - discussed in part 2:1. As in the case of housing, discussed in part 2:4, there is a discrepancy between the tendency of younger people to place less importance on these attributes, on the one hand while, on the other hand, showing more awareness of problems in their area; again, perhaps more tolerance of the problems is indicated. Older age groups attach particular importance to being safe from crime and this reflects relatively high levels of concern about burglary, car theft and robbery. Similarly, carers attach relatively high importance to the 'crime' and 'area' attributes and indicate a high degree of concern about problems and risks in their area.

Although the perception of problems and risks is high in both the Hawksworth Wood and Burley areas, the perceived importance of the 'crime' and 'area' attributes is lower in Burley (this reflects age structure and the distribution of 'carers'). This indicates that problems relating to local environment and crime are more of an issue in Hawksworth Wood. Similarly, crime can also be seen as an important issue in the Vespers area.

Environment: Perceptions of Professionals and Community Representatives

We asked the professional workers and community representatives for their views about the physical environment in the study area. As with housing this was an issue about which they had plenty to say. Generally their views echoed those of the local residents.

Access to facilities

Access in Burley was generally felt to be good by local professionals. Because of its location it is easy to get into the town centre, there are plenty of buses and an access bus. Hills in Burley are a major problem for older people who tend to use public transport even for very short distances.

There are two health centres and plenty of chemist shops in Burley. Views on local shopping facilities differed between those who think they are reasonable and those who think they are small and expensive and there is not much choice. There are no good supermarkets in Burley although the 'Asda bus' goes through the area. It was widely felt that there was a problem of access to shopping facilities for people who do not have a car or who have mobility problems especially in the area between YTV and Kirkstall Lites. In some cases this means that they travel into town more often, thus increasing their expenditure on travel.

Bus services to and from the city centre are felt to be good but it is more difficult to travel from north to south eg. to the Belle Vue area or Kirkstall leisure centre. It was widely felt that Kirkstall leisure centre is not ideally situated for use by residents in Burley and the area as a whole lacks adequate sports and leisure facilities. The design of the swimming pool at Kirkstall Leisure Centre (with floor to ceiling windows) deters use by the Asian community and there is a problem of child care at the international pool. It is feared that the Kirkstall Valley development will decrease leisure activities by doing away with areas currently used for informal leisure activities. There is some open/green space (Burley Park) but local people feel that it is unsafe for children and women and needs a warden. There is only one proper children's playground and there are fears that children playing there run the risk of assault.

It was felt by some that there are particular problems of access, and barriers to services and facilities for ethnic minority groups in Burley due to language and cultural differences. Another dimension of this cultural difference is reflected in the comment by one community activist that Asian people's concept of distance and what is 'local' may be different from that of white people; it is based on life in traditional villages and therefore much more local in perspective eg. a class at the Brudenell Centre may not be considered local to Burley. It was felt that there is generally a lack of facilities for the Asian community who make use of the Burley Lodge Centre but require more specialist facilities. A local vicar also commented that although the Cardigan Centre provides a strong community focus, Burley lacks a community centre appropriate to the needs of the Asian community. For example, the Cardigan Centre is too small for funeral wakes and weddings. Young people, women and the elderly need a place to go.

There is no senior school in the Burley area so children may have to take two buses to get to school (one to the city centre and another out again). It was also felt that special needs education is not adequately catered for and there is a lack of adequate specialist language teaching.

Ideas for improving services and access to facilities in Burley included the following:

• Benches for people to sit down on the way to the shops, and trees that are 'vandal-proof'

• Better access to shops for elderly people through a shop on the sheltered housing site, a mobile shop and organised trips to the supermarket.

- Better maintenance of kerbs eg. clearing of wet leaves in autumn and winter, and more ramps.

- A cafe/meeting place/drop-in centre in Burley and a community centre for the Asian community.

- Translation and interpreter facilities to benefit the Asian community.

A somewhat different set of concerns emerged in relation to Hawksworth Wood. Here there was general consensus that there is a lack of adequate shops and the local shops that do exist are small, expensive and often closed. In particular it was felt that chemist shops don't stay open long enough and there is a particular problem after 6pm and at weekends (according to a local GP). Furthermore it is difficult to get into town especially with young children.

A particular problem that emerged not mentioned elsewhere concerned public phones. There are few working public phones in Hawksworth Wood and it is rare for people to have their own phone: BT demand high advance payments because of the reputation of the estate.

Community health workers felt that there is a problem of access to health services for people on the Hawksworth Wood estate. Kirkstall Health Centre is the nearest but is difficult to get to for those with no car. Also some GPs are reluctant to take families from the estate. There is no dentist locally.

A number of people mentioned the shortage of child care on the Hawksworth Wood Estate. Only those children thought to be 'at risk' are allocated a place in local authority nurseries. This prevents mothers from getting jobs according to a local youth worker.

The main suggestion for improvements to services in Hawksworth Wood focussed on the need for a drop-in/meeting centre/coffee shop that is more accessible than the existing YMCA.

Facilities in the Kirkstall area were generally regarded as quite good although the heavy traffic on the local roads was seen as hindering access. Crossing facilities were frequently mentioned as inadequate. Disrepair of pavements and kerbs creates difficulties for people with mobility problems

and can result in falls and fractured hips etc. There are insufficient ramps
and crossings (resulting, it is claimed, in three deaths in the last four years
in the St Annes Parade area).

Bus services are reasonably good although not always reliable. Drivers are
not as patient as they might be and often do not give older people enough
time to get on and off buses. The access bus does not meet all the needs
of the physically disabled - it has to be booked in advance and is not
always available.

Elderly people in particular have mobility problems and have difficulties
getting to facilities such as shops. The biggest problem faced by the
elderly is isolation according to the officer-in-charge of an elderly
persons' day centre. The over 80s tend to be ostracised by those in their
60s. There are currently community rooms in sheltered housing which are
not being used but could be used for 'drop-in' facilities. New day centres
and health centres are being built but the real issues of isolation and
inadequate services are not being addressed.

According to a local head teacher there is a lack of facilities for children,
especially teenagers. There is some under-age drinking. A lack of open
space results in children playing in the street.

Suggestions for improvements included:

• More pedestrian crossings with sound for blind people on Queenswood
  Drive, Burley Road, Abbey Road, Beecroft Street, St Annes Parade,
  Kirkstall Lane/Morris Lane and Haddon Road/Kirkstall Road.

• A paid worker attached to a community centre (eg. drop-in centre) to
  offer advice and information on financial problems, unemployment and
  services for children and an extended luncheon club and evening
  classes.

• More account to be taken of the needs of residents by planners
  especially when commercial areas are developed in residential/mixed
  areas.

Problems and Risks

Traffic and/or busy roads was mentioned as a problem in all three areas. For example, one head teacher in Kirkstall was concerned about the effects of traffic noise and fumes on children in school and the dangers of children running into Kirkstall Road. Several people said that heavy traffic created problems for pedestrians trying to cross the road at the junction of Kirkstall Lane and Morris Lane. 'Rat-running' was mentioned as a particular problem for the Hawksworth Wood estate and for Burley.

Parking was another issue that gave cause for concern both in Hawksworth Wood where the problem was badly-parked or dumped cars, and in Burley where the problem is caused by commuters parking in the area causing access problems for local residents. For example, it was stated that 'people who travel by car to work in the city centre use the Burley area as a park-and-ride scheme'. This creates problems for access by emergency services and for children forced to play in the street.

Noise was also thought to be a problem in all areas. In Burley it was felt that noise was caused mainly by children playing in the streets and from students playing loud music. Noise was also thought to be a problem between neighbours living in maisonettes in the Graysons.

There are many complaints to the Environmental Health service about domestic noise because much of the housing is high density. Complaints relate to TVs, radios, stereos, shouting and animals. There are also complaints about industrial uses eg. about factories, pubs and clubs. Kirkstall Forge is the largest industrial site in Leeds and works through the night resulting in complaints from nearby residents. The area is also in the flight path of Leeds/Bradford airport but there do not appear to be too many complaints.

The lack of open space was mentioned as a problem especially in the Burley Lodge area and around Kirkstall school. Concern was expressed by the area housing managers about the lack of play spaces for children in the areas around flats and maisonettes.

There was also concern expressed about the safety of play areas for children. A youth worker in Hawksworth Wood identified the problem of lack of safe and stimulating play areas; children play on a disused quarry which is a 'dumping ground'. In the Burley area, Burley Park was thought to be unsafe because of glue-sniffers.

Dogs are a problem in Hawksworth Wood where strays roam around and attack people and foul the streets, pavements and grassed areas and create noise. Dogs were also mentioned as a problem in the Burley Lodge area where they make a mess of the streets and chase people.

Vandalism was mentioned as a problem by a majority of those interviewed. The local MP thought it was mainly caused by youths and involved attacks on property, breaking windows, fences, gates, attacks on shops and parked cars, the latter being a particular problem in Hawksworth Wood. The local councillor also mentioned vandalised bus stops and burned allotment sheds.

In Hawksworth Wood a youth worker also reported high levels of vandalism - 'anything moveable moves; anything breakable is broken'. Trees, telephone boxes and bus stops are damaged; a chemist shop has been burnt out (rocket put through letter box). All shops have to have steel shutters; they often have to be boarded up after being 'bricked'. Houses get 'bricked', especially if people are not liked. The chapel is often vandalised; it is a 'hanging out' area for young people and substance abusers. The YMCA is vandal proof, with a steel roof, no gutters, well alarmed and all doors are locked. Burglaries are not particularly high but theft is a problem.

In Burley there was a feeling on the part of some community activists that Asians are a particular target for vandalism and harassment resulting in damage to their houses and shops. Other examples of vandalism in Burley mentioned by the police were broken windows and street lights, graffiti and damage to empty houses. In Kirkstall the only area which has a problem with vandalism is Argie Avenue.

Lack of facilities for children was also a major concern in all areas. Although some examples of good facilities were mentioned, eg. the Family Services Unit in Burley and the YMCA in Hawksworth, it was nevertheless widely felt that there were not enough activities for children especially after school and at weekends. It was felt by many that the traditional 'uniform' groups no longer had wide appeal and that young teenagers, especially those from disadvantaged families 'miss out on a close family environment and are disenchanted with school and youth clubs'. This was seen as creating a problem of harassment from youths and burglaries eg. youths knocking on doors and running away and conning the elderly out of money. This is a major problem causing fear and stress. The police 'do very little' according to an officer-in-charge of an elderly persons' day centre.

Where play areas do exist it was claimed that they are not maintained so that there is broken glass in the play grounds and the grass is not cut. 'Informal' play areas such as the woods near Queenswood Drive were not considered safe (it was suggested that children were at risk from attack by glue-sniffers). Other areas where children play such as the canal and railway are hazards for children. The lack of facilities for children exacerbates the problem of annoyance to other residents.

It was felt that children and young teenagers need activities which 'arise out of the community'. The Community Association in Kirkstall mentioned the need for a fenced communal garden for children to play. In Hawksworth Wood the Community Association has played a role in obtaining a play area for children. A problem is that sports and leisure facilities (eg for swimming) are prohibitively expensive to many people.

Rubbish and litter were thought to be particular problems in Hawksworth and Burley. In Burley this was mainly rubble, household refuse and old furniture not collectable by normal service. It was felt by the local MP that failure to remove such rubbish creates a 'vicious circle' so that people perceive it as being an area that is run-down and so take less pride in it. Also, there have been problems with communal bin-yards for back-to-back housing. There have been some initiatives to remove these and pave them over. Some of this work has been done in the past by community programme workers.

In Hawksworth Wood the problem was thought to be created, in part, by failure to maintain fences so that dogs get at rubbish bags. However there is also a problem of dumping of rubbish by the old power station in the Kirkstall Valley.

On the whole, rundown buildings were not felt to be a particular problem in any of the three areas. The only sites that were mentioned as giving

cause for concern were the corner of Beecroft St and Commercial Road
and a small area on Argie Avenue and the Burley Lodge area.

Burglary was the most widely mentioned concern although the local MP
did not think that its incidence was higher in this ward than elsewhere. In
Burley the police said that there was some evidence that young people
indigenous to the area target students for burglaries, car-related crime and
personal attack because they are identified as having things that are worth
stealing, they are away during the holidays and there is a feeling that they
are more advantaged than local youth.

Car-related crime is recognised by many to be a major concern in all
areas. In Hawksworth there was concern about juvenile car theft. A local
youth worker said that people are at risk from fast, reckless driving of
stolen cars through the estate. Stealing cars gives status to young men.
Children grow up in a culture of stolen goods and stolen vehicles. High
speed police chases are seen as exciting.

In Burley the problem was thought to be break-ins to parked cars often
those belonging to commuters. In Kirkstall, car theft is mainly a problem
in the leisure centre car park and in nearby pub and club car parks. The
police and community activists thought that most of this form of crime
was committed by juveniles aged between 13 and 17.

Violent assault was thought to be a particular problem in Hawksworth
Wood where, according to some of those interviewed, there is a high
incidence of domestic violence and violence between members of
extended families and rival gangs. These are not reported to the police
according to local health workers. It was also suggested that the area has
become notorious so that people are afraid of the area and don't go into
the pubs if they are not local. Many people living on the boundaries of the
estate see it as a 'no-go' area. It was felt that some professionals also feel
uneasy about going into the area because of hostility towards them. This
has the effect of reducing their input.

A youth worker reported a high incidence of physical and sexual child
abuse in Hawksworth Wood. There are generational divisions: young and
older residents 'hate each other'. Older residents are not afraid of the
young; they shout and wave sticks at them resulting in verbal abuse from
the young. The divisions are clear in the use of the YMCA centre - some

parents see the work of the centre as a threat and ban their children from attending.

In general it was felt by one head teacher that Hawksworth Wood is poorly policed resulting in considerable 'petty crime and intimidation'. This view was reiterated by a home care worker who commented on the lack of police foot patrols.

However this view of the estate was not endorsed by the police who argued that there are not really any major problems on the Hawksworth Wood estate. Although the area was described as 'a self-contained patch where strangers are not welcome in the pubs' it was felt that the perceptions of residents that they live on a bad estate are now outdated. In fact, it was suggested that conditions on the estate are very good compared to other estates, with more facilities available than anywhere else in the patch. The police also claimed that although robbery, assault and sexual attack are probably perceived as being high risks in the Burley area the incidence of these is actually quite low.

Racial harassment was mentioned as a problem in Burley and on the Hawksworth estate. In Burley racial harassment was described by a community health worker as 'a constant aspect of the lives of Asians living in the Burley Lodge area' resulting in feelings of low status and not being respected. The police thought that the Pakistani community suffered the worst racial harassment but that it was a problem faced by all races. It was argued that racial harassment is a particular problem for shopkeepers and for people in their homes eg. broken windows, graffiti on doors, 'things' through letter boxes. Youths come to Burley from other areas because the black youth is less well-organised here than in other areas. Racial harassment is the biggest problem for those affected although it is not great in scale. Street lighting is poor especially in the streets of back-to-back housing and this encourages racial harassment and burglary.

There are very few black people on the Hawksworth Wood estate but Asian and Chinese shop-keepers are subject to racial harassment which was thought by one health worker to be very bad in Hawksworth. It was also claimed that there was racism towards ethnic minority children from teachers in schools. A local clergyman mentioned the presence of a 'National Front contingent' on the estate. He described how he had had to take in an Iraqi family during the Gulf War for their protection.

When asked about the problem that was the greatest cause for concern, the answers centred on crime and vandalism including, in Burley, racially motivated crime. Other concerns included lack of safe, open space for children (especially in Burley) and traffic and busy roads (especially in Kirkstall).

Environment: Public Meetings

In general people attending the public meetings felt less strongly about issues relating to the physical environment than they did about other issues. The exception to this pattern was, perhaps, in Kirkstall where the view was expressed that the police and city council were more concerned about traffic than people and the plea was made 'You have to do something to help us in this area... you've got to help us improve the lot of people in Kirkstall'. This is surprising in that Kirkstall residents were least likely to report problems and risks in the local area, but can probably be explained by the increased level of awareness of environmental issues as a result of recent plans to redevelop the area.

Participants in the meeting at Hawksworth Wood reiterated the view that the estate suffered particular problems of isolation exacerbated recently, it was claimed, by the loss of bus routes. Difficulties of access to the health centre, the lack of shops, dentist and a police station were all raised again. There was a general feeling too that the estate was under-policed and that there was a growing problem of drugs among children and young people on the estate. This view, strongly expressed, is in marked contrast to the view of local police that Hawksworth Wood no longer had a particular crime problem.

Crime and fear of crime was discussed at the meeting in Burley where it was felt that the elderly were particularly at risk since it was easy to spot where elderly people lived and for criminals to con their way into their homes.

Environment: Key Issues

The relationship between physical environment and well-being is a complex one. However our survey shows that there is a clear link between perceptions of problems and risks in the local area and poor general health, stress, anxiety, depression and sleeplessness. Codified knowledge is a poor guide to the characteristics of the physical environment, its problems or risks since there is little information available and what does exist ignores the subjective dimension. For example, it is as important for well-being that people feel that they are safe from acts of crime as it is for them actually to be safe from crime. So perceptions about levels of crime may be as important, if not more so, as figures for actual crime levels.

Not surprisingly, perhaps, the study area is highly differentiated in terms of the characteristics of the physical environment. In the areas furthest from the city centre, residents are likely to mention the attractive, open environment in positive terms whereas in the areas nearest to the city centre convenience for local facilities is most likely to be mentioned positively. However, the pattern of dislikes is much more varied with, overall, traffic and busy roads emerging as the main concern, followed by litter, dogs and vandalism. In the Vespers, while traffic was the main concern, proximity to Hawksworth Wood estate was also a problem for a significant number of residents. In Hawksworth Wood itself neighbours were likely to provoke the most negative comments followed by the area being run-down. Kirkstall was much closer to the average with traffic, litter and vandalism being the 'top' three dislikes, as was Burley where litter, traffic and dogs provoked the most negative comment.

In all areas access to certain facilities was seen to be a problem. However, overall Hawksworth Wood appeared to suffer the most acute problems with most facilities presenting access problems. In Burley the elderly experienced particular problems of access due to hills and the Asian community faced barriers as a result of culture and language. However, in all areas lack of facilities for children and young people emerged as a particular issue and was seen to be connected to other problems giving rise to concern such as crime, vandalism, glue-sniffing and drug-taking. In Hawksworth Wood and Burley, especially, crime was seen to be a problem by local residents - a view endorsed by local professionals although not necessarily by the police themselves.

In Kirkstall, Burley and Hawksworth Wood the issue of community centres, drop-in centres and meeting places was raised. It was widely felt by residents and professionals alike that current provision did not meet needs. For example it was generally thought that the Asian community in Burley needed their own community centre since the new Cardigan Centre did not have a room large enough to accommodate wakes or weddings. Similarly, in Hawksworth Wood it was felt that the YMCA had good facilities, but was in the wrong place, had developed a bad reputation and so was under-used. In both of these cases, it would seem, provision has been made and has proved unsuccessful because of a failure to adequately take account of local people's needs and wishes.

Figure 17
Satisfaction with health services

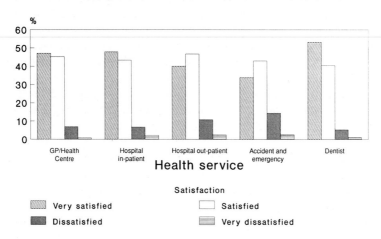

2:6. HEALTH CARE AND WELFARE SERVICES

Health and autonomy can both, potentially, be improved through access to appropriate health care and welfare services. In this chapter we first review the existing data on helath and welfare services before looking at residents' own perceptions of health and welfare services and also experiences of being carers or cared for. Then we examine the observations of local professional workers on existing services before summing up the main issues and priorities.

Health Care and Welfare Services: Codified Knowledge

For the purpose of health services Kirkstall ward was, until recently, a part of Leeds Western District Health Authority. There are seven hospitals within the district health authority with a total of 2,524 beds. This figure is more meaningful if expressed as a ratio to the numbers of residents in the health authority. Based on 1988 population estimates this gives a figure of 69 beds per 10,000 population.

Community health services such as ante-natal clinics, child health services, chiropody, dentistry and so on are provided from 16 health centres and other places in NHS and non-NHS premises as well as in patients' own homes. An examination of the staff profile of Leeds West DHA (in March 1989) shows that there is one member of medical and dental staff to 1010 population and one member of nursing staff to 110 population. In addition Leeds has just over 400 general practitioners with an average list size of 1,776 patients (88 per cent of the national average). It is also better supplied with women GPs than the rest of the country: 29 per cent of Leeds GPs are women compared with 22 per cent nationally.

This information relates to health care inputs. It is not a measure of need. In addition there are commonly used measures of the utilisation of services: numbers of hospital discharges and numbers of specific treatments or health care procedures carried out. The Standardised Deaths and Discharges Ratio (SDDR) expresses the number of hospital discharges of residents from each ward as an index number calculated in relation to the population of Leeds as a whole. Thus an SDDR of 100 would mean that the ward is typical of Leeds as a whole, taking the age and sex distribution of the ward into account. The SDDR index represents the use of hospital services by residents of different wards. It is not a measure of need: a relatively low SDDR could reflect less need of hospital services, poor access, or use of hospital services outside Leeds.

Nearly half of total deaths and discharges in Kirkstall relate to three specialities: general medicine, general surgery and gynaecology. The SDDR for Kirkstall is above 100 for 'all specialities' and for each of the major specialities shown with the exception of general surgery. In other words the amount of hospital services used by the population of Kirkstall is disproportionately high given its sex and age structure. The SDDR is particularly high for urology (144) and paediatrics (137). The highest rank positions of Kirkstall are of SDDRs for general medicine (27) and paediatrics (27): for each of these two specialties there are only six wards in Leeds with higher SDDRs than Kirkstall.

A survey of self-reported use of health services shows that 24 per cent of Leeds West respondents in the Yorkshire Healthy Life Survey had attended hospital as an out patient during the last 12 months, and 80 per cent had seen a GP. Fifty-seven per cent of respondents in the same survey had visited a dentist within the past year (45 per cent within the last six months). In a survey of 14-year-old children in Leeds schools in 1986/87, a somewhat higher proportion, 80 per cent, of 'white' children claimed to have regular dental check-ups and none reported that they had never been. The proportion of 'Asian' and 'Afro-Caribbean' children who report having regular check-ups is somewhat lower.

Finally, the Yorkshire Healthy Life Survey asked respondents about screening/prevention. A majority of women (59 per cent) reported having had a cervical smear test within the last 5 years (25 per cent within the past 12 months). However 27 per cent had never had a test.

Welfare Services

We now turn to welfare services for the elderly, mentally and physically handicapped and mentally ill adults. (Services for children are also dealt with in part 2:9.)

The data presented relates to social services inputs or resources (staffing and places provided in the form of residential provision and day care) and activity (active cases of social work staff). There are no direct measures of need for welfare services or of the outputs or outcomes of these services. The number of elderly people in the population, for example, provides a rough measure of need in that a larger number of elderly implies a greater amount of need, but it does not indicate the specific needs that the elderly have. Equally, the number of elderly people cared for in residential homes is a measure of output but it does not indicate the type or quality of care provided or its adequacy in meeting the needs of residents.

Leeds City Council Social Service administrative areas referred to in this section do not correspond closely with Kirkstall Ward or postal districts 4 and 5. The city is divided into three divisions and nine area offices. Data will be presented relating to Leeds as a whole, Division 3, and Buckingham House Area Office which covers postal areas 1-6 plus part of areas 7 and 16: Kirkstall, Burley, Woodhouse, Headingley and Weetwood. So far as possible information relating to the voluntary and private sectors is also given.

As regards Leeds City Council Social Services Staffing, approximately half of social services staff consist of home care assistants and care assistants in homes and day centres (excluding those for young people and children). There are some 135 home care assistants per 10,000 elderly people in Leeds. There are some 370 field social workers in Leeds, about five per 10,000 total population.

Statutory and voluntary child care and supervision accounts for 20-25 per cent of the active caseload of social work staff. 'Children and families, Other' is a 'catch-all' category embracing marital, financial, housing and health problems. Work with elderly people accounts for 18 per cent of the caseload in Leeds as a whole and a rather higher proportion (26 per cent) for Buckingham House. Almost all of these cases involve social work supervision. Mental health and physical handicap cases represent a much smaller proportion of the total caseload of Buckingham House (11.6 per cent) than Leeds as a whole (23.7 per cent). Caseload statistics indicate the range of work in which social work staff are engaged and this may be thought to more or less reflect the pattern of need in the population. However, the figures in effect indicate the pattern of response to need as assessed by social work staff and not the pattern of need itself.

Under the heading of mental health resources is included provision for people with a mental handicap (learning difficulty) and the mentally ill. There are some 700 residential places for mentally handicapped people in Leeds, half provided by the local authority and some 41 per cent by the voluntary and private sectors. In addition there are three hospital units managed by Leeds Eastern Health Authority with a total of 477 beds providing residential care to people with a mental handicap on a city-wide basis, there being no residential provision by Leeds Western Health Authority. Thus, there is a total of over one thousand places in residential care for people with a mental handicap in Leeds including public, private and voluntary provision and supported group homes. Nearly one thousand mentally handicapped people are registered with the seven adult training centres providing day care. Day services are also provided by the NHS at one of the hospital units (Meanwood Park).

These figures relating to the level of provision of residential and day care need to be set against an assessment of the amount of need in the population. In this connection it has been estimated that there are approximately 2,100 adults and children in Leeds who can be defined as being severely mentally or multiply handicapped. The Leeds Mental Handicap Planning Register includes all those who live in Leeds and are receiving or have received specialist services for their learning difficulty in the city or are receiving such services outside the city, and those from outside Leeds who are receiving specialist services for their significant learning difficulty in the city. The register does not include all mentally handicapped people but its coverage is sufficient to provide an indication of the amount of need in the population. At 20 September 1990 consent had been sought to register 2,055 people and of these 1,815 were fully registered. Of these 110 (7.6 per cent) were within the area covered by Buckingham House Social Services office, the lowest of all areas.

The NHS is responsible for 20 per cent of the clients registered. The distribution of clients by Community Mental Health Team (CMHT) Area closely matches the population distribution: registered mentally handicapped clients constitute 0.26 per cent of the population of Leeds as a whole and of the population of the Buckingham House Area.

There are places in residential homes (including supported group homes) for approximately two in three mentally handicapped people and the same ratio of daycare (ATC) places to mentally handicapped adults (age 21+).

Just over half of clients on the mental handicap planning register live in the community. The vast majority (90 per cent) of these live with one or two parents. 'An area of concern is the number of community based clients living with elderly carers...21 per cent of community based clients are living with a carer aged 61 to 70 years with a further 11 per cent of clients with carers aged 71 and over' (Leeds City Council, 1991).

At 31 March 1990 there were four local authority staffed homes and eight local authority supported group homes providing a total of 119 residential places for mentally ill people in Leeds. Accommodation in one of the social services hostels is obtained through referral by a social worker or other professional. None of these hostels is located in Kirkstall ward. Local authority supported group homes involve a small group of people living independently but sharing some facilities with support provided in the form of visits by social workers and other care staff. In addition to this provision three voluntary organisations (MIND, St Anne's Shelter and Housing Action, and South Leeds Community Health Project) provide specialist housing for people with mental health problems with support provided by social workers and other care staff.

At April 1991 there were four day centres in Leeds (none in Kirkstall) requiring professional referral, plus a range of drop-in centres and self help and support groups.

There are three hospitals providing services for mentally ill people in Leeds. The principal facility is High Royds Hospital in Leeds West which provides 626 acute, rehabilitation and long stay beds (Moore, 1989). One hundred and nine beds for the treatment of mentally ill adults aged under 65 are located at St James's University Hospital (Leeds East) (Services for Mentally Ill People' Leeds Eastern Health Authority). A number of acute and long stay beds located at Stanley Royd Hospital (Wakefield Health Authority) are used by Leeds residents. Day care, outpatient services and community psychiatric services are also provided by the health service. There is no equivalent for mental illness of the Leeds Mental handicap Planning Register and thus no way of assessing the amount of need in the population.

These are some 3,100 residential places for the elderly in Leeds - one place for every 37 elderly people. There is one home for the elderly in Kirkstall ward (Burley Willows) providing 40 places. Almost 2,000 older people are registered to attend one of the day care centres run by the local authority. Burley Willows provides 40 day care places and the Hyde Park and Queenswood Drive Day centres, which serve the Burley and Kirkstall areas, provide 80 places.

More important than residential or day care in terms of numbers of elderly people receiving care is the home care service. In Leeds, 17,467 home care cases involve elderly people, that is over 90 per cent of the total homecare caseload. The homecare elderly caseload represents 15 per cent of the elderly population. It is clear that the vast majority of elderly people live in the community and have no contact with local authority day care or the homecare service. The figures presented here refer only to the level of provision of services for the elderly. In particular it cannot be presumed of the large number of elderly who do not come into contact with local authority or voluntary services that there is not significant need.

Health Care and Welfare Services: Experiential Knowledge

We asked residents in the Kirkstall ward about their usage of health and welfare services. Specifically we asked whether or not they had used a range of health and welfare services, whether they were satisfied with them and the problems they experienced in accessing them. In addition we asked about people's experiences of being carers or cared for.

Health

Eighty-seven per cent of respondents had used a health centre or visited a local doctor during the past 12 months, with 92 per cent of those being satisfied or very satisfied with the services they had received, and eight per cent dissatisfied or very dissatisfied (Figure 17 - see p158). The second most used service was dental care although a significantly smaller proportion of the sample had visited their dentist in the past year (52 per cent). Once again the level of satisfaction was very high (93 per cent) with only 6 per cent of users being dissatisfied or very dissatisfied.

Thirty-five per cent of the sample had been a hospital out-patient in the past 12 months, with 18 per cent being in-patients, and 15 per cent having used the accident or emergency services. The latter attracted the highest rate of dissatisfaction (14 per cent dissatisfied, 2.5 per cent very dissatisfied). Other services with a higher than average rate of dissatisfaction were hospital out patients (13 per cent) and those using psychiatric care: although only three per cent of the sample had used this service, 11 per cent were dissatisfied with it. Of the other services, those using alternative medicine such as homeopathy or acupuncture (four per cent of the sample) were most likely to be very satisfied with the service they had received (58 per cent).

More women have used more of the services than men, with a noticeable difference in usage of health centres, or doctors, (women 98 per cent, men 80 per cent), chiropody (women 13 per cent, men six per cent), dentists (women 56 per cent, men 47 per cent) and, not surprisingly, family planning (women 11 per cent, men three per cent). In the majority of services men are more likely to be satisfied with the service they have received than women, although only slightly. The exception was in relation to psychiatric care where 69 per cent of males compared to only 61 per cent of females were satisfied. More women (87 per cent) than men (57 per cent) were satisfied with the family planning service, five per cent of men were very dissatisfied.

The use of doctors or health centres increases slightly with age as does the level of satisfaction with services received. The use of hospital services (both in-and out- patients) is equally spread across the age groups, as is the level of satisfaction. The use of emergency services, dentists and as might be expected, family planning decreases with age, with levels of satisfaction being roughly equal across age groups.

A comparison of health service usage between the white and non-white populations shows that no ethnic minorities (in the sample) have used psychiatric care services, chiropody, or family planning, although no firm conclusion can be drawn from this due to the small sample size. Where members of ethnic minorities have used health services the incidence of use is comparable between whites and ethnic minorities. Levels of satisfaction with health services vary significantly, however, non-whites being less satisfied. Thus, 82 per cent of non-whites compared to 92 per cent of whites were satisfied or very satisfied with the service they received from doctors or health centres. An even greater disparity emerges when looking at hospital services, with 73 per cent of non-white hospital in patients expressing satisfaction compared to 91 per cent of whites, and

63 per cent of non-white hospital out patients expressing satisfaction compared to 87 per cent of whites using these services.

Those looking after home and family are most likely to have used health services and not surprisingly, we find that this disparity includes a majority of women who have, or are about to have, children. Of those caring for home and family 98 per cent have visited their doctor or health centre in the past 12 months, and 75 per cent have visited their dentist. They are also at least twice as likely to have used psychiatric care services than any other group in the sample. The use of services by those in paid work, the unemployed or retired is roughly equal. In terms of levels of satisfaction however differences do occur. Retired respondents are more likely than others to be satisfied with doctor's services confirming the increased incidence of satisfaction by age. Those in paid work or at home caring are less likely to have been satisfied with hospital in patient services (84 per cent) compared to the others (93 per cent). Unemployed respondents express greater dissatisfaction with hospital out-patient services, 75 per cent say they are satisfied compared to 90 per cent of the retired. Finally, unemployed respondents are less likely to be satisfied with dental services (87 per cent) than the rest of the sample (93 per cent).

Residents in Hawksworth Wood have used the main services slightly more frequently than residents of other areas except for dental services where only 42 per cent of residents have been to a dentist during the past 12 months (perhaps reflecting the difficulties of access discussed in part 2:5). Residents in Burley are least likely to be very satisfied with the service they have received at health centres (40 per cent), and 10 per cent of residents in the area are dissatisfied with in-patient services. Fifteen per cent of residents in Kirkstall and Burley were dissatisfied with out-patient services compared to 9 per cent of residents in Hawksworth Wood and the Vespers. Residents in the Vespers and Hawksworth Wood are more likely to be dissatisfied with the dental services they have received (10 per cent).

Twenty-four per cent of those who have visited their GP or health centre during the past year report poor (20 per cent) or very poor (4 per cent) health. Twenty-nine per cent have or are suffering from a long standing illness. A higher than average proportion of those who think they drink too much, and do not get enough exercise have visited their doctor in the past year, although smokers and non-smokers have an equal incidence of GP or health centre visits.

Those respondents who have been hospital in-patients or out-patients over the previous 12 months report a poorer standard of health than the rest of the sample and are likely to suffer from a long standing illness (40 per cent). Ten per cent of those who have used hospitals in the period are registered disabled. Hospital patients are also more likely than others in the sample to report problems with stress, anxiety, and depression.

Health services users cannot be differentiated from the others in the sample in their views on the importance of their general standard of health to their quality of life with 98 per cent of both groups considering this to be fairly or very important. Health service users are equally as likely as others to consider that having access to health care in the form of doctors, dentists, and hospitals is important, although those that have used these services are more inclined to see this provision as 'very' important as opposed to fairly important.

The two most commonly reported problems in using health services were 'waiting to be seen' (39 per cent of respondents), and 'getting an appointment' (26 per cent). Car parking and lack of information were also reported as problems by about 10 per cent of respondents.

Waiting time and getting appointments were the two most common complaints irrespective of age, sex, economic activity and ethnicity. Of the other problems: car parking (11.1 per cent), lack of information (10 per cent), getting time off work (8 per cent) and waiting room facilities (7 per cent), the incidence varied between respondents. Women are more likely to report problems with waiting time, making an appointment and childcare, than men. A higher proportion of men reported difficulties with getting time off work, car parking and poor public transport. A higher than average incidence of problems in using health care services are reported by those aged 18-34 in all cases, except difficulties with access for the disabled, and problems with poor public transport, which are more prevalent among those aged over 65.

Getting an appointment and waiting to be seen are the most commonly reported problems among non-white respondents with the latter being reported by non-whites significantly more (52 per cent) than by whites (38 per cent). Ethnic minority respondents also report above average problems with translation facilities (13 per cent), an unwelcoming atmosphere (13 per cent), and getting care for children (13 per cent).

Those in paid work are more likely to find that getting time off work is a problem (17 per cent), whereas for the unemployed, 22 per cent reported lack of information as a problem, and a higher than average incidence of problems with waiting room facilities. For those looking after home and family, child care (25 per cent) was a problem as was waiting time (54 per cent). For retired respondents, although the greatest problems were appointments and waiting time, the incidence of these was far lower than for other groups, 11 per cent and 25 per cent respectively. Car parking (10 per cent) and poor public transport (5 per cent) were also problematic.

Respondents in Burley and the Vespers are more likely than those in other areas to report problems with waiting to be seen and getting an appointment. Residents in the Vespers also report problems with car parking (11 per cent), poor public transport (17 per cent) and waiting room facilities (11 per cent). In Burley lack of information (12 per cent) is the most common problem reported after waiting and getting an appointment.

The effect of experiencing problems using health services becomes apparent when looking at levels of satisfaction with services used. Whereas 92 per cent of health centre or GP visitors were satisfied with the service they received, only 66 per cent of those who had experienced difficulties with translation and 78 per cent an unwelcoming atmosphere were satisfied with this service. However, a slightly lower incidence of satisfaction with GP and health centre services is also reported by those facing problems with lack of information (81 per cent) and getting an appointment. Satisfaction levels are similarly affected by a lack of waiting room facilities, information and an unwelcoming atmosphere by the users of hospital out-patient services. Lack of access for the disabled and translation facilities affect the satisfaction ratings of the users of dental services.

Those residents in the Vespers and in Kirkstall who reported problems with transport also report that health centres and dental practices are not conveniently situated near their homes. This is also mentioned by some residents in Hawksworth with regard to dentists' surgeries. Problems of transport and childcare are particularly mentioned by those respondents with children, and especially by those with three or more dependent children.

The broad range of concerns about health care services was reflected in the individual interviews. Waiting times were a major concern both for hospital and GP appointments and also the length of time spent waiting when patients attended for their appointments. One elderly resident said: 'I object to having to make an appointment. Sometimes you have to wait two days. If you're ill you should be able to see a doctor on the same day'. Another complained about three-hour waits at Leeds General Infirmary (LGI) out-patient clinics. People were also dissatisfied with facilities in waiting rooms especially at LGI. A number of women with young children were particularly concerned about the lack of child care and play facilities at hospitals and health centres. Another frequently mentioned cause for concern was the lack of car parking at LGI, described as 'very bad' by one elderly person and 'ridiculous' by a woman with children. A number of people complained about the length of time it took for ambulances to arrive.

Welfare Services

Welfare services are relatively infrequently used by the majority of the population. The most frequently used services are social workers (7 per cent) and home helps (5 per cent). There is a very high level of satisfaction with all the services, the lowest being 50 per cent for adoption/fostering services but the small number of users of this service means that no firm conclusion can be drawn from this. Those rating the greatest level of satisfaction are social services day centres (93 per cent), support or self help groups (94 per cent) and home helps (90 per cent). The proportion of those very satisfied varies from a low of 29 per cent with meals on wheels, and 35 per cent with drop-in centres, to a high of 70 per cent of the users of day centres, and 63 per cent in support or self help groups.

The frequency of use of welfare services is greater among women than among men. Twice the proportion of women (8 per cent) than men (4 per cent) have seen a social worker in the past year. For all services except social services day centres women are more satisfied with the service they have received than men. The greatest disparity arises in relation to social workers with 81 per cent of women expressing satisfaction compared to 70 per cent of men.

The use of different services varies significantly with age (Figure 18). Respondents under the age of 65 do not make use of home care or meals on wheels services. 33 per cent of those over 65 have used the former and 15 per cent the latter. 21 per cent of those over 65 have seen a social worker in the past year compared to 5 per cent of younger respondents. Older people are also more likely to have made use of a day centre (10 per cent, against less than 1 per cent of those under 65 years). Younger respondents are more likely to be dissatisfied than older respondents with the service received from social workers. Moreover, the level of dissatisfaction of those using support or self help groups falls as age increases, although there is a very high overall level of satisfaction (88 per cent).

Assessing the use of welfare service by ethnic group is problematical due to the very small number of non-white users. Only four of the non-white respondents had used a social worker. In nearly all cases non-white users of welfare services reported satisfaction with the services they had used but again one must be cautious given the small numbers involved.

Use of welfare services varies considerably with economic activity. Those in paid work are highly unlikely to have used any of the services we asked about with only three per cent having used a social worker and two per cent social services nurseries. Among unemployed people seven per cent have used a social worker. A different picture emerges if we turn to those looking after home and family. This group makes most use of drop-in centres (4 per cent), adoption services (2 per cent), social services nurseries (6 per cent) and social workers (13 per cent). Fourteen per cent of retired respondents use home helps, six per cent meals on wheels, 10 per cent social workers and five per cent social services day centres.

The use of welfare services is noticeably lower in the Vespers than in any of the other areas of the ward. A higher proportion of residents in Burley and Hawksworth Wood have seen a social worker in the past year than in the other areas (roughly 8 per cent in both areas).

Users of social services are more likely than others to consider that having access to social services is important to their quality of life - 94 per cent of users of meals on wheels, 92 per cent users of social workers, and 91 per cent of users of home helps consider this to be important compared with 89 per cent of all respondents. In particular, the elderly are more

Figure 18
Use of welfare services by group

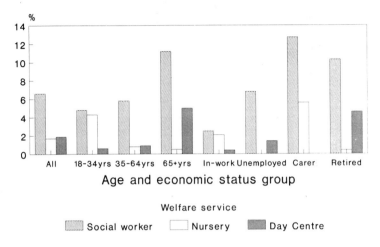

likely to consider welfare services as important, more likely to use them and more likely to be sastisfied with them.

Few of the people we interviewed had made use of welfare services. One of the few comments made (by a woman with young children in Hawksworth Wood) was that 'social workers at the advice centre didn't want to listen and gave no real constructive advice'. Another resident in Kirkstall complained that social workers 'keep changing' and 'never show you any reports'.

Carers and Cared For

In addition to care from health and welfare agencies, people also give care to, and receive care from, each other in the community. seven per cent of our sample said they were being cared for by a friend or relative and 10 per cent said they were involved in caring for a sick, elderly or disabled person. The amount of time this caring work entailed varies between those who spend less than two hours a day on caring activities (20 per cent of all carers), those who spend three to 10 hours a day (27 per cent of all carers) and those who spend 11-24 hours a day (25 per cent of all carers).

Carers live in all areas of the ward although in our sample there were slightly more living in Hawksworth Wood (12 per cent) and Kirkstall (11 per cent) than in the Vespers (9 per cent) and in Burley (7 per cent). Carers tend to be older rather than younger with only four per cent of the 18-34 age-group having caring responsibilities compared to 14 per cent of those aged 35-64 and 65 and over. As one might expect carers are more likely to be retired (39 per cent of all carers) than in paid work (29 per cent) or unemployed (6 per cent), and more carers are women (67 per cent) than men.

The kind of care provided varies according to the time spent caring. As one might expect those who spend least time on caring activities tend to undertake the less personal or intimate tasks such as shopping and those most involved tend to undertake tasks such as bathing and dressing. While shopping is the most commonly undertaken task (with 77 per cent of all carers saying they shop for those they are caring for) a high proportion of all carers (68.5 per cent) also say they provide friendship and support.

Carers' responsibilities are, perhaps, reflected in their responses to other questions. For example they are more likely to say that their home is not conveniently situated for leisure and shopping facilities and that the bathroom and toilet in their home are not adequate for their needs. Carers are more likely than non-carers to have made use of health care services in the previous 12 months but are less likely to report problems in using health services. However, to the extent that problems are identified waiting times and getting appointments are the main difficulties encountered although a significant number of carers also mention access for the disabled and lack of information. Carers are more likely than non-carers to say they suffer from stress (27 per cent) or depression (12 per cent).

Carers were asked to indicate which of a range of things would make their caring responsibilites easier. Again the responses varied to some extent according to the time devoted to caring activites. For all carers having more money was the item identified most often. After this, having better advice and information was the item mentioned most frequently (30 per cent of all carers). Interestingly this was the case among all groups of carers but especially among those caring longest. What is perhaps most interesting about these results is that relatively few carers want assistance with the caring work itself (only 12 per cent of all carers and of those caring 10-24 hours a day) nor by and large do they want help with housework (mentioned by 14 per cent of all carers). It appears that carers want help in a form that will enable them to continue with their caring responsibilities - more money, advice and information and, to a lesser extent, aids and adaptations.

A number of people we interviewed were caring for sick or elderly friends or relatives. In two cases relatives were being cared for at home in preference to residential care because 'you look after your own family'. Despite clear needs for nursing assistance, home helps and aids and adaptations, several of these women were getting no assistance at all because, as one of them expressed it, 'I don't want to put on anyone'.

Health Care and Welfare Services: Perceptions of Professionals and Community Representatives

Health

Comments about health care services by professional workers who we interviewed focused on three issues: access to facilities, delivery of services and coordination of services.

Hawksworth Wood was singled out as an area where access to health care facilities was especially problematic. There is no local dentist and only one GP. The nearest health centre is at Kirkstall (although there is a GP surgery on Vesper Road) and is difficult to get to with children if you do not have access to a car. As a result, one community worker claimed that 'children are not in regular contact with dentists and doctors'.

Inadequate resources allocated to care in the community resulted in poor services for the elderly and those discharged from institutional care. According to a local GP there is a 'permanent shortage' of health visitors, district nurses and community psychiatric nurses resulting in poor morale in the community health services because staff are over-stretched. The same GP commented that the present service 'does not amount to a comprehensive nursing service in the community'.

Difficulties of access to hospital services focused largely on long waiting times. Areas where there seemed to be especially long waiting times were orthopaedic, opthalmic and general surgery. One community health worker commented on the frustrations of nursing patients at home who were in need of surgery or who had been discharged too early and whose condition had deteriorated as a result. Another commented that since 'there will never be enough resources to meet demand' the service providers ought to find out what people in the area need in order to formulate priorities and meet needs more fully. Other factors inhibiting access to services include the timing of clinics. For example it was argued that evening clinics for sight and hearing tests for children were necessary.

The way in which services are delivered also provoked comment. The attitudes of doctors and dentists were thought to be a problem for some. For example a community dental officer said that since dentists tend to be middle class professionals they might find it hard to relate to their less well educated customers and therefore fail to provide a welcoming, user-friendly service. Conversely, the officer-in-charge of a day nursery thought that people are afraid of seeking help because they are intimidated and afraid of criticism and losing control. A health promotion officer thought that people lacked awareness of patients' rights.

Poor delivery of services was also reflected in the location of GPs in buildings of unsuitable design with no play facilities. This, it was suggested, deters women from seeking medical advice especially for themselves. The particular needs of older people were also not fully addressed in the way services are delivered according to the officer-in-charge of an elderly person's day centre who mentioned the difficulties of getting people seen by community nursing staff. It was felt that older people needed to be visited at home more often.

Another group or residents who were disadvantaged by the way in which services are delivered is the ethnic minority population. The manager of a day centre for elderly Asians complained of too few doctors who speak Asian languages; lack of interpreters which often meant another family member being present during discussions with doctors and a consequent lack of privacy; and a failure by hospitals to cater for the particular dietary needs of Asian people.

Lack of coordination of services notably between health and social services was a major cause for concern. Community health workers in Kirkstall felt that inadequate social services provision meant that community nurses were taking on work which was really the province of social services which in turn meant they had less time to give to the work which they regarded as rightfully their responsibility. In general it was felt that lack of liaison between service providers resulted in a poorer service to clients. The officer-in-charge of an elderly person's day centre argued that joint care planning between health and social services should be implemented immediately in order to avoid waste of resources but that social services were not prepared for this and 'people are hoping it will go away'.

Suggestions for ways in which existing health care services could be improved included the following:

- Encourage more public discussion of health issues so they are seen as collective not individual problems.

- Provide better health education and promotion to enable people to take control of their health and reduce dependence on health services.

- Make health centres the focus for a range of health-related activities aimed at prevention rather than cure.

- Give more consideration to the needs of parents with young children in the planning and design of local health centres.

- Commit more resources to community health services, especially district nursing services.

- Make more self-help and alternative health measures available at health centres eg. acupuncture.

- Ensure regular visits (eg. twice a year) by GPs to the elderly in their homes and provide better transport for the elderly to health centres and hospitals.

- Make available more interpreters speaking more languages at health centres; provide information about prescriptions and medicines in Asian languages; ensure better training for health workers in the health needs of ethnic minority groups; provide hospital food appropriate to the needs of Asian people.

- Provide better care for psychiatric patients leaving hospital eg. help with personal hygiene, cooking and cleaning and put more resources into community health services.

- Ensure better liaison between health and social services to ensure joint planning and provision for community care, also liaison between nurseries and health centres and between different sectors of the health service.

- Provide better dental health education; encourage attendance at dentists and provide better and more mobile facilities; provide systematic annual oral health examinations for school-children and elderly; provide financial encouragement for the establishment of General Dental Practices in areas of greatest need eg. Hawksworth Wood; address the needs of ethnic minority people by recruiting Asian auxiliary staff and taking service to the community.

Welfare

Comments from local professional workers about welfare services focussed on similar issues namely the adequacy of existing resources and facilities, access and liaison. Perceptions about the adequacy of existing services varied between areas and groups. For example the officer-in-charge of an elderly persons' day centre thought that social services provision for older people was generally good. However another day centre manager thought that there were not enough social workers for older people and that elderly people with similar needs did not necessarily get a similar service. Other services for the elderly that were seen as being inadequate were luncheon clubs (only one on Hawksworth Wood Estate) and day care provision.

Services for children were seen to be more problematic. The officer-in-charge of a day nursery thought that social services stigmatised people making them reluctant to seek help and since the publicity over the Cleveland child abuse cases, they were particularly fearful of their children being taken into care.

Similar more general problems of image were seen to be a factor in determining access to certain services. One police officer commented that the welfare service was 'too big and bureaucratic'; another thought that social workers were seen as middle class and therefore lacking in credibility with working class people.

However it was liaison and lack of coordination between agencies that was seen to be the main issues and that there was no general knowledge of what services were available in any one locality. The police were especially concerned about their relationship with social services and perceptions of their role, for example, in relation to children in trouble. A comment was made that many police officers felt that social workers didn't want to work with them. Similar concerns were voiced by a local clergyman and community leader who thought that some of the difficulties in forming inter-agency relationships arose from 'the constant restructuring of local authority departments' leading to a lack of continuity in the area.

Specific suggestions of ways to improve welfare services included:

- Increase staffing for home care and support services to provide care in the community.

- Make more resources available to fund additional social work staff.

- Make more social workers available after 5.00 pm to permit outreach work in the evenings to prevent youth coming into contact with the police.

- Recognise the crucial role played by front-line workers and ensure stability in front-line services, eg. home care, and give these workers a more positive role in decisions on service provision.

- Establish better networks of support for people in their communities based on a proper understanding of their needs eg. women's and pensioners' groups to develop a common sense of issues which need addressing.

- Make services more locally-based.

- Find out what are the needs of local people through welfare agencies listening to people more to gain greater understanding of their problems.

- Get away from the fragmented case-work approach of welfare services.

- Ensure better liaison between social services and the police eg. as part of training they should spend time in each others' service to find out how they work. There is also a need to create police/social work liaison posts.

- Provide a drop-in advice centre for older people in Burley.

Informal Caring

In all three areas of the ward informal care is seen as being vital since without it many people would not be able to remain in their own homes. Informal carers provide a very significant proportion of care at home and many do so without help from district nurses. One community health worker thought that sometimes the carers themselves don't recognise how much they do: 'There is nothing a carer doesn't do'.

In addition to caring for elderly or sick friends and relatives it was also mentioned that, for example, on Hawksworth Wood Estate, extended families do 'look out for each other'. Also babysitting circles and support groups are seen as essential, having developed as a result of inadequate statutory provision.

Although informal care is seen as being very important it was argued by a day centre manager that some informal carers provide assistance for financial motives such as access to an elderly person's money - a particular worry for those who are confused and have no family. Some carers, it is claimed, won't let dependent older peole go into hospital because of loss of benefits.

Informal care is seen as being particularly essential for elderly Asian people - without their families looking after them it would be very difficult for them to survive.

When asked what they thought were the main problems faced by carers, professional workers echoed the views of carers themselves by emphasising their need for financial assistance. The point was made that not all carers are eligible for attendance allowance and that loss of earnings, together with additional costs for heating and food, may be a consequence of taking on caring responsibilites. There was some recognition of the need expressed by carers themselves for advice and information although this was mentioned in the context of providing counselling for carers and setting up carers' support groups.

Other problems identified by professional workers were the adverse effects on health of carers; the isolation of many carers and the inability of carers to get away or leave the situation permanently without feeling guilty or selfish. However none of these issues emerged from carers' own comments. Other remarks of a more general nature related to the policy of care in the community. For example concern was expressed about the lack of resources to underpin care in the community and the principle of the policy in relation to older people - the promotion of independence and enabling them to remain within the community was questioned. Some older people, it was suggested, preferred residential care and it was feared that current policy changes would take that choice away from them.

Suggestions of ways to improve the position of carers included the following:

- Carry out an audit carers' needs

- Choice should be provided as to whether services are provided in the community or through a hospital.

- More equipment needs to be made available to help with caring eg. lifting

- Houses need to be built or adapted to cater for the needs of those being cared for at home.

- Allowances to patients and their carers should be increased to enable them to afford nursing home costs or additional care in the home.

- Promote a 'sitting' service to give carers a break.

- The problem of abuse by carers needs more attention.

- Information about what is available for both carers and cared for should be made available in the appropriate languages.

- Provide holidays away from home for carers leaving cared for at home with respite carers.

Health Care and Welfare Services: Public Meetings

Health and welfare services and informal caring were discussed by participants at all three public meetings and, to some extent, similar issues emerged. In general there was a feeling that the NHS was under threat and that this was reflected in the service provided. In all areas too, the view was expressed that what was required was a multi-agency centre that offered housing, health, welfare and advice services under one roof.

During the meeting in Kirkstall the view was expressed by a local resident that there was 'no community spirit' in the clinic and a lack of communication between professionals and people. In response it was suggested by a community health worker that it was difficult to engage in constant debate with the local community and they could only respond to specific requests. It was also argued that where attempts had been made to solicit the views of 'users' through a series of forums, 'real people' didn't turn up. The meeting at Hawksworth Wood ended by a representative from the health authority saying that she had noted people's views and would like to see a further meeting organised in 18 months' time to review the extent to which the health authority had addressed the issues raised.

Health Care and Welfare Services: Key Issues

Existing information on health and welfare services focuses by and large, on the numbers of facilities and staff available relative to the population and the outputs of those resources in terms of numbers of patients treated or clients using a particular services, ie. responses to need rather than need itself. This kind of information does permit some broad comparisons to be made with other areas in relation to levels of provision relative to population size and take-up of services. However we gain little understanding of the degree to which services available meet needs and whether or not the form in which services are delivered are appropriate or acceptable. A further difficulty with codified information is the now familiar one of the lack of consistency between administrative areas. This is especially an issue in relation to social service areas which do not match ward or health authority boundaries.

Our research shows that in general people are satisfied both with widely used health care services and welfare services which are used less extensively. However, it is significant that people from ethnic minority groups express lower levels of satisfaction with services used than do white people and identify particular difficulties in using services (notally lack of translation facilities). Interviews with professionals also highlighted the difficulties faced by ethnic minority groups.

Use of some services such as dentists, seems to be directly related to their availability. The lack of a dentist in Hawksworth Wood is almost certainly a factor in infrequent visits and the poor dental health of residents. Again, this issue was identified by professional workers. There was also concern about low levels of awareness about dental health and, more generally, relatively low levels of health education.

Despite high levels of satisfaction with most health and welfare services a number of difficulties were encountered; for example, difficulties in getting appointments, the length of time spent waiting and, for women in particular, problems of child care. Also of note is the relatively low perception of the importance of welfare services especially amongst younger people.

A new issue that emerged from the public meetings was that services that were seen to be related were delivered by different agencies from different sites resulting in frustration and duplication. The idea of a multi-agency, locally-based centre providing a range of health care, welfare and related services attracted widespread support. The issue of coordination of services was one that was also raised by professionals. There seemed to be a quite widespread feeling that there was no single source of information about facilities and services available.

Care in the community especially in relation to the elderly, also emerged as a major issue. This was also an area where it seemed that the professional view of carers' needs was out of line with carers' own perceptions. Carers themselves expressed the view that they wanted assistance in the form of extra money and advice and information. Professionals, however, seemed to emphasise respite care and holidays which came fairly low down carers' own list of needs. Our work suggsts that a detailed audit of carers' needs might be an important project for the future.

2:7. WORK AND ECONOMIC SECURITY

An adequate income and a reasonable assurance that income will continue and will be sufficient for one's needs is an important precondition for health and autonomy. As we have already seen general health and the incidence of problems such as depression, anxiety, sleeplessness and stress are likely to be affected by one's employment status.

In this chapter, we look at existing data relating to employment and income. We then examine the findings of our survey of residents' perceptions of their employment and financial situation and the perceptions of local professional workers and community representatives before summing up the key issues and priorities.

Work and Economic Security: Codified Knowledge

The availability of 'official' data on work and on work and economic security at a local level is notoriously inadequate.

Ideally one would like to have information on a ward, or better still at a community level. In practice, however, at a local level, this type of information is extremely difficult to obtain. Information on, for example, employment status except for numbers unemployed is not available. Even the data for unemployent is poor - in reality it refers only to the numbers of people in receipt of benefit not those who seek work and are unable to find it. No data at all exists for income or expenditure except from rare specially commissioned local studies. Occupational data is available but only for census years, next available in 1993.

However, we do have information on the numbers of unemployed and long term unemploymed for the Leeds travel-to-work area and the numbers unemployed in Kirkstall. In July 1991 there were 1,119 people registered as unemployed in Kirkstall Ward. Some 29 per cent of the unemployed in Leeds had been out of work for longer than one year. Clearly this information tells us very little about work and economic security in Kirkstall.

Similar difficulties are encountered when we look at statistics relating to social security benefits. We do know that in May 1991 there were 63,957 people in Leeds receiving income support, 4,940 in receipt of sickness benefit, 15,439 on invalidity benefit and 5,374 on family credit. In addition we know that a total of £181,412 was paid out in social fund payments to 2,144 people and that £73,547 was paid out to 1,383 people as community care grants. However, this tells us nothing about the quality of life of people on benefits.

Work and Economic Security: Experiential Knowledge

In our survey of residents we tried to fill some of these gaps by asking people a range of questions relating to employment and economic security.

About 46 per cent of respondents indicated that they are in paid work, the proportion varying between 40 per cent in the Hawksworth Wood area and 60 per cent in the Vespers area. The proportion unemployed is five per cent, and unemployed people are more likely to be male, non-white and residents of Hawksworth Wood and Burley. Overall, some 71 per cent of those in work have full time jobs and 29 per cent part time; however, 94 per cent of men work full time whereas 46 per cent of women have part time jobs. Older workers and non-whites are also more likely to work part time, and the proportion of part timers in the Hawksworth Wood area, at 36 per cent, is significantly higher than in other areas which average 26-29 per cent.

We compared the occupational breakdown of respondents in work with the structure for Leeds as a whole as indicated by the 1990 Leeds Skills Audit (Policy Research Unit 1990). Our sample comprises rather above average proportions in associate professional and technical, personal and protective services (eg. health, catering, hairdressing) and 'other' occupations and below average proportions of managers and administrators, clerical and secretarial and sales occupations.

There is a significant difference in occupational structure between women and men. Women are over-represented in clerical and secretarial, personal and protective services, sales and associate professional and technical occupations, whereas men are over-represented in the manager and administrator, craft and related and plant/machine operative categories. Management, professional, clerical/secretarial and sales occupations are over represented in the Vespers area, and professional and clerical/secretarial in the Burley area; Kirkstall has above average proportions in clerical/secretarial and craft occupations whereas Hawksworth Wood is above average in craft, personal service and plant and machine operatives.

Overall, 87 per cent of those in work indicate that they are satisfied or very satisfied with their work, and the degree of satisfaction tends to be rather higher for women than for men, for older than younger age groups, for white than for non-white respondents, and for those in the Vespers, Kirkstall and Burley areas than for residents of Hawksworth Wood. The level of job satisfaction is rather higher amongst managers and administrators, associate professional and technical, clerical and secretarial and personal and protective service occupations than amongst sales, plant and machine operatives, craft and other occupations. Also, there is an above average degree of dissatisfaction amongst professionals.

We compared responses on job satisfaction with those on general health and incidence of 'mental health' problems. First, it is notable that reported dissatisfaction with work is more prevalent amongst those who report poor or very poor health than amongst those whose health is good or very good. Thus, 11 per cent of those in good or very good health are dissatisfied with their work compared with 23 per cent of those in poor or very poor health. Moreover, those who report experiencing problems of stress and worry in particular are more likely to be dissatisfied in their work than those experiencing no such problems. For example, nearly a quarter of those reporting stress are dissatisfied with work compared with some eight per cent of those reporting no problems.

Respondents were asked whether or not they have 'serious difficulties' paying for various household expenses. Over half of all respondents reported serious difficulties paying the poll tax (see Figure 19). This is consistent across age groups but particularly prevalent amongst non-whites, the unemployed (68 per cent), those looking after home and children (69 per cent), and residents of Hawksworth Wood (64 per cent) and Burley (58 per cent). The incidence of difficulties with other items varies between groups. Thus, in addition to the poll tax, the elderly tend to show most concern about fuel and phone bills whereas younger people report most difficulty paying for clothes, furniture and housing costs. Relatively high proportions of the unemployed report difficulties with fuel bills, clothes, food and furniture, whereas clothes and furniture

Figure 19
Financial difficulties by age group

Figure 20
Financial security by autonomy

figure most prominently for those looking after home and family. For all items, difficulties are more prevalent for non-whites than for white people, and for residents of Hawksworth Wood and Burley than for those in Kirkstall and the Vespers areas.

Those who report difficulties paying these various household expenses also report above average incidence of worry, sleeplessness, stress and depression. This is particularly marked in the cases of food, clothes, fuel bills and mortgage/rent. The highest levels of reported incidence of these problems occur in the case of people having difficulty paying for food. For example, nearly a third of such people report depression compared with 12 per cent of all respondents.

When asked how secure they felt financially, only 4.5 per cent of all respondents answered 'very secure' but 55 per cent feel 'secure'. Nevertheless, some 37 per cent feel insecure or very insecure. Older people tend to feel more secure financially than younger people and white people more secure than non-whites. Over three quarters of the unemployed feel insecure or very insecure, and a majority of those looking after home and children similarly feel insecure. Residents of Hawksworth Wood tend to feel the least secure financially (45 per cent feel insecure or very insecure), and this is consistent with the relatively high proportions of unemployment, part time working and lower skill jobs in this area. Conversely, the Vespers area has the highest proportion of respondents feeling financially secure and this reflects relatively high levels of home ownership, low unemployment and above average proportions of residents in managerial and professional occupations.

If we examine the relationship between responses on financial security and general health, we find that those experiencing poor or very poor health are more likely to feel financially insecure or very insecure. Thus, a half of those in poor or very poor health feel financially insecure compared with a third of those in good or very good health. Moreover, those feeling financially insecure are more likely to indicate experience of stress, depression, worry and sleeplessness. Figure 20 shows that the reported incidence of stress, worry and depression in particular is significantly higher than average for those experiencing financial insecurity. This supports the relationship discussed above with difficulties paying household expenses.

These findings are consistent with those on the correlation between job satisfaction and reported health status, given a relationship between job satisfaction and financial security. Thus, only eight per cent of those who feel financially secure or very secure indicate that they are dissatisfied or very dissatisfied with their work; the proportion is 22 per cent for those who feel financially insecure.

Comparison with the findings discussed in part 2:1 indicates that the increase in the feeling of security with age is consistent with the increase in the perceived importance of such security with age. Thus, while the young feel more insecure, it is less important to them; this is also the case for non-whites. Conversely, financial security takes on greater importance for the unemployed and residents of Hawksworth Wood, and these groups report above average feelings of insecurity suggesting that financial problems are of great concern to them. This is consistent with the reported incidence of difficulties paying for various household expenses and of problems of stress, depression, worry and sleeplessness. The same pattern, although less marked, applies to those looking after home and children.

Respondents were asked to indicate the main thing which they are prevented from doing due to lack of money. Overall, 46 per cent of respondents indicated that they are prevented from doing 'something important', and the proportion is rather above average for women (48 per cent) and significantly above average for younger people aged 18-34 (60 per cent), for non-whites (63 per cent), for the unemployed (71 per cent), for those looking after home and family (56 per cent), and for council and private tenants (57 per cent). The main things which people are prevented from doing, indicated by a half of the respondents, are improvements to house and contents and holidays and visits to friends and relatives.

People's fears and insecurity with regard to work and money were elaborated on in the course of the follow-up interviews. The women with children spoke of the difficulties involved in getting jobs that fitted with school hours and of finding appropriate and affordable child care. Many were struggling to make ends meet. The interviews confirmed the survey results that the poll tax was a major cause of financial worry. However women were also concerned about providing for their children both in terms of necessities like shoes and clothes but also in terms of 'treats' like days out and holidays. One woman spoke of her 'bitterness' that she couldn't afford to take her children on trips or holidays. Another source of stress was financial insecurity. A number of women made comments like 'we can never plan ahead'.

The combination of low income, debts and inability to afford certain major items was clearly having a negative effect on quality of life. This was particularly the case with respect to lack of holidays. Comments such as: 'You get depressed when you've got nothing to look forward to like a holiday when you've worked all year,' were typical. Another woman who had taken a second job at nights in order to pay the poll tax said: 'I miss out a lot with the children. There's no time to talk, discuss their problems. I feel guilty about this.'

The concerns of the elderly people who we interviewed were slightly different although again, the poll tax and lack of holidays figured significantly in their list of concerns. In several cases the burden of the poll tax was exacerbated by high fuel bills entailed by the need to maintain a high level of heating because of a sick or disabled person in the household. Paying for essentials such as these meant there was little left over for 'treats' such as holidays. One elderly person said she felt aggrieved that 'after both working all their lives their standard of living was being reduced because of the poll tax'. Others who were clearly dipping into savings were worried about the future. One said there was 'no spare money to provide peace of mind'. Another expressed concern that her only daughter would have to bear the cost of her funeral while another said: 'Sometimes I lay awake at night and wonder if we will last longer than the money.'

The lack of money for holidays and visits were a major source of unhappiness among elderly people. The following comment is not untypical: 'We haven't been away for five years. It was something to look foward to'. Others were unhappy because they were unable to give financial assistance to their own families. For example one elderly lady said that she had hoped she would be able to help her grand-daughter who was going to medical school but couldn't afford to do so now because of the poll tax.

Work and Economic Security: Perceptions of Professionals and Community Representatives

In our interviews with professional workers and community representatives we focused on money - the extent of financial hardship, the consequences of financial hardship and what is needed in order to alleviate the problems people face.

A number of specific groups were identified as being especially likely to suffer financial hardship - the elderly, single parents, the unemployed and those on low incomes - and those living in Hawksworth Wood and Burley were seen as being particularly vulnerable.

It was widely thought that many elderly people suffered financial hardship. According to the manager of a day centre for the elderly, about 50 per cent of people using his centre experience some financial hardship because pensions are too low to live on. Another view was that elderly people have just about enough money to survive but have to watch every penny which is stressful and may result in risks to their health. For example, they may not turn on the heating during cold weather because of fear of high fuel bills. The local MP described pensioners as managing 'brilliantly' on meagre resources but having to do without 'luxuries', eg. travel to visit people. This echoes the sentiments of the elderly themselves. A number of people mentioned the stigma that elderly people felt was a consequence of getting help with bills. Most people agreed that the poll tax had caused particular difficulties for elderly people resulting in considerable stress and anxiety.

Elderly members of the Asian community were thought to face particular financial problems. Many were dependent on younger relatives, and if younger family members were unemployed the elderly also faced difficulties. Elderly people who had not been in employment in this country are not eligible for pensions and so are dependent on income support. However lack of knowledge about entitlements and lack of information together with language difficulties makes claiming very difficult. They often have to be accompanied by other family members increasing the sense of dependency. Again the issue of pride was mentioned - elderly Asians may conceal their needs because they do not want to make demands on their sons and daughters.

Financial hardship among single parents was thought to be especially prevalent in Hawksworth Wood. One police officer claimed that some single mothers are working as prostitutes in order to pay their bills although this was not mentioned by anyone else who we spoke to.

In general it was thought that many of those experiencing financial hardship managed their incomes well although others were thought to need assistance with financial management. There was a general consensus that benefit levels were too low and that the social fund - described as 'cruel' by a clergyman - did not help. One consequence of the failure of the Social Fund was that many households found it difficult to pay for furniture and other large items. As a result, according to the officer-in-charge of the family nursery centre, some families on Hawksworth Wood estate do not have a fridge, washing machine or vacuum cleaner. Some people were able, with the help of social workers, to obtain money from charities to pay for such items. Others turned to 'loan sharks' who charged as much as 700 per cent p.a. interest. Concern about loan sharks was widespread among those interviewed but they were not mentioned by local residents. However it was claimed by more than one person that some people have made themselves homeless to get away from moneylenders.

Another form of debt occurred through buying clothes and furniture from catalogues on credit. This was thought to be a particular problem for households with children. One community psychiatric nurse described how loans or credit were taken out at Christmas to buy toys leading to problems with debts by Easter. A youth worker said that 'Christmas is a very unhappy time for mothers'. Payment of rent or mortgage was thought to be a particular problem for households where the breadwinner is in low paid work. Rent arrears leading to evictions were thought to be a growing problem. Interestingly it was suggested that paying telephone bills on Hawksworth Wood is not a problem since many households can't afford to have a phone at all.

The effects of financial hardship were thought to be extensive both in terms of physical health and general well-being. A number of health problems were traced back to low income especially those connected to or caused by, poor diet and inadequate heating. (Damp housing was seen to be a particular problem for those on low incomes since extra heating and ventilation were necessary). However stress, anxiety and depression were mentioned more often in connection with financial hardship.

Particular concern was expressed about the effects on children growing up in a household experiencing financial hardship. For example, community health workers mentioned the lack of money available for books and toys contributing to a 'poor learning environment'. The officer-in-charge of a nursery described the situation of parents unable to cope with the stress created by financial problems also finding it difficult to cope with demanding children who then become even more demanding.

Solutions to the problem of financial hardship and its consequences not surprisingly focused on increasing people's incomes especially through raising the level of benefits.

The local MP and a probation officer both thought that even where people were getting their full benefit entitlement they still have insufficient resources. This view was endorsed by a youth worker who also wanted to see the abolition of Social Fund loans and their replacement with grants. More information on welfare rights was also thought to be necessary as was education and practical help with money management if this could be provided in a 'non-patronising way'.

Other suggestions included funding training opportunities for women, providing child-care to enable women to work, stimulating the local economy through investment (eg. in housing improvements), banning advertising on TV particularly that aimed at children as this creates enormous pressure on low income families, the setting up of credit unions, more rigid controls on money lenders, a statutory minimum wage linked to average wages, a change in the structure of fuel bills (eg. standing charges), getting rid of the poll tax, giving people food vouchers 'to ensure that money is spent on food rather than cigarettes' and 'getting rid of this government'.

Work and Economic Security: Key Issues

Our study, working on the basis that economic security is an 'intermediate' need, sought to assess the extent of economic security and insecurity and their effects on health and well-being. What we found out was that the highest levels of financial insecurity are felt by ethnic minorities, the unemployed, people looking after home and family and generally among residents in Hawksworth Wood and Burley, and that there is concern among professionals about 'hidden' hardship among the elderly who, in the postal survey, indicated that on the whole they felt more secure than younger people. However financial security is significantly more important to the elderly than to the young suggesting that the elderly are more likely to be concerned about the financial difficulties which they do experience, notably the poll tax and fuel bills - both large items which confound their usually careful financial management.

The poll tax emerged as a major cause of financial hardship but for those on benefits or low incomes almost all regular expenditure caused difficulties at some time including fuel bills, rent or mortgage, clothes, furniture, transport and even food. Those people experiencing financial insecurity and difficulties in paying bills are more likely to report that they suffer from stress, worry, depression and sleeplessness.

The effects of financial insecurity on mental health were a matter of considerable concern to professional workers who recognised that it could also result in family tensions, a poor environment for children and even violence and abuse.

Financial security is linked to employment. Unemployment is above average in Hawksworth Wood and Burley and among ethnic minorities - the same groups that also report high levels of financial insecurity. Similarly job security and job satisfaction are lowest among ethnic minority groups, women and residents of Hawksworth Wood which not only has the highest level of unemployment in the ward but also of part-time working and of workers in manual and lower skilled occupations. The above average levels of dissatisfaction in Hawksworth Wood can be related in particular to lower skill, male, manual occupations.

Dissatisfaction with one's job was also found to be more prevalant among those who feel financially insecure and, again, there is a correlation between both lack of job satisfaction and financial insecurity and stress, worry, depression and sleeplessness.

In terms of approaches to addressing these problems an important issue was seen to be the adequacy of the level of benefits available. It was widely argued that levels of support should be increased, the Social Fund loans should be replaced by grants, that better information should be made available on rights and entitlements, and that more attention should be given to the needs of ethnic minorities.

Another important issue related to work prospects. The need for better job prospects and training opportunities was referred to and the issue of childcare was considered important. In Hawksworth Wood, one professional referred to the need for investment in the local economy to generate activity and jobs; more local jobs would be particularly beneficial in view of the relatively high level of difficulties reported by respondents of Hawksworth Wood in terms of access to work (see part 2:7).

In terms of a response to high levels of debt and the use of money-lenders in Hawksworth Wood, it was suggested that there should be more controls on such activities and also efforts to establish a Credit Union. More generally, the issues of Credit Unions and investment to stimulate the local economy raise a broader issue of locally-generated and community-based initiatives to regenerate the economic and social life of the area. This would also subsume initiatives to address problems in the local area and the lack of facilities (see part 2:5).

This issue also relates to approaches to improve and manage the local housing stock (see part 2:4). Local investment in housing improvement could generate local jobs and such improvements would address the problem of 'fuel poverty' highlighted above. Thus, although changes in the structure of fuel tariffs would help to alleviate difficulties for some, a more fundamental solution would involve the improvement of houses to a high standard of insulation such that problems of inadequate heating, dampness and difficulties with fuel bills were alleviated simultaneously.

2:8 SOCIAL CONTACT AND COMMUNITY PARTICIPATION

Relationships with other people - family, friends, neighbours - that are mutually satisfying are thought to be an important element in maintaining health and well-being. Similarly, a sense of 'belonging' to a community and participation in the affairs of that community are also seen as likely to affect one's sense of well-being.

Not surprisingly, there is little or no 'hard' information of relevance to this issue especially at the local level. In the postal questionnaire we asked people to comment on the amount of time they spent with family and friends, whether there was someone they could rely on in a crisis and about time spent on leisure activities. We also asked about membership of community, voluntary and political organisations, 'civic' activities and people's sense of their ability to influence the decisions of the government, local authority and private companies.

This chapter reports the findings from the survey and follow-up interviews and comments made during interviews with local professional and front-line workers.

Social Contact, Community Participation: Experiential Knowledge

When we asked people to say how important a number of different factors are to their quality of life and well-being, the least likely of all the factors listed (with the exception of 'having access to social services') to attract 'very important' responses (part 2:1) were: 'having close friends and relatives who can be relied on', 'having spare time for personal and leisure activities', and 'having an influence on the decisions of organisations that attach your life'. However, the perceived importance of having close friends and relatives increases with age, and tends to be higher for women than for men.

We then asked people to say whether or not they had as much contact as they would like with friends and family (other than those they lived with). Seventy-nine per cent said they did, although slightly more women than men, especially those in the 35-64 age group with caring commitments, said this was not the case. For men the most common reason given for insufficient social contact was work commitments.

Younger people were more likely than older people to say they did not have enough social contact as they would like: 29 per cent of 18-34 year olds said this was the case compared to 13 per cent of those over 65. However, both these groups - the young and the elderly - are affected by geographical mobility. Many younger people had moved to Leeds, away from their families, in order to work or study; while older people had seen their own families move away from Leeds for similar reasons.

Some variation between areas was also apparent with people living in Hawksworth Wood expressing higher levels of satisfaction with the amount of social contact they had than residents of Burley, reflecting, perhaps, the fact that, as we saw earlier, Hawksworth Wood is a more settled area than Burley.

We also asked respondents to the postal questionnaire whether there was someone close to them who they could rely on in a crisis. Overall, only seven per cent of respondents felt they had no-one to rely on. However among ethnic minority respondents this figure rises to 16 per cent, among the unemployed to 15 per cent and among those caring for home and family the proportion was 11 per cent. Moreover those reporting poor or very poor health are more likely to lack such support (11 per cent) than those whose health is good or very good (6 per cent). The difference is even more pronounced if we compare the responses of those in very good and very poor health. Just four per cent of those in very good health say they have no one they can rely on in a crisis compared to 16 per cent of those with very poor health.

Overall, 28 per cent of respondents think that they do not have enough time for hobbies and leisure interests and slightly more women (29 per cent) than men (26 per cent) said this was the case. Again the reasons given for lack of time varied between men and women: among men the main reason was work commitments whereas among women the main reason was a combination of paid work and domestic commitments. There was a significant difference in responses between the different age-groups with 44 per cent of the 18-34 age group saying they did not have enough time compared to 29 per cent of the 35-64 age group and just seven per cent of the over 65s. The difference in responses between white and ethnic minority respondents was even more marked: 50 per cent of ethnic minority respondents said they did not have enough time compared to 25 per cent of whites.

We asked people a series of questions relating to community participation. First we asked whether they were members of a range of different organisations. Overall, levels of membership are relatively low: 21 per cent were members of a trade union (38 per cent of those in paid work), seven per cent were members of a community, tenants, or residents' association, four per cent belonged to a pressure group, three per cent to a political pary, two per cent to a self-help group and one per cent were school governors.

As regards the variation in membership levels by different groups, in general membership is higher amongst men than amongst women with the exception of community associations and self-help groups, amongst middle age groups, and amongst those in paid work. Ethnic minority respondents are least likely to be members of the listed organisations, with the exception of trade unions.

We went on to ask people to indicate whether they had engaged in a range of political and community activities. Overall the activity most commonly engaged in was voting in local elections (63 per cent of all respondents said they had voted), this figure remaining roughly constant across all areas. However, significantly, more men (66 per cent) than women (60 per cent) said they had voted and this pattern of greater activity by men was generally true except in relation to signing petitions and undertaking voluntary work. Voting was also relatively low among the youngest (18-34) age group and among ethnic minority and unemployed respondents and among those looking after home and family.

After voting the next most common activity was signing a petition: 46 per cent of all respondents said they had signed a petition in the last 12 months. However only 31 per cent of elderly people, 35 per cent of unemployed people and 39 per cent of Hawksworth Wood residents had done so. Sixteen per cent of all respondents had engaged in some form of voluntary work, in particular, women and residents in Burley.

Overall, those participating most in political or community activity are more likely to be male, white, aged between 35 and 64, in paid work and living in Burley. The only significant exceptions to this pattern are in relation to writing a letter to a newspaper where the writer is more likely to be over 65 and/or unemployed; going on a march or demonstration where participants are more likely to be aged 18-34; and undertaking voluntary work where volunteers are likely to be women looking after home and family.

Our final question in this section asked respondents to indicate how much influence they thought they had over decisions made by the government, Leeds City Council and private companies. Overwhelmingly, people think they have little influence over any of these organisations. Eighty-one per cent think they have no influence over central government, 80 per cent think this is true in relation to private companies and 68 per cent in relation to the City Council. Less than one per cent of respondents think they have a lot of influence over any of the organisations mentioned. In general, the belief that they have some influence over government decisions is most prevalent amongst women, those aged between 18 and 34, from ethnic minority groups and living in Burley or Vespers. (Only nine per cent of Hawksworth Wood residents think they have some influence over government compared to 19 per cent of residents in the Vespers and 14 per cent in Burley). The belief that they have some influence over the City Council is greatest amongst the young, non-whites, those in paid work and living in the Vespers or Burley. Finally the belief that they have some influence over private companies tends to be highest amongst males, those aged 18-34, whites, those in paid work and living in Hawksworth Wood.

These views on social and community activities were elaborated upon during the interviews where differences between the elderly and women with young children become apparent. Many of the elderly people did not have as much social contact as they would like because their family lived too far away. For this group the telephone was seen as an important means of keeping in touch. (This is consistent with the concern of the elderly in relation to the payment of telephone bills which we discussed in 2:6 above). For others, poor health limited the range of social contacts.

In contrast, social contacts for many of the women with children were limited by lack of money to pay babysitters and the difficulties of travelling on public transport with young children. One ethnic minority interviewee mentioned language as a barrier to social contact.

For most of the elderly interviewees lack of time for hobbies and leisure activities was not considered to be a problem. The only exception was a woman caring for her sick husband. However many of the women we spoke to were concerned at the lack of time available for leisure activities. For most it was the combination of paid employment and child care responsibilities which resulted in lack of time. One woman said she never had time for herself because she was 'always somebody's mum or wife'. One Asian interviewee commented that although he had very little leisure time he didn't regard it as a problem since he preferred to work.

With regards to community activities and political participation, the views of the two groups - the elderly and women with children - were much more homogeneous. Overwhelmingly voting was seen as the most important activity and the following comments were typical:

> 'You've got to vote to have a democracy - a say in
> who runs the country' (Elderly Hawksworth Wood resident)

> 'If you don't vote, don't complain' (Woman resident in Kirkstall)

An untypical but interesting comment about voting came from an elderly woman resident in Burley:

> 'Why did Emily Pankhurst get chained to the railings if
> we don't vote. I think it's important that women vote'

However, despite the strength of feeling in favour of people exercising their right to vote interviewees were much less sure about how effective it was to do so. For many people whether they had 'achieved' anything by voting was seen in terms of whether or not 'their candidate' had been elected. Others felt even more strongly that voting was actually ineffective:

> 'I shan't vote again. They are all a lot of useless gits -
> they couldn't do a rice pudding'. (Elderly Burley resident).

Other than voting, voluntary work was regarded positively for both volunteers and recipients, providing social contacts for the former and help to those in need for the latter.

In general people's assessment of their ability to influence government, the City Council or private companies was low. Interviewees felt most positively about Leeds City Council (although it was still a minority who felt they could exert an influence) and thought that lobbying councillors could be effective. A few people thought that you could have some influence on private companies either by being a shareholder or as a consumer by boycotting companies' products. No one who we interviewed felt that one could influence central government, which is interesting given the strength of feeling in favour of voting. The degree of cynicism about government - both central and local - politics and politicians was interesting and was common to both elderly people and women with children. Typical comments were as follows:

'The government is too far removed' (Elderly resident of Hawksworth Wood)

'Leeds City Council and the government do what they like regardless of what their constituents think' (Elderly resident of Hawksworth Wood)

'You can vote for a candidate but you can't tell him what to do' (Elderly Kirkstall resident)

'[Political activity] is hard work and I don't have the energy for it' (Woman with children in Burley)

'MPs are not there to look after your interests but their own' (Woman with children in Burley).

The general feeling with regard to influence over private companies was that 'money talks' and ordinary people had little or no opportunity to influence their decisions.

Despite the widespread cynicism and sense of powerlessness, the majority of people we interviewed thought they should have more influence and despite the contradictory views held in relation to voting, one of the commonest ways mentioned of achieving greater influence was through the use of referenda on important issues such as the poll tax. Most people we interviewed thought that as individuals they were quite powerless but that through collective action they had some potential influence. In general there was a feeling that power should be more devolved. Typical comments included the following:

'They should give people the power to control and regulate their own lives' (Elderly Hawksworth Wood resident)

'More power should be given to local councils. People would get more involved if government was more local'. (Resident of Hawksworth Wood with children).

'We need local action groups'. (Woman resident in Kirkstall).

'Councillors should ask people what they think' (Resident of Burley).

Social Contact, Community Participation: Perceptions of Professionals and Community Representatives

We asked professionals and front-line workers in the area to comment on the level of community activity and factors contributing to it, how community and voluntary activity helped in meeting needs and what else needed to be done.

The level of activity in different parts of the ward varied quite considerably. In Kirkstall there was a general feeling that there was quite a lot of community and voluntary activity although there were also areas of inactivity. According to the officer-in-charge of a local day centre for the elderly there was little activity in the area, which she regretted.

Perceptions of the level of activity in Hawksworth Wood varied between those who thought there was an average or good level of activity (supported by observations that there are lots of volunteers to do youth work and the quota of governors for both schools in the area are filled) and those who described the level of activity as 'poor'. However all were agreed that there is a particular problem in relation to the YMCA centre on the estate which was underused. The problem was described by a local clergyman in the following terms: 'The weak spot is the YMCA. Everything is provided there in terms of the building and the input from welfare services but people don't use it. There are now few volunteers and little community involvement in running it. It has become a sort of Council club rather than a community centre...There is an idea on the estate that the YMCA caters for rough people because of work done with offenders there'.

Levels of activity in Burley were thought to be good although it was still a relatively small proportion of the population who were involved.

Perceptions of the reasons for differing levels of activity were interesting. In relation to both Burley and Kirkstall it was felt that there was a lack of knowledge about what local people wanted or needed. The director of a community centre in Burley commented that 'a detailed assessment is needed of people's needs to ensure that resources meet needs. Similarly more consultation is required with local people about how resources are used.' In Hawksworth Wood lack of community and voluntary activity was ascribed to poor education and financial problems which undermine motivation for community activities. A community health worker commented that there was more activity in Burley because 'there were more facilities, better educated people, living in the area' and the Asian community's presence was thought to attract more initiatives.

However local community workers in Burley did not altogether share this view. They argued that there was considerable passivity and a reluctance to get involved among local people and a feeling of subservience to professionals especially among ethnic minority groups. It was also felt that there had been some improvement in levels of participation because efforts had been made to involve people in the running of the Burley Lodge Centre and to recruit local people as paid workers. As a result 'power is beginning to shift'. However it was also felt by some that existing social and community activities focused on the Pakistani population which is closely knit and has a strong sense of identity, at the expense of the Afro-Caribbean population.

Views on the contribution of community activity in meeting needs focused in particular on the sense of empowerment that could result. For example a councillor commented that community activity 'gives people more say

in the decisions which affect their lives' and 'people learn from each other and get confidence in doing things together'.

Activity of this kind was seen to be especially beneficial to certain groups within the community, for example the elderly. The officer-in-charge of a day centre for the elderly commented that she had seen older people 'blossom' when community and voluntary activity had been available to them. A community psychiatric nurse observed that community activity helped to overcome the isolation felt by many older people living in Hawksworth Wood.

Suggestions as to ways in which the level of community activity could be enhanced varied between provision of physical resources such as a meeting or drop-in centre in Hawksworth Wood and a community centre specifically for Pakistani people in Burley, provision of confidence building and support for people and more channels for communication and consultation. A number of people mentioned that it would be useful to 'get people together to discuss and identify common problems' (MP) or to conduct on 'audit of needs' (local clergyman). A community worker summed up these kinds of feelings as follows: 'We need to expand and enhance local involvement and activity to promote devolution of power to communities through real consultation and addressing local needs. Local people must have ownership of initiatives. We need to empower local people and give them confidence'.

Social Contact, Community Participation: Public Meetings

The issue of community participation came up in different guises, at all three public meetings. In Burley the discussion centred on the crucial question of what is a community? In particular the issue (already raised in this report but in a different context) of the very different boundaries within which agencies operate was discussed. It was felt that this not only inhibited effective coordination of services but also contributed to a lack of a sense of community among residents. Not only did agency boundaries not fit with each other, but they did not fit with local people's own sense of what their community is. (It was also pointed out to the researchers that our division of the study area into four sub-areas did not reflect local understanding of where the 'frontiers' between communities lie.)

In both Hawksworth Wood and Kirkstall it was argued that the lack of an appropriate meeting place or community centre inhibited community activity. (The point about the YMCA in Hawksworth Wood being in the 'wrong' place was again made.) In Kirkstall recent involvement in the Kirkstall Valley campaign had led people to become more involved and to value local activities. In particular people wanted devolution of power to a local level eg. through parish councils or local forums. It was argued that 'if you empower people they can take care of local issues' themselves.

Social Contact, Community Participation: Key Issues

Of all the topics covered in our study, social contacts and community participation ranked lowest in terms of the importance people attach to them and this is, perhaps, reflected in responses to the postal survey. On the whole people feel that they get enough contact with family and friends, that they have someone to turn to in a crisis and that they have sufficient time for hobbies and leisure interests. However, only a minority of people are members of a community, voluntary or political organisation and, apart from voting in the local election only a minority of respondents report having taken part in any political activity over the previous year (although the figures are, nonetheless, higher than might be expected).

The reason for the relatively low levels of community and political activity might lie, in part, in the fact that very few people think they have any influence over the decisions made by government, local council (although 24 per cent thought they had some influence) or private companies. It is perhaps significant that this sense of powerlessness is strongest on Hawksworth Wood estate - probably the most disadvantaged part of the ward on a number of criteria - and this sense of powerlessness is reflected in particularly low levels of political activity.

The follow-up interviews revealed enormous cynicism about politics and politicians but at the same time there was a view that voting was the most likely means of achieving any influence. Also it became clear that many people did want more influence and saw the way to achieving this through community activity - a view expressed at one of the public meetings.

Professionals and community representatives tended to see community activity in terms of physical resources like community centres although there was a recognition among some of the importance of residents' perceptions of their own power.

2:9   CHILDREN'S NEEDS

For adults to have health and well-being their childhood must also be a period of general health and well-being. In this chapter we try to assess the needs of children by looking first at the data which already exists relating to children in the city and, where possible, in the Kirkstall ward and secondly by looking at the perceptions of residents in the study area of the extent to which the needs of their own children are being met. Finally we report the views of local professionals and front-line workers on children's needs before summarising the key issues.

Children's Needs: Codified Knowledge

This section deals with provision in Leeds for the under 5s and the care and supervision of children. The index of child deprivation (University of Kent, Personal Social Services Research Unit) is intended to identify areas of high malaise relating to children, these being areas of high vulnerability of children to entry into care. The index is calculated on the basis of the following census variables:

- Population density (persons per hectare)
- Children in households that are not self contained
- Children in households that lack basic amenities
- Children in overcrowded households (more than one person per room)
- Children in single-parent families
- Children in households where the head was born in the New Commonwealth or Pakistan

The index value for Leeds Census wards (using 1981 data) are grouped according to the national classification so that Group 1 signifies the top 10 per cent of wards nationally (the least deprived) and Group 10 the bottom 10 per cent (the most deprived). Kirkstall is one of the most deprived wards, falling into Group 10 along with six other, mainly inner city wards.

There is a variety of forms of day-care provision for children under 5 in Leeds. Family nursery centres (FNCs) are provided by the social services department and a charge is levied according to income. They cater for children aged 0-5 years on five days a week between 8.00am and 6.00pm, all year round. Care is also provided for some 5-7 year olds before and after school and in school holidays.

In April 1991 there were 31 FNCs in Leeds with 1,748 children registered. Each of the postal districts 4 and 5 which cover the study area has one FNC. Together they provide a total of 80 places and have 111 registered children. However, at the end of April 1991 there were 169 children on the waiting list for these FNCs, a ratio of children waiting to those registered of 1.52. This indicates significant unmet need although it is better than the Leeds average ratio of 1.77.

All other forms of day-care provision are registered with and supervised by social services department and charge for their services. Community nurseries are run by elected committees of local parents. None of the three community nurseries in Leeds is located in postal district 4 or 5. The most important elements of day-care provision for children under 5 in Leeds in terms of number of places provided are childminders and playgroups. Playgroup places exist for one in 10 of the under 5 population in Leeds. Education nursery provision is provided in three nursery schools (none of which is located in Kirkstall) and in 114 nursery classes in primary schools. Children aged 3-5 years usually attend for half days during school terms. At December 1989, 6,758 places were occupied, that is equivalent to about 14 per cent of the under 5 population.

Child health clinics, whose main function is to advise on the child's progress and to prevent illness, are provided by the health service throughout the city. There is one child health clinic located in Leeds 5. (See part 2:6 for details of rates of immunisation).

Statutory and voluntary child care and supervision constitutes a significant proportion of the active caseload of community based social work staff in Leeds. Voluntary and statutory child care and supervision represent 22 per cent of the active caseload of community based staff at Buckingham House. Of the 250 cases, 100 involve statutory child care and, of these, 52 are cases of actual or probable neglect or ill treatment.

Children's Needs: Experiential Knowledge

In order to supplement this information which essentially focuses on facilities for children, we asked respondents to the postal questionnaire to comment on their children's health and any special needs that arise as a result of ill-health or disability; the adequacy of their income and home to their children's needs; their children's safety; satisfaction with services for children; and their concerns about their children's health, well-being and future.

Of the total sample 24 per cent have dependent (ie. under 18) children. However children are not spread evenly throughout the ward. 36 per cent of children live in Burley, 30 per cent in Kirkstall, 24 per cent on Hawksworth Wood and 13 per cent in the Vespers. Of those with children 79 per cent are married or living as married, 12 per cent are divorced or separated and eight per cent are single parents. The majority of households with dependent children (83 per cent) contain one or two children although larger families tend to be concentrated in Burley and Hawksworth Wood.

We asked parents to state whether any of their children suffered from a long-standing illness, repeated bouts of illness, a physical disability or severe learning difficulty. Figure 21 gives the responses.

However these problems are particularly prevalent in certain parts of the study area and among certain groups. For example:

- 21 per cent of ethnic minority respondents say that one or more child has a long-standing illness
- 13 per cent of parents in Hawksworth Wood say that one or more child has a long-standing illness (compared to 2 per cent in the Vespers)
- 15 per cent of parents in Burley say that one or more child has suffered repeated bouts of illness (compared to 6 per cent in the Vespers)
- 13 per cent of unemployed parents have one or more child with a severe learning difficulty.

Those parents who indicated that they had a child or children with a health or disability problem were asked what kinds of additional help they needed to care for their children. Their responses included the following:

'Better housing'
'My son has asthma; our house is damp and cold'
'My flat has condensation and damp'
'More heating'
'More information concerning the illness; we had to find out ourselves'
'My eldest has asthma. I need more help in finding out how to cure it'
'After school activities for special needs children'
'Special needs teaching in mainstream school'
'Extra tuition in schools'
'More speech therapy at an early age'
'My child has behavioural problems. I can't get financial help with replacing furniture or bedding that he regularly destroys'.

It is interesting that none of these suggestions involves medical intervention.

When we asked people about the adequacy of their housing in relation to their children's needs, 25 per cent said that their home was not adequate. Younger parents (18-34) were more likely to say that their housing was inadequate (30 per cent) as were the unemployed (44 per cent). There is, again, a stark contrast between areas: eight per cent of parents in the Vespers expressed dissatisfaction with their housing compared to over 30 per cent in Burley. Those responding that their home was not adequate for their children's needs were asked to explain the reason why. Thirty-four per cent replied that their home was too cramped. A particular concern was voiced about older children having to share bedrooms. Typical comments were as follows:

'[our home is] not big enough for privacy, doing home work or having friends round'.

'My two daughters aged 15 and 5 have to share the same room'.

Twenty per cent of parents said that there was insufficient outside space. This was particularly true of those living in Kirkstall and Burley. Seventeen per cent (half of whom lived in Burley) reported that their

FIGURE 21
Children's health problems

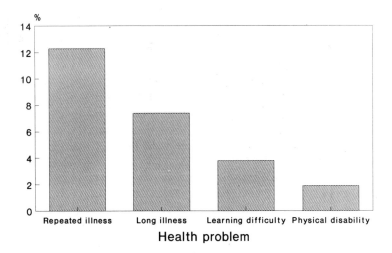

Health problem

home was damp or cold, with several stating that there was no heating in the upstairs rooms; 20 per cent reported a combination of at least 2 of these reasons, particularly in Hawksworth Wood and Burley.

Of respondents with dependent children, 38.5 per cent said that they did not have sufficient income to provide a reasonable standard of living for their children and 64 per cent of unemployed parents said this was the case. Similarly households with children are quite likely to feel financially insecure (45 per cent said this was the case) and to feel that lack of money prevents them from doing something important.

Respondents were asked to state whether they thought that their children were generally safe in certain situations. Figure 22 shows that the majority of parents think that their children are generally not safe in the streets, in local parks, or in the city centre. Respondents aged 18-34, who are more likely to have young children, were particularly likely to feel that their children were unsafe in the street. Those fears were confirmed when respondents were asked: 'If you have any worries about your children's health and well-being what is the main one?' A wide variety of responses was given but worries about children playing outside, and the fear of violence against children - either by adults or other (usually older) children - were the most common.

Other common worries were busy roads and traffic, particularly in Kirkstall, and, again, housing problems. Several respondents feared illness and infection, particularly through contact with dog faeces, and pollution in the environment on a wider scale with one respondent saying: 'I fear the effects of food/water pollution in years to come on my children'.

Other concerns centred on experiences with health services and having to wait long periods to get specialist referrals. Fears for health provision in the future were expressed more generally: 'I fear the dismantling of the N.H.S. will mean poor health care in the future'.

Respondents were also asked the more general question: 'If you have any worries about your children's future what is the main one?'   Several responses centred on health and in particular fear of Aids, but far greater concern was expressed regarding   standards of education and job opportunities. The following comments are typical:

'The cuts in spending . mean my child will not receive a good education'.
'The general state of schools and unemployment levels'.

Over 45 per cent of respondents with children gave education and/or employment as their main worry regarding their children's future. Again, fears of crime against children featured as a concern both in terms of children being subject to violence from adults, and their children getting involved in crime through the bad influence of other children. Pollution at a local level in terms of traffic pollution and dog faeces, and at a global level, in terms of the greenhouse effect, were mentioned by several parents.

Respondents were asked to assess services for children in their area. From Figure 23 it can be seen that pre-school nursery care and creche facilities produce the highest levels of dissatisfaction, with baby clinics and ante-natal clinics giving high levels of satisfaction. Interestingly a high proportion of respondents replied 'don't know' in relation to these services.

Finally respondents were asked to indicate what facilities were needed for children in their area. The responses focused firstly, on pre-school nursery provision, or creche facilities, and secondly, on facilities for older children such as youth clubs or other organised activities. Finally parents in all areas in the ward wanted more playgrounds and playspace. For young children several respondents wanted supervised play areas, with better equipment. Many commented that parks were not conveniently situated. As one respondent explained: 'We need a well-lit play area away from roads and preferably nearer home'. Several respondents commented that their children had to cross busy roads to get to existing play areas.

The highest number of parents wanting pre-school nurseries was in the Kirkstall and Burley areas with respondents implying that the scarcity and expense of pre-school care facilities were preventing women from going out to work. Typical comments included:

'More nursery places for 3-5 years olds and cheaper childcare for single working mothers'
'Extra nursery/pre-school places especially for mothers who need to work'.

Figure 22
Safety of children in and outside home

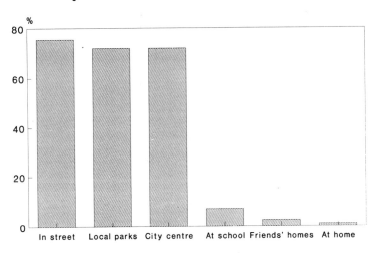

Figure 23
Satisfaction with services for children

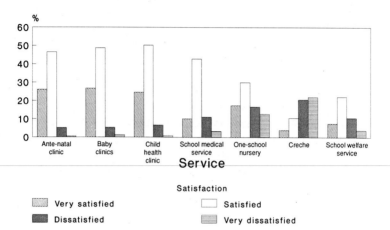

For older children parents wanted: 'More youth groups - the children here have nothing to do on an evening'. One parent suggested: 'A junior arts centre, with facilities for music, art, craft and drama'. Some had reservations that existing youth clubs were 'church or school based', and thought that the children should get more involved in running clubs for themselves. Some parents wanted holiday clubs and activities for children with working parents.

Several references were made to the fact that sports fields were only available through private clubs or leisure centres which were expensive. Some parents suggested that leisure facilities such as clubs and cinemas should be located in the area so that their children didn't have to go into the centre of town.

During the interview stage we followed up in greater depth some of these issues. Those women with children who had expressed dissatisfaction with services available to help children with long-term health problems were asked to expand on the causes of their dissatisfaction. One mother of a dyslexic child was concerned that state schools didn't recognise the problem and so treated her son as 'backward' or 'difficult'. Another cause of concern was the length of time it takes for the emergency doctors to come out; one woman said it could take up to four or five hours.

The interviews with women with children confirmed the view that for families in the Burley area lack of space, especially play space, was a particular problem. Most people thought that the only solution would be to move to a larger house but they were, in most cases, prevented from taking this action by lack of money. Some thought that it was the responsibility of the local authority to make appropriate provision.

Respondents to the postal questionnaire who had indicated that their income was insufficient to provide a reasonable standard of living for their children were asked during the follow-up interviews to elaborate on what they were prevented from doing. In general, holidays, outings and new clothes were the items identified. However some women also said they couldn't afford good quality food. One said she couldn't afford childcare. An Asian woman wanted to be able to send her children to private school; another wanted to be able to take her children to visit relatives abroad. Many of the women who expressed concern over the level of household income saw little prospect for improvement in the future. For others the prospects for improvement were dependent on them being able to work, or work full-time.

Levels of concern about children's safety were vey high among the women we interviewed. We asked them to elaborate on why they are worried. The majority are most worried about their children when they are outside the home in public places. Traffic and busy roads are one cause for concern as are dogs, and dirty and vandalised play grounds. However, overwhelmingly, concern focused on strangers in public places who might molest or abduct their children. Many women spoke of 'strange people', 'funny people' and 'perverts'. Other women were worried about bullies, glue- and gas sniffing.

Proposed solutions focused especially on increased levels of policing particularly 'bobbies on the beat' and stiffer sentences for offenders. Others wanted dog wardens and supervised, safe play areas. Many people thought the answer lay in education of parents and children. For example:

'Parents ought to be more involved in what the children
are doing. Spend more time with them. Educate your child
to kick and run.'
'Make sure children understand not to speak to strangers'.

Several women wanted action taken to reduce the speed of traffic eg.
speed bumps or even pedestrianised streets.

When asked their main concerns about their children's future, responses
focused on education and prospects for employment. Typical comments
were as follows:

'I am worried about the children getting qualified
enough for employment. Employers can pick and choose now.'

'What work will there be? There doesn't seem to be any skilled
manual work with proper apprenticeships'.

'Changes in the educational curriculum worries me'.

'A lot of teachers seem to have lost hope. There's not
enough money put into education.'

Others were worried about the availability and quality of childcare.
Proposed solutions focused on better funding of schools, increased job
opportunities and more facilities for children eg. after school clubs.

Mothers who had expressed dissatisfaction with services for children were
asked to say why they were dissatisfied. The main area of dissatisfaction
was the lack of nursery and childcare provision. Typical comments
included the following:

'Not enough creche facilities and the times are not right
especially for one-parent families working in evening jobs'.

'Not enough nursery schools. Everyone should have the right to send
their children to nursery without having to pay.'

'Twenty-eight months I've waited for a nursery place.'

'To get my youngest into nursey school at 18 months old I had to put his name down at two days old.'

Other comments on specific services included the following:

'School welfare service doesn't meet the needs of families on income support. There's no choice regarding school lunch. I would prefer my children to have sandwiches but the only option is the school meal which the children don't eat'.

'They [ante-natal clinic] have forgotten they are dealing with people'.

Suggestions as to how services could be improved were wide-ranging, but focused on increasing the amount of facilities available eg. more creches, nurseries and play groups and play areas or creches for children in waiting rooms. Other suggestions related to the way in which services are delivered. For example:

'Dentists should have more patience with young children'.

'A more caring service'.

There was also a concern about the lack of information about what services were available.

Children's Needs: Perceptions of Professionals and Community Representatives

We asked professionals and front line workers in the study area to comment on the main problems facing children, the priorities in terms of children's health and welfare, the short-comings of existing services, and to make suggestions as to what ought to be done to address children's needs.

Problems Facing Children

An education welfare officer summed up the problems facing children as follows: 'Children and teenagers are growing up in a general climate of neglect in terms of quality of housing, physical environment and the types of areas they live in. They can be at risk in terms of hazardous roads or from abuse within the home. Financial problems lead to a poor quality of life and affect access to leisure facilities and a good diet. There are a whole range of problems which impact at any time and affect children both in the short and long term. Their quality of life is also affected by school and opportunities for work in the future'.

Others interviewed expanded on this general comment. Road safety was seen as a particular issue for children due to the Hawksworth Wood estate being used as a rat-run to avoid traffic in Headingley and heavy peak time traffic in Burley.

The lack of facilities for children came up as an issue time and time again. In Burley it was argued that all forms of child care were in short supply - pre-school, child-minders, 'latch-key' clubs, holiday care and support for teenagers. In general it was felt that facilities for children in the area were very bad - there are no decent youth clubs so older children 'hang around the parks'. Sports facilities which do exist are very traditional - no efforts have been made to involve young people or to assess what they need. Young people cannot afford the prices charged by the sports centres. There is also a lack of child-oriented activities. Facilities that do exist are aimed at supporting parents (eg. nursery, creche, family support unit). It was felt that there was a particular lack of opportunities for young Asian women - the environment is not seen as safe and there is a problem of harassment if they go out.

A number of those interviewed spoke of the risks children faced within the home. One health worker said that some children are forced out on to the street because of pressure in the home: 'They want to get away from their parents' stress and drunkenness and parents want children out of the house because they can't cope with them.' A head teacher was particularly concerned about children in single-parent households and households where both parents work. It was claimed that as a result some children come to school at 8am and at the end of the day young children play in the streets. Other children faced difficulties as a result of broken homes or reconstituted families which may lead to behaviour problems. In such cases the problems may not be a result of lack of love but rather the lack of 'stable, supportive homes'. In such circumstances, according to one head teacher, school can be an important source of security.

However poor parenting was also seen to be a problem by some. A police officer interviewed spoke of 'indifferent and apathetic parents' who provide poor role models for their children giving more encouragement for 'negative' behaviour than for 'positive'. Head teachers described children's 'under-developed social and inter- personal skills' leading to violent responses to difficult situations due to a lack of knowledge of anything else.

A poor home environment was linked to the problem of juvenile crime. Many juvenile offenders, a police officer suggested, come from broken homes. Also juveniles can't get jobs but they need money to keep up with expectations - 'they have nowhere else to turn apart from crime'. Peer group pressure was also a problem: 'when all your friends are criminals there is pressure to turn to crime or lose your friends'.

A youth worker described children on the Hawksworth Wood estate as being at risk from male abusers who try to gain access to children even when barred from seeing them. Men, it was felt, are generally not helpful as parents. Children experience stress as they want to see their fathers but don't want the abuse. Women come to be grateful for not being abused - rather than making demands. Not being beaten up means they have a 'good deal'.

Girls are described as growing up very quickly on Hawksworth Wood; they are often primary carers within the family. As a result they miss out on other activities. For example a youth worker described how girls were unable to go to a girls' club without bringing a younger sibling and while fathers complained if boys miss school, girls are expected to take time off to look after younger members of the family and their mothers. Despite a recognition of the difficulties faced by their mothers, many girls see having a baby of their own as 'brilliant' as it is the only time anyone looks after them and gives them some attention.

The community in Kirkstall was described by one head teacher as being very fixed and stable with families who have lived there for generations. This, it was suggested, results in a narrow band of experience and type of resident. The average IQ is average to low and parents are not interested in involvement with the school and have low expectations of what the children will gain from it.

A poor standard of living was seen to be a particular problem for children on the Hawksworth estate who were described by a local clergyman as having the 'estate look' - pallor and hair doesn't shine - probably as a result of bad diet and poor hygiene. Community health workers also spoke of lack of stimulation especially for pre-school children; few children attend mother and toddler groups and there was little in the way of out-of-school activities especially at the weekends and during school holidays.

A head teacher interviewed thought that many parents are wary of going into schools because of their own bad experiences. However, she was also concerned that too much is expected from schools and this leads to a conflict between time spent on personal and social education and time spent on academic work. 'There is a danger of taking responsibility away from parents in educating their children for life. The welfare state has led to passiveness and opting out of this responsibility by parents.'

Other people mentioned the difficulties teachers faced 'trying to lift children out of a negative situation' in spite of what were seen as the appalling physical conditions of some schools. In general it was felt that schools are overstretched and under-resourced and that classes are bigger so children don't get enough attention.

Children on the Hawksworth Wood estate were seen as facing a particular problem arising from what is seen to be a very insular culture. Children don't get taken off the estate; there is a lot of inter-marriage and in-breeding and incestuous relationships, which limits the personal freedom of children; they have a narrow perception of what society is about and have low expectations about what they can get out of education. At the same time complex family relationships and inter-family feuds may overflow into school according to a head teacher.

In general it was thought that Hawksworth residents have a low self-image so that children who do try to improve themselves face difficulties. It was felt that education, both in and out of school, was needed to challenge childrens' poor self-image ie. of being a 'loser' and to shift behaviour away from violent responses.

Asian community leaders expressed concern at the low level of 'A' level passes and a feeling that schools are not up to standard and that ethnic minority children suffer from poorer job prospects as a result.

A local head teacher described the low standards of general health, cleanliness and hygiene and appalling dental health of children at her school. In particular children from poorer families were thought to be smaller and more susceptible to illness than those from better-off families. An education welfare officer spoke of the lack of proper care of children by parents. So, for example, children will go to the doctors' surgery themselves and others are sent to school when not well. Poor diet was a cause for concern with the school meal being the only balanced meal for many children according to a head teacher. A youth worker mentioned the repeated incidence of dysentry, meningitis and salmonella poisoning on the Hawksworth Wood estate, with asthma also prevalent among babies and under 5s.

In addition to physical health problems it was thought that the mental health problems of children are underestimated. In particular it was thought that many children are understimulated due to lack of exposure to different settings and experiences and too much time spent watching TV and videos.

Shortcomings in existing services and proposed solutions

When asked to comment on the shortcomings of existing services, professional workers and community representatives overwhelmingly focused on the lack of resources and shortage of facilities. It was widely felt that under-resourcing of education and social services, in particular, was resulting in services becoming over-stretched. One example given was that too few teachers had time to visit parents at home in areas where parents were unwilling to go into school. Shortage of facilities focused on lack of childcare (preventing women taking up training, employment and further education opportunities), inadequate, safe play areas and lack of facilities for older children and teenagers. A few people thought that the type of service currently offered was inappropriate. For example one person lamented the fact that the social work service operated on the basis of crisis intervention rather than prevention and a police officer thought that existing measures for dealing with juvenile crime were ineffective.

Proposals for improving facilities and services for children focused, not surprisingly in view of the above, on providing additional resources and facilities and improving existing facilities. Specific suggestions included the following:

- Enough money should be put into education to pay teachers at a level to maintain motivation and morale

- Schools should be seen as part of the community, eg. for teachers to live in the area. If children and parents saw teachers sharing the same environment and problems this would go a long way to reducing the gap between 'professionals' and residents.

- More facilities for children are needed including play space and organised leisure activities. A safe environment needs to be created so children can be out of the home but safe eg. play wardens, play streets. At least streets need to be free of litter and broken glass

- Children need secure, stable homes; without this they lack self-esteem resulting in bad behaviour

- More support and counselling are needed to prevent families from breaking up

- People 'with good listening skills' are needed to work with parents in Hawksworth Wood

- An enhanced multi-agency approach is required involving parents, police, probation, education welfare, social services, youth workers, youth groups and churches. Inter-agency co-ordination and liaison needs to be improved

- Health centres should have accessible drop-in facilities for mothers where they can discuss problems informally

- A community worker on the Hawksworth Wood estate thought that in order to improve the health of children it was necessary to give support to mothers many of whom have been in care themselves and need advice and information (on child care, health, welfare rights etc) given in ways that are 'non-threatening and don't put them down'. At the same time girls ought to be encouraged to see themselves in roles other than mother/carer

- A youth centre is needed in Burley with decent facilities catering for all ages of children involving coordination and cooperation with schools, social services and police

- There should be greater recognition of children's needs laid down as statutory policies including minimum agreed levels of services for children

- A service is needed to intervene with families and draw up contracts to enable young people to return home where appropriate

- We must break the cycle of crime by providing alternative experiences that are exciting and learning opportunities that enable people to develop skills and value themselves

Children's Needs: Public Meetings

Views on children's needs expressed at the public meetings followed a similar pattern to that established by parents and professionals. Lack of facilities was mentioned in all areas - child care, before and after school clubs, facilities for older children and teenagers to replace youth clubs which are no longer popular, play schemes and lack of safe play space.

During the meeting at Hawksworth Wood there was a debate about the nature of family responsibility. For example some people present felt that people ought to take responsibility for their own families and not be dependent on outside services. However it was also pointed out that women - especially single parents -needed to work and so needed reliable child care. Others present at the meeting mentioned the large, informal child care network on the Hawksworth Wood estate involving extended family or women looking after each others' children. Some people were concerned about older children being left in charge of younger siblings and that some children were the victims of 'poor parenting' - an issue that had also been raised by professionals.

Children's Needs: Key Issues

Some information is already available on children in Leeds. For example the index of child deprivation developed by the Personal Social Services

Research Unit suggests that Kirkstall ward is one of the more disadvantaged areas for children in Leeds. Furthermore, examination of child care provision in the study area and the number of children on the waiting list shows a considerable shortfall between provision and need. Nevertheless this information give us little insight into the form that deprivation takes among children in the study area nor does it help very much in formulating policy to address children's needs.

Our survey shows that a majority of children in the study area live in Burley and Kirkstall, with a concentration of larger families in Burley. Approximately 25 per cent of children in the study area are described by their parents as having a long-standing illness, a physical disability, a severe learning difficulty or suffering repeated bouts of illness, and that these problems are particularly concentrated among the children of ethnic minority groups, the unemployed and in Hawskworth Wood.

A significant proportion of parents were concerned that their incomes and/or housing were inadequate for their children's needs. In particular parents said they lacked money for holidays, outings and treats. While a majority of parents thought their children are safe while at home, at school or in friends' homes, they fear for their children's safety when out in the street, in local parks or playgrounds or in the city centre. When asked to elaborate on why they were concerned it became clear that the main worries are traffic and molestation by strangers. This concern was also demonstrated by the dissatisfaction voiced at the lack of safe play space for children and safe but stimulating activities for older children. Parents' fears for their childrens' future focus on the quality of education their children will receive and their opportunities for employment.

On the whole parents are satisfied with child health services, while there was considerable dissatisfaction about creche and nursery facilities. However during the interviews it became clear that the cause of dissatisfaction was not the quality of care their children received in creches and nurseries but the difficulties of getting a place.

A similar set of concerns emerged from our interviews with professional workers and community representatives. Lack of play facilities, child care and out-of-school care was a dominant theme as was the risk to children from, for example, traffic that resulted because of their absence. However, professionals also mentioned the risks to children from within the home either because of inadequate diet and/or housing or parental stress or as a result of poor parenting and/or abuse. This was seen to be a particular problem on Hawksworth Wood estate where, the impression was given, many children are 'at risk' in one way or another.

Behavioural problems and crime amongst older children were seen as an important issue and this related to lack of facilities, and poor expectations.

2:10   KEY ISSUES AND PRIORITIES

From all aspects of the 'Knowing About Leeds' project - existing sources of information, the postal survey and follow-up interviews, interviews with professionals, front-line workers and community representatives, and public meetings - it is possible to identify a set of issues and priorities relating to each of the basic and intermediate needs we have examined. Although, in this chapter, we discuss them separately it is worth pointing out the extent to which they are inter-connected. Many other studies have already demonstrated how factors such as income, housing and employment status affect health and well-being. Our work reinforces that message suggesting that the best way of addressing ill-health and the absence of well-being in the longer term, may not be through medical intervention but through measures aimed at alleviating the problems that appear to lead to ill-health and lack of well-being. The issues identified in this chapter offer an outline agenda for action.

Factors Influencing Well-Being and the Quality of Life

In general residents in the study area, professionals and community representatives agree that the set of basic and intermediate needs we identified are important for well-being and quality of life. However there are some differences between groups as to the degree of importance attached to the various needs listed. Among residents in the study area some differences emerged on the basis of age, gender, employment status, race and level of educational attainment.

Although we found certain differences between the priorities of local residents on the one hand, and professionals and community representatives on the other, differences between groups of professionals appear to be more significant. These differences raise an important issue in that they emphasise the importance of inter-departmental and multi-agency responses to problems and the need to encourage participation by local communities in order to ensure maximum agreement between the priorities of professionals and those of local people. Our findings suggest that single agency or single departmental responses are likely to result in measures that are out of tune with residents' own perceptions of needs and priorities. Furthermore dependence on input into policy formulation from community representatives may actually widen the gap between people and policy since their view of what is important to quality of life and well-being was further from that of local people than that of professionals.

Physical Health and Autonomy

Examination of existing information on physical health shows that Kirkstall ward is the ninth most deprived ward in Leeds according to the Jarman Index which identifies areas of disadvantage where the GP workload is likely to be heavier. Overall mortality rates for the study area are about average for the country as a whole (taking account of age and sex structure). The main causes of death for the area are cancer, heart disease, strokes and diseases of the respiratory system. However in the study area deaths from cancers and diseases of the respiratory system are above average.

A survey of dental health of children in Leeds in 1986/87 found that children attending school in Leeds 4 and 5 (which cover the study area) had significantly worse dental health than Leeds as a whole.

Two other sources of information are worth noting. Firstly a survey of self-perceived health in Leeds West in 1986/87 showed that 80 per cent of people thought they were very or reasonably healthy while only eight per cent thought they were not very healthy or in poor health. Thirty-one per cent indicated that they have a long term illness or disability. This compares with the 1987 Leeds City Council Population Survey in which people were asked whether they have a disability that affects them in terms of work or mobility or generally looking after themselves. Just under three per cent reported a disability defined in this way.

Our survey shows that 78 per cent of respondents think that their health over the past year has been good or very good. The incidence of ill-health is highest among the elderly, ethnic minorities, the unemployed and residents of the Hawksworth Wood estate. Nineteen per cent of respondents said they had suffered a major illness or injury over the previous year. Again this figure is significantly higher among the elderly and Asian populations.

Twenty-seven per cent of respondents (but 44 per cent of those over 65) say they suffer from a long-standing illness, and 20 per cent say that their current state of health places a major limit on how they live their life with the most common relating to mobility.

Interviews with professional health workers showed a high level of concern about coronary heart disease and other smoking related health problems which is consistent with mortality statistics although they, perhaps, have a different perception of the relative importance of heart disease as compared to cancers and diseases of the respiratory system. The issue of poor dental health was also picked up by professional health workers.

Considerable concern was voiced by professionals about the health of children in the area generally but especially on the Hawksworth Wood estate and, to a lesser extent, in Burley. Sickness and diarrhoea and persistent colds and coughs were thought to be common. Ill-health amongst children was linked to poor housing conditions and financial hardship. At the other end of the age spectrum there was also concern over the failing health of the elderly.

In addition to physical ill-health our survey shows that a significant proportion of people in the study area experience serious problems with stress (18.5 per cent), depression (13 per cent), anxiety/worry (23.5 per cent) and/or sleeplessness (22 per cent). Less than half of all respondents say they experience none of these problems, with residents of the Vespers and those in paid work most likely to fall into this category. The incidence of stress and anxiety is highest among women, young people, ethnic minority groups, the unemployed and those living in Burley and Hawksworth Wood; depression is highest among women, those looking after home and family and the unemployed; and sleeplessness is most likely to be experienced by the elderly and the unemployed. Other people for whom one is responsible appear to be a cause of anxiety or worry according to our interviews. Elderly people tended to worry about their own or a dependant's health while women worried about their children.

Professional workers showed considerable awareness of the 'fragile mental health' of many local people and how this related to physical health problems - a point borne out by our survey.

It is clear, then, that problems with physical health and autonomy are connected with a wide range of factors relating to housing and environmental conditions, financial circumstances, dietary and smoking habits and levels of health education. Concern among local GPs about coronary heart disease and other smoking-related health problems (cancer, respiratory and circulatory) is consistent with the available mortality and morbidity statistics, although there is perhaps a rather different perception of the relative importance of heart disease as opposed to respiratory diseases and cancer.

Poor dental health is a major issue. The combination of poor diet, smoking, poor oral hygiene, lack of regular visits to the dentist and a shortage of local dentists, particularly for residents of the Hawksworth Wood area, suggests the need for action on a number of fronts related to education and provision. A particular focus for attention is the problems and needs of Asian children.

Certain groups in the community are particularly vulnerable in terms of problems of health and autonomy. It is clear that unemployed people are especially vulnerable. An increasing number of elderly people suffer multiple problems of physical health exacerbated by worry, depression and sleeplessness related to loss of mobility, isolation, loneliness and financial difficulties. Problems for the Asian elderly are aggravated by language and cultural differences which create problems of access to health services.

There is evidence of particular problems experienced by women with young children (especially young single parents) in the Hawksworth Wood area. At issue here is a complex set of problems involving financial difficulties, problems of access to work (due in part to lack of affordable childcare facilities), poor diet and smoking, isolation and lack of parenting skills leading to worry and depression. In some cases this is exacerbated by gynaecological problems.

Diet and Lifestyle

Seventeen per cent of respondents think their usual diet is not good for their health with men, younger people and the unemployed being the groups most likely to think this is the case. Reasons given most commonly for not eating more healthily are lack of access to shops selling good quality food, lack of motivation and lack of money. Thirteen per cent of people think that food bought in shops is generally not safe to eat and

25.5 per cent that water is generally not safe to drink. In both cases a significant proportion of people said they 'didn't know'. Poor quality drinking water is seen by some to be related to the outbreaks of sickness and diarrhoea mentioned above.

Thirty-six per cent of respondents are smokers with younger people and residents of Hawksworth Wood most likely to smoke. Of those who smoke, 60 per cent think they smoke too much for the good of their health - with more women than men taking this view. Smokers are more likely than others to report poor general health.

Seventy-one per cent of respondents drink alcohol with a higher incidence among men, younger people and those in paid work. Of those who drink, only 10 per cent think they drink too much for the good of their health. Younger people are most likely to think this is the case.

Some 40 per cent of respondents do not think they get enough exercise for the good of their health. Women, younger people, those looking after home and family and residents of Burley and Kirkstall are most likely to think this is the case.

Discussion at the public meetings demonstrated the extent to which an unhealthy lifestyle was related to other factors such as stress or unemployment which needed to be taken account of by health educators. The generally low level of health education is a problem, particularly in relation to diet and smoking. An important issue relates to the limits of written material in health education due to literacy and language problems indicating a need for alternative media including TV and local discussion groups.

Lifestyle is also affected by culture, and cultural differences must be acknowledged if people are to be successfully encouraged to adopt lifestyles less damaging to health.

Housing

Both the local authority waiting list and our interviews with professionals and community representatives indicate that there is a considerable shortage of housing affecting certain groups in particular. Firstly there is a shortage of larger houses in the Burley area which can accommodate extended families common in the Asian community. Secondly, there is a shortage of housing for young, single people and for those suffering from a mental illness or with a mental handicap. In addition there are insufficient homes adapted to the needs of the physically disabled.

A second issue concerns housing quality. Existing information suggests that there is a considerable number of homes that are unfit or in need of renovation in Leeds as a whole but that overcrowding is not particularly a problem. Our survey showed that in the study area a significant number of people report serious problems with damp, condensation and poor heating. These problems are prevalent among younger people, the unemployed and those looking after home and family especially in Hawksworth Wood and, to a lesser extent, Burley.

Although overcrowding is not indicated as a major problem in Leeds, lack of space - both internal and external - emerged as an issue among respondents to our survey. In particular too few bedrooms, lack of play space and absence of laundry facilities were mentioned as problems.

Residents, professional and community representatives alike all drew attention to the impact on health of living in damp, poorly heated housing and this relationship was demonstrated by survey responses. Those experiencing housing problems are more likely to say that they are in poor general health and that they suffer from stress, worry, depression and sleeplessness.

A key issue therefore concerns the need to improve housing conditions, particularly addressing problems of dampness, condensation and poor heating in local authority housing on the Hawksworth Wood estate and in the more mixed tenure housing in the Burley area, where lack of space and noise affect those living in back-to-back housing in particular.

Resources to effect such improvements are an important issue since the local authority is restricted in its ability to spend on improvement programmes, housing repairs, new building to replace housing of inadequate standards and to provide additional housing to meet needs of particular groups and to finance grants for improvements in the private sector. The future of the back-to-back housing in the Burley area is clearly an important issue in view of concern about lack of space and amenities.

This raises the issue of the role of the local authority in social housing provision both in terms of new building relative to housing associations and the private sector, and in terms of the management of their existing stock where the issue of tenant participation arises.

An important issue relating to the broader social problems which exist in certain areas (especially on the Hawksworth Wood estate) concerns the local authority's allocation policy particularly in relation to 'problem tenants', and the problem of the bad reputation of the Hawksworth Wood estate. Tenant participation in management is also relevant to this issue.

Physical Environment: Access and Security

Problems of access emerged in relation to dentists (especially in the Vespers and Hawksworth Wood), shops (in all parts of the ward but especially the Vespers and Hawksworth Wood) and community centres (in all parts of the ward).

Residents on the Hawksworth Wood estate appear to suffer considerable isolation which is exacerbated by relatively low car availability. The elderly and women with young children are particularly affected. This raises the issue of the need for more responsive public transport.

The lack of community centres was a matter for comment in all areas although in some cases the problem is not the absence of a centre but inappropriate existing provision. For example the YMCA in Hawksworth Wood is widely seen as being 'in the wrong place' creating problems of access and having acquired a bad reputation. Similarly it was felt that existing community facilities in Burley do not cater adequately for the needs of the Asian community.

In all areas lack of facilities for children and young people was mentioned and was seen to be a causal factor in other problems such as vandalism.

In terms of environmental problems, the main issues to emerge are traffic and busy roads, litter, dogs and vandalism. However in Hawksworth Wood people are also likely to mention difficulties with neighbours. Concern about crime was especially prevalent in Burley and Hawksworth Wood although in the latter this was not a view shared by the police.

Again the relationship between the physical environment and health and well-being was apparent. Respondents who perceive their environment in negative terms or who feel at risk from crime are more likely to also suffer from stress, worry, depression and sleeplessness.

Health Care and Welfare Services

Existing information on health care services shows that GPs in Leeds have fewer patients than the national average and a higher than average number of women GPs. Residents in Kirkstall ward make disproportionately high use of hospital services especially urology, paediatrics and general medicine. The study area has below target uptake of child immunisation services.

Our work shows that 87 per cent of respondents had visited their GP or health centre during the past year; just over half had been to the dentist and just over a third had been a hospital out-patient. In general levels of satisfaction with health services are high. The highest level of dissatisfaction is expressed in relation to hospital out-patient and accident and emergency services. The main problems experienced are getting an appointment and waiting to be seen. Dissatisfaction with health services is disproportionately concentrated among ethnic minority respondents and may relate to lack of translation facilities.

Use of dentists is below average in the Hawksworth Wood area which is likely to be related to the problems of access mentioned earlier.

Dissatisfaction with GPs and health centres is above average in the Burley area. Women in all areas expressed dissatisfaction with the lack of facilities for children in waiting rooms.

Among professional workers there was concern expressed about the inadequate resourcing of community care - especially community nursing services - and lack of clarity about the division of responsibility between health and welfare services. Liaison and lack of coordination was also an issue in relation to the work of different agencies such as the voluntary sector, police and social services.

The adequacy of care and support in the community for elderly and handicapped people is clearly a major issue. If inadequate resources are devoted to front-line staff and equipment, an extra burden falls on families and GPs. Inadequate care can aggravate health problems of both the cared for and carers and inadequate respite care increases the burden on carers. Inadequate support for the mentally handicapped places them at risk of exploitation by private landlords and homelessness.

Existing information on welfare services focuses almost exclusively on resources - staffing and places provided in the form of residential provision and day care - and activity - active cases of social work staff. There are no direct measures of need for welfare services.

Our survey shows that welfare services are infrequently used by the majority of the population. However those services that are used generate very high levels of satisfaction among users.

Use of welfare services by respondents is heavily concentrated among the elderly and, to a lesser extent, among those looking after home and family. Ten per cent of our sample said they were involved in caring for a sick, elderly or disabled person and seven per cent said they were being cared for. The most common tasks undertaken by all carers are shopping and providing friendship and support. However those involved in caring for more than ten hours a day are also likely to undertake tasks such as bathing, dressing and assisting with mobility.

When asked what would make their caring responsibilities easier the most commonly mentioned item was more money followed by better advice and information. Relatively few carers wanted assistance with caring itself although a significant number of those caring ten hours a day said they would like time off.

Carers are more likely than non-carers to suffer from stress and depression and to have made use of health care services over the previous 12 months.

Professional workers and community representatives recognised the importance of informal caring and acknowledged the range of tasks undertaken by carers. Some concern was expressed about people who undertook caring duties for financial gain. Informal care was seen to be especially important in relation to elderly Asian people.

When asked about carers' needs and services to support carers, professional workers and community representatives gave a rather different set of responses to those given by carers themselves. Given the increasing importance of informal care arrangements this suggests an in-depth audit of carers' needs might be useful.

At the public meetings people spoke strongly in favour of more localised health and welfare services and, in particular, they wanted multi-agency centres that offered housing, health, welfare and advice services under one roof. Another issue concerns the participation of communities in discussions about health problems, needs and issues.

Work and Economic Security

Official statistics tell us that the study area has a level of unemployment higher than that for the city as a whole and contains more retired people. Our survey shows that unemployment is disproportionately concentrated among men, ethnic minorities and residents of Hawksworth Wood and Burley. Part-time working is concentrated among women and, according to interviews, this is clearly related to the lack of childcare.

For those in paid work levels of job satisfaction are high in general but especially so among women, younger people, and those employed in white collar occupations.

There is a correlation between dissatisfaction with work and poor general health and with problems such as stress, worry, depression and sleeplessness. And, as we have seen, the unemployed suffer disproportionately from ill-health and mental health problems.

Over half of all respondents report serious difficulties in paying the poll tax and this is especially the case among the unemployed and people looking after home and family, ethnic minorities and people living in Burley and Hawksworth Wood. In addition certain groups experience other difficulties: the elderly mention fuel and phone bills; younger people have problems paying for clothes, furniture and housing costs; and the unemployed report difficulties with fuel bills, clothes, food and furniture. In general financial difficulties are more common among ethnic minority groups than among the white population. Difficulties paying for large items such as furniture were seen by professionals to have become more acute since the introduction of the Social Fund.

Over a third of respondents said that they felt financially insecure and this insecurity is disproportionately concentrated among the unemployed, people looking after home and family and residents of Hawksworth Wood estate. Those experiencing financial insecurity are more likely to suffer from stress, worry, depression and sleeplessness and to be in poor general health.

Almost a half of all respondents say that they are prevented from doing 'something important' because of lack of money, most commonly home improvements, holidays and visits to friends and relatives and, during the interviews, this was linked to feelings of depression.

Professional workers and community representatives mostly recognised the financial difficulties faced by sections of the community and the impact of these on health and well-being. Many were also admiring of people's ability to cope on limited budgets but others thought that some people needed assistance to develop skills in financial management.

While much of the blame for financial security was laid at the door of too low benefit levels, there was also a recognition among some professionals and community representatives of the difficulties faced by those on low wages.

Concern was expressed by residents and professionals alike about the effect on the well-being of children growing up in low income households.

A key issue relates to measures to address and alleviate problems of financial hardship and insecurity: suggestions included raising the level of benefits and income support; replacement of Social Fund loans with grants for essential expenses; better information on rights and entitlements and particularly, more attention to the specific problems and needs of ethnic minorities; better job prospects and training opportunities; more attention to the training and childcare needs of women; credit unions to address debt problems.

The issue of credit unions raises that of the prospect for local community-based initiatives to regenerate the economic and social life of the

Hawksworth Wood area, including investment in local job generation, training opportunities and childcare facilites. This is related to issues of local housing and environmental improvement and the role of the local community. A development strategy formulated by the local community in partnership with relevant agencies (including the local authority, health authority, police, probation etc) could address interrelated problems of ill-health, poor housing, social and environmental problems and financial hardship by focusing on how to secure investment and action in the local area to meet local needs.

Social Contact and Community Participation

Over a fifth of respondents do not get as much contact as they would like with family or friends. This was more likely to be the case for women, those with caring commitments, and younger people.

The majority of people said they did have someone who they could rely on in a crisis. However those for whom this is not true are likely to be unemployed or looking after the home and family.

Over 70 per cent of respondents think that they have enough time for hobbies and leisure interests. However this is significantly less likely to be true for younger people and ethnic minority respondents.

Consequently, there appears to be an issue of the relative 'social isolation' of the unemployed and those caring for home and family, particularly the latter in view of the higher proportion of 'carers' who regard the support of friends and relatives as important to their well-being and quality of life (see part 2:1). This conclusion is strengthened by the relatively high proportion of 'carers' who do not get sufficient time for hobbies and leisure interests due to caring commitments.

In general, levels of community participation are relatively low. Around 40 per cent of those in paid work are trade union members but less than 10 per cent are members of community or tenants' associations, pressure groups, political parties or self-help groups. Nevertheless 63 per cent of respondents said they had voted in the local elections and almost half said they had signed a petition in the last 12 months.

Activities of this kind are disproportionately undertaken by white people, men, those in paid work and residents of Burley. However women are more likely to engage in voluntary work.

Broadly speaking, there is something of a division in socio-economic and age terms in the level and type of community and voluntary activity. Those in the middle and older age groups, in work and looking after home and family, tend to be involved in 'community building and support' activities epitomised by community associations and voluntary work. Younger people, and especially the unemployed, are rather more inclined towards 'protest' type activities such as signing petitions, going on marches and demonstrations and attending public meetings.

Overwhelmingly people think they have no influence over the decisions of central government, the City Council or private companies. However, rather more people think they have some influence over the City Council than the other two. In the course of the interviews people expressed considerable cynicism about politics and politicians. Nevertheless they showed, at the same time, considerable faith in the idea of democracy, which was often equated with voting, and in locally based collective action to achieve change.

Professional workers and community representatives tended to think about community activity in relation to physical resources such as community centres. However there was also the view expressed by several people that power ought to be devolved to communities or that better channels of communication ought to be established in order to find out about local needs. Many voices supported the notion of empowering local communities to develop initiatives to address their needs and, clearly, this relates to the broader issue raised above of the potential for community-based initiatives to address inter-related housing, environmental, economic, social and financial problems.

Children's Needs

The index of child deprivation (developed by the Personal Social Services Research Unit, University of Kent) shows that Kirkstall is one of the most deprived wards in the city and, as such, is an area where children are vulnerable to being taken into care.

Existing information focuses in particular on services for children which shows considerable under-provision of nursery places.

Our survey shows that children in the study area are concentrated in particular in the Burley and Kirkstall areas. Twenty-five per cent of parents say that one or more of their children have a long-standing illness, a physical disability, a severe learning difficulty or suffer repeated bouts of illness. These problems are most likely to be found among children of ethnic minority groups, the unemployed and residents of Hawksworth Wood.

A significant number of parents expressed concern that their incomes and/or housing were inadequate for their children's needs.

Parents are likely to fear for their children's safety when they are away from home (the exception being when they are in school) and to be concerned about the future well-being of their children in terms of the education they will get and the employment opportunities open to them.

Lack of childcare including nurseries, creches, pre-school and after-school care was a major source of dissatisfaction for parents as was the lack of safe play space.

Professionals echoed many of the concerns voiced by parents but also expressed concern about what they saw as 'poor parenting'.

Priorities

This summary of the key issues to emerge from all aspects of the Leeds audit gives a comprehensive picture of the range of needs of people in the study area and shortfalls in terms of service provision. In addition we asked all interviewees - residents and professionals alike -what they thought were the priority needs in the area.

Overwhelmingly residents, especially those with children, saw their priority need in terms of having more money, and freedom from financial insecurity and debt. Professionals and community representatives recognised that lack of money was a pressing need for many local people but gave greater emphasis to other issues as well.

Among older residents maintaining good health was seen to be a priority. However, this tended not to be mentioned by younger people interviewed nor by professionals, with the exception of one GP who saw smoking-related ill-health as a pressing problem.

For younger residents, especially those in Burley and Hawksworth Wood, housing was seen as a priority need. Most of these people wanted to move house. However many professionals prioritised housing in terms of repairs and renovation to existing housing, and provision of more sheltered housing.

Other interviewees saw increased or better provision of health and welfare services as a priority. In particular increased services for the elderly were seen as a priority by several people.

The needs of children and young people were mentioned as a priority by a number of professionals, in particular child safety, facilities for young people to divert them from crime and other anti-social behaviour, child abuse and education for parents to enable them to care for their children better.

Another issue which was mentioned by a number of residents and professionals relates to the empowerment of local communities. This includes things like consulting with local people, giving people choice over local services and creating community spirit and the feeling that people can change things for themselves. Also mentioned were the setting up of a tenants' management board in Hawksworth Wood and the development of a comprehensive local plan in Burley.

Poor education and lack of employment prospects was another issue mentioned as a priority by several professionals.

Appendix

<u>**Professionals, 'Front-Line' Workers and Community Representatives Interviewed**</u>

Leeds West Community Health
Services:

Nursing Officer
Health Visitors (x3)
School Nurse (x2)
Nursing Auxiliary
District Health Promotion Manager
Community Health Promotion Officer
District Dental Officer
Assistant District Dental Officer
Community Psychiatric Nurses (x3)

GPs/Health Centres:

GPs (x2)
Nurse Manager
Nursing Sisters (x2)
Nurse
Nursing Auxiliary

Women's Health Matters: Coordinator

Community Health Link: Community Health Development
                                     Worker

Leeds City Council, Social
Services Department:

Officers-in-charge, Family Nursery
Centres (x2)
Managers, Day Centres for the
Elderly (x3)
Social Workers (x3)
Home Care Team Leaders (x6)
Home Care Managers (x3)

Burley 88 (umbrella group for
voluntary organisations):   Representatives (x4)

**Leeds City Council, Department of
Housing:**   Area Housing Managers (x2)
                                        Area Environmental Health Officer

**Leeds City Council, Department of
Education:**   Head teachers, Primary (x2)
                                        Head teachers, Middle (x2)
                                        Education Welfare Officers (x5)
                                        Area Education Welfare Officer

West Yorkshire Police: Juvenile Liaison Officers (x2)
                                        Community Constables (x4)
                                        Community Liaison Officers (x2)
                                        Policy Constable - Tutor.

**West Yorkshire Probation
Service:**   Probation Officers (x3)
                                        Probation Service Assistant

Burley Lodge Centre: Chair of Directors
                                        Continuing Education Workers (x3)
                                        Staff member

YMCA, Hawksworth Wood: Senior Youth and Community Worker
                                        Adult Education Development and
                                        Youth Worker

Leeds City Council: Councillor, Kirkstall Ward

Member of Parliament, Leeds West

**Kirkstall Hill Community
Association:**   Representatives

**Hawksworth Wood Community
Association:**   Representatives (x9)

Leeds Muslim Council: Representative

Afro-Caribbean Community: Representatives (x2)

**Azad Kashmir Welfare
Association:**   Representative

**Church of England Parish
Church:**   Vicar

REFERENCES

Audit Commission (1989), *Managing Services Effectively - Performance Review*, Management Paper No 5.

Barrett S and McMahon L (1990), 'Public Management in Uncertainty: A Micro-Political Perspective of the Health Service in the United Kingdom', *Policy and Politics* Vol 18 No4 p257-68.

Bayley M, Seyd R and Tenant A (1989), *Local Health and Welfare -Is Partnership Possible?*, Gower.

Berry L (1988), 'The Rhetoric of Consumerism and the Exclusion of Community', *Community Development Journal*, Vol 23, No 4 p267-72.

Bradshaw J (1972), 'The Concept of Social Need', *New Society*, 30 March.

Burns D (1991), 'Ladders of Participation', *Going Local*, No 18, p14-15.

Callaghan, B et al (1990), *Meeting Needs in the 1990s: The Future of Public Service and the Challenge for Trade Unions*, IPPR.

Cave M et al (1990), *Output and Performance Measures in Government*, Jessica Kingsley.

Cochrane A (1991), 'The Changing State of Local Government - Restructuring for the 1990s', *Public Administration*, Vol 69, No 3 p 281-302

Coote A (1990), 'The Future of Welfare and the Challenge for Trade Unions' in Callaghan (1990) op. cit.

Coote A (Ed)(1992) *The Welfare of Citizens: Developing new social rights*, London, Rivers Oram Press

Croft S and Beresford P (1990), *From Paternalism to Participation: Involving People in Social Services*, London, Open Services Project.

Department of Health (1991), *Moving Forward - Needs, Services and Contracts*, NHS Management Executive.

Doyal L and Gough I (1991), *A Theory of Human Need*, MacMillan.

Gaster L (1991), *Quality at the Front Line*, School for Advanced Urban Studies, Bristol.

Griffiths H (1990), 'Community Resource Development; A strategy for the 1990s' *Policy Studies*, Autumn, Vol 11 (3).

Habermas J (1970), *Towards a Rational Society*, Beacon Press, Boston.

Halliday M (1991), *Our City, Our Health, Ideas for Improving Public Health in Sheffield*, Healthy Sheffield Planning Team.

Hambleton R (1988), 'Consumerism, Decentralization and Local Democracy', *Public Administration*, Vol 66, No 2, p 125-47

HMSO (1991), *The Citizen's Charter: Raising the Standard*, CM 1599.

Hoggett P (1991), 'A New Management in the Public Sector?', *Policy and Politics*, Vol 19, No 4 p 243-56

Hoggett P and Hambleton R (1987), *Decentralisation and Democracy - Localising Public Services*, Occasional Paper No 28, SAUS, University of Bristol

Hudson B (1991), 'Thrown Back Into Troubled Waters', *The Health Service Journal*, 30 May p 24-5.

Leeds City Council (1987), *Health in Leeds*, 1987, Health Unit, Leeds City Counil.

Leeds City Council (1991), *Leeds Mental Handicap Planning Register; Project Report:12*, Department of Social Services, Leeds City Council.

Leeds Eastern Health Authority (undated), *Better Services for People in Leeds with a Mental Handicap: Strategic Plan 1987-88 to 1995-96*, Leeds Eastern and Western Health Authorities with Leeds City Council

Maslow A (1943), 'A Theory of Human Motivation', *Psychological Review*, Vol 50, p 370-96.

Moore SRW (1989), *Health in Western Leeds, The Report of the Director of Public Health*, Leeds West Health Authority.

National Housing Forum (1989), *Housing Needs in the 1990s: an Interim Assessment*, National Federation of Housing Associations.

Percy-Smith J (1992), 'Auditing Social Needs', *Policy and Politics* Vol 20, no1, p29-34,

Pfeffer N and Coote A (1991), *Is Quality Good for You?*, Social Policy Paper 5, IPPR.

Sanderson I (Ed) (1992 forthcoming), *Management of Quality in Local Government*, Longman.

Stewart J (1984), 'The Role of Information in Public Accountability', in A Hopwood and C Tomkins (Ed) *Issues in Public Sector Accounting*, Philip Alan.

Stewart J and Clarke M (1987), 'The Public Service Orientation - Issues and Dilemmas', *Public Administration*, Vol 65, No 2.

University of Newcastle-upon-Tyne (1991), *Walker Riverside Study*, Department of Social Policy.

Wain EA and Moore SRW (1990), *Health in Leeds 1990*, The Report of the Directors of Public Health.

Walker A (1991), 'No Gain Without Pain', *Community Care*, 18 July.

Walsh K (1991), 'Quality and Public Services', *Public Administration*, Vol 69, No4, p503-14.

Webb A (1991), 'Coordination - A Problem in Public Sector Management', *Policy and Politics*, Vol 19, No 4 p229-41.

NEHRU

A Political Biography

MICHAEL BRECHER

Abridged Edition

LONDON
OXFORD UNIVERSITY PRESS
NEW YORK   BOMBAY   TORONTO

Oxford University Press, Ely House, London W. 1

GLASGOW NEW YORK TORONTO MELBOURNE WELLINGTON
CAPE TOWN SALISBURY IBADAN NAIROBI LUSAKA ADDIS ABABA
BOMBAY CALCUTTA MADRAS KARACHI LAHORE DACCA
KUALA LUMPUR SINGAPORE HONG KONG TOKYO

© Oxford University Press 1959

First edition June 1959
Reprinted November 1959 *and* 1960
This abridged edition first published in OXFORD PAPERBACKS 1961
Reprinted 1968 *and* 1969

PRINTED LITHOGRAPHICALLY IN GREAT BRITAIN
AT THE PITMAN PRESS, BATH

To my
Father and Mother

FROM THE PREFACE TO THE FIRST
EDITION

Time moves swiftly in contemporary Asia. At the turn of the century Western Powers held sway almost without challenge. Since then new ideas and forces have come to the surface, inducing change among the ancient peoples of the area. The result has been the still-unfinished Asian Revolution, worthy of study not only for its human interest but also because it has shattered the traditional relations between Asia and the West. The present work is, in part, an attempt to view that revolution in its Indian setting. The story is many-sided and complex. Many persons played a notable role. But only one, Jawaharlal Nehru, links the years of promise and fulfilment, of nationalist agitation and national construction. Indeed, the life of Nehru is admirably suited to serve as the binding thread in an account of recent Indian history and politics. Hence, I have employed the technique of biography to shed light on political events, ideas, and movements. At the same time I have used the Indian revolution as the background for a study of Nehru the man and the statesman. The book is, then, both a biographical history and a political biography. The approach is chronological and topical, covering the period from the 1880's to the summer of 1958 and ranging widely over the panorama of Indian politics.

A biography of a living statesman can never be entirely satisfactory. Some of the source materials are not available, some major themes in the plot remain incomplete, and one's judgements do not have the benefit of perspective. Yet there are compensations: the opportunity to talk at leisure with men who have lived through and have helped to shape the events analysed in this book, especially important because Indians, for the most part, are reluctant to write memoirs; the opportunity to capture the spirit of a society in motion and of the man about whom one is writing; and the possibility of breaking new ground.

If this book provides some clues to the tortuous course of recent Indian history and politics it will have served one major purpose. If it succeeds, at least in small measure, in making Nehru more intelligible to his admirers and critics alike, it will have served another. If it provides some insight into the role of the outstanding individual in history, it will have accomplished a third goal. Finally, I hope that it may contribute to the understanding of the state of mind among 'the uncommitted billion'. I leave the final verdict on Nehru to the historians. My concern is with the living, with the actions of statesmen when and as they take place, and with their implications.

Many have contributed to the making of this book. The Nuffield Foundation made possible the basic research by the award of a Travelling Fellowship which enabled me to spend the academic year 1955–6 in England and India. McGill University kindly granted a year's leave of absence and the McGill Research Committee assisted me to return briefly to India at the beginning of 1958. The Canadian Social Science Research Council was generous in its support of this return visit to complete my research.

Friends and colleagues were generous with their time and advice. One in particular, who regrettably seeks anonymity, read the entire manuscript with great care and expert knowledge and provided invaluable comments at every stage of the work. Although his views were not always accepted, they compelled me to rethink my interpretations. The bulk of an earlier draft was also read, with much benefit to the author, by Mark Gayn and by Freda and B. P. L. Bedi of New Delhi. Specific chapters have undergone the careful scrutiny of my colleagues, Professors Irving Brecher, Keith Callard, and Saul Frankel, and of Professor Richard L. Park of the University of California. To many friends on three continents I owe a debt for their sympathetic interest in the book during the past four years.

Most of all, I owe a profound debt of gratitude to my wife. She cheerfully undertook a year of travel to far-off lands with two small children under the most trying conditions. At every stage she was a source of inspiration and encouragement. She read and re-read the manuscript with a critical eye, constantly forcing me to present my ideas clearly and to reassess my conclusions. Patient and determined, she was a devoted companion on the long voyage of discovering Nehru and India. As on an earlier venture in scholarship, her contributions to this book were greater than even she realizes.

MICHAEL BRECHER

McGill University
Montreal
November 1958

CONTENTS

MAPS

CHAPTER I

PORTRAIT OF THE MAN

Nature and circumstance were kind to Jawaharlal Nehru. He was born into the Kashmiri Brahmin community, one of the most aristocratic sub-castes in the Hindu social system. His father was a distinguished and wealthy barrister, modern, urbane, highly cultivated and lavishly generous. As an only son—and the only child for eleven years—Jawaharlal was the focus of concentrated affection. He had, too, the leisure and learning of an English aristocrat in the secure atmosphere of the Edwardian Age—private tutors, Harrow, Cambridge and the Inner Temple. When he was drawn to the political arena soon after his return to India, his path was eased by the guidance and support of his father and Gandhi. Prime Minister Nehru recalled this head-start in a modest portrait of his past seen forty years later. 'My growth to public prominence, you know, was not by sharp stages. It was, rather, a steady development over a long period of time. And if I may say so,' he added dryly, 'I began at a fairly high level.'[1]

Nehru was also favoured with a strikingly handsome appearance, both by Indian and Western standards. Pictures of him at the age of twenty or sixty reveal the slim, chiselled features which stamp the Kashmiri Brahmin. The later ones reveal much more: expressive eyes, sometimes pensive or sharp with irritation or gay and self-satisfied and, at other times, intent and alight with resolve; the high, full temples suggestive of two of Nehru's outstanding qualities—stubbornness and intellectual curiosity; the wide mouth and sensuous lips which pout shamelessly during moments of ill-temper; the soft-moulded chin; and the long, delicate fingers. His smile is captivating, at times disarming. His face is oval-shaped and his profile classic Greek, making Nehru one of the most photogenic

[1] To the author in New Delhi on 30 January 1958.

statesmen of the century. He exudes the magnetic charm which has swiftly won individuals and crowds alike. Although he lacks the emphasis of height—he is about 5 ft. 8 in.—his straight back and good posture express the vigour and youthfulness for which he was justly famous. With years the lines of age have begun to score his face. Nevertheless, he remains an unusually attractive man.

The benefits of aristocratic background and education were not without price. Security was accompanied by an overweening paternalism and a tendency to depend on strong, decisive and older men. Indeed, it was not until his early sixties that Nehru emerged completely from the shadow of his father and Gandhi, the two men who exercised the greatest influence on his character. The legacy of that habit is still visible. In part, his indecisiveness is due to the intellectual in Nehru who sees all points of view and therefore hesitates to act boldly. But in large measure it must be traced to the circumstances in which his character was moulded.

Other elements in his background helped to shape the character of Jawaharlal Nehru. Alone among Indian nationalist leaders of his generation he was a true aristocrat. He remains a Brahmin with everything that this status connotes.

His education in the West marked him in other ways. For one thing, it set him apart from his colleagues in the Indian National Congress, a solitary figure in a middle-class, traditional-minded General Staff, guiding a petty-bourgeois and peasant army. Nehru's approach to strategy and tactics revealed the Western rationalist. This explained, in part, the constant struggle as he fought to reconcile his own conception of the right line of action with that of Gandhi, notably in the methods of pursuing civil disobedience. In a wider sense it made Nehru alien in his own society, a Hindu out of tune with Hinduism, 'a queer mixture of the East and the West, out of place everywhere, at home no-where'.[1] His was merely an extreme case in a whole class of young, Westernized intellectuals. But as the first to achieve prominence he carried a heavy burden of adjustment.

From his father Nehru acquired an intense pride, the root of his resentment against British rule—for his initial response to politics

---

[1] Nehru, J., *Toward Freedom: The Autobiography of Jawaharlal Nehru* (John Day, 1942), p. 353. Unless otherwise indicated, all subsequent references to the autobiography are taken from this edition.

was emotional, not intellectual. Like Motilal Nehru, too, he is quick to anger, but his outbursts are usually short-lived. They are the reaction of an over-sensitive man to anything which violates his high standards of integrity. Nehru is a perfectionist, which compounds the sources of irritation with people and things about him.

The Indian leader is a most affable and charming man. He is also inclined to aloofness, in private affairs. His early life in Allahabad strengthened a natural reticence and so did a British public-school education. Nehru himself underlined this element in his make-up in a letter to an Indian friend: 'Yes, we did not discuss personal matters. You ought to know me sufficiently to realize that I never discuss them unless the other party takes the initiative. I would not do so even with Kamala [his wife] or Indu [his daughter]. Such has been my training.'[1] So it continues down to the present day.

This trait should not be construed as mistrust or indifference to the welfare of others. On the contrary, Nehru is sustained in trial by a strong faith in man. Moreover, colleagues, friends, and subordinates speak in glowing terms of his kindness and consideration, in matters vital and trivial. According to one official who has worked closely with the Indian Prime Minister for some years, 'Nehru is not a demonstrative person; in that respect he is very much the English public school type. He will never tell you that he appreciates your work but he shows his affection and kindheartedness in indirect ways.' Prestige and power have not hardened him or made him neglect those little acts of kindness for which he was well known in pre-Independence days.

Nehru's natural reserve makes him feel uneasy in the company of a few, detached, almost withdrawn from those about him. An intangible but very real barrier seems to assert itself. But not so in the presence of a crowd. There his personality is transformed. He becomes alive, relaxed, uninhibited, as if infused with the collective energy of the group. He never loses himself completely, for the aristocrat in his make-up prevents a complete fusion with the mass. He is in the crowd but never of it, stimulated but not absorbed.

For thirty years he has been the idol of the Indian masses, second only to Gandhi. They literally adore him. From distant villages they come in thousands to hear him, more to see him, to

[1] To Dr. Syed Mahmud, 24 November 1933. Unpublished Nehru-Mahmud Correspondence.

have a *darshan* (communion) with their beloved 'Panditji', successor to the Mahatma, champion of the oppressed, symbol of the new India of their vague dreams. They may not understand everything he says, but no matter. He has come to talk to them, to inspire them and to make them forget, even for a little while, their misery and their problems. And he, in turn, feels a bond with the masses. They are not simply the clay with which to fashion a new society, his primary goal since Independence. Their simplicity and credulity and belief in him draw him out from the shell of reticence which normally encases his personality in the city. Their faith touches his vanity, giving him a sense of power—power to alter the grim poverty which they have always known. But most of all they provide him with an inexhaustible source of energy.

Remarkable indeed is the mutual impact of Nehru and the crowd. They seem to transmit waves of energy to him. The larger the audience the more exhilarated he feels, the more determined he becomes to persevere in the face of great odds. By periodic tours and almost daily speeches before crowds, large and small, his storehouse of energy is constantly replenished, not depleted. He, in turn, transmits his buoyant enthusiasm and irrepressible optimism to the masses, maintaining the precarious 'hope level' which enables them to press ahead in the long, difficult task of improving their way of life.

No one has recognized this unusual emotional link between Nehru and the masses better than the Prime Minister himself. 'Delhi is a static city with a dead atmosphere,' he has often remarked. 'I go out and see masses of people, my people, your people, and derive inspiration from them. There is something dynamic and something growing with them and I grow with them. I also enthuse with them.'[1]

*   *   *   *

Some personal insight into this and other aspects of Nehru's character emerged from my tour with the Indian Prime Minister in the spring of 1956. It was pleasantly cool when I drove through the deserted streets of the capital towards Palam Airport. Nehru was late in arriving, just a few minutes; but even this is a rare

[1] To a conference of irrigation and power engineers in New Delhi, 17 November 1952. *Indian Express* (Bombay), 18 November 1952.

occurrence, for the Indian leader has a typically Western mania for punctuality. As one colleague of very long standing remarked, 'he insists that his programme at all times be orderly, with precise arrangements for every function and appointment. Nehru is not averse to relaxation and leisure, but these too must be fitted into an orderly schedule. He must fill his day with purposeful activity. By comparison, however, Gandhi was a much more ruthless disciplinarian.'

After brief, formal introductions, we boarded the luxurious Viscount and headed south to Hyderabad City on the first lap of our journey. A very small party accompanied the Prime Minister from Delhi, the faithful Hari who had been adopted by Motilal Nehru more than fifty years ago and has served as the 'young Nehru's' devoted valet since the early 1930's.

The flight was swift and uneventful. Nehru withdrew immediately to the private compartment which serves as bedroom, sitting-room and office during his travels within India and abroad. There he passes the time in one of three ways: dictating letters, minutes and memoranda; reading official files or a book which has lain by his bed in Delhi, neglected for want of time; or resting his weary mind and body. On this occasion he slept throughout the two-hour flight which followed a week of conferences with the American, French and British Foreign Ministers who had descended upon the capital in rapid succession. His penchant for sleep while travelling is well known.

Presently we found ourselves at Begumpet Airport on the outskirts of Hyderabad City where the local élite had gathered to pay their respects to the uncrowned king of the Indian Republic. After the usual garlanding ceremony, with the ubiquitous photographers surrounding the Prime Minister like ants, we were herded into a caravan of old American cars for the short trip to the railway station. As his open car approached the entrance a mighty roar went up, 'Pandit Nehru ki jai, Pandit Nehru ki jai' ('Hail Pandit Nehru, Hail Pandit Nehru'). Here was genuine affection for India's first citizen. Being accustomed to this adulation for the past thirty years, Nehru took it in his stride, smiling to the crowd and reciprocating their warm greeting with the traditional *namaste* salutation—holding his hands together palm to palm and moving them towards his forehead.

There was further evidence of this hero-worship. At one village

10,000 had gathered to greet the Prime Minister. As our caravan rounded the bend they broke into a frenzied run towards the opposite side in order to get another look at him. The race for a *darshan* was like an instinctive, compelling drive, a craving for association with an exalted man, however brief. Throughout the journey there was a mumble among the crowds which was translated for my benefit. 'We saw him, we saw him', they were saying in ecstasy to their families. In the evening, on the return journey, the road was again lined with people. There was not the slightest possibility of seeing Nehru, for he was in a closed car travelling at fifty miles per hour in the dark. Yet they stood patiently to see the car go by. And frequently there arose the cry, 'Pandit Nehru ki jai'.

Watching this scene and others like it in the next few days recalled some passages in a 'portrait of Nehru' which was published anonymously in 1937:

Jawaharlal ki jai! [Hail Jawaharlal!] The Rashtrapati [President] looked up as he passed swiftly through the waiting crowds; his hands went up, and his pale, hard face was lit up with a smile. . . . The smile passed away and the face became stern and sad. Almost it seemed that the smile and the gesture accompanying it had little reality; . . . Steadily and persistently he goes on increasing his personal prestige and influence. . . . From the Far North to Cape Comorin he has gone like some triumphant Caesar, leaving a trail of glory and a legend behind him. Is all this just a passing fancy which amuses him . . . or is it his will to power that is driving him from crowd to crowd. . . . What if the fancy turns? Men like Jawaharlal, with all their capacity for great and good work, are unsafe in a democracy. He calls himself a democrat and a socialist, and no doubt he does so in all earnestness . . . but a little twist and he might turn into a dictator. . . . Jawaharlal cannot become a fascist. . . . He is too much an aristocrat for the crudity and vulgarity of fascism. His very face and voice tell us that. . . . And yet he has all the makings of a dictator in him—vast popularity, a strong will, energy, pride . . . and with all his love of the crowd, an intolerance of others and a certain contempt for the weak and inefficient. His flashes of temper are well known. His overwhelming desire to get things done, to sweep away what he dislikes and build anew, will hardly brook for long the slow processes of democracy. . . . His conceit is already formidable. It must be checked. We want no Caesars.

The purpose of this critique was to persuade the Indian National Congress not to re-elect Nehru as President for a third successive term. The author—Jawaharlal Nehru.[1]

[1] This article first appeared as 'The Rashtrapati' by 'Chanakya' in *The Modern Review* (Calcutta), vol. 62, November 1937, pp. 546–7. The quoted passages are taken from excerpts which were reprinted in *Toward Freedom*, Appendix E, pp. 436–7.

Most of the qualities mentioned in this remarkable self-analysis are still with Nehru: his command of the crowd; the actor's finesse in the centre of the stage; popularity; prestige; influence; impatience, and the like. Some have been tempered by time and experience, notably anger and intolerance of others' failings. Perhaps the most important trait suggested in his self-portrait has been belied by Nehru's own actions since Independence. He still possesses 'the makings of a dictator' but he is no Caesar. Jawaharlal *is* safe in a democracy. In fact, the Indian experiment in constitutional democracy owes more to Nehru than to anyone else or to any combination of factors. Few men with his talents could have resisted the inducements to exercise dictatorial powers. Some frustrated Indians regret his reluctance to do so.

Lunch was an informal affair in the Prime Minister's 'private car', very modest by any standards. Unlike Gandhi, Nehru has no fads regarding food. Typically, he partakes of both Indian and European dishes, with a preference for the latter, particularly English cuisine. His tastes were spelled out in an official note from his Delhi office in an effort to reduce the ostentation which greeted him everywhere in the land: 'The Prime Minister is anxious that no special and out-of-the-way arrangements might be made for his meals. He would like to have the normal food of the place he visits. The only thing that might be remembered is that he likes as simple food as possible, whether Indian or after the European style, and that he is not used to spices and chillies at all. While he eats meat, he does so sparingly and has far more vegetables. He likes a full vegetarian meal. . . . Normally he takes coffee with hot milk in the morning and a cup of weak tea in the afternoon.'[1]

After lunch Nehru retired for a brief nap. At that point one member of the group suggested a change in the itinerary so as to reduce the Prime Minister's discomfort. It was absurdly simple—to spend more time on the train the following day in order to shorten the dusty journey by car to the rendezvous with Vinoba Bhave, the *Bhoodan* leader, in a remote village. Anywhere else in the world the staff would have done this without consulting the Prime Minister—but not in India. For half an hour the pros and cons were weighed with due solemnity. Finally the great decision was made—to let sleeping dogs lie, even though the change would

[1] Issued on 18 June 1956. A copy was made available to the author by a member of the Prime Minister's Secretariat.

have been wiser. The reason: 'He has already seen the itinerary and might become irritated by any change.'

At last we arrived in Nizamabad for the conference of the *Bharat Sevak Samaj* (National Service Organization). Ostensibly this was the primary purpose of the tour, though the meeting with Vinoba was far more important.

Nehru spoke twice in the afternoon. He was in excellent form, speaking in his typical conversational manner. As he came forward to address the delegates he was surrounded by photographers. He was patient for a few moments but then waved them aside with annoyance. The following day he demonstrated his quick and sometimes petulant temper more emphatically. Emerging from the private conclave with Vinoba he was approached indirectly for a statement to the press. 'I won't be bullied by these people. Who do they think they are? Who asked them to come?' Then, after a brief pause, 'What do they want anyway?'

The highlight of his speech to the delegates was a derisive reference to the *sadhus* (Hindu holy men) who were trying to curry favour by mobilizing their ranks for 'national service'. Nehru remarked at one point that there were 50 lakhs (hundred thousands) of *sadhus* in 1931 and 78 lakhs at present. A prominent *sadhu*, sitting on the dais, interjected that there were only 10 lakhs now. 'What happened to the rest of them?' the Prime Minister asked. 'Did they go to Pakistan?' The audience roared with laughter and Nehru himself joined in, slapping his knee in delight.

The scene then shifted to the huge throng of peasants who had trudged from surrounding villages for a *darshan* with 'Panditji'. There they sat, passive and quiet, stretched out as far as the eye could see. They had assembled early in the morning and had waited patiently for six hours or more in the burning heat—it was well over 100 degrees. They were not disappointed, for Nehru communicated his sympathy with their problems. Even though they could not understand his language—he spoke in Hindustani and his words were translated into Telugu—they watched him intently, as if transfixed by his presence.

To observe Nehru talking *with* his people makes it possible to penetrate the intangibles of his popularity. There he stands in his typical pose, bent slightly forward as he surveys the audience, his hands now resting on the podium, now gripping the microphone, sometimes folded behind him, with a crumpled handkerchief tucked up his right shirt sleeve. He is no natural orator and rises to great heights only on rare occasions, such as on Independence Day and the death of Gandhi. His voice is soft and relaxed. He does not rouse his listeners by thundering pronouncements. He talks to them like a teacher to his pupils, showing them the errors of their ways, pointing out the proper path of conduct, stressing the need for discipline, hard work, unity, tolerance and faith, drawing on the inspiration of Gandhi and the freedom struggle, painting a picture of the India of the future, pledging himself to their welfare, calling for rededication to the cause of a good society.

Candour and spontaneity are the outstanding qualities of his speech. He talks as he thinks and feels at the moment. His words flow as in a stream of consciousness and therefore into endless side channels. He comes to his main points very slowly and indirectly, his words reflecting the variety of thoughts and emotions which filter through his mind as he speaks. The result is a rambling, ver-bose, repetitive and, very often, woolly speech, especially in the last few years. This is inevitable because of the mode of his public speaking. Nehru's habit of thinking aloud about all manner of subjects is not confined to the village crowd. Whether it be in Parliament or to a party gathering, before a group of sophisticated intellectuals or university students, among foreign visitors or even at a press conference, his approach remains the same. His speeches, then, provide insight into his way of thinking as well as into what he is thinking.

Nehru speaks in public more frequently than any statesman of the age. And the vast majority of his speeches are extemporaneous. Until the early 'forties his important speeches were thoroughly prepared and were models of clarity, such as his presidential addresses to the Congress in 1929, 1936 and 1937. Later, however, the pressure of time, and the practice of almost daily speeches, made spontaneity inescapable.

Some persons decry the free flow of ideas and the endless number of Nehru's speeches. There can be no doubt that they would benefit from greater organization and clarity. But this would require a marked reduction in his public appearances. And this he is reluctant to make. One reason is that in a pre-dominantly illiterate society the spoken word is the most effective means of communication between the governors and the governed.

Another is the legacy of the pre-Independence period when Gandhi and Nehru created a personal bond with the Indian people by incessant tours of the countryside. Moreover, Nehru feels strongly that only in this manner can he continue to feel the pulse of the common man. By constantly appearing before different segments of society he also acts as a great unifying force. Finally, as suggested earlier, he needs the crowd, perhaps no less than they need him.

The tour also revealed Nehru's penchant for reading. Books were a constant companion on his travels before Independence. It was comforting to have them, he used to say, even if he could not read them all. The habit and his strong attachment continue.

On this occasion he was absorbed by Dr. Oppenheimer's *Science and the Common Understanding*. The literature of science is, indeed, his favourite reading—almost a passion with him. In part this may be traced to his education at Cambridge, as indicated in a chance remark over lunch: 'Where I differ from Indian Socialists is that I have a scientific background and am more aware of the impact of science on social evolution.' Over the years he has acquired little interest in fiction. But he is still a great admirer of English poetry, especially of Keats. 'He constantly talks about the lack of time for good reading; in fact he bemoans it,' remarked a member of his staff. This has been part of the price of power and responsibility. Yet he continues to find time almost daily for a half-hour or more before he retires and while travelling.

Despite the arduous road journey the Prime Minister showed no signs of fatigue. Throughout the tour, in fact, he demonstrated a youthful vigour which seemed astonishing for a man in his mid-sixties. Indeed, Nehru's daily routine is such that few men twenty years his junior could stand the strain.

*　　*　　*　　*

During the winter months he rises at 6.30 in the morning (in the summer half an hour earlier). The next hour is devoted to a glance at the Delhi press and to yoga exercises. The habit of daily exercise dates to the 1920's, and Nehru retains the firm belief that it is essential to his physical health. Only under severe pressure of work does he forgo the pleasure of standing on his head. Among other benefits, he has remarked, one cannot take problems too seriously from that position.

By 7.30 he is ready to meet the formidable challenge of a typical day. It begins with half an hour in his private study reading cables that arrived during the night and signing papers and letters dictated the previous evening. So heavy is his correspondence and comments on sundry matters of state that typists work around the clock to keep up with the flow of words.

Breakfast generally takes no more than fifteen minutes, for Nehru does not believe in tarrying over meals. Usually it is of the typical Western variety—with fruit juice, cereal, eggs, toast and coffee. His daughter, Indira, who lives at the Prime Minister's Residence, is almost always present, along with her two sons when they are on holiday from school. Frequently there are guests, persons whom Nehru feels he must see but whom he cannot fit into his schedule for the day. For the most part they are friends and political colleagues, occasionally foreigners seeking an interview or acquaintances revisiting India.

From his living-quarters he descends to the office on the ground floor at about 8.15. There are always people to see him, 'gate-crashers' who try to catch him before he leaves the Residence. They may be peasants with grievances, politicians with requests or just sightseers. Sometimes they take fifteen minutes, sometimes less. Then he pays a brief visit to his four pet pandas, exquisite-looking Himalayan cat-bears which are kept in a specially constructed cage behind the Residence, surrounded by the lovely pleasure-gardens which add lustre to the estate.

By 9 o'clock he is at his desk in the Ministry of External Affairs, located in the South Block of Delhi's reddish-sandstone Secretariat. With the President's House (*Rashtrapati Bhawan*) in the background these government buildings are an impressive but dull sight, a legacy of the British *Raj*. They stand in splendour at the head of Kingsway (*Rajpath*) which leads down to the war memorial of India Gate.

When Parliament is not in session Nehru remains at his office in External Affairs throughout the day, i.e. from 9 until 1.30 and, after lunch, from about 2.45 until 6.30 or 7. There he receives diplomats, visiting dignitaries, Cabinet colleagues and party workers in a seemingly endless flow. There he pores over a mountain of files and deals with many matters requiring immediate decision, either domestic or foreign. Interviews and paper work are co-ordinated. Appointments are fixed on the half-hour; many of them, however, are brief courtesy calls, and others frequently do not occupy the allotted time. Between appointments Nehru dictates to stenographers who are constantly at his beck and call. This, indeed, is the key to his formidable pace of work. Moreover, Nehru takes notes while persons are talking with him so that he can take action immediately following the interview.

During parliamentary sessions the pattern of work remains essentially the same, but the physical locale shifts from the Secretariat to the Prime Minister's office in the parliament building a few minutes away by automobile. The legislature convenes at 11 a.m. If it is a question hour he remains in the House until noon; if an unimportant matter is on the floor, he leaves after fifteen minutes or a half-hour; during a key debate, especially on foreign affairs, he stays on until its conclusion. For the remainder of the day he conducts affairs from his office on the second floor of Parliament. Here, the routine of file-reading, conferences, interviews and dictation is repeated. Because of the pressure of time during the session, Cabinet meetings, party conclaves and the like are held before 11 in the morning or at his home in the evening.

When he returns to the Residence at 6.30 or 7 in the evening more appointments are waiting. Normally, they are fixed at quarter-hour intervals and continue until 8.30; between interviews he takes up the broken thread of dictation. Dinner varies from the purely informal family gathering—a rare occurrence—to the formal state banquet in honour of a distinguished guest. Colleagues or diplomats whom he could not see during the crowded day are frequently invited to dinner at the Residence. On these occasions he will remain a full hour or more; at state functions he is usually engaged until about 10.30 in the evening. In either event he returns to his desk at home and carries on with affairs of state until midnight or later. Previous to 1957 he continued until 1 or 1.30 and then read until 2 a.m. Since that time, however, he has reduced the normal daily workload one hour at night. This concession was made in response to persistent pleas of family and friends to conserve his energy for the years ahead.

Such has been the normal routine of Jawaharlal Nehru since Independence. There are, of course, frequent public appearances in Delhi. And while on tour the schedule is of necessity more flexible. Nevertheless, the workload is not fundamentally different. The average workday is about seventeen hours, with about five hours' sleep and, in the summer months, a half-hour rest after lunch. This routine applies throughout the year.

Not that Nehru is averse to holidays. Before Independence he loved to wander in the hills and valleys of Kashmir or in the Kulu valley of the Punjab or in the isolated splendour of the Himalayas viewed from the hill stations of the United Provinces. But the demands of public office have pressed him forward relentlessly. Even when in the hills he does not rest; there are speeches to the local population, inauguration ceremonies, correspondence and party gatherings.

This pace would have felled most men somewhere along the road. Certainly, few statesmen pursue their work with such un-remitting vigour. What makes it possible is Nehru's storehouse of energy and the benefits of excellent health. 'I have always attached importance to bodily health and physical fitness', he wrote from prison in the early 'thirties.[1] This is not surprising in the light of family experience. During his formative years at home his mother was fragile and sickly, indeed, a semi-invalid throughout her adult life. Later he saw his wife struggle in vain against the ravages of tuberculosis. And his only child, Indira, has never enjoyed robust health. Hence, Nehru's concern became a veritable compulsion, a stimulus to guard against severe illness. His devotion to yoga exercises is a continuing reflection of this concern.

In this ceaseless preventive battle he has been very successful. Nature was kind, endowing him with a resilient and powerful constitution able to cope with the privations of long years in prison. His only known serious illnesses were a severe bout of typhoid in 1923 and a brief attack of pleurisy in prison during the spring of 1934. Since Independence Nehru has rarely been compelled to cancel an engagement because of indisposition. The odd cold, fatigue and an occasional bout of fever have been the extent of his sickness. It is this bountiful good health which enables him to maintain his furious pace of activity.

What makes it necessary lies more in the realm of speculation. The heart of the matter would appear to be Nehru's temperament: he is a man who feels compelled to do things himself. This was true during the struggle for independence when, by his own admission,

[1] 'Prison-Land' in *Recent Essays and Writings*, p. 88.

Nehru as Congress President also 'functioned often as a secretary or a glorified clerk'.[1] This has also been true of Nehru as Prime Minister. His attention to trivia is startling for a man in his position. He continues to act as Congress draftsman. He also insists on handling his vast correspondence direct. And on the minutest affairs of party and government he must be informed. It is not because he desires to occupy the centre of the stage at all times, though his vanity is ill-concealed. Rather, his enthusiasm and curiosity get the better of him.

Much more than temperament, however, is responsible for Nehru's all-embracing direction of affairs. For one thing, he is acutely conscious of his place in history and is driven to act in all spheres. For another, the disappointments of the 'thirties led him to believe that 'one must journey through life alone; to rely on others is to invite heartbreak'.[2] Moreover, Nehru is essentially a Westerner in his intellectual make-up, and an impatient one at that. He becomes easily annoyed at evidence of inefficiency or an unruly audience and feels constrained to put things right. Lack of order and organization irritate him, as does the Indian indifference to time.

Even if he were not inclined to act at every level, objective circumstance would impose similar pressures. The sense of dependence on Nehru since 1947 is no less than was that of Nehru and others on Gandhi during the freedom struggle. This is due partly to the authoritarian tradition of India, partly to Nehru's status as Gandhi's successor, and partly to his towering position among his colleagues—especially since the death of Sardar Patel in 1950.

Nehru has many positions of responsibility in the Government and the Congress. Since 1947 he has been Prime Minister and Foreign Minister of India, as well as Head of the Atomic Energy Department; since 1950 he has also served as Chairman of the Planning Commission. From 1951 to 1954 he held the post of Congress President as well; and throughout the period he has served on the party's Working Committee. On various occasions, too, he has filled a gap created by the death or resignation of a Cabinet colleague; he held the Defence portfolio in 1953, and the Finance post in 1956 and 1958.

[1] Letter to Subhas Bose, 3 April 1939. Unpublished Nehru Letters.
[2] *Toward Freedom*, p. 312.

As Prime Minister, Nehru is more the 'giant among pygmies' than 'first among equals'. He is also the last hero of the freedom struggle, the visible link with Gandhi and the national movement. For the Congress, now in decline, he separates the party from electoral defeat. And to the masses it is he who offers the promise of a higher standard of living (except for twelve million who voted Communist in 1957).

THE SHOW MUST GO ON

R. K. Laxman: *The Times of India* 27.7.1956

The cumulative effect has been to place Nehru on a pedestal, to rely on him for guidance, direction and decision. Colleagues and subordinates feel the necessity of consulting him on a host of issues which should never reach the desk of a Prime Minister, partly because they do not want to risk incurring his displeasure, partly because he has set the pattern by involving himself in matters beyond his normal jurisdiction, and partly because it is obviously easier to let 'Panditji' himself bear the responsibility. Members of the Congress High Command have been in the habit of consulting

Nehru for thirty years or more; it is comforting to have his advice today as well.

*   *   *   *

The tenth year of Independence, 1956–7, was, in many respects, a turning-point in the life of Nehru. It was a year of turmoil following a period of relative calm, a year of continuous crisis which tried his faith as no other time since the aftermath of Partition. A few months earlier had come the storm of States Reorganization which undermined the foundations of Indian unity —riots in Central India and Orissa, violence and bloodshed in Bombay, tension between Sikh and Hindu in the Punjab, threats and squabbling over the Bengal-Bihar border area. For Nehru it was a bitter personal blow. How often had he preached the virtues of unity to his people. Yet at the first severe test they had failed him.

Amidst the outburst of regional and communal passions came the Hungarian uprising and the spectacle of Soviet repression. This, too, was an event for which he was unprepared. Had not the Russians loudly trumpeted their support for non-intervention and the *Panch Shila* (Five Principles) during the tumultuous reception accorded him in Moscow only sixteen months earlier? How could they violate their pledge with such impunity? At first the lack of direct knowledge and Soviet flattery inclined him to disbelieve Western reports of Russian perfidy and ruthlessness. But as the evidence accumulated he moved towards a mild censure of Soviet actions, reluctantly it appeared. His performance during this tragic affair disappointed many persons, both within India and abroad.

The decline of faith in Soviet sincerity was coupled with a mixture of anger and sadness as the Anglo-French assault on Suez unfolded. Was this not a symbol of Western Imperialism reborn? Was this the behaviour to be expected from the leader of a commonwealth which India had joined as an independent state? The deep wounds of the past, which had healed so slowly, were now reopened by what he considered to be a dastardly act against a weak, non-white people asserting its rights. Yet along with this disappointment came a more friendly attitude to the United States which censured its allies and seemed to champion the Egyptian cause.

A few months later the Indian general elections brought new sources of anxiety. The Congress was returned to power at the Centre and in all but one of the States. The results, however, were not entirely reassuring. The Communists had come to power in Kerala through the ballot box. They also showed signs of strength in the country as a whole. Even more disquieting was the evidence of how deep was the rot which had penetrated the once-mighty Congress. What would happen to the experiment in constitutional government once Nehru passed from the scene? The future looked bleak as he surveyed the results of the 1957 elections.

There was little time to ponder the significance of the elections. Suddenly, it appeared, India was confronted with a twofold economic crisis. On the one hand, floods and drought had played havoc with food production, causing serious hardship in many parts of the country. At the same time, large imports helped to cause a grave shortage of foreign exchange—precisely at a time of need for industrial development projects. Only two years earlier India appeared to have almost reached self-sufficiency in food, a pre-condition to economic progress. And only one year before, the Second Five Year Plan had been launched with high hopes of success. Now the Plan was in jeopardy unless the sum of $1·4 billion could be raised abroad as loans or gifts. The spectre of failure on the vital economic front began to haunt Indian minds. Even if the short-term financial problem were solved, the crisis indicated how steep and rocky was the road to economic development. Thus, as India moved into the second decade of independence Nehru had ample reason for concern.

The effect of these crises on the Prime Minister was profound. His buoyant spirit and vivid enthusiasm have been less in evidence since 1956. They have largely given way to a more sober appreciation of the facts of Indian and international life. It is as if Nehru discovered India afresh, not in a romantic setting but in all its harsh realities. With this rediscovery there came deeper insight, a greater awareness of the intractable nature of certain problems.

The 'new' Jawaharlal is less confident about the future, less exuberant and less temperamental than the 'old'. He has mellowed a great deal. He is inclined to be more patient with colleagues and subordinates, and more tolerant of human failings. An air of almost philosophic calm appears to have descended upon the mercurial Indian leader. The spark is not yet gone. Given the right stimulus, he can still respond pungently; but on the whole he is more restrained.

Nehru is not a defeated man. Rather, he is wiser, less quick to anger and more balanced in his attitude to men and affairs. More particularly, he appears to have fewer illusions about the Soviet Union and greater regard for the United States, partly because of the Hungarian tragedy and Suez War, and partly because of his unexpectedly warm reception in America and his conversations with President Eisenhower at the end of 1956. In sum, the crises of 1956–7 produced a rounding off of the edges and, ironically, a greater sense of inner calm in the face of external turmoil.[1]

Inevitably the advancing years have deepened Nehru's sense of loneliness. One by one fellow pilgrims to independent India have passed from the scene, including the few persons with whom he had a genuine intellectual and/or emotional friendship: first Gandhi and then Sarojini Naidu, the 'nightingale of the Congress'; then Rafi Kidwai, and most recently Maulana Azad. The few colleagues of long standing who remain either were never intimate friends, like the President of India, Dr. Rajendra Prasad, or have drifted away for various reasons, like Rajagopalacharia, who indulges in Olympian criticism from his retreat in the south,[2] and Jaya Prakash Narayan, the former Socialist leader, whom many considered Nehru's heir-apparent until the mid-1950's. Nor have younger men emerged to fill this vacuum, even in part.

Nehru has always loved to indulge in quick repartee. Nor is he averse to gaiety and laughter. Apart from family birthday parties, including his own, his *joie de vivre* readily comes to the fore in the company of children, notably his daughter's two sons, Rajiv and Sanjay. Until a few years ago they lived at his home with their mother and provided a constant source of joy and relaxation. Even now, during holidays from school, they add a much-sought element of lightheartedness to the otherwise forbidding atmosphere of the palatial Residence.

Nehru's attachment to children is well known. His shyness seems to evaporate as he descends to their level and joins them in carefree play. Never is he more relaxed than with youngsters,

[1] The events of 1959, notably the Tibetan revolt, China's border incursions, and President Eisenhower's visit to India, strengthened these tendencies.

[2] Rajagopalacharia moved to formal opposition in 1959 when he founded the Right-wing *Swatantra* (Freedom) party.

whether at a house party or at the National Stadium in Delhi on November 14th, his birthday, celebrated as Children's Day since 1954. 'Chacha Nehru', uncle Nehru, they call him, and his face glows as he watches them, the future hope of India. Their continued faith in him is also a source of happiness, and he responds with spontaneous affection. In recent years he has developed the habit of writing warm and sensitive letters to the children of India and the world.

Another result of 'the year of crisis' was the beginning of disenchantment with Nehru's political leadership. The masses continued to adore him. But in the vocal section of India's population questioning and critical voices multiplied. Since 1956 he has not been accorded universal adulation. The conviction of indispensability has ebbed. Indeed, it became fashionable for intellectuals and middle-class Indians openly to criticize him, a healthy development for Indian democracy.[1] The decline in popularity has been marginal in numbers and influence. But even this contributed to the change in mood, weakening, however imperceptibly, his drive and dedication. Beyond specific issues, there was a somewhat muted feeling that after ten years in power Nehru should give younger men an opportunity to bear some of his responsibilities. Yet, when he expressed the desire to resign as Prime Minister in the spring of 1958, there was an outcry among his party followers, and he was persuaded to yield.

Despite the strain of recent years, Nehru retains a zest for life and an abundant supply of energy. He retains, too, his love of nature, his fondness for animals and his interest in games. Whenever he goes to the hills, he indulges his childhood pleasure in riding and walking. Nevertheless, he has aged considerably since 'the year of crisis'. He moves more slowly and reacts less quickly than the Nehru of old. The river of time, which seemed to stand still for him mentally and physically until a relatively advanced age, has moved at a rapid pace since 1957.

* * * *

The change in Nehru's mood, the decline in popularity, the ageing process in recent years—all this became apparent to a

[1] Criticism by these groups increased dramatically in the wake of the border crisis with China during 1959.

foreign observer in India at the beginning of 1958. These insights were gleaned from interviews with well-informed Indians, from the press and from the atmosphere of India. Most of all they emerged from another lengthy interview with the Indian Prime Minister which I was privileged to have.[1]

When I was ushered into his spacious office in External Affairs he was standing behind a huge, neat desk, poring over some papers. The first impression was that age had caught up with him at last, that he had begun to look elderly. A handsome man still, but no longer with the youthful appearance which I recalled vividly from my first meeting with him two years earlier. The lines on his face were more pronounced, the eyes seemed sadder, the general expression was one of fatigue. He moved slowly to his seat, placed his hands under his chin and waited for me to begin. His mind seemed far away, preoccupied with one or another of the many problems besetting India in this, the eleventh year of independence.

After glancing at a list of prepared questions he moved forward in his chair, a faded rose prominently displayed in his brown *achkan* jacket.[2] A sword-like letter-opener in his left hand served as a diversion while he thought aloud in his usual manner. This time, however, he spoke more slowly and softly, with longer lapses for thought. As he reflected on the past and the future he moved the 'sword' in and out of its scabbard, an apparent outlet for nervous energy. Frequently his right hand was raised to his head in a stroking motion. At times he moved forward and stared straight ahead as he spoke; at other times he sat back in his chair while his mind wandered back to the great events in his growth to public prominence. It was a moving performance, an intensely human self-analysis by an extraordinary person.

He swung his chair to the side and ran his fingers through his

[1] The following account is based on the author's notes, taken immediately after the interview.

[2] For some years Nehru has always worn a rose in the button-hole of his tunic. The habit began as the result of a curious incident. One morning, as he was leaving the Residence for his office, an admirer tried to present him with a rose. At first she was prevented from doing so by the guards. But the lady persisted. Every morning she waited at the gate with a fresh flower. She was finally rewarded; Nehru accepted the gracious gesture. When the gardener at the Residence noticed this he assumed that the Prime Minister was fond of wearing flowers in his tunic. Hence he prepared a fresh rose each morning from the lovely gardens in the estate. The habit has continued ever since, even when Nehru is away from the capital.

fringe of white hair. There was a pensive, withdrawn expression on his face as he searched out the past, the long eventful road to his position of eminence in India and the world at large. After what seemed like an unusually long silence, a slight, almost embarrassed smile appeared, his eyes lit up, and the glow of pride transformed his expression of fatigue. One could almost observe his memory at work, with an endless flow of impressions, of persons and places and experiences in the moulding of his character and outlook—and the moulding of independent India.

He began, somewhat self-consciously, by referring to the special position he occupied at the outset of his career by virtue of his father's prominence and Gandhi's fondness for the young man. 'At that time I didn't think very much about myself', he continued. 'We were so involved in the struggle, so wrapped up in what we were doing that I had little time or inclination to give thought to my own growth.' His words exuded warmth, sincerity and humility. They were simple words, gentle words, gently spoken in an honest portrait of his past.

Certain landmarks are deeply rooted in Nehru's memory. The first to be mentioned was *Jallianwalla Bagh*—the Amritsar Tragedy in 1919—the effect of which has been feelingly described in his autobiography. Along with this, 'my visit to the villages'—his discovery of the peasant in 1920—and 'my first close contact with Gandhi'. In 1920–1, 'I lived my intensest,' he continued, referring to the first civil disobedience campaign. Then came prison, 'a period with no peaks of experience'. Despite the sharp change from a life of activity and fulfilment, 'I adjusted very well. I have that capacity, you know. I was much less agitated than my colleagues by events outside; there was nothing I could do about it so why get involved. I was interested, of course, but I adjusted very well to the changes which prison brought.' Later, he returned to his prison experience. As he talked freely, he conveyed more poignantly than anything he has written the lasting effects of the nine years of enforced isolation from the outside world. 'I did a lot of reading and writing', he remarked casually. He also learned the art of self-discipline and used his time to think through the next phase of the struggle for Indian freedom. There was no hint in his words of anger at his captors. A Gandhian spirit of forgiveness seemed to permeate his attitude as he reflected on the lonely days and nights behind the walls. But he has not forgotten them.

The next milestone was the Lahore Congress in 1929 'which remains vivid in my memory'. Understandably so, for this was the year Nehru came of age politically, the first time he was elected Congress President. Suddenly he remembered his European sojourn in 1926–7, 'which gave me time to think, to broaden my outlook, to see India from afar, to think on life itself. Until then I was so involved in Indian affairs that I had little time to think about the broad world or about life's problems in general.'

He turned next to 'whither India', to the probable course of Indian society in the next generation. His tone was one of cautious optimism, but clearly optimistic. 'We shall certainly have our ups and downs, but I have no doubt that we shall go forward, perhaps a little more slowly than we should like, but forward none the less.'

Nehru is one of those men who refuse to lose hope. He has had good reasons to be disappointed with the trend of many events in India and abroad. His faith in man—everywhere—remains. He has moments of doubt, but his deep belief in the ability and desire of India and the world to solve their problems dispels misgivings. Caste would gradually fade away, he said, though the process would be slow. So too with economic development. Although tired and seemingly aware that he may have entered the final stage of his public life, Nehru showed that he retains a determined faith in the future.

Little time remained, for he had dealt with his early life at leisure. But he seemed oblivious of the clock and began a discourse on the world situation. I asked if he had reason to feel optimistic in the light of the preceding year. 'There are some hopeful features', he began. 'Take Hungary, for instance. The events of 1956 show that Communism, if it is imposed on a country from outside, cannot last. I mean to say [a characteristic expression] if Communism goes against the basic national spirit, it will not be accepted. In those countries where it has allied itself with nationalism it is, of course, a powerful force. As in China; in Russia, too.

'The events in Suez also brought out an important fact. It is no longer possible for strong, former colonial powers to return to areas they once ruled.' His discussion of Suez underlined the continuing influence of Colonialism on his thought.

He then turned to Eastern Europe. He seemed convinced that the Russians would ease their grip on the entire area 'once this wretched Cold War is ended'. 'Once, perhaps, Eastern Europe

was of benefit to Russia, economically and strategically. But now
—well, look at Hungary—and Poland. It is a major cost to the
Russians; strategically, it is of little value, and they have lost a
great deal in world opinion. They will give it up, but not as long as
they feel threatened.'

That the Soviets still laboured under the psychology of siege,
Nehru appeared to believe at the beginning of 1958. 'As Khruschev said to me, "for forty years we have had to defend ourselves".
They have never had a chance to settle down. If only they were
allowed to do so, this fear would give way and then they could
give up their hold on Eastern Europe.'

'I cannot see the value of a military approach to these problems,' he continued. 'This approach can no longer solve any
problems. Besides, I do not see why some people in the West think
the Russians are out to conquer other peoples. They are not
interested in this. It is only when a neighbour is hostile that they
try to weaken it. The Russian people want peace. So do the
Americans. In fact, they are so similar, the Russians and the
Americans. If only they could agree to end the Cold War.'

On the world situation in general he remarked, 'Viewed logi-
cally, there is much to be pessimistic about—but looked at in a
human way there is a good deal to be optimistic about.' By this he
meant that people everywhere were yearning for peace and that
the force of public opinion in all lands would make itself felt. On
this note the interview came to a close.

Nehru had aged since I last saw him a year before. He also
seemed more mellow, more troubled, more tired. But the most
vivid impression was a quality of deep sincerity, a human touch
which breathes warmth and tenderness. Throughout the interview I felt that here was a sensitive man who had succeeded in
absorbing the shocks of life without coarsening his mind, character
and personality.

CHAPTER II

THE YOUNG BRAHMIN

The Kashmiri Brahmins are a small community renowned for their learning, their handsome men and beautiful women—and their pride. The Nehru family was seven generations removed from their ancestral home. But they looked upon Allahabad as a place of self-exile from the fabled Vale.

Motilal Nehru, the father of India's Prime Minister, was born in 1861 in the city of Agra, site of the exquisite Taj Mahal. Until the age of twelve, he was educated at home, largely in Persian and Arabic. Thereafter he attended the Government High School in Kanpur and Muir Central College in Allahabad. Although he failed to take the B.A., Motilal led his class in the *vakil* (lawyer) examinations. After his apprenticeship in Kanpur, he settled in Allahabad in 1886 to practise law at the High Court. By sheer talent and a capacity for work, he rose rapidly in his profession. Within a few years he was recognized as one of the outstanding lawyers in Allahabad. It was there that his only son was born, on 14 November 1889. His name: Jawaharlal, the red jewel.

His parents doted upon the youngster, and with good reason. Motilal had been married once before, there had been a child, and both mother and child had died. A child had been born to his second wife but it too had died in infancy. Hence Jawaharlal was the object of their complete devotion and love. And as the only child of a wealthy barrister for eleven years, he was spoiled in a princely fashion.

Until Jawaharlal was three the family lived in the city proper, near the *chowk* (market), amidst congestion and crowds. Then as his father's practice became increasingly lucrative, they moved to the exclusive residential area known as 'the Civil Lines'. Only one other Indian family lived there at the time. The Nehru home at 9 Elgin Road was unpretentious, but luxurious compared to those of almost all other Indians in Allahabad. In 1900, when Jawaharlal was ten, his father purchased a palatial home which he named *Anand Bhawan* (Abode of Happiness). Thus, for all practical purposes, the young Nehru lived in comfortable surroundings throughout the formative period of his life. Moreover, apart from the period of infancy, he lived amongst Europeans until the age of twenty-two, first in Allahabad, then at Harrow, Cambridge and in London. And even at home the atmosphere was more typically English than Indian. In his early education, too, the young Nehru was subjected to European influences. From the pre-school age until he left for England at the age of fifteen he was trained at home by private tutors, most of them British. As a result, though 'I was filled with resentment against the alien rulers of my country who misbehaved . . . I had no feeling whatever, so far as I can remember, against individual Englishmen. . . . In my heart I rather admired the English.'[1]

Life at home was not unpleasant. An atmosphere of luxury and security pervaded *Anand Bhawan*. Every material comfort was available. There were two swimming-pools, one in the palatial garden, another in the house itself. One of the more impressive stables in India enabled the young Nehru to become a proficient horseman and to develop a taste for riding which persisted throughout his adult life. Nothing was spared in Motilal's effort to emulate the ways of English aristocrats. He entertained royally, and maintained three separate kitchens.

All who knew him agree that he was a formidable and commanding figure, in appearance very much like a Roman senator, with a remarkable strength of character and rock-like will. Motilal had little imagination and was in no sense an original thinker, but he possessed an uncommon common sense. He was intensely practical, and disdainful of theoretical subtleties. He was not particularly eloquent, but he was lucid, logical, precise, witty and sarcastic, interspersing his remarks with pointed quotations from Persian and Arabic poetry. He was affable among friends and guests, and an entertaining raconteur. He was, according to all who knew him, a complete man, with many-sided interests and activities. In every sphere of life in which he was interested he towered above those about him. He was acknowledged to have no peer at the Allahabad Bar; he set the fashion for contemporaries

[1] *Toward Freedom*, p. 21.

of his class; he was more advanced than anyone else in the United Provinces in his liberal social ideas; and he was responsible for a secular outlook in the Congress organization of his province.

Typical of the attitude of British officials in India who knew him is a portrait of Motilal Nehru by Sir Frederick James, sometime member of the Central Legislative Assembly:

He was a nationalist, but a cosmopolitan; at home in any society and with every race. He was a distinguished lawyer and a powerful advocate; also a man of charm, culture and tolerance. He represented in many respects the highest type of civilization. He was, in fact, a Grand Seigneur —such as those who have appeared in all the great epochs of history. . . . I remember particularly his exquisite courtesy and delightful deference to youth. No wonder he was adored by his family. He was the perfect host. His hospitality was generous and of a high order. . . . His home, which was always open, was the Mecca of all who enjoyed the good things of life and who looked to him as a great lawyer and national leader. Motilal had the dignified, clear-cut features and fair skin of a Kashmiri Brahmin of ancient lineage. He was always immaculate in dress whether in European or Indian style. . . . What struck me most [about his speeches in the legislature] was his tolerance towards his political enemies. No querulousness, irritation or bitterness marred his reasoned statement of his case, whether legal or political. . . . Motilal was generous in everything that he did. There were no half-measures.[1]

All of Motilal Nehru's children acknowledged his predominant influence within the family. The youngest, Mrs. Krishna Hutheesingh, described her father 'as a tower of strength to his children . . . with a certain grandeur and magnificence that was bound to command the respect of all who knew him. . . . His one fault was his temper . . . a fault handed down to him from a long line of ancestors and not one of us is immune from it. . . . Whilst he was alive, we lived a happy, carefree life, knowing he was there to guard and protect us.'[2]

Jawaharlal's attitude to his father was ambivalent. He, too, experienced this sense of security. He 'admired [his] father tremendously', saw him as 'the embodiment of strength and courage and cleverness, . . . but feared him also. . . . His temper was indeed an awful thing, and even in after years I do not think I ever came across anything to match it. . . . But, fortunately, he could control himself as a rule. . . .'[3]

[1] Extracts from an unpublished memoir kindly made available to the author by Sir Frederick in London in October 1955.
[2] Hutheesingh, Krishna, *With No Regrets*, pp. 75–77.
[3] *Toward Freedom*, pp. 21–22.

Many years later, on the ninety-fifth anniversary of his father's birth, Jawaharlal referred to him as 'something like a Renaissance prince. . . . I have no doubt that he would have succeeded in any other activity of life which he had undertaken.'[1]

The contrast between father and son in those early days, left lasting impressions on Jawaharlal Nehru. The shy, reticent, aesthetically-inclined son stood in awe of his father's personality. There was no inducement to make decisions, for his father provided the symbol and substance of security. Doubt and vacillation date from this early association. So, too, it would appear, does his respect for decisive and strong men—men such as Gandhi and Mountbatten. Thus, too, the duality in his later years, of lucid thought along with constant doubt about the appropriate course of action.

Still another legacy of his home in Allahabad was a broad secular outlook. Three cultural strands pervaded *Anand Bhawan* during his formative years: Hindu, Moghul and British. Of all the Indian languages the only one which Nehru has mastered with reasonable competence is Urdu, the Moghul derivative of Persian and Hindi. And he has always felt more at ease in English, for both the written and spoken word. In fact, all his works have been written in English, in a fluent, sensitive style.

Both parents were immensely proud of their son, though his mother was more demonstrative in her show of affection. Even after the arrival of her two daughters, Jawaharlal remained the favourite. Of Swarup Rani Nehru little has been written. Like her children, she lived in the shadow of Motilal Nehru. Unlike the Nehrus, hers was an orthodox family which had descended to the plains from the Valley of Kashmir only two generations before. She had little formal education, never spoke English well, and never fully approved of her husband's Western habits, though she adjusted to them in time. According to her elder daughter, 'Mother was a charming and delicate person, a fragile woman, afflicted with ill-health; she was a good, gentle Hindu wife whose life was wrapped around that of her husband. Yet, as I think back, I realize now that mother did influence us all, though indirectly.'[2]

From her marriage, at the age of thirteen, she occupied a submissive vital role in the Nehru home. Of fair complexion and

---

[1] An interview with Prime Minister Nehru, on All-India Radio, 5 May 1956.
[2] Related to the author by Mme Pandit in London in October 1955.

hazel eyes, she was tiny and doll-like with small beautifully shaped hands and feet. She was born and bred in luxury and was pampered by everyone about her. She had a devoted husband, a famous name, wealth, leisure, comfort and three children upon whom she could dote to her heart's content. Yet, later in life, she became a semi-invalid and was confined to her bed for many months at a time. Most of her life was absorbed in her children and home. However, with the change in the Nehru way of living in 1920, when her husband and son joined Gandhi's non-co-operation movement, she gave up many comforts and joined in the fray, even to the extent of participating in demonstrations and courting arrest.

There are few references to his mother in Nehru's lengthy auto-biography. Because of his father's preoccupation with work, and his mother's protective love, he was drawn to her in the early years. 'I had no fear of her, for I knew that she would condone everything I did, and, because of her excessive and indiscriminating love for me, I tried to dominate over her a little. I saw much more of her than I did of father, and she seemed nearer to me, so I would confide in her when I would not dream of doing so to father.'[1]

The young Nehru's leisure hours were whiled away in games—swimming, cricket, tennis, riding and the like. He also enjoyed an occasional dip in the Ganges, journeys to a distant town for a family marriage, and the many Hindu festivals. But religion proper 'seemed to be a woman's affair'. Later this was to blossom into agnosticism. At home, he imbibed some of the classics of Hindu mythology, as well as the stories of the 1857 Rebellion, related by a family retainer, Munshi Mubarak Ali. It was this composite environment that shaped his later attitude to Muslims and the communal problem in general.

What the young Nehru lacked above all was companionship. He found himself surrounded by his elders, people who could instruct, discipline and guide but who could not share his youthful world. This, too, had a lasting effect, for in his adult life Nehru never confided completely in anyone, except Gandhi.

Among his tutors, only one, Ferdinand T. Brooks, had any significant effect. Of mixed Irish and French extraction, Brooks was a moody, sensitive, gifted young man when he joined the

[1] *Toward Freedom*   . 22.

Nehru household. He was also a devout follower of theosophy. Jawaharlal was ten years old at the time. Under Brooks's inspiration he developed a taste for serious reading and an attachment to English poetry. He also acquired an avid interest in science. Inevitably the tutor's spiritual bent penetrated the curious and receptive mind of his pupil. Jawaharlal began to read, with respect, the Hindu classics, such as the *Bhagavad Gita* and the *Upanishads*. He was also attracted to his tutor's faith. And so there occurred at the age of thirteen, the young Nehru's initiation into the Theosophical Society. But his infatuation was short-lived, for Brooks parted from the Nehrus soon afterwards.

*　　　*　　　*　　　*

The time was rapidly approaching to leave the sheltered atmosphere of *Anand Bhawan*. Motilal had long ago decided that his son should attend an exclusive British public school before proceeding to the university. Thus when he was fifteen, the Nehru family embarked for England—and Harrow.

It was the first time that Jawaharlal Nehru was on his own. He remained at the famous public school for two years, a period in his life which was relatively uneventful but not unhappy. He was a quiet, reserved, studious boy who managed to fit into the school life but 'was never an exact fit'. Only those who took an active interest in school sports were likely to leave a lasting impression on their contemporaries—and he was not the rugger type. Yet he was not entirely averse to games: in 1906, in the track and field competition for the Headmaster's House, to which he belonged, Jawaharlal won the half-mile race and was placed third in the mile event. More noteworthy, he was awarded the prize for topping the examination list in his form during the third term in 1905 and again in the first term of 1906. Among his other interests were local British politics and the pioneering developments in aviation. In his autobiography he recalled having written to his father, anticipating a week-end visit to India by air.

Like so many Harrovians before and after him Nehru retained an emotional attachment to his public school. Some years ago, this association provided the setting for an act of personal and political interest.

Another Harrovian Sir Winston Churchill had always opposed

the transfer of power to 'men of straw', as he termed the Congress leaders. Indeed, he was the symbol of the most reactionary aspects of British life for most Indian nationalists. In the early 1950's, however, Churchill was Prime Minister of Great Britain while Nehru was Prime Minister of India, and India was now a full-fledged member of the Commonwealth. Although they differed in many respects, both wore the same old school tie. And so a group of Old Harrovians anxious to bring about a reconciliation arranged a dinner in Nehru's honour early in 1953.

Churchill consented to attend and to propose Nehru's health. Unfortunately, he was called away at the last moment to an un-avoidable state function. Sir Walter (later Lord) Monckton sub-stituted for Churchill; hopes of a reconciliation were rapidly fading. But soon after Nehru replied to the toast word was re-ceived that Churchill would be able to come after all. Churchill was at his best. He paid tribute to Nehru's courage and integrity. He spoke rapturously about Nehru's magnanimity in remaining within the Commonwealth after the experience of subjection. Nehru accepted the gesture and the formal reconciliation took place.[1] It is doubtful, however, that the emotional antagonisms of thirty years were waved away by a few generous words, even between two Harrovians.

Nehru went up to Cambridge in the autumn of 1907, when England basked in the glory of the Edwardian era, and when the first stirrings of nationalist agitation were heard in India. Three years he remained, years of mental growth, and of comfort and pleasant living. By one of those quirks of fate he was enrolled at Trinity College, famous among other things as the training ground of Prime Ministers.

His formal studies were in the natural sciences, chemistry, geology and botany, but his intellectual interests ranged far and wide—into literature, philosophy, economics, politics, history and Greek poetry. No one exerted a very marked influence. At Cam-bridge, he first came into contact with socialist ideas; Fabianism was then very much in the air. But his interest was academic. Twenty years were to elapse before Nehru acquired a genuine attraction to socialism.

Of his political thoughts and moods while at Cambridge, Prime Minister Nehru remarked fifty years later: 'So far as political

[1] Related to the author by Lord Monckton in London in October 1955.

matters were concerned, I was, if I may say so, an Indian nationalist desiring India's freedom and rather inclined, in the context of Indian politics, to the more extreme wing of it, as represented then by Mr. Tilak. I felt like any average Indian student would feel. There was nothing peculiar about it.'[1]

Cyrenaicism was then the rage, and Nehru was inclined to its philosophy of pleasure. His allowances were ample, his responsibilities a thing of the future. 'I enjoyed life, and I refused to see why I should consider it a thing of sin. . . . Work and games and amusements filled my life, and the only thing that disturbed me sometimes was the political struggle in India.'[2]

As at Harrow, he did not impress his contemporaries. Indian classmates recall him as a typical public-school product, polished, urbane, somewhat snobbish. There was no evidence yet of his future greatness. His Cambridge experience had a lasting influence, as Nehru himself testified. On the eve of his second imprisonment, in 1922, he declared: 'Less than ten years ago, I returned from England after a long stay there. . . . I had imbibed most of the prejudices of Harrow and Cambridge, and in my likes and dislikes I was perhaps more an Englishman than an Indian. I looked upon the world almost from an Englishman's standpoint . . . as much prejudiced in favour of England and the English as it was possible for an Indian to be.'[3] More than thirty years later he told the members of the Cambridge Union that wherever he goes he tries to make himself receptive, and 'coming to England it is far easier for me, because a part of me, a fairly important part of me, has been made by England, by Cambridge'.[4]

Nehru took his degree in the summer of 1910, with second-class honours in the natural science tripos. There arose the question of an appropriate career. It is ironic that serious consideration was given to the I.C.S. (Indian Civil Service), the 'steel-frame' of the British *Raj*. The idea was finally abandoned, largely because such a career would have involved almost constant absence from his family within India. There was, too, his father's preference for the law. Thus in the autumn of 1910 he went down to London to read for the Bar at the Inner Temple.

[1] To the author in New Delhi on 6 June 1956.
[2] *Toward Freedom*, p. 34.
[3] Dwivedi, R. (ed.), *The Life and Speeches of Pandit Jawahar Lal Nehru*, pp. 4–5.
[4] *Manchester Guardian*, 11 February 1955.

During his two years in London, Nehru lived the life of an English gentleman. He was a very handsome, slim young man, with black hair and a moustache, debonair in his Bond Street clothes. He frequented the proper clubs and restaurants, whiled away his time at the theatre and at social functions of the young aristocrats. His law studies took up relatively little time, as did serious intellectual pursuits, though he dabbled in Fabian ideas and was interested in the suffragette movement. In the summer he did Europe, as was fashionable then and now.

He was called to the Bar in 1912. With his education complete, he returned to India after seven formative years in the country against which he was to struggle much of his adult life. But this was in the future. 'I am afraid,' he wrote later, 'I was a bit of a prig with little to commend me.'[1]

*   *   *   *

The India to which Nehru returned was essentially unchanged. The British were still undisputed masters of the sub-continent. Political consciousness was still confined to the intelligentsia in the cities, though the lower middle class had been aroused by Tilak and the agitation against the partition of Bengal, from 1906 to 1910. The Congress remained a timid annual gathering, loyal to the British connexion. The extremists had been subdued and their leaders were in prison or in self-imposed exile. The peasant masses continued to slumber. Gandhi was still in South Africa. Indeed, India in 1912 was a land of political apathy.

Within his own family little had changed. Another sister had arrived in his absence, Krishna, by name, or Betti as she was called. Swarup, the beautiful one, or Nan as she was nicknamed, was now twelve, but the difference in age prevented any real communion. Motilal's practice was as lucrative as ever, and *Anand Bhawan* had become the social and intellectual centre of the town.

Allahabad seemed terribly provincial to the young Nehru. The scope of activity was severely limited: the club; family gatherings at *Anand Bhawan*; and the Bar library, for he began to practise his profession soon after his return. 'Gradually the life I led began to

[1] *Toward Freedom*, p. 39.

lose all its freshness, and I felt that I was being engulfed in a dull routine of a pointless and futile existence.'[1]

Nor was his legal practice inspiring or inspired. His qualifications and assets were impressive—intelligence, a legal training at one of the great English inns of court, and the benevolent guidance of Motilal, the acknowledged leader at the Allahabad High Court. But the young Nehru showed little initiative or promise at the Bar. He remained a junior to his father for eight years, rarely pleaded a case on his own, and made no impression on his colleagues. Many years later he recalled this period without any enthusiasm: 'There was little that was inviting in that legal past of mine, and at no time have I felt the urge to revert to it.'[2]

Nehru's early ventures into the political arena were amateurish. At the end of 1912 he attended the annual session of the Congress. He joined the United Provinces Congress organization in 1913 but remained inactive for some time. Two years later he served as secretary of a fund drive for Indians in South Africa. During this period, too, he participated in the agitation against the system of indentured labour for Indians in Fiji. But these activities were peripheral to his essentially placid life.

Of all the events during the war the one which stirred him most was the internment of Mrs. Annie Besant in the summer of 1917. A fiery Irish lady devoted to Indian freedom, Mrs. Besant was an intimate friend of the Nehru family. And as a leading theosophist, she had excited considerable influence on the young Nehru. He was galvanized into political action and became joint secretary of the Allahabad branch of the Home Rule League. 'I was a pure nationalist,' he wrote of this period, 'my vague socialist ideas of college days having sunk into the background. . . . They were vague ideas, more humanitarian and utopian than scientific.'[3] Throughout his adult life these two ideologies, nationalism and socialism, were to vie for primacy in his thought and action. Nationalism was invariably to be the more compelling drive, though he has maintained his allegiance to both.

*   *   *   *

[1] *Toward Freedom*, p. 40.
[2] 'The Mind of a Judge', September 1935, in *India and the World*, p. 130.
[3] *Toward Freedom*, p. 44.

It was on the eve of his political awakening that Jawaharlal
Nehru was married. He was then twenty-six and among the most
eligible young men in India. It was an arranged marriage, for a
love marriage in the Western tradition was rare in India at that
time. Motilal chose Kamala Kaul, daughter of a prosperous
Kashmiri businessman of the same caste. She was seventeen, tall,
slim, with classic Kashmiri features, and the picture of health at
the time of her marriage. But her appearance of health proved to
be tragically deceptive. She was also shy, somewhat awkward in
social company, and like Jawaharlal sensitive and high-strung.
Coming as she did from an orthodox family, she was educated in
the traditional Hindu manner. From the beginning there was an
intellectual gap between them but with the passage of time she
more than compensated for this with her understanding, sympathy and devotion to her husband. Although she was overshadowed by him throughout their married life, she revealed
much courage and inner strength, which won the admiration of all
who knew her.

The marriage took place in Delhi, in February 1916, after
Kamala had spent a few months in Allahabad under the tutorship
of the governesses of Nan and Betti. It was a lavish affair, with
pomp and splendour. At first it was difficult for Kamala to fit into
the Westernized surroundings of *Anand Bhawan*. However, she followed her husband dutifully and gracefully. She was a favourite
of Motilal—causing some jealousy on the part of Jawaharlal's
elder sister. Her only child, Indira Priyadarshini, better known as
Mrs. Indira Gandhi, was born on 19 November 1917. It was at
that time that the first evidence of Kamala's fatal disease appeared.

As his attraction to politics increased, Nehru devoted less and
less attention to the Bar. An alternative interest had kindled his
imagination, and without regret his legal practice faded away.
And yet, his urge to political action remained only partially
expressed until the Mahatma appeared on the scene.

CHAPTER III

'AND THEN CAME GANDHI'

Mohandas Karamchand Gandhi was India's most illustrious son since the Buddha. Unlike Jawaharlal, the 'Father of the Nation' came from a relatively plebeian social background. The Gandhis belong to the third highest of the four traditional Hindu castes; their sub-caste, the *Modh Bania*, has long been identified with money-lending and commerce, an object of derision and envy in Indian society. Yet both his father and grandfather had served with distinction as Chief Minister of a tiny princely State in western India. It was there, on 2 October 1869, that the Mahatma was born.

The young Gandhi was physically weak, timid and self-conscious. Like his most prominent political disciple he admired and feared his father. Gandhi completed his studies in Rajkot and then proceeded to London to read for the Bar at the Inner Temple —in the very year that Nehru was born. Both men lived and dressed like fashionable young Englishmen of the day. Both imbibed the spirit of English law and the sense of British justice. But whereas Nehru was profoundly influenced by his contact with British culture, habits and thought-processes, Gandhi remained essentially untouched by the experience.

Nehru had gone to England as a young boy whose home life was permeated with the modern, secular atmosphere of the West. His real mother-tongue was English. Seven years at Harrow, Cambridge and London deepened his attachment to the British way of life, with the result that he returned to his native land 'more an Englishman than an Indian'. By contrast, Gandhi's mother-tongue was Gujarati. And by the time he left for England his personality and outlook had already been moulded. Thus, two years in London merely provided him with a legal training. He returned to India in 1891 entirely an Indian, in no sense an Englishman.

After a few years at the Bar Gandhi went to South Africa, to plead a case on behalf of the Indian community. He expected to remain a year but stayed on for almost twenty. It was there that he experimented successfully with *satyagraha* or non-violent non-co-operation, a technique which was to revolutionize Indian politics. He returned to India in 1915 but remained a silent spectator of events for the next three years. His triumphant campaign in support of indigo plantation workers in 1918 and his leadership of an agrarian struggle in Gujarat began to rouse the peasants from their apathy. Gandhi rapidly emerged as the champion of the oppressed. But during the first world war there was a virtual moratorium on serious political action.

As the war drew to a close, discontent was increasingly felt in India. Wilson's principle of self-determination for all peoples, stirred the imagination of the intelligentsia. Closer to home, its hopes had been raised by the British pledge of ultimate self-government for India, contained in the Montagu Declaration of 1917. The first instalment was promised soon after the war. A similar ferment was evident among other classes of Indian society. The forced pace of industrialization enhanced the influence of Indian businessmen. Returning soldiers were beginning to demand equal treatment and a better way of life. Even the dormant peasantry showed signs of unrest. And in the Punjab, in northern India, revolutionary groups like the *Ghadr* Party were actively challenging British authority. Such was the political state of India in the summer of 1918 when the Montagu-Chelmsford Report proposed partial self-government for the provinces.[1] The Congress replied with a demand for 'self-government within the Empire', fiscal autonomy for India and a declaration of Indian rights. And yet this was hardly a revolutionary group. The constitutional Old Guard was still in control. Only a traumatic experience and a dramatic call to action could set the Congress—and the young Nehru—on a new path.

The necessary shock was provided early in 1919 by the Rowlatt Bills and the Amritsar Tragedy; the leadership, by Gandhi. The Rowlatt Bills, which granted sweeping powers of preventive detention of all suspected political agitators, were received with dismay by every section of Indian public opinion. But only Gandhi responded with a direct challenge. He first requested the Viceroy

[1] Cmd. 9109, 1918.

to withhold his assent from the 'black bills'. When this failed he formed a *Satyagraha* Society and proclaimed *Satyagraha* Day, a day of *hartal* (suspension of all business), a day of fasting, a day of mass meetings to protest against the hated legislation. In major cities and provincial towns alike the call to non-co-operation evoked a widespread response.

The main centre of unrest was the Punjab, 'the land of the five rivers', the home of the Sikhs and the reservoir of the Indian Army. The spark which set the Punjab ablaze in 1919 was the detention of two popular Congress leaders. As word drifted through the bazaars, crowds gathered quickly and began to march to the Civil Lines to demand their release. Police barred their way, a skirmish occurred, and a few demonstrators were killed. Bitter and angry, the others retaliated with arson and mob violence, in which five Europeans were killed. A few days later similar scenes of violence occurred in nearby towns. Martial law was proclaimed and all public meetings were banned in Amritsar. Tension mounted hourly.

In the heart of the city is a public park known as *Jallianwalla Bagh*, enclosed on three sides by high walls which form the boundaries of adjoining houses. The only exit is wide enough to allow but a few persons to pass at a time. Despite the ban on public gatherings, the Congress organized a mammoth meeting on 13 April, the Hindu New Year Day. An estimated 20,000 people gathered in the *Bagh*. Suddenly there appeared at the entrance 150 soldiers under the command of General Dyer. The crowd was ordered to disperse, but there was no way out; the military blocked the only exit. Within three minutes, an order was given to fire at point-blank range on the unarmed mass. Panic enveloped the crowd; they were caught in a veritable graveyard. Some tried to scale the eight-foot walls, but in vain. A hail of bullets cut them down. Blood flowed freely on that tragic day.

According to the Hunter Committee of Inquiry, 379 were killed and about 1,200 were wounded. The only reason the others were spared, according to Dyer's own testimony before the Commission, was that he had exhausted his ammunition.[1] It was perhaps the worst crime in the annals of British rule in India, a massacre of defenceless people. Matters were not improved when the Lieutenant-Governor of the Punjab gave his official approval.

[1] See Cmd. 681, 1920.

In his determination to 'teach the natives a lesson' Dyer ruled
Amritsar with an iron hand. Public floggings were not infrequent.
Detention of all nationalist leaders was the order of the day. But
the most degrading measure was a 'crawling order' imposed on all
Indians who passed a narrow lane in the city where a medical
missionary had been assaulted during the disturbances. The
humiliation of crawling on all fours to and from one's home, for
many lived in this lane, was not to be forgotten. A wave of anger
swept the land. *Jallianwalla Bagh* became hallowed ground and the
shooting a day of remembrance.

The British were to pay dearly. As one well-known British historian of India remarked, the Amritsar Tragedy was 'a turning-
point in Indo-British relations almost as important as the Mutiny
[1857]' primarily because of 'the assumption, implied in the
behaviour of responsible Englishmen and in their evidence before
the Hunter Committee, that Indians could and should be
treated as an inferior race'.[1] A former senior civil servant put the
issue more pungently: '. . . from now onwards the whole situation
was changed. Government had been carried on with the consent
—usually apathetic and half-hearted, but still consent—of the
governed. That consent was now changed to active mistrust.'[2]

For Nehru, among many others, the Punjab tragedy was a profound insult to the national honour, pride and self-respect. When
he first learned about Gandhi's proposed *Satyagraha* Society he
'was afire with enthusiasm and wanted to join . . . immediately. I
hardly thought of the consequences—law-breaking, jail-going,
etc.—and if I thought of them I did not care.'[3] But in deference to
his father's wish he did not do so. According to his youngest child,
Motilal 'was furious with Jawahar for joining Gandhi. Once, in a
rage, he ordered [his son] out of the house.'[4] Finally Gandhi's
intervention was sought by the elder Nehru, and Jawaharlal was
persuaded to relent, temporarily.

The cleavage lasted about eighteen months, when Motilal
yielded. 'It was perhaps a triangle: Mr. Gandhi, my father and
myself; each influencing the other to some extent. But principally,

[1] Thompson, Edward & Garratt, G. T., *Rise and Fulfilment of British Rule in
India*, p. 610.
[2] Woodruff, Philip, *The Men Who Ruled India: The Guardians*, vol. ii, p. 243.
[3] *Toward Freedom*, p. 48.
[4] Hutheesingh, 'Nehru and Madame Pandit' in *Ladies' Home Journal*,
January 1955, p. 77.

I should imagine, it was Gandhi's amazing capacity to tone down opposition by his friendly approach. . . . [No less important, father] was forced to think because of my own reaction. I was his only son; he was much interested in me.'[1]

At the end of 1919 the Congress met in annual session at Amritsar, a symbolic act of defiance of the *Raj*. Motilal Nehru presided, but Gandhi was rapidly emerging as the dominant figure. Jawaharlal was present but as a passive spectator of events. Ironically, it was Gandhi who pressed for acceptance of the Montagu-Chelmsford Reforms, though acknowledging their inadequacy. As for the atrocities, he told the delegates, 'the Government went mad at the time; we went mad also at the time. I say, do not return madness with madness, but return madness with sanity and the whole situation will be yours.'[2] Here in essence was the Mahatma's philosophy of *satyagraha*.

A new issue now blazed across the Indian horizon and stirred the emotions of the Muslim community—the *Khilafat* agitation. The defeat of Turkey in the first world war caused genuine disquiet. More particularly, the Allied decision to dismember the Ottoman Empire aroused anger and hostility because it allegedly violated a pledge of Lloyd George during the war. Deputations were sent to the Viceroy and even to London, but in vain.

The result was the creation of a powerful politico-religious movement headed by the Ali brothers, Mohammed and Shaukat. More important, this episode led to an alliance between the Congress and the Muslims. Gandhi correctly perceived the measure of Muslim feeling and succeeded in combining forces on the two entirely unrelated questions of 'the Punjab Wrongs' and the preservation of the Khaliphate. Underpinning these was the positive goal of *swaraj*, self-rule or independence. The stage was being set for the first civil disobedience campaign.

*   *   *   *

Jawaharlal Nehru did not play an important part in these developments. Yet 1920 was marked by an episode of great

---

[1] Mende, Tibor, *Nehru: Conversations on India and World Affairs*, pp. 22-24.
[2] As quoted in Sitaramayya, P., *History of the Indian National Congress*, vol. i, p. 181.

personal significance—his first direct contact with the Indian peasant. Like other members of the Indian élite, the Nehrus were in the habit of spending part of every summer in the hills, away from the extreme heat that parches the plains and dulls the mind. In May 1920 Nehru, his wife, and his mother were on holiday in Mussourie, in the United Provinces. Upon his refusal to pledge that he would not associate with an Afghan delegation staying at the same hotel, he was compelled to leave the area.

Soon after he returned to Allahabad, he agreed to return with a peasant delegation to their villages for a first-hand inquiry into their complaints. There he discovered a whole new world. 'I was filled with shame and sorrow—shame at my own easygoing and comfortable life and our petty politics of the city which ignored this vast multitude of semi-naked sons and daughters of India, sorrow at the degradation and overwhelming poverty of India. A new picture of India seemed to rise before me, naked, starving, crushed, and utterly miserable.'[1] This was an educational experience. Not only did it broaden his horizon. It also aroused his sympathy for the underdog, one of the key motives of his subsequent behaviour in politics. And his discovery of the peasant removed the mental block to public speaking. From that time dates Nehru's conversational method of public speech, his tendency to speak to his people 'like a schoolmaster; to try to explain things to them in as simple a language as possible; not to deliver, well, I can't deliver them, fiery orations, but just trying to get them to think and to understand'.[2]

In the meantime, preparations for civil disobedience had been completed. Strangely enough, it was the *Khilafat* Committee that took the lead. But it was not clear sailing. Almost all the prominent Congress leaders were still sceptical of *satyagraha*. Only one of the Old Guard sided with Gandhi—Motilal Nehru. His defection was sufficient to turn the scales. Gandhi's programme was simple. It consisted of a triple boycott—of the impending elections under the Government of India Act of 1919, of Government schools and colleges, and of the law courts. To the surprise of many, both officials and Congressmen, almost two-thirds of the electors stayed away from the polls in November 1920. Thus, when the Congress met in Nagpur at the end of the year the critics were won over.

[1] *Toward Freedom*, pp. 56–57.
[2] Related to the author in New Delhi on 13 June 1956.

The Nagpur session was a landmark in many respects. Gandhi's undisputed leadership was acknowledged for the first time. Moreover, the Congress goal was changed from 'self-government within the Empire' to 'the attainment of Swaraj . . . by all legitimate and peaceful means'. The Mahatma was 'delightfully vague' about the meaning of *swaraj*, which could be interpreted as Dominion status or complete independence. But the use of a Hindi term to describe the nationalist objective evoked an emotional response from people to whom the Western expression, self-government, was utterly foreign. This was Gandhi's way to convey ideas in traditional Indian symbols and thereby to reach the masses. Hence *swaraj* and *satyagraha*, not self-government and non-co-operation. Thus, too, the emphasis on *khaddat* (home-spun cotton cloth), his simple way of life, his renunciation and his founding of an *ashram* (a commune of teacher and disciples). All this appealed to the tradition-bound peasants, the overwhelming majority of India's population.

The most important development at Nagpur was the refashioning of the Indian National Congress. At the top of the organizational pyramid was the Annual Session, the 'legislature' of the Congress 'government', where, in theory, major policy decisions were to be taken. India was divided into twenty-one 'provinces' based on linguistic groups, each headed by a Provincial Congress Committee (P.C.C.). The 'provinces', in turn, were sub-divided into districts, *taluqs*, towns and villages, each lower body electing delegates to the committee immediately above it, ultimately to the All-India Congress Committee (A.I.C.C.), the highest executive organ in the party. The A.I.C.C., with a membership of three hundred to four hundred, conducted all Congress business between the annual sessions and was given wide discretion. It also elected the Working Committee, the real decision-making organ of the Congress. Popularly known as the High Command, it consisted of the President, the General-Secretaries, the Treasurer and about a dozen others. The President was elected annually by the P.C.C.s but remained only one of the élite, first among equals— with Gandhi as super-president until 1947.

With these constitutional changes, the Congress was transformed from an upper-class urban club into a nation-wide mass organization capable of penetrating the heart of Indian society, the village. 1920, then, saw the emergence of a new leader, a new method of political action, a more advanced goal and a mass party which in time was to rally millions to the cause of Indian freedom. The way was now paved for civil disobedience.

The campaign lasted about fourteen months but it gathered momentum very slowly. The first event of any consequence was the arrest of the Ali brothers in mid-September 1921, for a fiery speech inciting Muslim soldiers to sedition. Gandhi seized upon this issue and openly espoused the view of the *Khilafat* leaders. The challenge to legal authority was clear, but the Government hesitated to take action against him. For Gandhi's influence had already spread to almost all sections of the Indian people. As the pro-Government leader of the Indian Liberals remarked:

He is not a mere politician in the eyes of the masses. He has all the sanctity of a holy man attached to him . . . To the Muhammedans he has made himself invaluable. . . . With the labouring classes, he and his party un-questionably wield a most powerful influence which cannot be ignored. . . . I have also grave doubt as to whether we would be able to carry even the Assembly with us in regard to this matter [the arrest of Gandhi].[1]

Nehru was a mere observer at the Nagpur session. However, as the campaign unfolded, he was filled with elation. Indeed, he was so absorbed that he ignored certain unattractive features, such as the strange admixture of politics and religion, the artificial unity with the Muslims, and the lack of a clear-cut ideology. Like all true converts he had absolute faith in his leader.

What was it that attracted Nehru to the Mahatma? Many persons testify to Gandhi's magnetic personality. But that magnetism required an appropriate setting. Gandhi arrived upon the Indian political scene when the nationalist movement was devoid of imaginative thought or leadership. He created a new mood and provided a way out of the impasse. As Prime Minister Nehru put it many years later, 'We saw him functioning, functioning with success. It was so different from our method, which shouted a great deal and did little. Here was a man who didn't shout at all. He spoke softly and gently, and put forward what he thought were his minimum demands, and stuck to them. There was an element of great strength about it.'[2] Beyond that were Gandhi's courage in the face of a mighty empire, his serenity, his pledge to free India

[1] Confidential letter to Sir William Vincent, K.C.S.I., the Home Member, on 9 October 1921. Published with the permission of the Government of India.
[2] To the author in New Delhi on 6 June 1956.

through *satyagraha*, and his genuine renunciation of material comfort.

The Mahatma's personal influence at that time was remarkable. Nehru gave up smoking for five years and even flirted with vegetarianism, though only for a brief period. He began reading the *Bhagavad Gita* afresh, with its emphasis on right action, caring less for the consequences. His faith in the importance of means dates from this period, as does his stress on the ethical side of politics. In the broadest sense, his life was simplified and spiritualized. Calm and serene, yet firm and decisive, drawing people from all walks of life, Gandhi the man was a model of behaviour for Nehru.

Throughout the first civil disobedience campaign Jawaharlal was General Secretary of the United Provinces P.C.C., a not unimportant position then as now. All his energies were devoted to the struggle: the innumerable committee meetings; the establishment of Congress branches; the drafting of memoranda; the organization of *hartals* and demonstrations; public speeches by the score; and visits to the countryside. Like the Russian *Narodniks* in the 1870's, the Congressmen of 1921 turned to the village as the key to political success. Nehru himself felt 'the power of influencing that mass [and] began to understand a little the psychology of the crowd . . . I took to the crowd, and the crowd took to me, and yet I never lost myself in it; always I felt apart from it', a trait he retained over the years.[1]

Tension reached its peak with the arrival of the Prince of Wales (later the Duke of Windsor) for a goodwill visit. Gandhi proclaimed a nation-wide *hartal*. To the surprise and consternation of many it was a remarkable success, though marred by violence in Bombay, which the Mahatma severely criticized. At that point the Government struck, and struck hard. About 30,000 nationalists were sent to prison, most of them for short terms. Both Nehrus were seized in the first round-up of prominent Congressmen and were sentenced to six months' imprisonment. The younger Nehru's 'offence' turned out to be a perfectly legal act, and so he was released after three months.

While they were in prison Gandhi abruptly decided to terminate civil disobedience—because of the killing of twenty-two policemen in a remote village. The Mahatma was appalled by

[1] *Toward Freedom*, p. 76.

this violation of his creed and summarily called off the campaign. His colleagues were stunned by his decision. Many were hurt and angry. Years later, Nehru asked: 'Must we train the three hundred and odd millions of India in the theory and practice of nonviolent action before we could go forward?'[1]

Gandhi's action seemed all the more regrettable because the campaign was advancing throughout the country. As the Viceroy reported to the Secretary of State for India:

The lower classes in the towns have been seriously affected by the non-co-operation movement. . . . In certain areas the peasantry have been affected. A large proportion of the Mahommedan population throughout the country are embittered and sullen as a result of the Khilafat agitation. . . . Religious and racial feeling at the same time is bitter . . . *It has not been possible to ignore the fact that the non-co-operation movement has to a large extent been engendered and sustained by nationalist aspirations.*[2]

The Governor of Bombay at the time summed up the reaction of British officials more pungently: 'He gave us a scare. Gandhi's was the most colossal experiment in world history, and it came within an inch of succeeding.'[3]

Thus, when Nehru emerged from the Lucknow District Jail in March 1922, he was forlorn and depressed. He hastened to Ahmedabad where Gandhi was on trial for sedition. Then he returned to Allahabad and focused his attention on the boycott of foreign cloth, one of the few items of the non-co-operation programme still in effect. He was charged with criminal intimidation and the abetment of extortion, for which he received a sentence of eighteen months' rigorous imprisonment. Hence, after six weeks of freedom, he was back behind the walls.

To court imprisonment deliberately and openly was the supreme obligation of those who followed the creed of *satyagraha.* To be sent to jail was a mark of distinction. But the reality of life in prison was completely unknown to Nehru in 1921. With the passage of time it was to become a second home, for he returned nine times, some of them for short terms. Altogether, he spent about nine years away from family, home, friends and work.

As he approached the Lucknow Jail the first time he was

[1] *Toward Freedom*, p. 82.

[2] Telegram dated 9 February 1922 in *Telegraphic Correspondence regarding the Situation in India.* Cmd. 1586, 1922, paras. 7–8. (Emphasis added.)

[3] Lord Lloyd, as quoted in Andrews, C. F., 'Heart Beats in India' in *Asia*, vol. xxx, No. 3, March 1930, p. 198.

gripped with a natural feeling of tension. Fortunately he was not alone. His father and two cousins were there, along with many colleagues and friends from the Congress. Nor were conditions unduly harsh for political prisoners under the British *Raj*, though they were far from pleasant. Especially was this true when the first great wave of Indian nationalists descended upon the bewildered jail officials. The sheer number confounded them, but even more, the type of convict, which was utterly foreign to their experience—respectable middle- or upper-class professional men, many of them distinguished leaders in community life, proud of their violation of the law. Political prisoners comprised a separate class. They were kept apart from ordinary convicts and received special amenities.

During his first stay at the Lucknow Jail, Nehru, his father, and two cousins lived alone in a small shed, 16 ft. by 20 ft., with a large enclosure. Free contact with other barracks was provided, as were ample books, newspapers, interviews with relatives, and the right to supplement prison food from beyond the walls. Much time was spent in political discussions. The routine was rather simple: the morning was spent cleaning the shed and washing his own and his father's clothes, and spinning; for a few weeks there were literacy classes conducted for uneducated political prisoners; the afternoon was occupied with volleyball and occasional reading. Prison life did not involve serious privation.

When he returned after six weeks of liberty, Nehru found that conditions had deteriorated. His father had been transferred to another prison, and all politicals were now crowded together in the inner jail. Interviews were reduced in frequency, but reading and writing materials remained.

The most disconcerting aspect was the almost complete absence of privacy. Prison existence 'was the dull side of family life, magnified a hundredfold, with few of its graces and compensations. . . . It was a great nervous strain for all of us, and often I yearned for solitude.'[1] He was later transferred with a few friends to a remote section of the prison where he had time and peace of mind for serious reading. But this life was monotonous, dreary and cold. Finally, at the end of January 1923, he walked through the prison gates to freedom.

Only four years had passed since Gandhi had unfurled the

[1] *Toward Freedom*, p. 88.

banner of *satyagraha*. But in Nehru's life this was a crucial period, a phase of mental and emotional growth. He came under the influence of the Mahatma, a relationship which profoundly shaped his future as a man and a statesman. He had also discovered the peasant. He had overcome his aversion to public speaking. And he had tasted the bitter fruit of prison life. No longer was he the dilettante. His future was now clearly charted, a life of politics in the quest for national freedom.

*   *   *   *

There was confidence in the air during 1921–2 and hope—hope in a resounding victory. The magic word of *swaraj*, self-rule, had fired the imagination of millions. A new era in Hindu-Muslim friendship seemed at hand. But what had been achieved? The first wave of civil disobedience had broken on the rock of Gandhi's insistence on pure non-violence. The movement had disintegrated. So too had the communal alliance, and Hindu-Muslim tension reappeared. Within the Congress there were petty squabbles and intrigues. India had withdrawn to its submissive shell. Nehru, too, became despondent in the face of defeat. The years of disenchantment were upon him.

Factional strife began soon after Gandhi's imprisonment in March 1922. The crucial question was the proper attitude to the forthcoming general elections. One group, led by C. R. Das and the elder Nehru, favoured entry into the Legislative Councils—to paralyse the experiment in semi-constitutional government. The *pro-changers*, they came to be called, for they deviated from Gandhi's programme of complete non-co-operation. Strongly opposed were the *no-changers*, the pure Gandhians, who advocated total boycott of the elections and concentration on the Mahatma's Constructive Programme—spinning, communal harmony, abolition of untouchability, etc. Their leaders were C. Rajagopalacharia (C.R. or Rajaji), the last Governor-General of the Dominion of India, and Rajendra Prasad, first President of the Republic of India.

Rajagopalacharia is probably the most astute intellectual among the élite of Indian nationalists. He is also the only south Indian to achieve nation-wide prominence as a Congress leader. A Madrassi Brahmin of fair complexion, Rajaji's delicate appearance belies his intellectual vigour. Short, slim and completely bald, he walks with a slight stoop. Perhaps the most striking physical characteristics are his protruding chin, an impassive expression on his long, thin face, and the ever-present dark, horn-rimmed glasses which conceal his eyes from the viewer. There is a cold, almost icy reserve about him, a pronounced aloofness and stern composure. Precise in thought and speech, he is also capable of biting satire. His is a quick, razor-sharp mind, less given to emotion than that of any of his colleagues in the nationalist movement. Now in his late seventies, he is one of India's Elder Statesmen, having served with distinction as Chief Minister of Madras and Governor of Bengal, as well as Governor-General of India and Home Minister in New Delhi.

By contrast, Prasad is a kindly, gentle-looking man. He is sturdy and tall, heavy, slow-moving, with a ruddy complexion and an impressive, bushy moustache. Simple in dress and manner, never without his Gandhi cap, he looks very much like the father figure which he is to many Indians today. An orthodox Hindu and a devout believer in pure non-violence, Prasad was, among all of Gandhi's leading political disciples, the most spiritually akin to the Mahatma.

Twenty years later Rajaji was to clash with Gandhi over the issues of Pakistan and active co-operation with the Allies in the war. Prasad has been loyal to his mentor throughout his public life. On this occasion they were united in support of the Mahatma's policy of total non-co-operation.

Gradually the Congress split into these two factions. It was, indeed, sick in mind and body, floundering in a morass of tactical disagreement. The battle of words was only terminated by a face-saving formula in the autumn of 1923 which allowed the pro-changers to stand for election. Nehru played a key role in working out the compromise solution. His sympathies lay with Gandhi and the no-changers, but he did not hold strong views. His primary concern was to reconcile the warring factions. This led him to join a middle-of-the-road group within the Congress, the Centre Party.

The controversy between no-changers and pro-changers marks Nehru's *entrée* into the inner politics of the party. It also witnessed his earliest performance as a mediator, a role which he was to play with increasing skill in the struggle for national freedom, in independent India, and in world affairs after 1947. Ideologically, he was a Gandhian *par excellence* during this period: 'I believe that the salvation of India and, indeed, of the whole world will come through non-violence. Violence had had a long career in the world. It has been weighed repeatedly and has been found wanting.'[1]

In the midst of the Congress squabble, Nehru had a curious and unpleasant adventure in the Sikh princely State of Nabha. It culminated in his third, short-lived imprisonment.

At the end of September 1923 he and two colleagues were invited to observe anti-British demonstrations there. They were ordered to leave the State at once, but demurred. They were then arrested and were paraded down the main street of the town, handcuffed and chained to a policeman. For Nehru this was a severe shock, since his previous encounters with the police had been relatively civilized. To make matters worse they were kept in a foul, insanitary cell, with rats for companions. After a farcical trial they were given a six months' and an eighteen months' sentence; the sentences were suspended, however, and they were allowed to leave.

The Nabha experience was of great educational value for Nehru. From it dates his genuine interest in the conditions of the States' subjects. But the price of this education was high. Along with his colleagues, he contracted typhoid in the Nabha jail. For a month he lay seriously ill at home, rare for one who has been strengthened by a robust health throughout his adult life. And yet there were compensations: 'my mind seemed clearer and more peaceful than it had previously been. . . . It was in the nature of a spiritual experience . . . and it had a lasting effect on me and my way of thinking.'[2]

One aspect of Nehru's outlook at the time was reflected in his presidential address to the first conference of Volunteers, held as a side-show to the Congress session of 1923. 'Most of our weaknesses', he stressed, 'can be traced to our lack of discipline.'[3] Again and again, he was to reiterate this pre-condition of victory in the struggle for independence—party discipline. After 1947, however, the need for discipline applied to the nation at large. In

---

[1] For the text of this speech see Dwivedi, op. cit., pp. 17–36.

[2] *Toward Freedom*, p. 112.

[3] The text of his address is to be found in *Indian Annual Register*, vol. ii, 1923, Supplement, pp. 215–18.

town and village, party conclave and Parliament, Nehru has brought the full weight of his prestige to bear on the virtues of individual and collective discipline. Unity and discipline—these have been the twin pillars of his one-man educational campaign to ease India's transition to a modern, progressive society. The early 1920's provided him with dramatic evidence of their importance.

At the behest of Congress President Mohammed Ali, one of the towering Muslim figures in recent Indian history, Nehru was appointed a General Secretary for 1924. He was reluctant to accept the post. But Mohammed Ali persisted, and Nehru yielded. 'I . . . must "protest most indignantly" once more against your misplaced modesty,' wrote the Muslim divine. 'My dear Jawahar! It is just because some members of the Working Committee distrust and dislike your presence as Secretary that *I like it.* . . . So do be cheerful and let us start work.'[1]

Early that year came news which electrified the nation. Gandhi suffered an acute attack of appendicitis while in prison. The emotional impact on Nehru and millions of Indians was akin to a personal tragedy. But the Mahatma's life was spared. As so often in the future, the Government decided to release him lest he die while in detention. The two Nehrus rushed to Poona to visit Gandhi and then followed him to Juhu, a seaside resort near Bombay, where he went to recuperate. For Jawaharlal it was in the nature of a holiday, his first since the hectic days of civil disobedience. His father and Das engaged in serious talks with Gandhi. The Mahatma was adamant on the issue of principle: entry into the legislative councils was a deviation from the programme of non-co-operation. But he called on his followers to respect the Swarajists' right to continue their activities in the legislatures.

Jawaharlal had serious doubts about the value of a constitutional approach to politics. He also found Gandhi's leadership wanting at this stage, particularly the preoccupation with spinning. He agreed to stay on as Congress General Secretary another year, though there was little work in the circumstances. During the next four years the Swarajists dominated national politics.

What disturbed the younger Nehru even more was the sharp deterioration in Hindu-Muslim relations. During 1924 communal riots spread over the land, most of them over petty matters such as

[1] *A Bunch of Old Letters*, p. 33. (15 January 1924.)

the playing of music before mosques or cow-slaughter on the Muslim festival of *Bakr-id*. These had always been sources of friction. But to them was now added frustration resulting from the collapse of the *Khilafat* agitation.

The prelude was the tragic Moplah Rebellion of 1921, perhaps the bloodiest communal clash before the partition of India. The Moplahs are poor Muslim peasants and petty traders descended from Arab invaders many centuries ago. Fanatically religious, they had a reputation for periodic outbursts of violence.

Early in 1921 the message of civil disobedience was carried to the Moplahs by Congress and *Khilafat* spokesmen. At first the rebellion was directed against the Government. As it spread, however, it took the form of a peasant uprising against Hindu landlords. The provincial government moved thousands of troops into the area, and a full-scale military operation followed. Official casualty figures suggest its magnitude: 2,339 killed, 1,652 wounded, 5,955 captured and 39,348 'prisoners', of whom 24,167 were convicted of rebellion or lesser crimes.[1] The communal twist to the uprising inevitably affected Hindu-Muslim relations elsewhere in India. In 1924 it was to bear bitter fruit.

As Nehru surveyed the tension of the mid-'twenties from home and abroad, his hostility to orthodox religion crystallized. 'The communal frenzy is awful to contemplate,' he wrote to a friend. 'We seem to have been caught in a whirlpool of mutual hatred and we go round and round and down and down this abyss.'[2] About religion itself he was even more critical: 'No country or people who are slaves to dogma . . . can progress, and unhappily our country and people have become extraordinarily dogmatic and little-minded. . . . I have no patience left with the legitimate and illegitimate offspring of religion.'[3]

*   *   *   *

These were, in truth, lean years for Jawaharlal Nehru. In the autumn of 1923, he was elected Chairman of the Allahabad Municipality. Here was an outlet for frustrated energy. And there

[1] Figures given in the Legislative Assembly, 1923. H.O.R. No. 1749, made available by the National Archives of India.
[2] Unpublished Nehru-Mahmud Correspondence, 24 May 1926.
[3] Ibid., 12 June 1926 and 12 January 1927.

was much to do—enlarging the scope of social services, reducing taxes, infusing a moribund organization with efficiency and *élan*. He worked hard and was attracted to the challenge of local reform. Being a perfectionist by nature, he concentrated authority in his own hands, as he was to do in the Congress secretariat and in the Government of India after 1947. Memoranda flowed from his pen on issues great and small—education, sanitation, prostitution, the removing of billboards which disfigured the city, and the like.

His tenure of office was three years, but by the beginning of the second he was anxious to resign. At every turn his reform programme came up against serious obstacles. Nepotism and corruption were rampant in the permanent ranks of the service. The bureaucracy moved slowly, far too slowly for his mercurial temperament. The municipality was utterly dependent on the provincial treasury. No fundamental changes were possible. And Nehru has rarely been satisfied with palliatives. Yet the experience was highly instructive, for it brought the intellectual down to earth.

By all accounts his venture into the arena of local politics was successful. The provincial government commended his services. The machinery of local government was toned up. Corruption was reduced. And his colleagues were impressed.

While Nehru was engaged in local politics, his father was at the pinnacle of his career, as the Swarajist leader in the Legislative Assembly. During this period the younger Nehru found much solace and comfort in his family. He drew closer to his wife who had shown sympathy and understanding during the period of travail after 1920.

One source of dissatisfaction was his continuing financial dependence on his father. Nehru was then in his mid-thirties but had no regular source of income. In 1924 a way out of his dilemma presented itself, a proposal to pay full-time officials of the Congress. But Motilal Nehru was strongly opposed, for public work was *noblesse oblige*. The son yielded.

During 1925 Jawaharlal began to notice a tendency to baldness. He was anxious to stay the inevitable and consulted a friend, who recommended a special hair tonic. Nehru was appalled by the odour. 'It is a most evil-smelling concoction,' he wrote, 'and if offensiveness in smell is a measure of its efficacy, then I should have a thick crop of hair in the future!'[1] Alas, there was no correlation.

Another inconsequential episode at that time revealed the streak of vanity in Nehru's character. 'For heaven's sake don't call your son Jawahar Lal,' he admonished a friend. 'Jawahar by itself might pass but the addition of Lal makes it odious. . . . I cannot congratulate you on your aesthetic taste. I dislike my name intensely.'[2]

This relatively uneventful period in Nehru's life was brought to an end abruptly by the news that his wife's tubercular infection had become much worse. Nehru welcomed the opportunity to get away from the depressing atmosphere of Indian politics. Conditions were ripe for a change and he felt that a trip abroad would give him a new perspective. In this he was remarkably prescient, for his European sojourn in 1926–7 proved to be a turning-point in his intellectual growth.

---

[1] Unpublished Nehru-Mahmud Correspondence, 3 September 1925.
[2] Ibid., 24 May 1925 and 3 June 1925.

CHAPTER IV

NEHRU COMES OF AGE

On the whole Nehru's stay in the West was a quiet, peaceful interlude, a period for reflection and serious reading. Most of the time was spent in Geneva or at a nearby mountain sanatorium in Montana. But as Kamala's health improved, he was able to visit neighbouring countries. Before they returned to India he managed to pause in France, England, Belgium, Holland, Germany and the Soviet Union. Two of these excursions were to leave a marked imprint on Nehru's outlook, namely Brussels and Moscow.

While in Geneva he lived modestly, in a three-room flat, cared for by his sister, Krishna. From afar, he anxiously watched developments at home. He also observed with interest the changing moods of Europe in transition, the flow of ideas, the intellectual debates of the time and the struggles waged by the Powers. Ever in search of more satisfying answers to the basic problems of ethics and politics, he went on various 'pilgrimages' to Villa Olga, the home of Romain Rolland in nearby Villeneuve. Although he was impressed by the great French novelist, the highly spiritual tone of Rolland's social philosophy was too remote and abstract to inspire him. By contrast Nehru was immediately drawn to the sensitive, morose, passionate young German poet, Ernst Toller, whom he met at the anti-imperialist Congress in Brussels.

In the mountain resort where Kamala was undergoing treatment time moved slowly. There was no sense of urgency, no rigorous schedule, no commitments of any kind. Thus, with the approach of winter Jawaharlal indulged in sports—skiing, ice-skating and tobogganing, and climbing among the lofty peaks which reminded him of his beloved Himalayas.

The highlight of Nehru's European sojourn was an anti-imperialist conference in Brussels in February 1927. It was there

that he first came into contact with communists, socialists and
radical nationalists from Asia and Africa. It was there that the
goals of national independence and social reform became linked
inextricably in his mind. It was there, too, that the notion of an
Afro-Asian group of nations co-operating with one another was
conceived.

Nehru himself sees the Bandung Conference of 1955 in this
perspective. 'I will tell you an old story,' he remarked about
Bandung. 'Perhaps you have come across the fact that I attended
a conference in Brussels in 1927.' The Asian delegates wanted to
meet regularly thereafter but 'found that it was not possible for us
to meet anywhere except in some country of Western Europe.'
When I interjected, 'the world has changed since then,' his face
glowed and, in slow, measured words, he said, 'the world has
changed and of course we meet.'[1]

The idea for an anti-imperialist conference came from a small
group of revolutionaries in Berlin, then the European centre of
political exiles from the colonial world. It had strong moral support from Moscow. Many delegates had communist sympathies,
though the ideologies of those present varied considerably. Among
the most prominent figures were George Lansbury, the arch-
pacifist, Albert Einstein and Romain Rolland. The principal
sources of funds were the Mexican Government and the Kuomin-
tang.

For Nehru this was an informal début on the international stage.
As a mark of honour to the movement he represented he was
elected to the presidium of the conference and later served on the
nine-man Executive Committee of the newly formed League
against Imperialism.

His speeches at Brussels were typical of the radical socialist pronouncements then in vogue, angry critiques of Imperialism and
all its misdeeds, with special reference to India. In his report to
the All-India Congress Committee he referred to 'the rising
imperialism of the United States' which was acquiring a strangle-
hold in Central and South America. His account of the conference
was most favourable and he urged the Congress to maintain a link
with the newly established League against Imperialism. It was, he
wrote, a useful channel for propaganda and it offered facilities for
closer contact with other Asian nationalist movements.

[1] To the author in New Delhi on 13 June 1956.

Nehru's attraction to Communism was perhaps the most striking feature of his role at Brussels. It was not Marxist theory that influenced him at the outset; rather, an emotional aversion to the social democrats and faith in the Soviet experiment. And yet, 'communists often irritated me by their dictatorial ways, their aggressive and rather vulgar methods, their habit of denouncing everybody who did not agree with them.'[1] As early as 1927, then, the dichotomy in Nehru's attitude to communism was already visible. He was emotionally attracted to the vision of a classless society but he was emotionally repelled by the communist militant. From that time onwards this split mentality to communism is evident.

His doubts went far beyond these sources of friction. Then as later his primary loyalty was to Indian national interests. This vital aspect of Nehru's political outlook emerges clearly from a confidential report on the Brussels Conference which he prepared for the Congress High Command. 'The disadvantages [of affiliation with the League against Imperialism]', he wrote, 'might be *the socialist character of the League and the possibility that Russian foreign policy might influence it.* [Moreover] the boycott of Lancashire goods in India . . . is an example of a possible conflict between *our nationalistic interests* and the interests of the workers outside.'[2]

Nehru's relations with the League against Imperialism were excellent during the first two years of its existence. By 1929, however, dissension became apparent, for he had signed the 'Delhi Manifesto', a Gandhi-inspired compromise to render civil disobedience unnecessary if London granted Dominion status immediately. The League was appalled. In vain it urged him to withdraw his approval. Nehru's pride revolted against the slightest hint of dictation. 'Good advice is always welcome, but . . . people have a tendency to jump to conclusions without sufficient data', was his rebuke to the League. What incensed him even more was a circular sent to workers' and peasants' organizations in India criticizing Gandhi for 'chronic reformism and betrayal of the cause of workers and peasants'. This sealed the issue for Nehru —it was reprehensible interference. His loyalty to Gandhi and the

---

[1] *Toward Freedom*, p. 126.
[2] Extracts are in the files of the History of the Freedom Movement Project in New Delhi, File 1 (B.19). These were made available by the Government of India. (Emphasis added.)

Congress came first. For his 'deviationism' Nehru was expelled. He in turn severed all relations with the League. In 1930, as in the 1950's, he placed the interests of India ahead of extra-national considerations.

Nehru's initial exposure to communist views at Brussels was widened by a brief visit to Moscow early in November 1927. Although it lasted only four days, it helped to shape his attitude to communism and the Soviet Union, to Indo-Soviet relations and to Soviet foreign policy in the 'thirties.

Genuine sympathy for Soviet society is the dominant theme of his 'random sketches and impressions' which were published in the Indian press.[1] Read in the 1950's they appear incredibly naïve. Occasional reservations creep into his 'discovery of Russia', but on the whole he accepted what he saw and heard as indices of 'the good society'. In this he was not alone. And undoubtedly those impressions reflected his receptive mood at the time, a will to believe, and perhaps to find answers to some of the questions still troubling him.

Among his reflections on Russia at that time was a laudatory portrait of Lenin. He called on his readers to learn from Lenin's realism, flexibility and perseverance, and concluded with a tribute to the Bolshevik leader which resembles his estimate of Gandhi's achievement years later: 'By amazing power of will he hypnotised a nation and filled a disunited and demoralised people with energy and determination and the strength to endure and suffer for a cause.'

Apart from his emotional attraction to the Soviet experiment, Nehru was conscious, even then, of its practical significance for India. 'Even our self-interest compels us to understand the vast forces which have upset the old order of things. . . . *Russia again cannot be ignored by us, because she is our neighbour, a powerful neighbour, which may be friendly to us and co-operate with us, or may be a thorn in our side. In either event we have to know her and understand her and shape our policy accordingly.*' Although written thirty years ago, here is a lucid statement of one of the core elements in Nehru's foreign policy since Independence. As for Russo-Indian relations, he saw no danger from the north. 'It is inconceivable that Russia, in her present condition at least, and for a long time to come, will

[1] Nehru's articles were published in book form in 1929—*Soviet Russia*. (The Inter-Continental Library.)

threaten India. . . . The two countries are today too similar to be exploited by each other, and there can be no economic motive for Russia to covet India.' The continuity of thought and policy suggests that the roots of Nehru's foreign policy may be traced to the late 1920's. His infatuation with the Soviets later gave way to a more sober and mature attitude. Yet, it lingered on for at least twenty years and influenced his thought and action.

Nehru's visit to Moscow was the last noteworthy event of his European tour. There was nothing else to keep him in the West. Kamala's health was much improved. His own physical and mental condition was excellent after the prolonged holiday. The sense of inner conflict which plagued him on the eve of his arrival had been overcome. Through reading and discussion he had acquired a wider perspective, especially the conviction that political freedom had to be linked to socialism. Moreover, the political situation at home was showing signs of emerging from the doldrums. And so he returned to India towards the end of 1927.

*　　　*　　　*　　　*

The most striking feature of Nehru's return to the political wars was a sharp clash with Gandhi, the first of a series during the next two decades. The precipitating cause was a resolution which Jawaharlal moved at the Madras session in December 1927: 'The Congress declares the goal of the Indian people to be complete national independence.' The Mahatma was absent from the proceedings. But when he learned of it he exclaimed: 'By passing such resolutions we make an exhibition of our impotence. . . . We have almost sunk to the level of a schoolboys' debating society.'[1]

What disturbed Gandhi more than anything else was Nehru's surge to radicalism, and his apparent abandonment of nonviolence. It was as if a son had gone astray. The Mahatma rebuked the younger man but not in the spirit of anger. 'I feel that you love me too well to resent what I am about to write,' he began. 'In any case, I love you too well to restrain my pen when I feel I must write. You are going too fast. You should have taken time to think and become acclimatized. Most of the resolutions you framed and got carried could have been delayed for one year. Your plunging into the "republican army" was a hasty step.

[1] Tendulkar, *Mahatma*, vol. 2, p. 402.

[Nehru had presided over a Republican Congress, a one-day side-show at the Madras session.] But I do not mind these acts of yours so much as I mind your encouraging mischief-makers and hooligans.[1]

A few weeks later Gandhi wrote again. 'I see quite clearly that you must carry on open warfare against me and my views. . . . The differences between you and me appear to be so vast and so radical that there seems to be no meeting ground between us. I cannot conceal from you my grief that I should lose a comrade so valiant, so faithful, so able and so honest, as you have always been. . . . But this dissolution of comradeship—if dissolution must come—in no way affects our personal intimacy.'[2]

Despite the tone of Gandhi's letters an open break was not seriously entertained by either. It was as if the Mahatma were testing Nehru's loyalty. This play would be re-enacted often in the future. Invariably Nehru would remain loyal to the master.

The cleavage of 1928 centred on tactics, not on strategy. Nehru believed that they would have to launch another campaign of mass civil disobedience, even without the support of the wealthy and educated groups in the party. Gandhi agreed but he felt that conditions were not yet suitable. In general, Gandhi was cautious, moderate, restrained. Nehru was impetuous, exuberant and romantic in his approach to politics, with a strong will to action. It was, however, a healthy difference of opinion, almost always kept within bounds.

Encouraged by his victory at Madras, Nehru pressed forward with his 'mission' of educating colleagues and the rank and file. In 1928 he presided over five provincial party conferences, was elected president of the All-India Trades Union Congress, and addressed various gatherings of nationalist youth. Everywhere he hammered on one basic theme—the twin goals of the nationalist movement must be complete independence and socialism. Action was essential, he declared; even wrong action was better than no action at all. Industrialization was inevitable. Capitalism and Imperialism must be eradicated. The struggle against British rule must be waged on both the political and economic fronts. But he denounced violence as counter-revolutionary. As for communalism,

---

[1] Tendulkar, ibid., vol. 8, Appendix on Gandhi-Nehru Letters, p. 349. (4 January 1928.)
[2] Tendulkar, op. cit., vol. 8, pp. 350-1. (17 January 1928.)

it was a giant with feet of clay which would soon disappear. He urged the boycott of all foreign cloth and defended *khaddar* (home-spun cloth). Reformism was rejected as inadequate to the needs of India. Yet Nehru rejected the *methods* of communism and the dialectical theory of history. His attitude to Imperialism was based on emotional antipathy to colonial rule, not on orthodox Marxism. And on political tactics he followed Gandhi's lead, rejecting secrecy in negotiations and organization. From his speeches in 1928 it is evident that Nehru had not yet worked out a coherent ideology. It is questionable whether he has ever done so.

As he travelled throughout the land Jawaharlal detected a new spirit among the people, in town and village alike. The mood of defiance was sparked by a minor incident in Bardoli, in the northern part of Bombay Province. The issue was an increased land tax, which was greeted with anger by the small landlords of the area. To their rescue came a man who was later honoured as one of the three heroes of the Indian revolution, Vallabhbhai Patel. A lawyer by profession and a native of Gujarat, Patel brought the Mahatma's message to the sullen but fearful peasants of Bardoli. With Gandhi's blessing he organized a small-scale *satyagraha* against the government decree. Under his leadership they stood fast and refused to pay the tax. The Government gave way. In appreciation of his services, the people of Bardoli gave Patel the honorary title *Sardar* (leader) and his fame spread throughout the country.

The beginning of 1928 also saw the arrival of the Simon Commission to propose another instalment of constitutional reform. Indian political opinion was outraged by the exclusion of Indians from its ranks. The Commission was greeted everywhere with black-flag processions. In the autumn, Lala Lajpat Rai, Congress leader of the Punjab, died, a few weeks after he was severely beaten while leading a demonstration against the Commission in Lahore. Then it was Nehru's turn to feel the physical pain of *lathi* blows.

In Lucknow he led a column of *satyagrahis* towards the central meeting-ground—though all processions were prohibited. He was promised safe conduct if he requested it in writing. He refused. Suddenly, mounted police descended upon the group, swinging their clubs in all directions. Nehru's reaction sheds much light on his character. His instinct bade him to seek safety and he began to move away, 'but . . . I stopped and had a little argument with myself, and decided that it would be unbecoming. . . . I . . . could not tolerate the idea of my behaving like a coward. Yet the line between cowardice and courage was a thin one. . . .' The following day this scene was re-enacted on a larger scale. 'It was a tremendous hammering and the clearness of vision that I had had the evening before left me. . . . I felt half blinded with the blows, and sometimes a dull anger seized me and a desire to hit out . . . but long training and discipline held, and I did not raise a hand, except to protect my face from a blow.' What remained in his memory was a picture of 'those faces, full of hate and blood-lust, almost mad, with no trace of sympathy or touch of humanity!'[1]

At the level of high politics 1928 was dominated by the search for an acceptable 'nationalist' constitution. The result was the 'Nehru Report', drafted by Jawaharlal's father and adopted by all groups except the Muslim League, then an insignificant minority organization. One feature of the Report caused a sharp division within the Congress. The elder Nehru, supported by Gandhi and a majority of the Old Guard, called for Dominion status. Against them were ranged the radicals led by Jawaharlal and Subhas Chandra Bose, already the hero of Bengali youth. To press their demand, the 'young Turks' formed an Independence for India League. As Secretary of the All-India Council, the younger Nehru was its dominant figure. He virtually created the League and did most of the work, drafting its communications and preparing its constitution. Indeed, but for his interest the organization would have been stillborn.

The Independence League was merely a pressure group within the Congress. With the Congress acceptance of the goal of complete independence it disappeared. Despite its atrophy, British officials were disturbed by the League's propaganda effect. 'By the end of 1928', wrote the head of the Home Department's Intelligence Bureau, 'Jawahir Lal Nehru had established his Independence League, and the ideal of independence could command such a following that amongst the younger and more ardent spirits it completely swept away the more prudent counsels of the advocates of Dominion Status.'[2]

The debate reached a climax at the Congress annual session in

[1] *Toward Freedom*, pp. 135–8.
[2] A secret minute of 19 June 1929. Used with the permission of the Government of India.

Calcutta. Gandhi moved the adoption of the 'Nehru Report' in its entirety, i.e., including the Dominion status formula, if the British Parliament accepted the Report as a constitution for India before the end of 1930. Should Westminster balk, he proposed another mass civil disobedience campaign. The atmosphere was tense as the younger Nehru urged civil disobedience if complete independence were not granted by the end of 1929, i.e., only one year of grace. The party leaders held an emergency session in the evening. In an attempt to escape from the dilemma—displeasing Gandhi and his father or retreating from principle—Nehru absented himself from the open proceedings the next day. To many of the younger men this action seemed political cowardice. Bose, too, withdrew and Gandhi's motion was ultimately carried. As a concession to the radicals, London was given only one year to act.

In perspective, the controversy over Dominion status and complete independence was over a straw man. The elder Nehru was correct in identifying the two formulae. Why then the depth of feeling on this issue? Until the very end of the freedom struggle, Dominion status was genuinely misunderstood by many Indian nationalists, including the younger Nehru, who viewed it as a symbol of dependence on Britain and the Empire. Especially in 1928-9—before the Statute of Westminster had altered the meaning of Dominion status—the radical nationalists insisted on a total break with London as the visible expression as well as the reality of political freedom. This incident was forgotten but it revealed a number of Nehru's characteristics: vacillation, devotion to Gandhi and his father, and a conviction that party unity had the highest political priority.

The Calcutta compromise set the stage for a year of uneasy quiet, a lull before the storm of civil disobedience broke over the land. Individual terrorism reappeared, along with widespread labour unrest. The Government of India retaliated swiftly, notably by arresting thirty-two prominent trade unionists. Nehru himself sought to raise funds for the accused and termed the subsequent Meerut Trial 'a blow against the whole working class'.[1] The Government shared this view: '. . . The removal of the thirty leading Communist agitators from the political arena was

[1] History of the Freedom Movement Project. File on the League against Imperialism.

immediately followed by a marked improvement in the industrial situation. There can be no doubt whatsoever that the arrests . . . placed the authorities in a commanding position and created a vacuum in the leadership of the [trade union] movement which was filled by very inferior material.'[1]

Amidst this turmoil the Congress elected a president for the crucial year 1930. Gandhi declined the nomination and threw his weight behind Nehru, then only thirty-nine. Sardar Patel was persuaded to withdraw, though in terms of seniority and support by the Provincial Congress Committees he was the logical second choice. But the Mahatma had an instinct for the right political decision.

There were two basic reasons for this choice: namely to divert radical youth from Communism to the Congress; and to wean Nehru himself from the drift to the far Left. As formal head of the party, he would become aware of the necessity of compromise. This would take the edge off his extreme leftism. In any event the potential risk was minimal, for Gandhi would be at his side. 'Those who know [our] relations,' said the Mahatma, 'know that his being in the [presidential] chair is as good as my being in it.'[2]

To placate the Old Guard Gandhi wrote a moving panegyric to his protégé: 'In bravery he [Nehru] is not to be surpassed. Who can excel him in the love of the country? "He is rash and impetuous" say some. This quality is an additional qualification at the present moment. And if he has the dash and the rashness of a warrior, he has also the prudence of a statesman. He is undoubtedly an extremist, thinking far ahead of his surroundings. But he is humble enough and practical enough not to force the pace to the breaking point. He is pure as crystal, he is truthful beyond suspicion. He is a knight *sans peur et sans reproche*. The nation is safe in his hands.'[3] Nehru himself 'seldom felt quite so annoyed and humiliated . . . I appeared suddenly by a trap door and bewildered the audience into acceptance. . . . My pride was hurt, and I almost felt like handing back the honour.'[4]

*   *   *   *

[1] Government of India, India and Communism (Confidential) (1935), p. 72.
[2] Tendulkar, op. cit., vol. 2, p. 488.
[3] Ram Mohan Lal, L., *Jawaharlal Nehru, Statements, Speeches and Writings*, p. ii.
[4] *Toward Freedom*, p. 145.

A mood of sombre anticipation gripped the Indian political scene in the autumn of 1929. In an effort to stave off the impending clash, Lord Irwin (later Halifax), succeeded in persuading London to reaffirm the goal of Dominion status. He also proposed a conference between the British Government and representatives of all shades of Indian political opinion. Spokesmen for the Congress, the Hindu Mahasabha and the Liberals issued a joint manifesto accepting the Viceroy's declaration and the idea of a Round Table Conference. Nehru was dissatisfied but 'allowed myself to be talked into signing [after] a soothing letter from Gandhiji.'[1] How accurate was the Mahatma's appraisal, '. . . he is humble enough and practical enough not to force the pace to the breaking point'.

During a British parliamentary debate on India in November, Lord Irwin's pledge was seriously undermined by Conservative spokesmen. And the Labour Prime Minister, Ramsay MacDonald, made no effort to reassure Indian political opinion. At this juncture Nehru made a brief appearance on the stage of trade union politics, as President of the All-India Trades Union Congress for 1929–30.

The labour movement was then in the throes of sharp growing pains. On the eve of the meeting a split occurred; the Right-wing leaders decided to boycott the open session. Nehru's address was filled with socialist jargon. On the vital issue of the moment he adopted a typical middle-of-the-road position. Stand aloof from both Internationals, he advised, the Second International because it has become the exponent of a new form of Imperialism, and the Third because it would mean the adoption of communist methods in their entirety—something that Nehru opposed. It was an appropriate plea for moderation by an outsider more interested at the moment in rallying the trade unions to the impending civil disobedience campaign.

Tension was heightened by an attempt to assassinate the Viceroy on December 22nd, as his train approached New Delhi. The conference with Indian leaders was held as scheduled the following day, but to no avail. Within a week some 300,000 persons gathered on the banks of the Ravi River on the outskirts of Lahore where the Congress camp had been pitched. Nehru held the limelight. He was then barely forty, one of the youngest Presidents in

[1] *Toward Freedom*, p. 147.

Congress history. No one was more moved than his parents. Motilal handed over the chair to his son, like a king passing on the sceptre of the throne to his logical successor.

The issue at Lahore was war or peace. The key resolution was moved by Gandhi. In essence the party was called upon to authorize the All-India Congress Committee, 'whenever it deems fit, to launch upon a programme of civil disobedience, including non-payment of taxes'. The Right wing pressed for delay until another all-party conference considered the matter again. Then came the challenge from the Left: Bose called for the establishment of parallel governments based on local Congress committees and the effective organization of workers, peasants and youth for direct action. Gandhi remained firm and his resolution was carried. But the fissures remained. The Bose group expressed its displeasure by forming a Congress Democratic faction within the party.

Nehru was silent throughout the debate: emotionally he was sympathetic to Bose, but intellectually he was drawn to Gandhi's resolution. Yet he did speak his mind, in a moving presidential address.

'I must frankly confess that I am a Socialist and a republican,' he began. As was his habit then and now, he rambled over the political universe. Europe's traditional mastery was rapidly coming to an end, he said, and 'the future lies with America and Asia'. Although India desires independence, it was not narrow nationalism which animated the Congress. The influence of Marxism and his world perspective is evident throughout.

Turning to the Indian scene, Nehru stressed three problems— the minorities, the princely States, and the peasants and workers. Real communal differences have largely gone, he argued naïvely. As for the States, they are 'the products of a vicious system that will ultimately have to go'. Twenty years later this seed of opposition to the Princes bore fruit. Speaking as a champion of the peasants and urban workers he criticized Gandhi's theory of trusteeship (of wealth) and paternalism as 'equally barren. . . . The sole trusteeship that can be fair is the trusteeship of the nation. . . .' He also differed with the Mahatma on the question of violence. 'Violence is bad, büt slavery is worse.' Finally, he issued a call to action: 'Success often comes to those who dare and act; it seldom goes to the timid who are ever afraid of the consequences.'[1]

---

[1] The text is to be found in *Indian Quarterly Register*, vol. ii, 1929, pp. 288–97.

Here was Nehru's first major triumph in national politics. He was acclaimed by radicals and youth. He had delivered a forth-right address. He had presided over an historic Congress session when the long-sought goal of *purna swaraj*, complete independence, had become the official creed of the party. And the declaration of war had been issued. At the relatively young age of forty he became the rising star of India. The young Brahmin had arrived. Yet the real centre of power in the Congress was still Gandhi.

Looking to the future, Nehru was unperturbed. 'We have got a stiff time ahead of us here,' he wrote to an English friend. 'Probably the Labour Government will have the honour of sending some of us to prison before long.'[1] The shouting was over. The war was soon to begin.

[1] To Reginald Bridgeman, Secretary of the British Section of the League against Imperialism. (Unpublished.) History of the Freedom Movement Project.

CHAPTER V

PRISON BECOMES A HABIT

An air of uncertainty hung over the Indian political scene as the Lahore Congress drew to a close on New Year's Day of 1930. Everyone waited for the Mahatma's lead. But Gandhi was never disposed to hasty action. The strategy of *satyagraha* had a marked Fabian strain. To pave the way for mass civil disobedience it was first necessary to gauge the mood of his followers. All Congress legislators were urged to resign their seats. Most did so. Even more encouraging was the enthusiasm of the rank and file at 'Independence Day' gatherings fixed for 26 January. All over the country thousands adopted a pledge to *swaraj*. Yet Gandhi bided his time. Indeed, he seemed prepared to retreat. At the end of January he actually offered to desist from civil disobedience—if the Viceroy would concede eleven points which for Gandhi formed the 'substance of *purna swaraj*'. Lord Irwin took no notice, but many Congressmen were disconcerted. As Nehru wrote a few years later, 'what was the point of making a list of some political and social reforms—good in themselves, no doubt—when we were talking in terms of independence? Did Gandhiji mean the same thing when he used this term as we did, or did we speak a different language?'[1]

Another month passed while Gandhi waited for his 'inner voice' to point the way. At last he divulged his plan. He would disobey the salt tax, he said, for here was the most iniquitous of all laws in India, a burden on millions which taxed even the poorest peasants. This he would do by marching from his *ashram* (spiritual retreat) near Ahmedabad to the Arabian Sea, a distance of 241 miles, and there he would violate the law by taking salt from the sea. To ensure complete non-violence he would confine this initial act of civil disobedience to a group of hand-picked disciples from

[1] *Toward Freedom*, p. 157.

his *ashram*. Mass civil disobedience against the salt tax would follow.

Many like Nehru were stunned by this novel approach to political warfare. But time and experience proved the Mahatma's unerring instinct for tactics attuned to the temper of the Indian masses. A campaign of civil disobedience to achieve *purna swaraj* would not arouse the peasantry, for it was too vague to inspire self-sacrifice. But salt, an absolute necessity for everyday life, touched the very core of resentment against the *Raj*. Here was something tangible, on which there were no divided opinions. The very simplicity of the issue was its greatest strength. And with his flair for the dramatic—for Gandhi was a superb political artist—the Mahatma chose the technique of a long march from village to village, the only means of transport for millions of peasants in India. It was, too, an ideal method for attracting attention to the campaign throughout the country. Gandhi informed the Viceroy of his plans and reiterated his offer of co-operation on the basis of the Eleven Points. Lord Irwin was unimpressed. The way was now open to non-violent war.

As the sun rose on 12 March 1930 Gandhi and seventy-eight disciples set out for the sea. Day by day the tension mounted, as all India followed the elderly Mahatma—he was then sixty-one—plodding through the countryside on his crusade. Along the route Gandhi preached the message of non-violence, an article of absolute faith throughout his life. Everywhere he was greeted as a saint. Anxiously both Congressmen and Government officials awaited his arrival at Dandi on the sea.

Gandhi reached the sea on the morning of 5 April. He paused for prayers and then proceeded to break the law by picking up salt lying on the shore. The explosion followed with devastating effect. The pent-up emotions of thousands burst forth, and a nation-wide violation of the Salt Law followed. Giant public meetings were held in the major cities. The word salt had acquired a magic power. The operations extended to an effective boycott of British cloth—avidly supported by Indian cotton manufacturers—and picketing of liquor shops. The campaign rapidly gathered momentum and by early summer the 'revolt' had assumed mammoth proportions.

Nehru, however, was prevented from playing more than a token role in the struggle. During the first week he directed operations from Congress headquarters in Allahabad, issuing a stream of circulars to local organs on day-to-day tactics. For violating the Salt Law he was sentenced to six months in Naini Central Prison, just across the river from his home town.

In all logic Gandhi should have been the first to be taken into custody. But as in the past—and in the future—the authorities hesitated to do so for fear of dangerous repercussions. Only after he wrote to the Viceroy of his intention to demand possession of the Salt Works at Dharsana—which would have given added impetus to the campaign—was he taken into preventive detention. To avoid undue publicity he was whisked away in a car to prison in the middle of the night. No trial was held.

As expected, Gandhi's arrest led to demonstrations in every major Indian city. From the specific attack on the Salt Law the campaign developed into a general onslaught on British rule. The Government responded with mass arrests, estimated at 60,000 (official) to 90,000 (Congress) before the year was out. There was also a rigid press censorship on any news about the campaign and lavish use of the Viceroy's and provincial Governors' reserve powers. 'Between the middle of April and the end of December [1930]', wrote Lord Irwin's sympathetic biographer, 'Irwin had powers through no less than ten Ordinances—an unprecedented number representing a sum total of arbitrary rule which had been wielded by no previous Viceroy.'[1] Yet the campaign attracted a steady flow of recruits during the spring and summer of 1930.

Official quarters in Delhi attempted to minimize its scope and intensity—in their public pronouncements. But in their confidential reports they expressed concern.[2] Early in June the Viceroy informed the Secretary of State in London: 'All thinking Indians deeply resent racial inferiority with which they consider we regard them, and they passionately want substantial advance which will give them power to manage their own affairs. . . . I think every European and Indian would tell you that he was surprised at the dimensions the movement had assumed. I certainly am myself—and we should delude ourselves if we sought to underrate it.' The military were even more pungent in their appraisal. In a letter to the Chief of the General Staff, the G.O.C. Eastern

[1] Campbell-Johnson, *Viscount Halifax*, p. 268.
[2] The following extracts are used with the permission of the Government of India.

Command, General Shea, wrote: 'The general results have been a serious dislocation of trade . . ., a most highly organized attack by a gang of revolutionary terrorists, open rebellion in certain urban areas, the inflammation of the Frontier tribes, and systematic attempts to undermine the loyalty of the Army. . . . I am deeply concerned about the effect which is being produced in the minds of Indian soldiers by current events . . . they are being subjected to an insidious strain which is bound in time to have a far-reaching effect.'

On the whole the campaign of 1930 was non-violent, a testimony to Gandhi's remarkable hold on his followers. But in a movement of that size and intensity deviations from the norm were inevitable. There were three outstanding events. The first was a daring raid on the police armouries of Chittagong, a small port city of East Bengal. The second took place in the town of Sholapur in Bombay Province, when *satyagrahis* secured effective control for a few days and then clashed with the military.

By far the most dramatic event took place in Peshawar, capital of the North West Frontier Province, homeland of the warlike Pathan tribesmen. For five days this strategic gateway to the Khyber Pass was in control of the local Congress organization more particularly of the *Khudai Khidmatgars* (Servants of God) or 'Redshirts' led by Khan Abdul Ghaffar Khan, a devoted follower of Gandhi. The Peshawar episode caused grave concern among senior officials, this was the historic invasion route from central Asia. Even more dangerous was the refusal of two platoons to fire on the unarmed crowd. Although an isolated incident, it revived faint memories of the Rebellion of 1857.

All this Nehru followed with eager interest from his prison cell at Naini. Seven years had elapsed since his last enforced residence in this huge fortress-like jail. When he returned to Naini, he was the only important political prisoner there. Whether out of deference or the desire to prevent contact with criminal inmates, he was kept in isolation, in a small circular enclosure about one hundred feet in diameter, separated from the main prison compound by a fifteen-foot wall. 'The Doghouse' it was called, having been originally designed for dangerous criminals. Now it was used for distinguished nationalist politicians. For a month he had no companions of any kind, except a guard, a prison cook and a 'sweeper'. As long as he was alone the accommodation was not unbearable, two cells in a four-cell barrack. Yet it was a frustrating experience.

Time passed slowly in this confining atmosphere. Ever a believer in routine, particularly during the long years in prison, Nehru managed to fill out the day. Early to rise, about four in the morning, he spent about three hours a day spinning and another few hours weaving. He read voraciously, busied himself with household chores and tried to calm his restless mind. It was a rigorous schedule, self-imposed because of a self-created guilt complex. He derived some compensation from news of his wife's active participation in the struggle. Fragile though she was, Kamala took the lead in organizing the women of Allahabad and surrounding villages, particularly in the boycott of liquor shops and foreign cloth. As the campaign progressed she was appointed a substitute member of the Working Committee. A new dimension was added to their relationship.

For a month Nehru remained in virtually solitary confinement. Then he was joined by his father and an intimate friend, Dr. Syed Mahmud. The reunion was a source of much joy. But the discomforts of prison life and the extreme heat of the plains led to a rapid deterioration in Motilal's health. On the advice of doctors, he was released early in September. His son followed a month later. But he was to remain at liberty only eight days. For though civil disobedience had settled down to a war of attrition, he was too important and too dangerous to be allowed to roam unhindered throughout the country. Indeed, even before his release, the Secretary of the Home Department expressed 'the hope that the first opportunity will be taken *to put Jawahar Lal out of harm's way*'.[1] This was done as he and Kamala were returning home one evening after completing plans for a district-wide no-tax campaign. Altogether, he was sentenced to two years and four months.

Once again among familiar faces, Nehru settled down to his normal prison routine—spinning, reading and the like. There were, however, some additions, notably the facsimile of a tiny golf course—in 'The Doghouse' of Naini Jail! And the autumn had come, with its cool breezes and blue skies, a relief from the torpid heat of Indian summer.

The reimprisonment of Jawaharlal so soon after his release

[1] In the files of the National Archives of India, New Delhi. (Emphasis added.)

infused the flagging civil disobedience campaign with new vigour. Despite his grave illness, Motilal rose from his sick-bed and organized 'Jawahar Day' on 14 November, his son's forty-first birthday. All over India the Congress held public meetings at which were read those portions of his original speech which had caused his rearrest. To Nehru it was a 'unique birthday celebration', for about 5,000 persons were arrested on the occasion. Another source of pride was the news of Kamala's arrest.

*　　*　　*　　*

It was during this, his fifth term in prison, that Nehru began a series of letters to his daughter, later published as *Glimpses of World History*. A sense of parental obligation to Indira, whose normal upbringing had suffered from his preoccupation with politics and his frequent 'visits' to prison, provided the initiative for this informal survey of world history.

Nehru is not a trained historian, but his feel for the flow of human history and his capacity to weave together a wide range of knowledge in a meaningful pattern give to this book qualities of a high order. Perhaps its most impressive feature is the creative selection of significant facts on the many cultures of East and West and their orderly presentation in a simple style intelligible to a girl in her early 'teens. What makes it original and unique is its Asian-centred orientation. The lack of balance in historical writing is redressed.

This is no scholar's work, nor was it intended to be. Indeed, it is not a book in the proper sense. Rather, it is a series of thinly connected sketches of the story of mankind. It is rambling and repetitious, introspective and 'romantic'. There are errors of fact and dubious interpretations. It lacks 'objectivity', for Nehru cannot and does not wish to remove himself completely from his subject-matter. It also reveals his shifting moods; and his assessment of a particular epoch or situation shows the influence of his momentary reflections. It is, then, uneven in quality and perspective.

Written during the height of what he considered to be a life-and-death struggle with British rule, the sections dealing with British history are marked by an aggressive tone. Those on Indian culture are marked by deep sympathy and understanding, though he was not averse to sharp criticism of India's social and political ills, notably caste, the deadening effects of orthodox religion and near-perpetual fragmentation.

The French Revolution is for him, as for many others, the decisive force in modern European history. Strong men called forth much praise. The Russian Revolution evokes some of his most emotional observations. But it is in his many letters on nationalism, Indian and other, that Nehru reveals his basic outlook. For him it is the force of the century, the key to a new age.

Despite its shortcomings, the *Glimpses* is a work of great artistic value, a worthy precursor of his noble and magnanimous Autobiography. The canvas is as large as the record of man itself, the strokes are sweeping and multi-coloured. There is a sure grasp of detail, yet a breadth of outlook which distinguishes it from the standard 'history'. It can best be described as cultural history, though there is no dearth of political events. It is, too, a human document, a projection of Nehru the man on to the stage of societies in motion.

Nehru's theory of history, as expressed in these letters, combines three strands: the nineteenth-century belief in perpetual progress; a stress on the role of 'the great man'; and sociological analysis with a strong infusion of Marxist method. More than twenty-five years have passed since he completed his survey. Yet these three elements still influence his approach to historical change.

The *leitmotif* of Nehru's thought and action in this period of his life was the global struggle for freedom. In this sense the *Glimpses of World History* is a milestone, embodying in its purest form his international idealism. His analysis of the rise of Fascism and Nazism, the cause of the Great Depression, the growing disunity among the Western Powers, and the approach of war bears a marked resemblance to Strachey's *The Coming Struggle for Power*, though not quite as outspoken in its Marxism. Typical of his revolutionary fervour is the following passage: 'The reformer who is afraid of radical change or of overthrowing an oppressive regime and seeks merely to eliminate some of its abuses becomes in reality one of its defenders. We must therefore cultivate a revolutionary outlook.' Yet this was combined with Gandhian methods: 'Never do anything in secret or anything that you would wish to hide. It is no surprise, therefore, that orthodox communists considered Nehru 'unreliable' and 'petty bourgeois' at the time.

Typical of the Indian Communists' attitude to him is the

following declaration of 1930: 'The most harmful and dangerous obstacle to victory of the Indian revolution is the agitation carried on by the "left" elements of the National Congress led by Jawaharlal Nehru, Bose . . . and others. . . . The exposure of the "left" Congress leaders . . . is the *primary* task of our Party.'[1]

While Nehru was engrossed in reflections on history, the Round Table Conference opened in London. Agreement was reached in principle on an all-India Federation. The communal representation issue was not resolved, but enough progress had been made to adjourn the proceedings—in the hope that the Congress could be induced to abandon civil disobedience and co-operate in the plan. Thus, at the end of January 1931, the Viceroy passed the burden of decision to the Congress by releasing Gandhi and nineteen members of the Working Committee. Among them were Jawaharlal and Kamala. At that moment his father's condition took a sharp turn for the worse. 'There he sat,' wrote Nehru of his father during the last ten days, 'like an old lion mortally wounded and with his physical strength almost gone, but still very leonine and kingly.'[2] The news of his death spread quickly. Huge crowds gathered to pay homage to the nationalist leader. So too along the route as the procession moved towards Allahabad and cremation on the banks of the holy Ganges.

Nehru's feelings were perhaps best expressed in a letter to his daughter:

Millions have sorrowed for him; but what of us, children of his, flesh of his flesh and bone of his bone! . . . We sorrow for him and miss him at every step. And as the days go by the sorrow does not seem to grow less or his absence more tolerable. But, then, I think that he would not have us so. . . . He would like us to go on with the work he left unfinished. . . . After all, we have something of his fire and strength and determination in us.[3]

Nehru eulogized Gandhi in almost identical words after his assassination by a Hindu fanatic seventeen years later. This is not surprising because Gandhi succeeded Motilal as his mentor. The younger Nehru's respect for and dependence on the Mahatma now became almost filial.

They often disagreed on strategy and tactics. And their social, economic and political philosophies differed in certain fundamental

[1] 'Platform of Action of the C.P.I.', as quoted in Limaye, Madhu, *Communist Party: Facts and Fiction*, pp. 18–19.
[2] *Toward Freedom*, p. 184.
[3] 21 April 1931. *Glimpses of World History*, p. 54.

respects. Yet Gandhi and Nehru were tied to each other by personal bonds, as well as their complementary roles of leadership in the struggle for independence. Gandhi was the symbol of traditional India, capable of galvanizing the masses into action as no other man in Indian history, and few men in any country. Nehru was the spokesman of the radical, Westernized intelligentsia, bringing to the Indian scene the ideas of liberalism and socialism, the faith in science, and the vision of a new society. As such, he was capable of attracting the urban middle and working classes to the nationalist movement. Through his association with Gandhi and his programme of agrarian reform he appealed to the masses as well.

It may well be that both understood their historic roles: the Mahatma was the only conceivable leader as long as the struggle for freedom continued; and Nehru would succeed him once independence was attained. It is doubtful whether Gandhi, with his archaic ideas about economic policy, could have carried through the transformation of India into a modern state. This Nehru was pre-eminently fitted to do.

The passing of Motilal Nehru coincided with a crucial decision of the Congress—the abandonment of civil disobedience in favour of a truce with the *Raj*. Negotiations between Gandhi and the Viceroy followed the mediation efforts of Indian Liberals. There was much opposition on both sides. Many British Tories were aghast at what Churchill termed 'the nauseating and humiliating spectacle of this one-time Inner Temple lawyer, now seditious fakir, striding half-naked up the steps of the Viceroy's Palace, there to negotiate and to parley on equal terms with the representative of the King-Emperor'.[1] Left-wing Congressmen like Nehru questioned the practical value of such a personal meeting on the grounds that Lord Irwin was not a free agent. But Gandhi, with his complete trust in the 'enemy', saw the possibility of converting his opponents by persuasion.

Only in one respect did the Mahatma score a victory, however intangible it was. The Viceroy's willingness to negotiate was an implied recognition of the Congress as *the* representative of the Indian people. On specific issues, however, it was an unmitigated Congress defeat. By far the most significant concession was on the basic constitutional issue: Gandhi agreed that in the future

[1] Quoted in Campbell-Johnson, op. cit., p. 294.

scheme of Indian government London would have reserve powers in the fields of defence, external affairs, the position of minorities, the financial credit of India, and the discharge of obligations.

Until the very end Nehru pressed for rejection of the truce terms; and even after Gandhi signed the agreement he was opposed. But nothing could be served by holding out. Once it were known that Gandhi had signed the agreement, civil disobedience would collapse. It had already come to a virtual halt in the expectation of peace.

The memoirs of Lord Halifax shed much light on the value which Gandhi placed on morality in the pursuit of political objectives, so much so that it was more important than the goals themselves. The key stumbling-block to agreement was Gandhi's request for an inquiry into police activities. The Viceroy refused, on the grounds that nothing would be achieved except to aggravate feelings on both sides. 'This did not satisfy him [Gandhi] at all, and we argued the point for two or three days. Finally, I said that I would tell him the main reason why I could not give him what he wanted. I had no guarantee that he might not start civil disobedience again, and if and when he did, I wanted the police to have their tails up and not down. Whereupon his face lit up and he said, "Ah, now Your Excellency treats me like General Smuts treated me in South Africa. You do not deny that I have an equitable claim, but you advance unanswerable reasons from the point of view of Government why you cannot meet it. I drop the demand." '[1]

The informal atmosphere of the talks is illustrated by the following anecdote. Churchill's remark about the 'half-naked fakir' had caused a sensation. At the end of one of their conversations, when the Mahatma was about to leave without his shawl, the Viceroy picked it up and said, 'Gandhi, you haven't so much on, you know, that you can afford to leave this behind!'[2]

It remained only for the Congress as a whole to ratify the truce. This was done at the end of March 1931 at the annual session in Karachi, under the presidency of Sardar Patel, but under the domination of the Mahatma. Far more important, in the perspective of free India's welfare goals, was the Resolution on Fundamental Rights and Economic and Social Changes. There is still

---

[1] The Earl of Halifax, *Fulness of Days*, pp. 148-9.
[2] Campbell-Johnson, op. cit., p. 308.

some doubt as to who really drafted this resolution, but it is generally agreed that Nehru played the decisive role.

In essence, the Karachi Resolution laid down a programme of reform which the Congress was henceforth pledged to include in a constitution for independent India. Among them were the liberal freedoms of expression, religion, thought and assembly 'for purposes not opposed to law or morality'; equality before the law, regardless of caste, creed or sex; protection of regional languages and cultures; 'a living wage' for industrial workers, limited hours of labour, unemployment and old age insurance; the abolition of untouchability; the right to form unions; reduction of land revenue and rent; a system of progressive income taxes and graduated inheritance taxes; universal adult suffrage; free primary education; total prohibition; severe limitations on salaries of civil servants; a secular state; state protection of *khaddar* (hand-spun cloth), etc. The most important provision read: 'The State shall own or control key industries and services, mineral resources, railways, waterways, shipping and other means of public transport.'[1]

This was a moderate programme embodying various principles now enforced in many parts of the non-socialist world. Yet at the time it was considered a pioneering act, a broadening of the Congress programme beyond the purely political goal of complete self-government. As such, it was one of Nehru's major contributions during the struggle for independence. Indeed, the inauguration of national planning in 1951 and the Avadi Resolution on a 'socialist pattern of society' in 1955 may be traced to the Karachi Resolution of 1931.

Civil disobedience had suffered a setback. But the principle of far-reaching social and economic reform had now penetrated the ranks of the Congress. Within a few years Nehru's initiative was to reap rich rewards—in the elections of 1937.

*   *   *   *

The 'Delhi Pact' provided a respite to both parties in the long-drawn-out struggle of the early 'thirties. Nehru escaped from the political wars for seven weeks. With his wife he went to Ceylon,

[1] The text is to be found in *Report of the 45th Indian National Congress, at Kara 1931*, pp. 139–41.

where he overcame the weariness of recent months. It was his last holiday with Kamala. Writing many years later of this episode, he recalled, 'we seemed to have discovered each other anew. All the past years that we had passed together had been but a preparation for this new and more intimate relationship. We came back all too soon and work claimed me and, later, prison. There was to be no more holidaying, no working together, except for a brief while. . . .'[1]

In the interim the truce showed signs of cracking. Some Congress leaders, notably Nehru, doubted the wisdom of attending the Second Round Table Conference. Even Gandhi had second thoughts, but he finally consented. The Conference floundered in the quicksand of communal representation and finally adjourned in total deadlock. In the interim political conditions at home deteriorated.

The most critical area of tension was the United Provinces, where Congress politics had long been dominated by the Nehrus, father and son. Friction arose from agrarian discontent, almost endemic in that part of India. The crisis reached a head in November 1931. Under pressure from the *Kisan Sabha* (Peasant League), and with Nehru's whole-hearted approval, the Congress advised a no-tax campaign. It was this which led to Nehru's sixth imprisonment.

Such was the atmosphere which greeted Gandhi upon his return to India—ordinances in Bengal, the North West Frontier and the United Provinces, as well as the arrest of senior colleagues. More hurt than angry, he sought an interview with the Viceroy. Lord Willingdon refused and Gandhi reminded him that civil disobedience had only been 'suspended' under the terms of the 'Delhi Pact'.

The Government of India then struck and struck hard. Gandhi and Sardar Patel, the Congress President, were taken into custody. At the same time four new ordinances were issued. As the Secretary of State for India, Sir Samuel Hoare, told the House of Commons, 'I admit that the Ordinances that we have approved are very drastic and severe. They cover almost every activity of Indian life.'[2]

The most striking features of the onslaught were its precision, its

[1] *The Discovery of India*, p. 33.
[2] 24 March 1932. Gt. Brit. H.C., *Debates*, 1931–2, vol. 263, col. 1226.

thoroughness, and its scope, all of which strongly suggested pre-meditated action. The Congress was unprepared for all-out war-fare at this stage. No plans are evident in its actions at the time. No orders had been issued to local organs and no provision had been made for substitute members of its High Command.

The Government's campaign was devastating. Within a week almost every Congressman of any consequence was in prison. The party was outlawed, its records destroyed, its funds confiscated and its buildings seized. Moreover, some eighty affiliated or sym-pathetic organizations were declared illegal—youth leagues, *kisan sabhas*, Congress-supported schools, economic enterprises. Political meetings and processions were prohibited. The nationalist press was gagged. Severe fines and imprisonment were meted out. Land and property were confiscated in cases of failure to pay taxes. Civil liberties were suspended. It was nothing short of martial law.

The Congress never recovered from the initial assault. For eight months the semblance of mass civil disobedience was main-tained. But it was a desultory campaign and there was never any doubt as to the outcome. Bereft of leadership, funds and organiza-tion, the rank and file were compelled to fall back on their own resources. There was no lack of enthusiasm. Many courted arrest and many were arrested. According to the Congress, no fewer than 80,000 were imprisoned in the first four months of 1932.

All this Nehru observed from prison, with mixed emotions, sometimes with anger, at other times with detachment. One in-cident in particular stirred him deeply. At a demonstration in Allahabad, his mother received severe blows from a wooden cane and was bleeding badly. There were even rumours of her death, causing retaliation that evening by an angry crowd. When the news reached Nehru he was beside himself with rage. As he wrote some time later, 'the thought of my frail old mother lying bleeding on the dusty road obsessed me, and I wondered how I would have behaved if I had been there. How far would my non-violence have carried me? Not very far, I fear. . . .'[1]

He was at Bareilly District Jail from February to June 1932. The change from Naini was distasteful, partly because it meant leaving friends and familiar surroundings, partly because his new 'home' was surrounded by a twenty-five-foot wall. Aside from the

[1] *Toward Freedom*, p. 223.

feeling of claustrophobia which it produced, the 'Great Wall' reduced the hours of sunlight for reading and writing.

What disturbed Nehru even more was an unusual deterioration in health, both at Bareilly and at Dehra Dun Jail, in the United Provinces, where he spent the last fourteen months of this imprisonment. An unexplained daily rise in temperature plagued him for some months. It made him moodier than he is wont to be and temporarily reduced his interest in the struggle going on beyond the walls. But the illness passed and with it the mood of despair. With time Nehru's attitude to prison life mellowed. Writing to his sister Krishna in the autumn of 1933, he said: 'Those who have had the advantage of prison experience know at least the value of patience, and if they have profited by their experience they have learned adaptability, and that is a great thing.'[1]

His prison routine during 1932–3 was essentially the same as in earlier periods, with a heavy concentration on reading and writing. He resumed the letters to his daughter, and by the time he was released at the conclusion of his two-year term his reflections on world history were complete. But with the coming of spring 1933 his mind turned to the world crisis as he saw it from prison.

Hitler had come to power. Japan had completed its conquest of Manchuria. The Great Depression continued to wreak havoc the world over. The Western democracies appeared to him to be entering a stage of decadence. Only Soviet Russia seemed to offer a ray of hope. 'However, I do not approve of many things that have taken place in Russia, nor am I a Communist in the accepted sense of the word.'[2] Indeed, from the very outset of his flirtation with Communism he was sceptical, especially on the question of means. The Gandhian influence, as well as a streak of individualism and non-conformism, prevented him from embracing the creed completely. He never overcame his distaste for the authoritarian aspects of the Soviet régime.

What made Nehru sympathetic to Communism in the early 'thirties was the apparent polarization of ideologies. He saw the world entering a titanic struggle between Communism and Fascism and he found himself condoning the former's excesses. 'I do believe that fundamentally the choice before the world today is

[1] Hutheesingh, *With No Regrets*, p. 109.
[2] Nehru, *Recent Essays and Writings*, p. 123.

between *some form* of Communism and some form of Fascism, and I am all for the former, i.e. Communism. . . . There is no *middle road* . . . and I choose the Communist *ideal*. In regard to the methods and approach to this ideal . . . *I think that these methods will have to adapt themselves to changing conditions and may vary in different countries.*[1]

While Nehru was engaged in reflections on history and the contemporary world the struggle within India took a dramatic turn. In September 1932 Gandhi began a 'fast unto death' because of the 'Communal Award' of British Prime Minister Ramsay MacDonald. Among other things it provided for separate electorates for the Untouchables, a scheme which the Mahatma considered immoral.

Alarm and anxiety greeted the news of Gandhi's gesture. Nehru himself was tormented by the thought of Gandhi's possible death. 'I am shaken up completely and I know not what to do,' he wrote to his daughter. 'My little world in which he has occupied such a big place, shakes and totters, and there seems to be darkness and emptiness everywhere. . . . Shall I not see him again? And whom shall I go to when I am in doubt and require wise counsel, or am afflicted and in sorrow and need loving comfort? What shall we all do when our beloved chief who inspired us and led us has gone?'[2]

The fast began despite the pleas of friends, colleagues and even critics. The Government, concerned lest Gandhi die in prison, offered to release him under certain conditions. The Mahatma refused. A conference of Hindu leaders was hurriedly convened at his bedside. Three more days passed in tense discussion. On the fifth day of the fast, with Gandhi's life hanging by a thread, an agreement was reached. The British Government approved, Gandhi called off the fast, and the crisis ended.

The months in prison dragged on. Nehru was now at the small district jail in Dehra Dun, in the foothills of the Himalayas. It was a welcome change from Bareilly, where the temperature rose to 110 degrees and above. And the walls were lower. The nearby trees soothed him, and beyond were the mountains. Nehru has always been enamoured of the panoramic beauty of the hills of northern India.

In the stillness and isolation of his surroundings he had almost

---

[1] *Recent Essays and Writings*, p. 126. (Emphasis added.)
[2] On 15 September 1932. *Glimpses of World History*, p. 327.

forgotten the world outside. But suddenly another rude shock was administered by Gandhi. Early in May 1933, when civil disobedience was at its lowest ebb, the Mahatma began a twenty-one-day fast for 'self-purification'. Nehru's rational mind rebelled at the master's strange tactics. Nor has his attitude to the political fast changed these many years. In 1956 he remarked, 'Gandhi would go on a fast. I didn't understand it then—and I don't understand it now.'[1]

The fast marks the *de facto* end of the lengthy civil disobedience campaign, though it dragged on officially until the summer of 1934. In the meantime Nehru had been released. After a brief stay at his mother's bedside he hurried to Poona for the long-awaited reunion with the Mahatma. Much had happened in the intervening two years, much that was distressing. The time was more than ripe for serious conversation.

Their intimate talks and the exchange of letters which followed brought into bold relief the differences between the two men, as well as the many things they had in common. They seemed agreed on ultimate objectives. But their divergence on means laid bare the gap in social and economic philosophy. Nehru stressed complete independence and the abolition of vested economic interests. Gandhi agreed in principle but insisted that this be done by conversion not coercion. Here was the core issue of disagreement. Moreover, Gandhi, on principle, abhorred secrecy in political tactics while Nehru argued that it was permissible in special circumstances. Similarly, the Mahatma emphasized the 'constructive activities' of the Congress, notably spinning, the removal of untouchability and communal unity, while Nehru did not even mention them.

There was, too, a striking difference in their ways of thought. Nehru was a rationalist who felt the necessity of a clear statement of goals and the ideology from which they emerged. Gandhi, by contrast, arrived at decisions intuitively. Nehru's was the Western mind, thinking in terms of the long-run; Gandhi refused to be pressed beyond the immediate aim.

Nehru set down his thoughts more systematically in 'Whither India', a provocative series of articles on 'what do we want and why'.[2] In Western terms, he emerged as a left-socialist of the

---

[1] To the author in New Delhi on 6 June 1956.
[2] Reprinted in *Recent Essays and Writings*, pp. 1–24.

Austrian school, Marxist in theory, democratic in practice. These essays aroused considerable interest. Communists accepted his main line of argument but said it did not go far enough. Conservatives attacked his premises and angrily rejected his conclusions. Although 'Whither India' did not have any immediate concrete effect, it influenced some younger left-nationalists who in the following year were to form the Congress Socialist Party, a faction within the Congress. As such it was a milestone in Nehru's emergence as the hero of the Left in the middle and late 'thirties.

*   *   *   *

These were trying months for Nehru, a period of uneasy freedom between his two lengthy imprisonments in the early 'thirties. His mother's slow recovery was a source of continuing concern. There was the problem of arranging his daughter's university education. There were also renewed fears for Kamala's health. Nehru has never attached much importance to money, probably because his father had long ensured the family's economic security. He now felt the need for retrenchment. The position was improved, in the short-run, by the sale of family heirlooms, silverware and his wife's jewellery. Later his income was enhanced by the very considerable royalties from his books. To this day, they supplement his paltry salary of Rs. 2,250 (approximately $475) per month as Prime Minister of India.[1]

Early in the new year, 1934, Nehru and his wife went to Calcutta, partly to secure medical advice and partly because Jawaharlal was anxious to pay tribute to the Bengali role in the freedom struggle. They were there only a few days, but during that time he delivered three provocative speeches against the current policies of the *Raj*. He was not apprehended immediately, but it was merely a matter of time. Word was passed from the Home Department to the Government of the United Provinces: 'The Government of India regard him [Nehru] as by far the most dangerous element at large in India and . . . are definitely of the

[1] Up to 13 June 1957 all members of the Indian Cabinet received a monthly salary equivalent to $472.50 (after taxes $336), an allowance of $105 and a free furnished house. On that day the Prime Minister announced that he and his Cabinet colleagues agreed to a 10 per cent. cut in their salary and allowances. *New York Times*, 14 June 1957.

opinion that . . . it is desirable to institute a prosecution at once.'[1] Upon his return to Allahabad he was taken into custody to stand trial for sedition.

Normally Jawaharlal and Kamala took these separations stoically. This time it was different, perhaps because Kamala sensed the approaching end. Describing the scene many years later, Nehru wrote,'. . . Kamala went to our rooms to collect some clothes for me. I followed her to say goodbye. Suddenly she clung to me and, fainting, collapsed.'[2] The next time they met she was caught once more in the grip of her relentless disease.

And so it began again, the long nights in prison, the loneliness, the constant search for the 'right path'. During a period of almost four years, from the end of 1931 to September 1935 he was free only six months.

The first few days he spent in Presidency Jail, Calcutta, pending his trial. He offered no defence, only this statement of defiance: 'Individuals sometimes misbehave; officials also sometimes misbehave; crowds and mobs get excited and misbehave; all that is very regrettable. But it is a terrible thing when brutality becomes a method of behaviour.' At that point he was silenced by the Court and was sentenced to two years simple imprisonment. It was Nehru's seventh term.[3]

His next 'home' was a ten- by nine-foot cell in Alipore Central Jail, located within the city limits of Calcutta. There was the usual veranda and open yard, this time surrounded by a seven-foot wall. But close by were the kitchen chimneys which frequently wafted disagreeable smells into his enclosure. The regimen was no different from Nehru's normal prison experience: confinement to the cell from early evening to early morning; permission to walk about the open yard and to have reading and writing materials; occasional interviews with relatives.

Indian news was hard to come by. But early in April 1934 he learned of Gandhi's decision to terminate all forms of civil disobedience—primarily because 'a valued companion of long standing [not Nehru] was found reluctant to perform the full prison task, preferring his private studies to the allotted task'. 'This

[1] D.O. No. S-282/34-Poll./19 January 1934, in the Home Department (Political Section) files. Used with the permission of the Government of India.
[2] *The Discovery of India*, p. 34.
[3] Home Department (Political Section) files. Used with the permission of the Government of India.

seemed to me a monstrous proposition and an immoral one,' wrote Nehru. 'With a stab of pain I felt that the cords of allegiance that had bound me to him for many years had snapped.' And in this context he penned one of the most revealing disclosures about his personality: 'Of the many hard lessons that I had learned, the hardest and the most painful now faced me: that *it is not possible in any vital matter to rely on anyone. One must journey through life alone; to rely on others is to invite heartbreak.*'[1]

Another source of concern was a swing to the Right in Congress economic policy. In June 1934 the Working Committee condemned confiscation of private property and class war as contrary to the creed of non-violence. Nehru interpreted it as a retreat from the Karachi Resolution on Fundamental Rights and a direct rebuke to his socialist views.

By that time he had been transferred from Alipore to Dehra Dun Jail. His old cell, vacated nine months earlier, was now occupied, and so he was lodged in a refurbished cattle-shed with an attached yard some fifty feet long. But the surrounding wall was too high to allow him to gaze upon the nearby mountains. Nor was he allowed to take occasional walks outside his enclosure.

The long months in prison made him irritable. Relief came with the monsoon, but the restrictions on his movements and contacts remained. His depression was deepened as Kamala's health deteriorated rapidly. Under these pressures Nehru began the searching self-analysis which emerged as one of the memorable autobiographies of his generation. Though not its primary aim, *Toward Freedom* brought the Indian struggle for freedom to the attention of hundreds of thousands in the West. It also revealed Nehru to himself and to others—the mainsprings of his thought and action, the development of his ideas, the constant search for answers to questions both personal and political.[2] Suddenly came news that Kamala's condition had taken a turn for the worse. On the advice of Government doctors he was released temporarily to be with his wife.

Kamala was in the very painful grip of advanced pulmonary

---

[1] *Toward Freedom*, p. 312. (Emphasis added.)

[2] First published in 1936 under the title *The Autobiography of Jawaharlal Nehru* (John Lane, London). It was immediately acclaimed by many people in India and the West, including such British Conservatives as Lord Halifax, formerly Lord Irwin, who pronounced it indispensable reading for an understanding of modern India.

tuberculosis. As he sat by her bedside, Nehru thought back over the eighteen years of their married life. In his reminiscences, he reprimanded himself for his 'semi-forgetful, casual attitude' during the first years of their marriage. Now time was running out. 'Surely she was not going to leave me when I needed her most,' he wrote upon his return to prison. 'Why, we had just begun to know and understand each other, really. . . . We relied so much on each other; we had so much to do together.'[1] The reunion lasted only eleven days.

During his stay at home Nehru wrote at length about the 'state of the Nation' to Gandhi. All the pent-up emotions of years in prison came to the fore. Its main themes are dismay and anger at Gandhi's reasons for terminating civil disobedience; his feeling of loneliness and despair; the effects of prison; criticism of the Congress and of its attack on socialism; and hurt feelings about an alleged insult to the memory of his father. Of special interest are the passages about himself:

I have always felt a little lonely almost from childhood up. That loneliness never went, but it was lessened . . . Now (with Gandhi's abrupt decision to end civil disobedience) I felt absolutely alone, left high and dry on a desert island. . . .
The keenness of my feelings on the subject, which amounted almost to physical pain, passed off; the edge was dulled. But shock after shock, a succession of events sharpened that edge to a fine point, and allowed my mind or feelings no peace or rest. Again I felt that sensation of spiritual isolation, of being a perfect stranger out of harmony, not only with the crowds that passed me, but also with those whom I valued as dear and close comrades.'[2]

Gandhi's reply was firm but gentle. 'I understand your deep sorrow. You were quite right in giving full and free expression to your feelings.' But 'I am the same as you knew me in 1917 and after. . . . I want complete independence for the country in the full English sense of the term.'[3] The Mahatma's attachment to Nehru was also revealed in a letter to Patel explaining why he had decided to resign from the Congress: 'I feel that I am in no sense deserting one who is much more than a comrade and whom no amount of political differences will ever separate from me. . . . He is courage personified. . . . He has an indomitable faith in his mission. . . .'[4]

[1] *Toward Freedom*, p. 334.
[2] 13 August 1934. Tendulkar, op. cit. vol. 3, pp. 379–84.
[3] 17 August 1934, ibid., pp. 384–5.   [4] Ibid., pp. 386–8.

In other circumstances Nehru had managed to adjust to prison. As he wrote to his daughter, 'here all is different; everything is quiet and I sit for long intervals, and for long hours I am silent. . . . It is the life of a vegetable rooted to one place, growing there without comment or argument, silent, motionless. . . . [but] one gets used to everything in time. . . . And rest is good for the body; and quiet is good for the mind; it makes one think.'[1]

Now, however, the habit was becoming a drain on his health. He had lost ten pounds in a few months and was down to 130. He had some difficulty in breathing; and his condition was far below his norm of vigorous good health. Waiting for news about Kamala—he received a daily bulletin for a short while—was an ordeal. He was allowed to visit her occasionally. But there was no improvement.

Kamala was moved to the hills. In response to pressure both in India and in England, Nehru was transferred to the Almora District Jail close by her sanatorium. His new 'home' was spacious by comparison with his cell at Naini—a large hall, fifty-one feet by seventeen, with ample room to stroll about and fresh breezes penetrating the many openings in the walls. Yet it was lonelier than the normal prison cell, and with the approach of winter the 'mansion' became less attractive. Much of his time was spent completing his autobiography and waiting anxiously for news of his wife.

Kamala grew worse, and was sent to Europe for special treatment. Life returned to its dismal routine. A few months later came news that her condition had become critical once more. In a humane gesture, mixed with concern lest Indian feelings be alienated, the Government released him early in September. He rushed to her bedside at Badenweiler in the Black Forest of Germany.

There was little he could do at this stage, for her disease was now beyond cure. To it was added angina pectoris. Twice a day Nehru walked from his *pension* in town to visit her. Occasionally he read to her. At other times they reminisced about the past and old friends. For a very brief period there were signs of improvement, enough for Jawaharlal and his daughter, then studying in Switzerland, to visit England for a fortnight. The end came on 28 February 1936. And soon thereafter, 'that fair body and that

[1] Letter of 1 January 1933, in *Glimpses of World History*, p. 475.

lovely face, which used to smile so often and so well, were reduced to ashes'.[1]

Nehru set out for home, his thoughts engrossed by Kamala and the days gone by. Yet even at this moment of grief he could not entirely escape the limelight. It was a curious and irritating incident. Some weeks earlier, while his wife lay dying, he had been informed that Mussolini was anxious to meet him. Nehru had declined because of his strong antipathy to Fascism. But when his plane landed in Rome he was informed that the Italian dictator was expecting him in the evening. It was merely to convey condolences, he was assured. But Nehru persisted and the meeting was never held. When he reached Baghdad he cabled the dedication for his autobiography: 'To Kamala who is no more.' And then to Allahabad.

[1] *The Discovery of India*, p. 38.

CHAPTER VI

DAYS OF FERMENT

Many who saw Nehru on his return to India perceived his sense of loss. 'His face, which a few months ago had looked so youthful,' wrote his younger sister, 'was aged and lined with sorrow. . . . Though he tried hard to hide the anguish of his heart, his sad, expressive eyes held a world of agony.'[1] In moments of despair he has always found consolation in his life work—the struggle for Indian freedom and the creation of a 'good society'. On this occasion, in the spring of 1936, India was astir. Far-reaching events were on the horizon, and Nehru was to play the leading role.

The setting was far from propitious. The Congress was in the doldrums once more. The Old Guard was in control, impervious to new ideas. There was a sharp cleavage between them and the recently formed Congress Socialists who looked to Nehru for guidance.

It was Gandhi who had pressed Nehru to accept 'the crown of thorns'. For one thing, the Mahatma admired him much more than any other party leader. For another, he wanted to offer a token of sympathy for the loss of Kamala. Moreover, Gandhi realized that Nehru was the only other nationalist leader with genuine mass appeal. He was also concerned about his protégé's drift to the Left.

The basic motive, however, arose from the rift between conservatives and radicals which threatened to wreck the party. Gandhi knew that Nehru was the one person who could bridge the growing gap between Socialism and Gandhism. Nehru himself frankly admitted this special quality and seemed to relish the role of mediation—then as later. 'In a way I represented a link between various sets of ideas and so I helped somewhat in toning down the

[1] Hutheesingh, *With No Regrets*, p. 120.

differences and emphasizing the essential unity of our struggle against imperialism.'[1]

He had just returned from Europe troubled by the growing crisis in world affairs. The war clouds were gathering once more. An attempt would undoubtedly be made to drag India into the conflict. The only weapon at his disposal to forestall this development was the Congress. Hence the need to rebuild the party.

This sense of urgency was strengthened by disquieting conditions at home, notably the challenge posed by the 1935 Government of India Act. In essence it provided virtually complete responsible government in the provinces of British India and the framework for a loose All-India Federation of the provinces and as many of the six hundred-odd princely States as wished to join. It had taken eight years to produce the Act, from the Simon Commission through the three Round Table Conferences, the White Paper, the Report of the Joint Select Committee of the British Parliament, to the final document itself. Much care had been taken to ensure the ultimate authority of Great Britain in the affairs of India, through an array of special powers vested in the Viceroy and, to a lesser extent, in the Governors of the provinces. Over ninety articles conferred 'discretionary powers' on the Viceroy. There were, as well, 'reserve powers' which gave him exclusive control over defence, external affairs, ecclesiastical affairs and certain frontier areas. Finally came the 'safeguards' or 'special responsibilities' which were all-embracing, for example 'the prevention of any grave menace to the peace or tranquillity of India or any part thereof', the prevention of discrimination against British imports, corporations or individuals, protection of the rights of Princes, etc. Moreover, representation in the federal legislature was to be heavily weighted in favour of the Princes—and the States' representatives were to be *appointed* by the Princes themselves.

This Act, suitably amended, served as the constitution of the Dominion of India from 1947 to 1950 (and of Pakistan from 1947 to 1956). It is in fact the basis of India's present constitution. But in its original form the *federal* part of the Act was hedged by so many 'safeguards' as to deny complete self-government to *India as a whole*. Nehru had no strong objections in principle to contesting the elections but he was vehemently opposed to the idea of taking

[1] *Eighteen Months in India*, p. 64.

office under what he termed the 'slave' constitution. If he refused Gandhi's offer of the presidency, the Congress would certainly adopt this 'reformist' line. (It ultimately did so anyway.) And if the Congress waged an electoral campaign, unity was a precondition to success.

Beyond these specific factors was his desire to push the Congress to the Left. Conditions, he felt, were ripe for such a change, for beneath the surface of Indian politics new social forces were fermenting. The peasants had been galvanized into action during the civil disobedience campaign and had begun to organize *Kisan sabhas* (peasant leagues). The cry of land reform had now become too loud to be ignored. Urban workers, too, began to demand greater recognition from the nationalist movement. And even women, had been aroused by the years of political struggle.

Much of this ferment found expression in the Congress Socialist Party (C.S.P.), created in the spring of 1934 by a group of left-nationalists headed by Jaya Prakash Narayan. Nehru was in prison at the time, but his influence among them was great. Yet he never associated himself officially with this group, a source of disappointment to his admirers. The reasons are not entirely clear, but his action conformed to pattern. He agreed fully with its basic objective of converting the Congress to socialism. He felt, however, that the C.S.P. had rigidly adopted the language of Western socialism which was little understood by the rank and file. Moreover Nehru has always shown antipathy to factions of any kind, and the C.S.P. was clearly that type of organization; its membership was confined to Congressmen and it subscribed to the Congress programme and constitution. He also wished to avoid being classified as a sectarian. He was probably convinced that the cause of socialism itself could be pushed further within the Congress if he maintained his identity as a 'national' leader. Another likely factor was concern lest official membership of the C.S.P. alienate Gandhi and weaken his own position. Nevertheless he gave direction to the growing body of leftist opinion within the Congress and acted as the supreme spokesman of radical ideas in the late 'thirties. With this background and in this frame of mind Nehru took up the reins of office.

From the outset a clash with the Old Guard seemed inevitable. Nehru assumed that his election reflected a growing desire for change among the rank and file. Hence he sponsored a number of radical resolutions on the eve of the Lucknow session. Many were rejected or drastically modified. Nehru was bitterly disappointed and decided to resign, the first of three such 'decisions' in the next few months. After much mental conflict he changed his mind because party unity would have suffered.

If Nehru could not overcome the power of the Old Guard he could nevertheless express his radical views. This he did in his presidential address to the Lucknow session. It was free from the hackneyed phrases of so many of its predecessors. It had literary grace and a tone of passionate sincerity. It was sentimental but forceful, with a majestic sweep which none of his colleagues could match.[1] This speech also revealed the touch of the universal in Nehru's intellectual make-up which made him so attractive to the modernists in India. Yet it was precisely this quality which explains the hesitant response of the average Congressman.

The Left wing was pleased with his address, but the Right felt betrayed by his caustic attack. Gandhi himself was disturbed lest the bold proclamation of socialist ideas cause an irrevocable split within the party.

Despite his fiery words, Nehru was not prepared to force the issue with the Old Guard. As President of the Congress he had the right to pack the Working Committee with his own supporters, but he felt it would be 'improper' to act contrary to the spirit of the session; hence ten Right-wing leaders were invited to join the Committee and only four from the Left.

The reaction among his followers was dismay. 'I have passed the last few days in agony,' wrote Rafi Ahmad Kidwai, one of Nehru's oldest friends. 'Some people had their doubts as to how far you will be able to withstand the combined opposition and influence of Gandhism . . . the Working Committee you have formed is bound to prove more reactionary than the one it has replaced. It may be my vision is narrow. I rely more on the number of heads than on ideological discourses.'[2] During the next few months Nehru spent much of his time on tour. Everywhere he found a 'bubbling vitality' among the masses. His conservative colleagues in the High Command became alarmed by his socialist propaganda.

The clash came at the end of June 1936, when seven members

[1] The text is to be found in *Toward Freedom*, pp. 389–416.
[2] 20 April 1936. *A Bunch of Old Letters*, pp. 174–5.

of the Working Committee, headed by Prasad, Patel and Raja-gopalacharia, resigned. Gandhi intervened and the resignations were withdrawn. The leaders apologized for having hurt Nehru's feelings but did not retract their charges. How hurt Nehru really was becomes clear from his letter to Gandhi on 5 July: 'I read again Rajendra Babu's [Prasad's] . . . his formidable indictment of me. . . . The main thing is that my activities are harmful to the Congress cause. . . . However tenderly the fact may be stated, it amounts to this: that I am an intolerable nuisance and the very qualities I possess—a measure of ability, energy, earnestness, some personality which has a vague appeal—become dangerous for they are harnessed to a wrong chariot. . . . Perhaps the fault may lie with me . . . but the fact remains and today there is no loyalty of the spirit which binds our group together.'[1]

Gandhi replied: 'Your colleagues have lacked your courage and frankness. The result has been disastrous. . . . They have chafed under your rebukes and magisterial manner and above all your arrogation of what has appeared to them your infallibility and superior knowledge. They feel that you have treated them with scant courtesy and never defended them from socialists' ridicule and even misrepresentation.'[2]

Nehru agreed to withdraw his resignation as President, but for a different reason. While on tour he learned of the outbreak of the Spanish Civil War. 'I saw this . . . developing into a European or even a world conflict. . . . Was I going to weaken our organization and create an internal crisis by resigning just when it was essential for us to pull together?'[3] It was a typical example of the influence which international affairs have always exerted on Nehru's decisions at home.

As the date of provincial elections drew near, Congress leaders closed ranks. With Gandhi's backing Nehru secured approval for a Left-of-centre election manifesto. Its most striking feature was the special appeal to the peasantry in the form of a pledge to sponsor substantial agrarian reforms: immediate relief to the poorer peasants by a reduction of rent and land taxes: exemption of uneconomic holdings from all rent and taxes; a moratorium on debts; the scaling down of rural indebtedness; and the provision of cheap credit facilities.

[1] 5 July 1936. *A Bunch of Old Letters*, p. 183.
[2] Ibid., p. 197. (15 July 1936.)   [3] *The Unity of India*, p. 102.

On the eve of the election campaign there arose the question of choosing a Congress President for the year 1937. Nehru stated that he would welcome the election of any of his colleagues. The leading contender was Patel. But as in 1929 and again in 1946 he was persuaded to withdraw by Gandhi, this time probably because of the recognition that Nehru alone had a mass appeal. Lest his decision be misunderstood, the Sardar stressed that he did not endorse all of Nehru's views. And so it was done. In his presidential address at the end of 1936, Nehru set the tone for the election campaign by re-enacting his Lucknow performance— as the tribune of Left-socialism and a 'popular front'.

His election campaign can only be described as a fury of activity. Like an arrow he shot through the country, carrying the Congress message to remote hamlets in the hills and on the plains. He covered some 50,000 miles in less than five months, using every conceivable means of transport. Most of the time he travelled by car, train or aeroplane, occasionally by horse, camel, steamer, bicycle or canoe, and where necessary, on foot through the trackless dusty plains. Even the elephant was harnessed into service. All told, about 10,000,000 persons attended his meetings, and millions more lined the route to catch a glimpse of the Congress's crown prince. Many of the gatherings exceeded 20,000, some attracted 100,000, mostly peasant men and women who walked from distant villages to see and to hear their much-loved 'Panditji'. His average working day ranged from twelve to eighteen hours. It was a prodigious feat.

Then as later he enjoyed the sense of communion with large masses of people. Indeed, from this experience dates his genuine discovery of India. And from that time onwards he possessed, in only slightly less measure than Gandhi, a capacity to feel the pulse of the Indian masses. Their appeal differed: Gandhi was the incarnation of traditional India; Nehru was the symbol and hope of future regeneration.

Nehru's approach to the electors was ideological in the main, with very few references to individual candidates. The Congress election manifesto was explained in simple, straightforward terms, and a few core themes were stated *ad infinitum*: 'fight for Indian freedom: build the Congress into a mighty army of the Indian people: organize to remove poverty and unemployment.' The technique of hammering on a few key objectives is one which Nehru still uses in order to rouse his people from lethargy.

In 1937 this approach made a vital contribution to the party's victory at the polls. Of the 1,585 seats the Congress won 711. (It had contested only 1,161 seats.) The Congress sweep is all the more impressive when it is borne in mind that of the 1,585 seats less than half were 'General' or open, i.e., not allotted to a separate, closed electoral group. The balance was fragmented among Muslims, Sikhs, Christians, Europeans, Landholders and others. Of the eleven provinces in British India, the Congress won an absolute majority in five and was the largest party in three others. By contrast, the Muslim League, which was to win Pakistan only ten years later, secured only 4·8 per cent. of the total *Muslim* vote. Nor did it win a majority of seats in *any* of the four Muslim-majority provinces.

There were two fundamental reasons for the Congress victory: a broadly based organizational network throughout the country and the mass appeal of its election manifesto, especially its pledge of agrarian reform. To Nehru goes most of the credit for the Congress stress on land reform. And it was he who carried the message so effectively to the Indian countryside.

*   *   *   *

To accept or not to accept office—this was the question which confronted the Congress. A decision had become imperative. Nehru and the Left wing strongly urged rejection. But the majority of Congressmen hungered for power after many years in the wilderness. A compromise formula was finally evolved and Congress ministries were formed in seven (later eight) provinces. Nehru was unhappy with the decision, but he had no choice; the pressure among his colleagues was too great.

Flushed with success the Congress adopted an imperious attitude to all other political parties, for which it was to pay dearly in the years to come. Nehru set the tone with his haughty remark, 'There are only two forces in India today, British imperialism, and Indian nationalism as represented by the Congress.' Jinnah was quick to retort: 'No, there is a third party, the Mussulmans.' History was to bear him out.

The Congress went beyond contemptuous words. During the election campaign there developed a tacit understanding with the

Muslim League in the U.P. that a coalition government would be formed. However, it was no longer necessary to make concessions. The League offer of co-operation was met with a series of incredible conditions amounting to an ultimatum for its self-destruction. Jinnah replied in kind. Alarmed by the election results and the Congress arrogation of total power, he embarked on a country-wide tour with the cry, 'Islam is in danger'. Muslims began to respond. The opening shots had been fired in the calamitous Congress-League war which was to envelop north India in flames and ultimately result in partition.

In historical perspective Nehru's attitude was a grave error of judgement. Yet he was not among the most rabid foes of the League. Though denying its claim to act as the spokesman of *all* Indian Muslims, a pretentious claim at the time, he was prepared to meet the League half-way in an effort to reduce the growing friction between the two parties. This is evident from an exchange of letters with Jinnah during the early months of 1938.

Many exchanges were to follow, but this one set the pattern. It laid bare the basic difference in approach to the Indian problem: Nehru thought and acted in terms of Indian unity; Jinnah was concerned only with the position of Indian Muslims. Here were two explosive personalities in verbal combat. The most revealing disclosure is that Jinnah considered himself an *Indian* nationalist as late as 1938. 'It is the duty of every true nationalist', he wrote, 'to whichever party or community he may belong' to help achieve a united front.[1] Two years later, in the Lahore ('Pakistan') resolution, he 'discovered' a separate nation of Muslims in India.

Just as this correspondence drew to a close the League established a Committee of Inquiry into alleged Congress persecution of Muslims. The overall conclusion of the Pirpur Report was that the Muslim community was much better off under the British than under Congress rule. How much truth there was in its charges was never verified. The Congress offered to submit them to the (British) Chief Justice of India, but the League refused. In any event, 'The Viceroy felt that . . . it would be most difficult for Jinnah to prove any general anti-Muslim action on the part of the Congress governments (and) the [provincial] Governors . . . were satisfied that there was no basis for the allegations.'[2]

---

[1] *Indian Annual Register*, vol. i, 1938, pp. 363–76.
[2] Menon, V. P., *The Transfer of Power in India*, p. 71.

Among the sources of Muslim discontent was a fear for the future of Urdu, the *lingua franca* of northern India and the Muslims in particular. Fanatical Hindus were beginning to press the claims of Hindi which shares a common vocabulary with Urdu but is derived from Sanskrit and is written in *Devanagri* script, whereas Urdu uses the Persian script.

The character of the debate annoyed Nehru. 'It is curious how many things in our country take a communal tinge,' he wrote to a nationalist Muslim friend. 'For some mysterious reasons, Urdu is supposed to be the hallmark of the Muslims. With all due deference, I am not prepared to admit this. I consider Urdu as my language which I have spoken from childhood up.'[1]

Desirous of rescuing this controversial issue from the bigots, he prepared a comprehensive analysis of 'the language question'. To reassure the Muslims and regional linguistic groups, he proposed that the all-India language be Hindustani, a fusion of Hindi and Urdu, with equal status for the two scripts. State education and all public activities should be carried out in the dominant language of each area, with suitable provisions for minority language groups. Basic Hindustani, a complete language of about one thousand words, should be developed as an aid to mass education. University education should be imparted in the regional language, but a foreign language should be compulsory. Provision should also be made for the teaching of foreign and Indian languages in secondary schools.

The partition of India 'solved' the Hindi-Urdu squabble, with Hindi now the 'official language' of India and Urdu one of the two 'official languages' of Pakistan. At the time they were made, however, these proposals aroused considerable support. In response to growing pressure, the All-India Congress Committee declared that Hindustani in both scripts would be the national language of free India.

Another problem that occupied Nehru's attention was the relationship of the Congress to mass functional organizations. The *kisan sabhas* (peasant leagues), in particular, were beginning to rival local Congress committees in the countryside, causing alarm among the more orthodox sections of the party. Ever the mediator, Nehru undertook to 'reconcile the irreconcilables'. He welcomed the growth of labour and peasant movements; but since the party

[1] Unpublished Nehru-Mahmud Correspondence, 24 September 1936.

constitution did not permit collective affiliation, the only way to achieve harmony was by mass individual membership of the Congress. He also called upon the *kisan sabhas* to co-operate with the Lucknow resolution on agrarian reform and to join ranks in an 'anti-imperialist front'. By and large they accepted his advice.

It was at this period, too, that Nehru laid the foundations of economic planning which plays so important a role in India today. At his suggestion the Congress established a National Planning Committee. It met only eight times from 1938 to 1940, and accomplished little of concrete value. However, it made the Congress plan-conscious and thereby paved the way for the introduction of All-India economic planning in 1950. Most of the credit for this achievement was undoubtedly Nehru's.

Among the political problems of the late 1930's none caused more concern than the relationship of the Congress ministries to the party organization. On this vital question Nehru tried to steer a middle course. While asserting the supremacy of the party as a whole, he trod more cautiously on the provincial level: the P.C.C.'s should offer advice and criticism, but should not interfere in administration. In policy matters final authority lay with the Working Committee and its Parliamentary Board, consisting of Patel, Prasad and Maulana Azad. It was this concentration of power that gave rise to charges of Congress 'totalitarianism' and the obstruction of parliamentary government. 'To these charges there is really no reply—except the adequate one that it is not reasonable to expect nationalist movements to behave as parliamentary parties.'[1]

The problem of party–government relations has not been solved to the present day. At the Centre the Cabinet is supreme, primarily because of Nehru's commanding position. In the States, however, there are many examples of Congress Committees exceeding the bounds of 'friendly criticism'. And the Congress High Command continues to exercise great power over state governments and state party organizations alike.

On the whole the record of the Congress ministries was rather good. Relations with the Governors were smooth except for brief crises in Bihar and the United Provinces over the release of political prisoners. Their social and economic programme, though limited in scope, was in line with the party's pledge for reform: a

[1] Morris-Jones, W. H., *Parliament in India*, p. 67.

moratorium on debts in Bombay and the U.P.; tenancy legislation and remission of land revenue in various provinces; encouragement to trade unions; a 'Basic Education' scheme and limited
social legislation. By far the most important benefit was the valuable experience in administration for a number of Congress
politicians, the men who assumed power in India in 1947.

Nehru was not unaware of these attainments. However, 'they
are adapting themselves far too much to the old order and trying
to justify it. . . . What is far worse is that we are losing the high
position that we have built up, with so much labour, in the hearts
of the people. We are sinking to the level of ordinary politicians. . . .'[1] Hence he welcomed their resignations.

*   *   *   *

By the spring of 1938 Nehru felt the need for a change and
decided to make another 'pilgrimage' to the West. The precipitating cause was Hitler's occupation of Austria. It happened while
Nehru was at Khali, in the U.P., close by the mountains he loved
so well. For two weeks he 'drank deep of the mountain air and
took my fill of the sight of the snows and the valleys'. But the
escape was short-lived. 'Suddenly there came a rude shock. Hitler
was marching into Austria, and I heard the tramp of barbarian
feet over the pleasant gardens of Vienna. . . . There was no peace
for me then even in Khali, no escape.'[2]

Early in June he sailed for Europe. In Marseilles he was joined
by Krishna Menon, head of the India League in London and
already an admirer of Nehru. They hurried to Barcelona for a
five-day visit. Much of the time was spent in the front lines on the
outskirts of the city, where the International Brigade stood fast
against overwhelming odds.

Nehru's stay in the capital of the Republic remains vivid in his
memory. All the values of European civilization which he held
dear seemed to him to be at stake in the Spanish Civil War—
democracy, socialism, human dignity, self-determination, individual freedom. When the Republic was destroyed Nehru's faith in
the West was severely shaken. The depth of his feelings is evident
in his own writings at the time. The Republic, he wrote, was

---

[1] To Gandhi, 28 April 1938. *A Bunch of Old Letters*, p. 277.
[2] 'Escape', reprinted in *The Unity of India*, pp. 200-4.

killed by Britain and France; 'history long ages hence will remember this infamy and will not forgive them. . . . For Spain was not Spain only, but the new world locked in a death struggle with the barbarian hordes of reaction and brutal violence.'[1]

Much of his stay in Europe was devoted to pleading the causes of anti-fascism and Indian freedom. He divided his time between London and Paris, addressing gatherings on the iniquities of British rule, on the horrors of bombing open cities, on the Fascist menace in Europe, in the false security of appeasement. At the same time he served notice that the Indian National Congress would not accept meekly a British decision to drag India into a world war. And when Munich came he knew that the evil day had only been postponed.

Nehru returned to India in November 1938, only to find himself in the midst of another Congress crisis, one of the gravest in the party's history. The 'Tripuri Crisis' provides a dramatic example of his role as 'the mediator' in the nationalist movement. More important, it throws considerable light on Nehru's relations with Subhas Bose, the proud, ambitious, fiery hero of Bengal. By the time the crisis was over, Bose's power within the Congress was broken. Of all the participants only Gandhi had a clear and consistent objective—to oust Bose. This he did in the end.

It was a complex affair in that the ideological lines were blurred by a clash of temperaments and personal ambition: Bose and some Right-wing leaders, notably Patel, disliked each other intensely. The strong injection of personal factors explains much about what happened.

When Nehru returned from Europe he was asked by Gandhi to assume the presidency for the coming year. He declined, as did Maulana Azad. Bose decided to run for re-election despite advice to the contrary by Gandhi and Nehru. To the consternation of the Old Guard he was re-elected. So ended round one. The real struggle was about to begin.

Bose blundered by renewing a charge that some members of the old Working Committee were prepared to compromise on the Federation issue. He also prohibited the Committee from transacting any business in his absence. Taking this as a vote of no-confidence, twelve of the fifteen members resigned; their letter was 'believed to have been drafted by Gandhi'.[2] The three exceptions

[1] *China, Spain and the War*, pp. 20 and 92.   [2] Tendulkar, *Mahatma*, vol. 5, p. 56

were Bose himself, his brother, Sarat, and Nehru—who did not resign officially, but did issue a separate statement that he would not serve on the new Working Committee. Actually he was in isolation once more, trying desperately to maintain party unity.

The substantive point of conflict was the composition of the Working Committee. The Old Guard and Gandhi desired a 'homogeneous' High Command whereas Bose urged a Committee to represent various groups in the party. Nehru adopted a typical middle-of-the-road approach which reflected his role throughout the crisis.

The struggle for power shifted to the larger stage of the annual session held in the village of Tripuri. Gandhi's policy was accepted and a resolution was passed which 'requested' Bose to appoint the Working Committee in accordance with the Mahatma's wishes. Nehru's vote is unknown. The climax was still to come.

Throughout the 'Tripuri Crisis' Nehru and Bose carried on a spirited correspondence which reveals much about their differences and their frustrating roles—Bose in his inability to break down Gandhi's opposition, Nehru in his failure to mediate in the conflict. 'Personally, I have always had, and still have, regard and affection for you,' wrote Nehru in an illuminating letter, 'though sometimes I did not like at all what you did or how you did it. To some extent, I suppose, we are temperamentally different and our approach to life and its problems is not the same.'

Regarding the resignation of the Old Guard and Bose's allegations: 'It is obviously not good enough for . . . the Congress President to repeat press rumours or bazaar statements. . . . It was a fantastic statement and it hurt to the quick. . . . [It] was an effective barrier to any further co-operation between you and Gandhiji. . . . I pressed you therefore to clear this barrier and have a frank talk with Gandhiji [but you did not]. . . . It made me realize how difficult it was to work together with you. . . .'

As for Nehru's handling of party affairs: 'You say that "in the habit of interfering from the top, no Congress President can beat" me. I realize that I am an interfering sort of a person but . . . I do not recollect having interfered with the work of the office of the A.I.C.C. though I sought to influence it frequently. . . .'

About Bose's re-election Nehru wrote:

One personal aspect. . . . I felt all along that you were too keen on re-election. . . . it did distress me for I felt that you had a big enough position to be above this kind of thing.

In one of his more significant passages Nehru remarked: 'To my misfortune, I am affected by international happenings more than I should be. . . . I felt that we should not passively await events.'

About Nehru's traits as administrator and draftsman: 'You are right in saying that as President I functioned often as a secretary or a glorified clerk. . . . It is also true that because of me Congress resolutions have tended to become long and verbose and rather like theses. . . .'

Perhaps the most illuminating passage relates to Nehru's political philosophy: 'Am I a Socialist or an individualist? Is there a necessary contradiction in the two terms? . . . I suppose I am temperamentally and by training an individualist, and intellectually a socialist. . . . I hope that socialism does not kill or suppress individuality; indeed I am attracted to it because it will release innumerable individuals from economic and cultural bondage.'[1]

During the six weeks following the Tripuri session Nehru made strenuous efforts to heal the breach between Gandhi and Bose. Bose was markedly conciliatory and he relied heavily on Nehru's advice. But Gandhi seemed determined to oust him. 'I think now, as I thought in Delhi, that you should accept Subhas [Bose] as President,' wrote Nehru to Gandhi. 'To try to push him out seems to me to be an exceedingly wrong step.'[2]

Bose explored all avenues of conciliation, but the Mahatma was adamant. Hence the Bengali leader resigned, and Prasad was named his successor. The old Working Committee remained in office, except for Bose, his brother and Nehru. But Nehru pledged his co-operation. The Bose faction walked out and soon after he formed the Forward Bloc.

The epilogue came on the eve of the war. Bose was removed as President of the Bengal Provincial Congress Committee for indiscipline, and was disqualified from any elective office in the party for three years. The 'rebellion' had been crushed. Early in 1941 Bose left India, never to return.

Nehru was unhappy about this unsavoury affair. He was able to escape temporarily. The Indian National Congress had a standing invitation to send a representative to China. What better time than now, when China was in the midst of a death struggle with a foreign invader? The obvious choice was Nehru, the party's

[1] 3 April 1939. *A Bunch of Old Letters*, pp. 340–54.
[2] 17 April 1939. *A Bunch of Old Letters*, pp. 369–71.

acknowledged spokesman on foreign affairs. He had already served as 'ambassador to the east' on two occasions: in 1937 to Burma and Malaya and in 1939 to Ceylon in an effort to reduce the friction between Indian settlers and the Sinhalese.

Nehru intended to spend four weeks in Nationalist-held China, but the war intervened. He remained only twelve days. Most of his visit was spent in Chungking, where few visitors were greeted with such enthusiasm and respect, a symbol of the hoped-for alliance between India and China in the 'brave new world'. As usual he was brimming over with vitality. With boyish enthusiasm he insisted on walking, at times running, up the three hundred steps leading to the city; he was then just short of fifty. Nightly air-raids added a touch of realism to his stay in the Chinese capital.

Nehru's diary of this 'voyage of discovery' reveals a deep interest in Chinese civilization and perception of the dramatic changes to take place a decade later: 'A new China is rising, rooted in her culture, but shedding the lethargy and weakness of ages, strong and united. . . . '[1] Fifteen years after this 'personal visit', he returned to China as India's Prime Minister, to find, not without some concern, how accurate was this observation.[1]

[1] *China, Spain and the War*, pp. 11–53.

CHAPTER VII

THE WAR AND INNER TORMENT

'Munich' had come and gone, but the illusion of peace was soon to be dispelled. In the spring of 1939 the German army marched into Prague and occupied the remnants of Czechoslovakia, despite the solemn pledge of the Great Powers. The world was drifting rapidly towards war. 'We sit on the edge of a sword,' wrote Nehru, 'balancing precariously, and waiting for the succession of events.'[1]

On 3 September the uncertainty came to an end: the Viceroy proclaimed India a belligerent state. The legality of the act was beyond dispute, but it was done without as much as a gesture of consulting India's political leaders. To Lord Linlithgow and British officials generally it was axiomatic that 'the crown jewel of the Empire' would automatically come to the assistance of Great Britain in time of need. To Nehru and most Indian nationalists, however, the issue appeared in an entirely different light. A subject India, they had often declared, would not participate in an 'imperialist' war unless its right to freedom were acknowledged.

For Nehru the war crisis was an agonizing quest for an honourable settlement with Britain which would permit active Congress participation in the war on the Allies' side. He was emotionally and intellectually hostile to the Axis powers. At the same time he was devoted to the cause of Indian freedom. As a result, his was a constant torment between the polar attractions of anti-fascism and Indian freedom. They were never reconciled, for the forces ranged against him proved to be insurmountable. His role during the war may best be sketched within the framework of a five-act drama, for such was the character of the Indian war crisis. The climax was rebellion and mass imprisonments.

[1] 18 August 1939. *China, Spain and the War*, p. 17.

The first act opened with the Viceroy's proclamation. The Congress replied with a request for clarification—a statement of British war aims and their application to India. Instead of an unequivocal assurance of Indian freedom, the Congress was promised only 'consultation' at some future date, with the ultimate goal of Dominion status. For the duration of the war the Viceroy offered merely to include more Indians in his advisory Executive Council. Thus the Working Committee rejected his invitation and called on the eight Congress provincial governments to resign before the end of October. And yet the door to cooperation was left open.

Throughout the autumn negotiations Nehru performed a dual function; he was chief draftsman of party resolutions and the principal Congress publicist. In a series of articles he pleaded the nationalist case with supreme passion. Over and over again a few themes were cogently stated: India's sympathies lie with the Allies, as testified by Congress policy declarations in the 'thirties; only a free India can play a meaningful role in a war for democracy; England must demonstrate its sincerity by stating its war aims boldly, and these must include freedom for India; friendship is possible between India and England but only on equal terms.

There was an air of unreality about the Congress-British negotiations in the autumn of 1939. The Congress wanted tangible evidence of real power immediately, however limited it might be for the duration of the war. The British were extremely rigid in their approach. They acted as if this were still the age of Kipling, not of Hitler.

The Viceroy throughout this crucial period was Lord Linlithgow, of whom Nehru wrote with brutal candour:

Heavy of body and slow of mind, solid as a rock and with almost a rock's lack of awareness . . . he sought with integrity and honesty of purpose to find a way out of the tangle. But his limitations were too many; his mind worked in the old groove and shrank back from any innovations; his vision was limited by the traditions of the ruling class out of which he came; he saw and heard through the eyes and ears of the Civil Service. . . .[1]

More important than Linlithgow's failings was the fact that this was the period of the 'phoney war'. The threat to Britain was still remote, its Asian empire relatively secure. As long as these conditions prevailed neither the India Office nor the Viceroy was

[1] *The Discovery of India* (Signet Press, Calcutta), p. 528.

prepared to make any real concessions. Indeed, it seems that the Viceroy sought to weaken the Congress at this time and to strengthen the League. 'When . . . the Congress resigned [pro-vincial] office,' wrote V. P. Menon, a senior civil servant, 'Lord Linlithgow's attitude automatically changed. . . . [He] began to lean more on the support of the Muslim League. . . . For all prac-tical purposes Jinnah was given a veto on further constitutional progress. . . . The Viceroy even discouraged the efforts of certain well-wishers to bridge the gulf between the Congress and the Government.'[1]

An uneasy quiet descended upon the Indian political scene, the counterpart of military stalemate in western Europe. In both cases it was a lull before the storm. In both it gave rise to a tendency to seek a compromise. Nehru's fears in this regard proved to be un-founded for further talks with the Viceroy failed to resolve the deadlock. The stage was now set for the climax to Act I of the war crisis.

Although the Mahatma was not even a formal member of the party—he had resigned from the Congress in 1934—his power was absolute at this time. It was he who pressed for civil disobedience as the way out. All his conditions were accepted, including a period of delay until the organization was, in his view, ready for non-violent war. In reply to those who criticized his dilatory tac-tics, Gandhi declared: 'You must know that compromise is in my very being. I will go to the Viceroy fifty times if there is need for it.'[2]

While Congressmen waited for Gandhi's call to action, events moved swiftly in the West. Norway and Denmark, then Holland and Belgium, and finally France, fell before the *panzer* onslaught. Hitler's armies were poised at the Channel, and England stood alone, open to invasion. Nehru strongly opposed civil disobedience at this crucial juncture. The idea of using England's distress for political advantage was utterly repugnant. Indeed, the tide of battle in Europe provided the setting for the second, brief act in the drama.

The Congress Working Committee met in emergency session in mid-June and offered complete co-operation in the war effort—if two conditions were met. These were an unequivocal declaration

[1] *The Transfer of Power in India*, pp. 69–72.
[2] *Report of the Indian National Congress at Ramgarh 1940*, p. 90.

of Indian independence and the immediate formation of an all-party national government. The armed forces would remain under the control of the British Commander-in-Chief; the Viceroy's constitutional position would remain unchanged, though it was assumed his veto would not be exercised abnormally; and the civil administration would continue unhindered by the change at the executive level.

Of the Congress leaders' sincerity there can be no doubt. So powerful was their urge to align themselves with the Allies that for the first time since 1920 Nehru, Rajagopalacharia, Azad and others defied Gandhi on the crucial issue of violence. It was a heart-rending break between the master and his disciples. Nehru tried to minimize the significance of the split. 'The Congress of the past twenty years is his creation and child and nothing can break the bond.'[1] Gandhi was deeply moved by this expression of loyalty. Nehru stressed that there was a brief time limit to the offer.

The Viceroy's response was rigid and uninspired. The only innovation was an offer to create a War Advisory Council. The impasse was complete. There seemed nothing left but Gandhi's ultimate weapon. With the failure of conciliatory diplomacy Nehru receded into the background once more. The Mahatma returned to the leadership.

The most striking characteristic of Act III was Gandhi's moderation. Despite the free hand given him by the Congress, he restricted himself to the least effective weapon in his armoury—*individual* civil disobedience. It was a strange campaign indeed. Selected individuals were to recite in public a set formula of an anti-war slogan. No other action was prescribed.

The first *satyagrahi* was Vinoba Bhave, one of Gandhi's most devoted spiritual disciples. He was little known then, though highly respected in the 'inner circle'. His learning was impressive, including a dozen languages and the basic teachings of the great religions. A gaunt, spare man in his early forties at the time, Vinoba had renounced material comfort, in the tradition of India's sages, and had followed in the footsteps of his *guru*. Many years later, with the passing of Gandhi, he emerged from obscurity and achieved international recognition as the founder of the *Bhoodan* (land gift) movement, applying the Mahatma's message

[1] Tendulkar, op. cit., vol. 5, pp. 355–6.

to India's unsolved problem of land reform. Vinoba repeated the symbolic protest against the war in a number of villages and was arrested for sedition. His sentence—three months.

Nehru was to follow him, after giving notice to the authorities. But before he could do so he was arrested. He was tried for a series of speeches and was sentenced to four years' rigorous imprisonment. The nation was stunned by this severe sentence. So too was Churchill, who 'had to be assured that Nehru would . . . receive specially considerate treatment'.[1]

All over India protest meetings were held. The pattern was the same everywhere, though the reaction was spontaneous. Speakers railed against the Government, praised Jawaharlal's virtues, and called for a redress of grievances. Nor was the indignation confined to Congress followers.

The consequences of Nehru's imprisonment were clearly indicated in a confidential British account of the 1940 civil disobedience campaign: 'The immediate and local effect was good; it put an end to the sort of agrarian discontent that Nehru had been endeavouring to stir up. . . . On the other hand, it gave a handle to those, both in India, and also in England and the U.S.A. who desired to accuse Government of repression and vindictiveness. . . . It therefore caused some embarrassment in dealing with the less important people who followed in Nehru's footsteps.'[2]

Gandhi's original intention was to fast after the arrest of the third *satyagrahi*, but he was dissuaded by his colleagues. Instead, he extended civil disobedience to the entire élite of the party, as well as to volunteers from the provincial, district, *tehsil* and primary committees of the Congress. By April 13,000 of the 15,000 potential *satyagrahis* from these groups had been convicted. By early summer the campaign had petered out, though it continued officially until December. On the whole civil disobedience in 1940–1 was a tame affair with little public enthusiasm compared with the campaigns of 1930 and 1942.

*   *   *   *

Pearl Harbour marked the beginning of another act in the Indian war drama. The current of anti-fascism asserted itself.

[1] Menon, op. cit., p. 101
[2] Government of India: *History of the Civil Disobedience Movement 1940–41* (unpublished), p. 5.

Nehru came to the forefront, and a split with Gandhi occurred over the issue of non-violence. With the pendulum shifting rapidly towards active co-operation with the Allies, Gandhi asked to be relieved of the leadership. This was done in January 1942, when the A.I.C.C. made another offer of conditional co-operation.

In the life of Nehru this was an historic Congress session—because the Mahatma publicly designated him as his successor. Rumours were rife at the time of a fundamental split between them. 'It will require much more than differences of opinion to estrange us,' remarked Gandhi. 'We have had differences from the moment we became co-workers, and yet I have said for some years and say now that not Rajaji [Rajagopalacharia] but Jawaharlal will be my successor. He says he does not understand my language, and that he speaks a language foreign to me. . . . *I know this, that when I am gone he will speak my language.*'[1] It was a prophetic statement which even Nehru must have doubted at the time.

While the Congress re-examined its attitude to the war, the danger to India grew ominous. In rapid succession, Japanese armies overran Hong Kong, the Philippines and Malaya. Indo-China and Thailand were firmly under their control. Then, on 15 February 1942, the great bastion of Singapore fell. In Burma, too, the British were retreating. India lay open to invasion.

In the midst of this turmoil Chiang Kai-shek made a brief appearance on the Indian political stage. During a goodwill visit to India in February, he called for the immediate transfer of 'real political power' to the Indian people so that they would rally against the invader. Nehru reciprocated by paying tribute to Chiang as 'a remarkable man [who] has proved himself a very great leader and captain in war'.[2] The turning-point came early in March 1942, when Rangoon was occupied by the Japanese. It was only in the face of this imminent threat that London responded to the Congress offer. Sir Stafford Cripps was dispatched to Delhi with new proposals in an effort to break the deadlock.

The negotiations began hopefully but ended in complete failure, amidst mutual recriminations. Cripps offered full Dominion status after the war with the right of secession from the Commonwealth. To achieve this goal he promised the establishment of a

[1] *Indian Annual Register*, vol. i, 1942, pp. 282–3. (Emphasis added.)
[2] Bright, J. S. (ed.), *Before and After Independence*, p. 216.

constituent assembly immediately after the conclusion of hostili-
ties. He also pledged British acceptance of a constitution so
framed, subject to the right of any province to remain outside the
Dominion. Such non-acceding units would receive a status comparable to that of the projected Indian Union (the opening wedge
to a separate Muslim state of Pakistan). For the duration of the
war no constitutional changes were proposed. But Cripps expressed the hope that the principal political parties would co-
operate in a 'National Government'. Defence would remain the
prerogative of the British Commander-in-Chief. All parties
rejected the offer. Gandhi termed it a 'post-dated cheque'.

Sir Stafford Cripps was probably the ideal choice for the role of
mediator. But his task was a formidable one. It was made more
difficult by the oppressive political atmosphere in Delhi in the
spring of 1942. Indeed, the suspicions were so intense that the
gradualist, constitutional approach seemed doomed to failure.

Cripps's fundamental error was his assumption that Nehru held
the power of final decision in the Congress. In the dying moments
of the talks he sent a private note to Nehru. 'Let me make a final
appeal to you,' he wrote, 'upon whom rests the great burden of
decision. . . . The chance which now offers cannot recur. . . .
Leadership—the sort of leadership you have—can alone accom-
plish the result. It is the moment for the supreme courage of a
great leader to face all the risks and difficulties—and I know they
are there—to drive through to the desired end. I know your
qualities, and your capacity and I beg you to make use of them
now.'[1]

Nehru's reply is unknown but his candid assessment of the
Cripps Mission is revealing. 'Cripps surprised me greatly. I have
liked Cripps as a man. . . . But on this occasion I was surprised at
his woodenness and insensitiveness, in spite of his public smiles.
He was all the time the formal representative of the War Cabinet,
in fact he was the War Cabinet speaking to us with a take it or
leave it attitude. Always he seemed to impress on us that he knew
the Indian problem in and out and he had found the only solution
for it. Anyone who did not agree with it was, to say the least of it,
utterly misguided. Indeed, I made it perfectly plain to him that
there were limits beyond which I could not carry the Congress and
there were limits beyond which the Congress could not carry the

[1] *A Bunch of Old Letters*, p. 468.

people. But he thought that all this was totally beside the point.'[1]

There is no doubt that Gandhi tipped the Congress scales against the Cripps offer. But the responsibility for deadlock was shared by Churchill, Linlithgow and Cripps himself. Beyond these individuals was a climate of opinion which virtually assured deadlock. The Congress approach was legalistic, almost sectarian, but it had become so distrustful that concrete evidence of British sincerity was required there and then, not at some time in the future. Cripps and his superiors failed to cut through the clouds of suspicion with a bold gesture. If the British were going to part with total power at the end of the war a limited transfer could have taken place during the conflict. Ironically, Cripps had anticipated the basic cause of the collapse of his mission in a letter to Nehru three years earlier: 'The trouble is that, as always, it [a sympathetic British offer] is likely to come too late to save the situation.'[2]

From the moment the deadlock was announced bitterness mounted swiftly in the Congress. There seemed only one way out —the ultimate weapon of civil disobedience. But this course of action was fraught with danger, for the Japanese were poised to strike against eastern India. For Nehru, more so than any other nationalist leader, the spring and summer of 1942 were months of emotional turmoil. He loathed the idea of Japanese conquest. Intellectually, too, his course was clear, for Allied victory was a precondition to Indian freedom. But the issue was blurred in his mind by the cause of independence and his distrust of British intentions.

Of one thing Nehru was certain: total inaction was suicidal, both for the war effort and the struggle for independence. Hence he pressed for guerrilla war against the Japanese. Gandhi was opposed and termed it 'a nine days' wonder'. The Mahatma then took the lead and issued a provocative challenge to the *Raj*.

'Quit India' at once, he urged, so that a free India could mobilize its full strength against the Japanese menace. Beyond this slogan nothing was spelled out, though Gandhi was certainly thinking of mass civil disobedience if the British did not heed his call. The effect was electrifying. Throughout the country thousands

[1] To Evelyn Wood on 5 June 1942. Unpublished Nehru Letters.
[2] 11 October 1939. *A Bunch of Old Letters*, p. 387.

rallied to the cry. Some like Nehru were disconcerted by the prospect of civil disobedience at this critical period in the war. As a result he fought a strong rearguard action against the Mahatma's plan until the very last moment.

Nehru's dilemma in the summer of 1942 was described by Gandhi in a letter to the Viceroy: 'I have argued with him for days together. He fought against my position with a passion which I have no words to describe. . . . He yielded when he saw clearly that without the freedom of India that of the other two [China and Russia] was in great jeopardy. Surely you are wrong in having imprisoned such a powerful friend and ally.'[1] Having succumbed to Gandhi's logic, Nehru closed ranks with his mentor. It was he who moved the resolution calling on the British to quit India at once.

The 'Quit India' resolution contained an offer and a challenge. 'On the declaration of India's independence . . . a *Free India will become an ally of the United Nations* . . .' Further, 'The Committee resolves *to sanction* . . . the starting of a mass struggle on non-violent lines on the widest possible scale. . . .'[2]

The Government of India reacted at once. On the morning of 9 August 1942 Gandhi and all members of the Working Committee were arrested. Nehru was then staying at the home of his younger sister. The Mahatma was detained at the Aga Khan's palace in Poona, while the Committee members were taken to Ahmadnagar Fort, a Moghul relic in a remote corner of Bombay Province. There they were to remain until June 1945. It was Nehru's last and longest period behind the walls.

*   *   *   *

The arrest of the Congress leaders set off a nation-wide political explosion, the climax to the war drama. There was no need for directives and planning. For more than a week business life was paralysed in Ahmedabad, Bombay, Delhi, Madras, Bangalore and Amritsar. In almost every major city mass demonstrations mushroomed from the bazaars. Students and workers, shopkeepers and housewives marched through the streets, singing nationalist

[1] 14 August 1942. Government of India, *Correspondence with Mr. Gandhi, August 1942–April 1944.*
[2] The text is in *Congress Bulletin*, No. 1, 1 November 1945, Part I, pp. 10–13. (Emphasis added.)

songs and demanding the release of Gandhi and the Working Committee. They were peaceful at first. But the tension was great and the authorities were nervous. The pattern was the same every-where—protest meetings, police firing and arrests.

Students were in the vanguard. They walked out of the universities and started a campaign of sabotage—derailing trains, cutting telephone wires, instigating peasants to withhold payment of taxes. Later, cases of arson and bomb-throwing became common. Violence bred violence. According to the Congress account of the 'August Movement', about 600 persons were killed by police fire during the first few days. Perhaps the most dramatic episode occurred in the Midnapore district of Bengal, well known for radicalism in earlier campaigns. Two *tehsils* succeeded in expelling all officials, declared themselves part of 'Free India' and maintained their 'independence' for four months.

Everywhere government repression was harsh, for this was the gravest threat to British rule since the Rebellion of 1857. No quarter was given. None was asked. In addition to frequent police firing, there were mass arrests and extensive use of *lathi* charges. In short, it was the establishment of a police state or, as the Congress termed it, 'Ordinance *Raj*'. During the last five months of 1942 India was fired by the spirit of revolt.[1]

One of the most striking features of the campaign was the 'general conspiracy of silence'. 'The public as a whole is either apathetic or tacitly sympathetic [to the Congress]', wrote the Chief Secretary of Bombay. 'There is still general distrust of the British Government.' From all over India came similar reports. Not all groups were sympathetic. The League was jubilant about the arrest of the Congress leaders and continued its policy of passive support to the war effort. The Communists openly opposed civil disobedience. They blamed the Government for the revolt but criticized the nationalist response. The Hindu Mahasabha favoured the 'Quit India' demand but was not prepared to court jail for its goal.

The campaign was short-lived but intensive. By the end of August the rebellion was broken, though incidents continued for

[1] The Congress account is taken from All-India Satyagraha Council, *Report of the August Struggle* (unpublished). The following quotations from the official *Fortnightly Reports* are taken from extracts in the files of the History of the Freedom Movement Project in the National Archives of India.

months. According to the Secretary of State for India, the casualties from 9 August to 30 November 1942 were 1,028 killed and 3,215 seriously injured. These figures are almost certainly an underestimate. Moreover, within a few months about 100,000 nationalists were imprisoned, many of them for the duration of the war. And as the Chief Secretary of Bengal reported in September, 'all sections of Indian opinion may be said to be at one in support of the demand for the immediate transference of power and the establishment of a national government'. The campaign failed, but the feelings of politically conscious India had been expressed. The tragedy was that it assumed violent forms, against the will of Gandhi and at a delicate stage in the war. Five years later Independence came—without the need for another round of civil disobedience.

Seen in historical perspective, the 'August Movement' was the outcome of persistent British intransigence during the preceding three years. This created such frustration among Indian nationalists that the only, though unwise, course of action was civil disobedience, as a symbolic act of defiance. If, instead, violence ensued, it was precipitated by the Government of India's abrupt and repressive action on 9 August whch decapitated the Indian National Congress of its entire leadership. Thereafter the clash could not be averted.

It is difficult to gauge the effects of the revolt on the Indian war effort. According to General Sir Francis Tuker, G.O.C. in C., Eastern Command, in 1946–7, the riots accompanying the struggle 'nearly brought our armies to a standstill, fighting the Japanese on the Assam border'.[1] The Home Member of the Viceroy's Executive Council, Sir Reginald Maxwell, expressed a similar view.

The long-range political consequences were even more significant. For almost three years the Congress was outlawed, its leaders in prison, its funds seized and its organization virtually destroyed. In the political vacuum thus created the Muslim League was able to build a mass party, by appealing successfully to religious emotions and genuine Muslim fears. Between 1942 and 1945 the League increased its membership to two million with the result that by the end of the war it was able to put forward a strong claim to Pakistan. The Congress was to pay dearly for its 'Quit

[1] *While Memory Serves*, p. 154.

India' Resolution. Unwittingly it helped to pave the way for Partition.

In recalling the 'August Struggle' fourteen years later, Nehru remarked: 'I don't think that the action we took in 1942 could have been avoided or ought to have been avoided. It might have been in slightly different terms; that is a different matter. Circumstances drove us into a particular direction. If we had been passive then, I think we would have lost all our strength.'[1]

The Congress committed another blunder in September 1944, when Gandhi was persuaded by Rajagopalacharia to meet Jinnah in a further effort to break the deadlock. The talks proved futile but they strengthened the League; they enhanced Jinnah's prestige and gave him a status of virtual equality with Gandhi.

While the 'August Revolt' raged over British India Nehru remained in prison with his eleven colleagues of the Working Committee. The oldest of this unique band was the doughty, earthy Sardar Patel, organizing genius of the Congress. In appearance and dress the Sardar resembled a wise old Roman senator. He was a robust man, then in his late sixties, one of those Indians whose native male dress, the *dhoti*, gave dignity and nobility, an impression strengthened by his massive, strikingly bald head. His face was usually expressionless. But this mask concealed a clear, rational mind, forceful and determined. His piercing eyes and the hard lines around his mouth denoted strength of character and decisiveness, the dominant characteristics of modern India's most astute party politician. Yet he was not without a caustic wit which he exercised on occasion during the thousand days and nights at the Fort.

The most stimulating of Nehru's companions were: Maulana Azad, dean of the nationalist Muslims, a renowned Islamic scholar and a political comrade for twenty years; and Acharya Narendra Dev, gentle scholar and humanist, steeped in India's cultural traditions, a founder of the Socialist Party and a friend since pre-Gandhi days. There was Asaf Ali, later India's first Ambassador to the United States, with an alert mind and a lawyer's outlook. Another Muslim companion was Dr. Syed Mahmud, a close associate since the early 1920's.

Two members of the group later bolted from the Congress and became prominent figures in the Praja-Socialist Party: Acharya

[1] To the author in New Delhi on 6 June 1956.

Kripalani, in appearance the prototype of India's ascetics among
the politicians, a man of strong and often divergent views; and
Dr. Profullah Ghose, chemist by profession, a staunch Gandhian
pacifist during the war-time cleavages within the High Command.
An imposing figure was Pandit Pant, long-time leader of the
United Provinces, with his massive frame and walrus moustache;
though slow of movement, he was articulate and verbose. Later,
he became Nehru's right hand at the Centre as Home Minister.
From Maharashtra in Western India came Shankerrao Deo, devoted Gandhian, who was unique among Congress leaders in that
he never occupied a position in government. A storehouse of
information and an engaging raconteur was Dr. Pattabhi
Sitaramayya, historian of the Congress. The youngest was Hare-
krishna Mahtab, later Chief Minister of Orissa, Minister of Commerce at the Centre and Governor of Bombay, who added a touch
of lightheartedness to the discussions. It was an odd assortment.
Their temperaments varied, as did their cultural interests, their
habits of living, and their sensitivity to surroundings.

It was a mild imprisonment on the whole. The accommodation
was adequate. They had a series of adjoining rooms in a large
quadrangle set apart from the main prison and leading on to a
long-neglected garden. They were given a private kitchen, with
service performed by convict warders. The greatest punishment
was a confining atmosphere.

From all accounts Nehru was, as usual, a model prisoner and
companion. His presence brightened the gloomy atmosphere, and
his varied interests and vitality were sources of strength. Though a
voracious reader, he participated in most of the humdrum activities and took a leading interest in gardening. In short, he was the
soul of the party.

His routine was severely regulated. Early to rise, he began the
day with yoga exercises. After breakfast he settled down to work—
careful reading and painstaking notes. This lasted until 3 p.m.
with only a short break for lunch. Then, after a brief nap, there
was discussion on politics and culture with his fellow prisoners and
a spell of gardening. In the evening he strolled in the prison compound or played badminton. From nine to eleven at night he returned to his books.

According to Narendra Dev, he was utterly devoted to his companions and nursed his sick comrades with scrupulous attention.

He had a passion for order and cleanliness, and was a model of tolerance in political discussions. He was full of energy, boyish in his exuberance and vitality. Despite his periodic outbursts and fiery temperament, he always made an effort to see the other person's viewpoint and was open to persuasion.[1]

Thus, it was only after their release in the summer of 1945 that the full impact of events was brought home to the Congress leaders. In that sense these were utterly barren years. Nevertheless, this period of inaction was productive for Nehru personally. As so often in the past, prison provided leisure for contemplation and writing. He read voraciously and pondered with a fresh mind the problems which had long troubled him. It was another 'voyage of discovery', part of his endless quest for knowledge. From it emerged the last of his trilogy, *The Discovery of India*.

During the early 'thirties Nehru had explored the panorama of history on a grand scale, in his *Glimpses of World History*. From this he turned to self-analysis and related his own experience to India's struggle for freedom, in the celebrated *Autobiography*. Now he examined his heritage, in the form of a rambling and discursive history of his native land, social, philosophical, economic, political and cultural. Largely under the influence of Azad and Narendra Dev, he acquired a deep appreciation of the cultural tradition of India and of its influence on his own thought and action. He now sought and found the mainsprings of India's struggle for independence within India's historical experience.

The Discovery of India is not especially profound or original. Indeed, scholars question the accuracy of some of the facts and his interpretation of many controversial issues. Yet it is important for the light it throws on Nehru's new awareness of the specifically Indian influences on his character and outlook. Like most of his writings it is partly autobiographical in form. In essence it unfolds Nehru's discovery of his Indian antecedents, the flow of Indian history seen through the eyes of a person who had described himself earlier as 'out of place everywhere, at home nowhere'.

[1] *Nehru Abhinandan Granth: A Birthday Book*, pp. 111–12.

CHAPTER VIII

INDIA AT THE CROSSROADS

By the beginning of 1945 the outcome of the war was no longer in doubt. Within India discontent was rampant, though partly concealed by an air of resignation. In Bengal man and nature conspired to produce the most disastrous famine of the century. By official estimate 1½ million persons perished and 4½ million more suffered greatly during 1943 and 1944.

Nehru observed this spectacle of death from afar, and recorded his anguish in prison: 'Famine came, ghastly, staggering, horrible beyond words. . . . Men and women and little children . . . dropped down dead before the palaces of Calcutta, their corpses lay in the mud-huts of Bengal's innumerable villages and covered the roads and fields of its rural areas. . . . Death was common enough everywhere. But here death had no purpose, no logic, no necessity; it was the result of man's incompetence and callousness, man-made, a slow creeping thing of horror with nothing to redeem it, life merging and fading into death, with death looking out of the shrunken eyes and withered frame while life still lingered for a while. . . .'[1]

The British *Raj* was generally slow to respond to pressures for change. In mid-1945, however, India was expected to be the principal base of allied operations in East Asia and a long war with Japan was anticipated. Hence all members of the Congress Working Committee were released and a conference of political leaders arranged to discuss the Government's new offer: communal parity, i.e. equal representation of caste Hindus and Muslims, in a reorganized Viceroy's Executive Council, which would be completely Indian except for the Viceroy himself and the Commander-in-Chief.

The 1945 Simla Conference was really a contest between the

[1] *The Discovery of India*, pp. 2-3.

Congress and the Muslim League. The League insisted on the right to appoint *all* Muslims to the Executive Council and the Congress refused to abdicate its status as a national organization. Jinnah threatened to boycott the Executive Council unless his demands were met; and Lord Wavell acquiesced. The veto given to the League leader was a dangerous precedent that strengthened his hand in the crucial battles to follow.

Nehru's role at the Conference was of no importance. From Simla he went to Kashmir for a post-imprisonment holiday. His attachment to the Vale is perhaps best revealed in this passage: 'The loveliness of the land enthralled me and cast an enchantment all about me. I wandered about like one possessed and drunk with beauty, and the intoxication of it filled my mind. Like some supremely beautiful woman, whose beauty is almost impersonal and above human desire, such was Kashmir in all its feminine beauty of river and valley and lake and graceful trees. And then another aspect of this magic beauty would come to view, a masculine one, of hard mountains and precipices, and snow-capped peaks and glaciers, and cruel and fierce torrents rushing down to the valleys below.'[1]

In the meantime, the British Labour Party assumed office. Almost at once a new policy statement appeared: elections to the central and provincial legislatures were announced for the winter; provincial autonomy would be restored immediately after the elections; a constitution-making body for India would be established as soon as possible; and the Viceroy's Executive Council would be reconstituted in consultation with the principal Indian parties.

The Congress fought the elections with a catch-all programme similar to its manifesto in 1937. To allay Muslim fears it called for a federal constitution with autonomy for the constituent parts and a minimum list of common subjects. The Muslim League stressed the issue of Hindu domination in a united India and the consequent need of a separate Muslim homeland, i.e. Pakistan. The results were astonishing. The League won all 30 Muslim seats in the Central Assembly and 427 of the 482 Muslim seats in the provincial legislatures. Its only setback was in the North-West Frontier Province. Most of the remaining seats were won by the Congress. The trend to polarization was now evident; all other groups faded into insignificance.

[1] *The Unity of India*, p. 223.

The Congress formed provincial ministries in eight of the eleven provinces, the League in Bengal and Sind, and the Unionists, with Congress support, in the Punjab. The stage was now set for the reconstitution of the Viceroy's Executive Council and the convening of a Constituent Assembly. To achieve these goals London dispatched a three-man Cabinet Delegation consisting of Lord Pethick-Lawrence, Sir Stafford Cripps and A. V. Alexander. Another frustrating bargaining session was soon to begin.

In the midst of the elections, disaffection penetrated the military services. Ironically, it began in R.A.F. stations in India. These were followed by hunger strikes in the R.I.A.F. (Royal Indian Air Force) and minor cases of indiscipline in the R.I.N. (Royal Indian Navy). The explosion occurred in February 1946 in the form of a mutiny of naval ratings at Bombay. For five days the leading naval base in India presented the appearance of a minor battlefield, though there was little bloodshed.

There were strong political overtones to the mutiny. Left-wing parties called for a 'union of Hindus and Muslims at the barricades'. Communist influence was evident in the Sailors' Central Strike Committee. Congress leaders sympathized with the sailors' grievances but opposed their talk of violence. Patel persuaded the ratings to surrender unconditionally—by promising Congress aid against victimization and support for their legitimate demands. Nehru adopted a similar attitude. The mutiny spread to other naval bases, notably Karachi, but these incidents were less dramatic. Their political significance cannot be gauged accurately, but it seems more than a mere coincidence that the announcement about the British Cabinet Mission was made one day after the outbreak of the Bombay mutiny.

*   *   *   *

The fundamental principles of the Cabinet Mission scheme were deceptively simple. There was to be 'a Union Government dealing with . . . Foreign Affairs, Defence and Communications . . . [and] two groups of Provinces (Hindu and Muslim) . . . dealing with all other subjects which the Provinces in the respective groups desire to be dealt with in common. The Provincial Governments will deal with all other subjects and will have all the residuary Sovereign rights. It is contemplated that the Indian [princely] States will take their appropriate place in this structure on terms to be negotiated with them.'[1] Theoretically, all the warring parties could have been satisfied. The League was offered a *de facto* Pakistan. The Congress could find a united India, though somewhat emasculated, and an assurance of provincial autonomy. The plan also provided for the lapse of Paramountcy, thereby granting freedom of action to the Princes.

In the midst of the crucial negotiations, Nehru rushed to Kashmir to assist in the defence of his protégé at the time, Sheikh Abdullah, then on trial for treason. He was prohibited entry and was detained when he violated the Maharaja's order. The Viceroy intervened through the British Resident in Kashmir and Nehru returned though not without misgivings and only after he was assured that the Congress would make his cause their own. To many his behaviour seemed immature. Although it showed commendable loyalty to a friend the political battle in Delhi was far more important.

The climax was approaching. Gandhi advised rejection of both the long-term and short-term plans. His colleagues, however, were not completely persuaded. The Working Committee rejected the scheme for an Interim Government but accepted the long-term plan for an Indian Union—with its own interpretation of the disputed clauses. The League had already done the same. The Cabinet Mission ignored the harsh reality of continued deadlock, shelved its recommendations for an Interim Government and left for England at the end of June, having accomplished virtually nothing. The gap was as wide as ever.

During the talks the Congress held a presidential election, the first since 1940. Patel was in line for the post. Moreover he was the overwhelming choice of the Provincial Congress Committees. But as in 1929 and 1937 Gandhi intervened and Nehru was elected. The Mahatma remarked on another occasion, 'Jawaharlal cannot be replaced today, whilst the charge is being taken from Englishmen. He, a Harrow boy, a Cambridge graduate and a barrister, is wanted to carry on the negotiations with Englishmen.'[2] Moreover, Nehru could speak with greater authority for a united Congress than Patel, who was inclined to distrust nationalist Muslims in general. 'There is only one genuinely nationalist Muslim in India—Jawaharlal,' the Sardar reportedly said.

[1] Cmd. 6829, 1946, p. 3.   [2] On 1 June 1947. Tendulkar, op. cit., vol. 8, p. 3.

One month after the election the Viceroy invited Nehru (as Congress President) to form an Interim Government. If Gandhi had not intervened, Patel would have been the first *de facto* Premier of India, in 1946-7. The Sardar was robbed of the prize and it rankled deeply. He was then seventy-one while Nehru was fifty-six; in traditionalist Indian terms the elder statesman should have been the first premier; and Patel knew that because of his advanced age another opportunity would probably not arise.

The newly elected Congress President was dissatisfied with the Cabinet Mission plans. This is evident in Nehru's speech to the A.I.C.C. on 10 July, one of the most fiery and provocative statements in his forty years of public life. The Congress was committed to participate in the Constituent Assembly, he said, but nothing else. And the Assembly would be a sovereign body, regardless of policy statements from London. Of course, protection of the minorities had to be assured, as Congress had always pledged, but this would be done by the Constituent Assembly alone. As for a treaty with Britain, this would depend on the British attitude. About the grouping scheme he was brutally candid. It would probably never come to fruition, he declared, because section A, the Hindu-majority provinces, would be opposed, the Frontier Province would oppose it in section B as would Assam in section C, and provincial jealousies would thwart it. He also stressed the likelihood of a much stronger central government than that envisaged by the Cabinet Mission. 'The scope of the Centre, even though limited, inevitably grows, because it cannot exist otherwise.'[1]

There was much political insight in Nehru's speech. At the same time it destroyed the façade of agreement which the Cabinet Mission tried to maintain. In fact, it sparked the collapse of the Mission and was a serious tactical error. Jinnah was given an incomparable wedge to press more openly for Pakistan on the grounds of Congress 'tyranny'. At the end of July the League withdrew its acceptance of the Mission's long-run plan and called for 'Direct Action'. This was an ominous decision, for it set in motion the disastrous civil war which was to engulf the sub-continent for the next eighteen months.

Many persons regret that the Mission's long-term plan never came to fruition. But it was unworkable in the tension of 1946-7.

[1] *Indian Annual Register*, vol. ii, 1946, pp. 145-7.

Neither the Congress nor the League ever really accepted the plan, though both placed their formal approval on record for bargaining purposes. The basic drawback was its complexity and cumbersome procedure. The three-tier scheme (Centre, Groups, provinces) was an intellectual *tour de force* but it was impracticable in the environment of a deadly struggle for power. It would have led to endless friction between the Centre, the Groups and the provinces, and between the Congress and the League, making efficient administration impossible. Cripps was riding two horses at the same time, trying to find a solution on paper which both parties would accept. His proposal would have brought Pakistan in through the backdoor, by the group scheme, and would have maintained the façade of a united India. As long as the two Indian parties disagreed on fundamentals any plan was doomed.

They could not even agree on the composition of an Interim Government. After more frustrating negotiations, this was formed early in September with Nehru as *de facto* Prime Minister and Member for External Affairs and Commonwealth Relations. The League continued its boycott.

*   *   *   *

Amidst these 'summit talks' the poison of communalism penetrated deeper into India. The contest for power heightened the tension to boiling point. The 'War of Succession' was ready to begin. Its spark was Jinnah's proclamation of 'Direct Action Day'. The initial result was the 'Great Calcutta Killing'.

There is no evidence to suggest that Jinnah himself planned or even desired the holocaust, though he had no compunction about resorting to violence. Whether orders were dispatched to the Muslim League Ministry in Bengal is unknown. In any event they were unnecessary. 'The origin of the appalling carnage and loss . . . was a political demonstration by the Muslim League,' wrote the British-owned *Statesman* of Calcutta. 'The bloody shambles to which this country's largest city has been reduced is an abounding disgrace, which . . . has inevitably tarnished seriously the all-India reputation of the League itself.' Only after four days of lunacy, in which 4,000 were killed and thousands more wounded, did the city return to relative sanity.

'This is not a riot', wrote the *Statesman* when it was over. 'It needs a word found in medieval history, a fury. Yet "fury" sounds spontaneous and there must have been some deliberation and organization to set this fury on the way. Hordes who ran about battering and killing with eight-foot *lathis* may have found them lying about or bought them out of their own pockets, but that is hard to believe. . . . It is not mere supposition that men were imported into Calcutta to help in making an impression.'

Nothing comparable to the 'Great Calcutta Killing' had occurred in the annals of British rule. But this was only the beginning of a tidal wave of communal madness which was to sweep over India during the next year. As with all mass upheavals an irrevocable chain reaction was set in motion. Early in October 1946 the scene shifted to the Noakhali District of eastern Bengal where Muslim gangs went on the rampage, killing, looting, converting Hindus by force, and destroying Hindu temples and property indiscriminately. The official estimate was 300 killed and thousands made homeless; the Congress press kindled the flames with exaggerated reports of casualties. These spread like wildfire to the neighbouring province of Bihar where the Hindu majority wreaked vengeance with equal savagery. The estimates varied again, but not less than 7,000 Muslims were killed. 'There appears to be a competition in murder and brutality,' said Nehru in a report to the Central Assembly.[1]

The difference in approach of Gandhi and Nehru was brought into sharp relief during the 1946 riots. The Mahatma went on a prolonged walking tour of Bengal, addressing small groups at every village, bringing the message of communal harmony and appealing to their sanity. His soothing words were directed to the hearts of each individual; there was no recrimination. To some extent Nehru did the same in Bihar, though there was less of the personal touch in his passionate words to the crowds who gathered in thousands to hear him. He scolded the Hindus mercilessly for their brutal behaviour towards those with whom they had lived in peace for centuries. He appealed for a return to sanity but also threatened harsh punishment unless the killing ceased. Both had a quieting effect on the people, but their methods were basically different.

While the early battles of the 'War of Succession' raged in

[1] *Indian Annual Register*, vol. ii, 1946, pp. 212–14.

Bengal and Bihar the Interim Government entered on a stormy course in Delhi. Initially the experiment went well, for the League boycott permitted joint responsibility in the Executive Council. But Jinnah soon realized that a continued boycott would perpetuate the Congress monopoly of power at the Centre and would jeopardize the goal of Pakistan. He also wished to demonstrate that the two communities could not function in harmony and that Pakistan was the only way out of the impasse. Hence he relented in mid-October and five League nominees were added to the Interim Government.

Nehru was aware of the danger in such a coalition but he was powerless to alter the course of events. Jinnah added fuel to the flames in mid-November by declaring, 'We shall resist anything that militates against the Pakistan demand.' League ministers were instructed to oppose any Government action of substance which prejudiced this goal. He also delivered the death blow to the Cabinet Mission plan by ordering all League members to boycott the Assembly. Nehru replied: 'Our patience is fast reaching the limit,' and 'I cannot say how long we will remain in the Interim Government.'

There seemed to be no way out. At that point Prime Minister Attlee invited the Viceroy, the Congress, the League and the Sikhs to confer in London. The talks lasted four days but the deadlock remained. Then the British Cabinet issued a statement which pointed the way to the final solution. 'Should a constitution come to be framed by a Constituent Assembly in which a large section of the Indian population had not been represented [i.e., the Muslim League], His Majesty's Government could not of course contemplate—as the Congress have stated they would not contemplate—forcing such a Constitution upon any unwilling parts of the country.'[1] This was nothing less than a Pakistan Award. It invited Jinnah to stand fast and spelled the doom of a united India. The British Government had yielded to Nehru in constitutional *discussion* and had yielded to Jinnah in the matter of constitutional *decision* (by virtually assuring him Pakistan).

Nehru was stunned by this turn of events. Why then did he accept Attlee's invitation? The principal reason was to protect the Constituent Assembly. There were also the desires not to 'add to our enemies' and not to give anyone the opportunity to accuse the

[1] *The Times* (London), December 1946.

Congress of rejecting the British plan to transfer power. His intentions were sound but he had been outmanœuvred.

* * * *

A few days after the London Conference the Constituent Assembly was formally convened. The League was absent, but the Sikhs, initially opposed, had been persuaded by Nehru and Patel to attend. The Congress had an overwhelming majority—205 of the 296 seats allotted to British India. The Princes were still to join the proceedings.

It was a memorable event, a realization of the dreams of years gone by. It was indeed a moment of personal and national pride. It was also a time for reflection, at a turning-point in India's chequered history. Nehru rose to the occasion with an eloquent address, while moving the Objectives Resolution, which served as the Assembly's basic frame of reference.

'We are at the end of an era . . . and my mind goes back . . . to the 5,000 years of India's history. . . . All that past crowds upon me and exhilarates me and, at the same time, somewhat oppresses me. . . . When I think also of the future . . . I tremble a little and feel overwhelmed by this mighty task. . . . And now we stand on the verge of this passing age, trying, labouring, to usher in the new.' Here was a typical example of Nehru's stream-of-consciousness approach to public speaking. The mood was all-important.

He paid tribute to Gandhi, 'the Father of our Nation'. He acknowledged, as well, the inspiration of the American, French and Russian Revolutions. He pleaded with the League to abandon its boycott. To the resolution proper he attached the aura of the general will duly proclaimed: 'It is a Declaration. It is a firm resolve. It is a pledge and an undertaking and it is for all of us, I hope, a dedication.' There was also a spirit of defiance.

The objectives laid down in the resolution were general in character as befitted the occasion. The Assembly was called upon to declare its 'firm and solemn resolve to proclaim India as an Independent Sovereign Republic' and to draw up a federal constitution for British India and the princely States, in which the 'autonomous Units' would retain residuary powers. The liberal Western freedoms would be guaranteed in such a constitution 'subject to law and public morality', and safeguards would be provided for minorities and backward tribes and castes.[1]

Further debate on the Resolution was postponed until mid-January 1947 in an effort to placate the League. But the gesture was in vain. Jinnah's attention remained focused on the grouping scheme. Gandhi was still on his pilgrimage of faith. In the face of his refusal to return to Delhi, Nehru went to consult him in the heart of Bengal. More than anything Nehru needed solace. He seemed rejuvenated after the meeting. 'It is always a pleasure and inspiration to meet this young man of seventy-seven,' he remarked on his return to the capital. 'We always feel a little younger and stronger after meeting him and the burdens we carry seem a little lighter.'[2] But there was more than the Constituent Assembly to discuss.

A cleavage between Nehru and Patel had come into the open. The Sardar opposed Nehru's 'idle threats' of resignation from the Interim Government, which damaged the prestige of the party. This incident reveals a fundamental difference between the Congress and the League during the period 1945–7. The League spoke with one voice and its policy was determined by Jinnah alone. The Congress spoke with three or more voices and was subject to the strains of a more heterogeneous organization. Moreover, the Congress was inclined to negotiate in publc, with a variety of statements which perforce could not follow a standard line. These factors strengthened the League's bargaining power in the last stages of the constitutional battle.

When the Constituent Assembly reconvened it was clear that the League did not intend to lift the boycott. Hence the Assembly proceeded to pass the Objectives Resolution, unanimously. The League called on London to dismiss the Assembly. Its mood was defiant. Nothing less than Pakistan was acceptable. The Congress responded with a demand that the League Ministers should be removed from the Interim Government unless the League participated in the Assembly. At that critical juncture Attlee intervened with an historic proclamation about the transfer of power. The year of decision was about to begin.

[1] The text of the Resolution and Nehru's speech are in *Independence and After* pp. 344–53.
[2] *Hindustan Times* (New Delhi), 31 December 1946.

CHAPTER IX

1947: TRIUMPH AND ANGUISH

Nineteen forty-seven was a fateful year in the life of Nehru and in the turbulent history of India. For both it was a year of mixed fortunes. The coming of freedom and Nehru's accession to power were accompanied by a savage communal war in which half a million people died and millions more were uprooted from their ancestral homes. For Nehru and the Congress generally, the joy of Independence was tempered by the sadness of Partition. The moment of their greatest triumph was also the moment of their greatest defeat. A few months after the transfer of power the successor states were at war in Kashmir. And then there occurred the death of Gandhi, the beloved and revered master. For the first time in his political life Nehru was alone, leading his country through its greatest crisis. But no one could anticipate this sequence of events.

The year of decision began with an historic declaration in the House of Commons on 20 February 1947. Prime Minister Attlee announced that power would be transferred by June 1948 and that if the League refused to join the Constituent Assembly power would be granted to the central Government or the provincial Governments or in some other suitable way—which obviously meant partition. This statement was a logical continuation of the declaration of 6 December. Whether or not so intended it paved the way for partition. As for the princely States, paramountcy would end with the transfer of power in British India and would *not* devolve upon the successor Government(s).[1] It remained for Lord Louis Mountbatten, who was named Wavell's successor, to execute the withdrawal of the British *Raj*.

Tory spokesmen predicted disaster. 'India is to be subjected not merely to partition, but to fragmentation, and to haphazard

[1] Cmd. 7047, 1947.

augmentation,' declared Churchill. 'In handing over the Government of India to these so-called political classes we are handing over to men of straw, of whom, in a few years, no trace will remain.'[1] The Labour benches were unmoved.

More than a month passed between Mountbatten's appointment and his arrival in India. It was a crucial interregnum, because the struggle for power had moved from the conference room to the streets. By indicating a specific date for the transfer, the British Prime Minister had added a sense of urgency to the struggle. And by remaining vague about the successor(s) he galvanized the parties into vigorous action. The Muslim League was especially vulnerable because it controlled only two of the six provinces claimed for Pakistan, namely Bengal and Sind.

The kingpin of the Pakistan demand was the Punjab, the largest, most populous and wealthiest province in northern India. On communal grounds the claim was valid, for the Muslims comprised about 56 per cent. of the total population of 29 million. On political grounds the League claim was less persuasive but powerful none the less. It had swept the polls in the 1946 elections and was the largest party in the Punjab legislature. But it lacked a clear majority and was excluded from office. Constitutional government was virtually at a standstill because the coalition of Unionists, Congress and Sikhs was uneasy and had a majority of only three; the legislature met only when it was essential to pass the budget.

The most disturbing feature of Punjabi politics was the formation of private armies by the three communities. In January 1947 the League resorted to 'direct action'. Stealing a leaf from Gandhi's book, it launched mass civil disobedience against the Punjab Government's belated ban on these para-military organizations. The agitation continued for more than a month. Then came Attlee's statement. Seizing the pretext that it altered the political situation, the Premier resigned.

The Governor, Sir Evan Jenkins, called on the League leader in the legislature to form a ministry. The Sikhs responded with a mass rally at which their fiery leader, Master Tara Singh, added fuel to the flames: 'O Hindus and Sikhs ! . . . Disperse from here on the solemn affirmation that we shall not allow the League to exist. . . . I have sounded the bugle. Finish the Muslim League.'[2]

---

[1] Gt. Brit. H.C. *Debates*, 1946–7, vol. 434, cols. 673–4.
[2] Quoted in G. D. Khosla, *Stern Reckoning*, p. 100.

It was an idle threat, for the National Guards of the League were much better organized at the time.

The next day, 4 March, the struggle for the Punjab shifted to the streets; and Jenkins was compelled to take over direct administration of the province. The initial wave of communal killings, in town and village, lasted about a fortnight; because of its superior organization the League 'army' scored a major 'victory'. But the 'War of Succession' had just begun. Of its ferocious character, Nehru remarked after a tour of Lahore, 'I have seen ghastly sights and I have heard of behaviour by human beings which would disgrace brutes.'[1] Large-scale violence flared anew early in May. No quarter was offered. By the time the transfer of power took place, one-twentieth of Lahore had been destroyed by fire and many villages had murdered every member of the minority community. Yet these disturbances were mere skirmishes of a massive civil war.

Amidst the upsurge of communal violence, Nehru made his formal début on the stage of international politics. The place was the Purana Quila in New Delhi; the occasion was the first Asian Relations Conference. It was an impressive gathering, more than a score of nations, cultures and languages with little in common except the urge to assert Asia's place in the world political community.

Perhaps more than any other statesman of the age, Nehru responds to the mood of his immediate surroundings. On this occasion the urge for recognition and equality of status provided the main theme for his address. 'Far too long have we of Asia been petitioners in western courts and chancelleries,' he said. 'That story must now belong to the past. . . . We do not intend to be the playthings of others.' With obvious pride he referred to India's pivotal role in Asia but he pointedly denied any claim to Asian leadership. As for the Conference, 'This event may well stand out as a land-mark which divides the past of Asia from the future.'[2]

Nehru clearly dominated the Conference. Almost all his colleagues were too engrossed in the deadly struggle for power within India to be concerned. Typical of the indifference was Patel's alleged comment when asked if the Conference would take any formal stand on the Indonesian demand for independence: 'Indonesia, Indonesia, let me see—where is Indonesia? You

[1] Bose, D. R., *New India Speaks*, p. 133.   [2] *Independence and After*, pp. 295–301.

better ask Jawaharlal about that.' Gandhi appeared briefly to plead his philosophy of non-violence. The League leaders ignored the Conference completely; they, too, were obsessed with the great issues within India. Nothing concrete was achieved, except the creation of a pro-forma organization of Asian states. Nevertheless, the Conference reflected one of the most significant phenomena of the century, the re-entry of Asia into world politics. And Nehru's initiative was to reap for India the reward of international prestige.

*   *   *   *

While the spokesmen of Asia pledged their peoples to co-operation, the leaders of India were preparing for mortal combat. The struggle for power was intensified with the coming of Mountbatten in March 1947. The range of problems bequeathed to the new Viceroy was formidable indeed: communal frenzy in the Punjab; League agitation in the North West Frontier and Assam; virtual paralysis of the Interim Government; a sharp decline in the efficiency and *élan* of civil servants; a series of British Government pronouncements which could not be reconciled; a Congress demand for a united India; a League demand for Pakistan; evidence that the Sikhs would resist partition; and potential Balkanization of the country.

The new Viceroy plunged into a round of intensive interviews with the Big Five of Indian politics—Gandhi, Jinnah, Nehru, Liaquat Ali Khan and Patel. From the outset he was drawn to Nehru whom he had met in Malaya a year before. Both possessed charm, vanity, boundless energy, a patrician bearing and background. From this flowed mutual trust and candour. In time it developed into a warm and lasting friendship.

With none of the other leaders did Mountbatten establish such intimate relationship. Jinnah was too cold and aloof; Liaquat Ali was overshadowed by the League President; Patel was a man of few words. For Gandhi, the Viceroy had much respect but their outlooks were fundamentally different.

The most striking feature of Mountbatten's diplomacy was the rapidity with which he arrived at decisions. From the very beginning he was concerned lest the friction give way to total disintegration on the Chinese pattern. It had become obvious soon after his arrival, he suggested to the author some years later, that a united India could not be imposed except at the cost of a major civil war, for events had moved too far and too fast since the Cabinet Mission. The riots had indicated what could happen but a civil war would have been infinitely more costly. It remained only to persuade all the protagonists.

Nehru seemed resigned to the necessity of partition very early. 'The Muslim League can have Pakistan if they want it,' he declared in April, 'but on the condition that they do not take away other parts of India which do not wish to join Pakistan.'[1] Early in May, Mountbatten's Chief of Staff, Lord Ismay, flew to London to secure Cabinet approval of the partition scheme. Nehru raised certain technical objections, but a compromise was finally hammered out.

In this connexion the role of V. P. Menon, the Viceroy's Constitutional Adviser, was crucial. Indeed, without his help and advice the Partition Plan might have fallen through. When Mountbatten appeared on the scene he was committed to the Cabinet Mission Plan (Cripps's three-tier scheme) but soon decided that a united India was impossible. His next plan was to transfer power to the provinces. Menon proposed it to Nehru and met a blank wall. Finally, Menon persuaded the Viceroy to try his own scheme—Dominion status for both states. The die was cast when Menon succeeded in winning Nehru's consent. Patel had already approved. With their acceptance the Congress was virtually committed.

Jinnah muddied the waters by demanding an 800-mile corridor to link East and West Pakistan. Nehru termed the demand 'fantastic and absurd'. In the face of firm Congress opposition, Jinnah did not press the issue. Another disturbing note was contributed by Gandhi who told his prayer-meeting audience: 'Even if the whole of India burns, we shall not concede Pakistan, even if the Muslims demanded it at the point of the sword.'[2] But these were mere words, for power in the Congress now lay with Nehru and Patel. Finally, a bizarre element intruded. Jinnah said he could not give his formal consent, but he did agree to nod in approval when the Viceroy announced that Jinnah had given him acceptable assurances on the League attitude.

[1] Lumby, *The Transfer of Power in India*, p. 155.
[2] On 31 May 1947. Quoted in Lumby, op. cit., p. 161.

The principal merits of the Mountbatten Plan were clarity, brevity and simplicity, and the critical fact that it embodied the maximum agreement of the parties. In essence it provided a procedure to ascertain the will of the people living in those areas claimed for Pakistan. In Bengal, Sind and the Punjab the issue was to be determined by the provincial legislatures. But in Bengal and the Punjab the Assemblies would divide into two sections, representing the Muslim-majority and non-Muslim majority districts. If either favoured partition of the province, almost certain, this would be an irrevocable verdict. In the Frontier there was to be a referendum. Similarly, the Muslim-majority Sylhet district of Assam would hold a referendum if Bengal favoured partition and would be tacked on to east Bengal if it favoured Pakistan. The Plan also indicated a willingness to transfer power before June 1948—on a Dominion status basis.[1]

On the evening of 3 June the leaders announced their agreement to the Indian people. Nehru's mood combined sadness, resignation, reflection, almost detachment. 'It is with no joy in my heart that I commend these proposals though I have no doubt in my mind that this is the right course.' There was humility, too. 'We are little men serving great causes, but because the cause is great something of that greatness falls upon us also.'[2] Jinnah paid tribute to Mountbatten's impartiality and offered his co-operation. He also appealed to all communities to abandon violence. Baldev Singh, speaking for the Sikhs, succeeded in concealing the bitterness of his co-religionists.

The League Council granted Jinnah complete authority to accept the Plan. Formal Congress approval was emphatic and unequivocal, though there was opposition from the nationalist Muslims, Hindu communalists and Congress Socialists. Gandhi was present at the historic A.I.C.C. session in mid-June but he refused to challenge his two senior lieutenants, even though he remained firmly opposed to partition. Patel delivered the keynote address. He used the analogy of a diseased body and argued that if one limb was poisoned it must be removed quickly lest the entire organism suffer irreparably. The speech was typical of the man—pointed, brutally frank, unemotional. After two days of debate

[1] See Cmd. 7136, 1947.
[2] Quoted in Campbell-Johnson, A.: *Mission with Mountbatten*, p. 107 (British edition).

the Mountbatten Plan was approved. The nationalist Muslims felt betrayed. A rare photograph portrays Nehru's anguish as he pondered the meaning of partition.

To implement the enormous administrative tasks in connexion with the transfer, a complex machinery was created. At the top of the pyramid was the Partition Committee of the Interim Government, later the Partition Council. Then came a Steering Committee of two senior civil servants, which co-ordinated the work of expert committees and sub-committees, each charged with a specific facet of the Partition. Among the most important were those dealing with the armed forces, the civil service, economic relations, especially cash balances, and communications. Though not described as such, this structure was a parallel caretaker government; the Interim Government remained but it lost its *raison d'être* with the decision to divide the country. The most delicate task was the division of the armed forces. To its credit the Council carried through the operation with efficiency and speed, ascertaining the choice of every soldier, sailor, and airman.

By the middle of July all the disputed areas had made their choice. The results were a foregone conclusion except for the Frontier Province which, despite a Muslim majority of 92 per cent., was governed by the Congress-orientated 'Redshirt' Party. Geographically the Frontier was now isolated from the Indian Dominion. Moreover, the 'Redshirts' boycotted the referendum because it did not provide the alternative of independence. The result was a massive majority for Pakistan. The cry of 'Islam in danger' had penetrated deeply by the summer of 1947.

Amidst these developments the constitutional formalities were hastily completed in London. In a fortnight the Indian Independence Bill secured the approval of both Houses of Parliament. It was brief, only twenty clauses, but symbolic of the end of an epoch.

In accordance with the Mountbatten Plan, the Act provided for the creation of two new Dominions on 15 August 1947. As for the princely States, Paramountcy would lapse with the transfer of power, by inference granting them freedom of action to accede to India or Pakistan—or to proclaim their independence. The territories of the Dominions were defined, with appropriate qualifications for the areas about to determine their choice by referendum or by vote of their legislature. Each Dominion was to be headed by a Governor-General, but it was expressly stipulated that one person might serve in a dual capacity, in the hope that Mountbatten would be acceptable to both. The absence of a legally constituted Parliament was overcome by giving both Constituent Assemblies the dual status and function of legislature and constitution-making body. The 1935 Government of India Act and its accompanying Orders-in-Council would remain in force subject to the removal of the reserved and special powers vested in the Governor-General and the provincial Governors. All laws in force in British India on 15 August would remain in force until amended by the new Dominion legislatures. There was also a provision for continuity in the terms of employment of members of the Services. Indeed, the Indian Independence Act was remarkable for the degree to which it assured continuity in political institutions, the legal and judicial system and the constitutional fabric of British India.[1]

One provision of the Act gave rise to vigorous controversy. The Congress proposed Mountbatten as Governor-General of the Dominion of India and assumed that the League would do likewise. But Jinnah decided to occupy that post in Pakistan. This schism and Mountbatten's acceptance of the Congress invitation created widespread Pakistani distrust. To the present day it is alleged that the Viceroy was offended by Jinnah's action and that he used his authority to strengthen India's claims in the many disputes that arose, the boundaries of Bengal and the Punjab, and the Kashmir dispute. That the outward animosity lingered on became evident in 1956, when Mountbatten was forbidden air passage over Pakistani territory *en route* to India.

Within the Interim Government tension continued. Mountbatten solved the problem by splitting it into two provisional administrations for the successor states. Friction was intensified by uncertainty over the frontiers pending the reports of the Boundary Commissions for the Punjab and Bengal, headed by Sir Cyril Radcliffe, a noted English barrister. Apparently they were ready on 9 August, but Mountbatten decided to delay their publication for a week in order not to mar the celebration of Independence.

At last the 'Appointed Day' arrived. On the evening of 14 August huge, cheering crowds lined the main streets of New Delhi

[1] Indian Independence Act 1947, 10–11 George VI C.30. *Law Reports–Statutes*, 1947, vol. 1, pp. 236–55.

as Nehru, Prasad, Patel and others made their way to Parliament House for the solemn ceremony of dedication to a free India. Nehru rose to the occasion with an eloquent address.

Long years ago we made a tryst with destiny, and now the time comes when we shall redeem our pledge, not wholly or in full measure, but very substantially. At the stroke of the midnight hour, when the world sleeps, India will awake to life and freedom. A moment comes, which comes but rarely in history, when we step out from the old to the new, when an age ends, and when the soul of a nation, long suppressed, finds utterance. . . . The achievement we celebrate today is but a step, an opening of opportunity, to the greater triumphs and achievements that await us. . . . Peace has been said to be indivisible. So is freedom, so is prosperity now, and so also is disaster in this One World that can no longer be split into isolated fragments.[1]

After each member of the Assembly recited a pledge of service to India, Nehru and Prasad went to the Viceroy's Palace. Nehru handed Mountbatten an envelope containing a list of members of the Cabinet to be sworn in the following morning. The excitement of the day was, indeed, overwhelming—the envelope was empty!

All over India the coming of Independence was celebrated with unrestrained enthusiasm. It was a great *tamasha* (celebration) and the pent-up emotions of millions gave way to gay abandon. Parades and firework displays were everywhere, mass meetings with speech-making dotted the land. Gandhi was honoured as the Father of the Nation, Nehru and Patel were hailed as indomitable leaders in the freedom struggle and, in the exuberance of the moment, tribute was paid to Mountbatten as the bearer of Indian freedom.

For Nehru August 15 marked the great divide in his public life. Behind him were three decades of opposition to foreign rule. Ahead was the unknown, an opportunity to translate ideals into reality. It was also a time for leadership, for the 'War of Succession' was about to enter its most disastrous phase.

Independence Day itself provided a respite from the nerve-racking events of the preceding fifteen months. But it was a day of ceaseless activity. In the morning the official swearing-in of Cabinet Ministers took place at the Viceroy's House amid the pomp and splendour of Durbar Hall, followed by the unfurling of the national flag at the Council of States. Then he attended a

[1] *Independence and After*, pp. 3–4.

gathering of school-children, another flag-raising ceremony at the war memorial and a traditional 'crowning' by Hindu Pandits. In the evening there was a state banquet.

To his people Nehru addressed two messages. 'The Appointed Day has come,' he said, 'the day appointed by destiny, and India stands forth again after a long slumber and struggle, awake, vital, free and independent. . . . A new star rises, the star of freedom in the East. . . . May the star never set and that hope never be betrayed!'[1] In his broadcast to the nation he concentrated on the critical problems facing free India at its birth: the end of violence and internal strife; increased production and equitable distribution; and radical reform of the land tenure system.

The celebrations were brought to a close with an impressive flag-hoisting ceremony at the Red Fort, the majestic symbol of Moghul power and splendour in Old Delhi. A crowd estimated at half a million gathered for the occasion and a deafening roar greeted the unfurling of the Congress flag. They listened attentively as Nehru recounted the highlights of the freedom struggle and posed the challenge for the future. The time of rejoicing was brief, however, for the rumblings of communal war could be heard in the distance. Independence Day was not only a day of triumph. It was also the prelude to a spectacle of barbaric cruelty and wholesale migration.

*   *   *   *

The 'War of Succession' was resumed with increased ferocity on the morrow of independence. There were two great danger spots—Bengal and the Punjab. Largely due to Gandhi's presence, communal passions in Bengal were kept within manageable bounds. In the Punjab, however, they unleashed a full-scale civil war.

The immediate effect of the Radcliffe Award was to generate mass hysteria and paralysing fear in the Punjab. Hatred was already entrenched as a result of the March riots. But it was the formal announcement of the boundary lines that galvanized the communities into renewed action. It was as if the Award had closed the prison doors, trapping millions of frightened Punjabi peasants in two large concentration camps. The alternatives were

[1] *Independence and After*, pp. 5–6.

death or flight. They reacted with blind instinct and set out for the 'Promised Land', Pakistan for the Muslims, India for the Hindus and Sikhs. The leaders had offered assurances of protection to minorities but years of inflammatory words had roused communal passions; a monster had been created, no longer capable of being controlled by pledges of fair treatment. Thus, while the rest of the sub-continent celebrated the coming of Independence, the Punjab entered a period of horror.

In remote villages members of the minority community were killed, for no other reason than the accident of birth. Each atrocity bred response and, within days, the 'Land of the Five Rivers' was aflame with bestiality. It is impossible to apportion responsibility, nor is it easy to prove who set the chain reaction in motion. All communities share the blame for this black record in Indian history, though many individual Muslims, Sikhs and Hindus risked their lives to save friends in the minority group.

Rumour, fear and the desire for vengeance maintained the momentum of communal fury. Members of the minority fled from isolated villages to larger centres in the hope that numbers would provide a measure of security. Some were killed *en route*. No quarter was given—torture, mutilation, assault, conversion by force. It was nothing less than a war of extermination. The battle-field was everywhere, in village, town, road, temple and mosque. Trains going between Lahore and Amritsar were considered fair prey. The less fortunate began a trek by foot. In sheer numbers it was the greatest in history, about twelve million, equally divided between Hindus and Sikhs fleeing from West Punjab and Muslims from the East. Before the year was out half a million people died, or were murdered.

The crisis reached its peak within India early in September, when thousands of refugees poured into Delhi and wreaked vengeance on local Muslims. When the enormity of the disorders became clear, Nehru and his colleagues resorted to emergency measures. Under Mountbatten's direction, they formed an emergency committee along the lines of a military headquarters command. Gradually the response had the desired effect—to restore law and order, especially in the capital. Nehru's role during the crisis was vital. Mountbatten organized the administrative machinery but it was Nehru who inspired confidence and led his people back to the road of sanity. Both contributed to the victory over the riots, their efforts complementing one another effectively. Those who observed Nehru at the time noted that he had aged considerably. To a few intimates he confided his pain, disgust and disillusionment, but to the nation he was more resolute than ever.

Many are the stories of Nehru's personal courage during the riots in Delhi. On one occasion he rescued two Muslim children who had taken refuge on a roof. During the height of the riots he raced to the Connaught Circus, the commercial heart of the capital, where Hindus were looting Muslim shops with the police standing by as interested onlookers. Panic was enveloping the city. Without regard for his personal safety, he rushed unarmed into the midst of the angry mob and attempted, single-handed, to bring about a return to sanity. As a last resort he ordered the police to shoot the Hindu looters, an extremely unpopular decision at the time. It was this, perhaps more than anything else, that broke the back of violence in Delhi.

It required much courage, too, to declare repeatedly that as long as he was Prime Minister, India would not become a Hindu state. Indeed without his decisive leadership at the time the fate of millions of Indian Muslims would have been much worse. By the beginning of October the threat to Delhi had been overcome. By the end of the year both sides of the Punjab border had been denuded of the overwhelming majority of the minority communities, particularly in West Pakistan. The cost of Partition in human suffering was enormous.

Was the response of the authorities adequate? Could the loss of life have been reduced? Was the size of the migration inevitable? The crux of the answers to all these questions is that no one foresaw the magnitude of the Punjab migration. In part, this was due to the belief that once Pakistan was conceded, the basic cause of communal violence would vanish. It was as if the torrent of communal riots from the 'Great Calcutta Killing' onwards could be dismissed as unfortunate excesses of the struggle for freedom. When to this is added the fact that violence was normal in the Punjab for five continuous months, the belief of Mountbatten, Nehru, Patel and their colleagues that the transfer of power would be peaceful in the Punjab was a grave error of judgement. Even more, it was a tragic misreading of mass psychology.

One of the most painful features of the Punjab catastrophe for Nehru and others was the fact that after thirty years of preaching non-violence, millions of Indians behaved like brutes. Gandhi himself had the remarkable capacity to restore communal peace wherever he went. But no one else possessed this magic at the time. If there had been two Gandhis, things might have been different. But there was only one and he went to Bengal.

It may well be that the size of the migration was inevitable, given the haste with which the transfer of power was carried out. In seventy-three days from the acceptance of the Mountbatten Plan to Independence Day, a large number of complicated problems had to be solved, with resulting dislocation on a vast scale.

What persuaded him to puih the date of the transfer ahead from June 1948 to 15 August 1947? In Mountbatten's view there were two critical factors—the instability of the Interim Government and the decline of administrative efficiency. Issues were not decided on their merits, the vote invariably being 9 to 5, along party lines, thereby hampering the functioning of the central government. The longer the transfer of power was delayed, the greater the possibility of disorder in the country. Mountbatten also implied that the leaders' agreement to his plan for partition was precarious. And Gandhi was opposed to partition in any form. As Mountbatten remarked to the author, 'I heard about it in Karachi, on my return from London at the end of May, and so asked him to come and see me. It happened to be a day of silence for which I was grateful. In retrospect I think he chose to make that a day of silence to save him the embarrassment of accepting the Partition. For he had no other solution.'

Having succeeded in getting acceptance, it was important to maintain the momentum, almost, it would seem, to prevent them from changing their minds. What would have happened if the date had been set a few months later? The Interim Government might well have broken down, the administrative machine might have suffered serious harm, and the partition Plan might have been abandoned. Moreover, widespread communal violence might have followed.

*　　　*　　　*　　　*

These reflections have an added interest. They suggest that the timing of the British withdrawal was dictated by the compulsion of events within India in the spring of 1947. No less compelling was the weakened position of England as a result of the war and the enormous drain, economic and military, which continued control over India would have entailed. There was, too, growing pressure from the United States and the Soviet Union.

These factors and the absence of any real choice were emphasized in a candid speech by Sir Stafford Cripps to the House of Commons. 'One thing that was, I think, quite obviously *impossible was to decide to continue our responsibility indefinitely—and, indeed, against our own wishes—into a period when we had not the power to carry it out. . . . It would be politically impracticable, from both a national and an international point of view, and would arouse the most bitter animosity of all parties in India against us. . . .* [And] it is certain that the people of this country—*short as we are of manpower, as we all know—would not have consented to the prolonged stationing of large bodies of British troops in India.*'[1]

The choice, then, was coercion on a large scale or independence —and British resources were inadequate to retain power by force. The fact that a Labour Government carried through the withdrawal certainly hastened the process. More than that, it symbolized a fundamental change in British public opinion towards India during the preceding half-century. There were large and powerful segments of British society which had developed a guilt complex about continued British rule in India. There was, too, a growing sympathy for Indian nationalism. But only a realization that power could not be retained except at an excessive cost ensured the outcome in 1947.

Indian independence was inevitable in another sense. Viewed in the long perspective of history, it was the climax of a lengthy process inherent in the character of British rule. The key to its attainment was the creation of a common purpose. Once that purpose, the quest for freedom, penetrated most strata of Indian society, the transfer of power by the United Kingdom was inescapable. How, then, was this common purpose achieved? In part, it was an inadvertent legacy of the *Raj*: administrative integration and a transport system that united India physically for the first time in two thousand years; the penetration of English as a medium of communication for the intelligentsia throughout the sub-continent; and secular education, which broke down age-old barriers among Indians of different castes and classes. In part it was forged by the

[1] Gt. Brit. H.C. *Debates*, 1946-7, vol. 434, cols. 503-5. (Emphasis added.)

nationalist movement and especially by Gandhi who super-imposed upon these foundations the symbols of a common pur-pose, such as the nation-wide *hartals*, constructive work, a flag, an anthem, and most important, mass non-violent non-co-operation. The civil disobedience movements strengthened the common bonds and maintained a continuous focus on the goal of national freedom, welding diverse groups together in the common purpose. The growth of political consciousness among Indian peasants and workers hastened the process. The success of the Russian Revolu-tion also acted as a stimulus. Ultimately, the common purpose spread throughout the country and infected the Services with a sense of guilt and impending doom. It was at that point that the British had no choice but to transfer power. In short, indepen-dence was the natural outcome of the process of creating national consciousness and a common purpose, accomplished by the *Raj*, unwittingly, and by Indian Nationalists, deliberately, over an extended period of time. In this sense the British *Raj* contained within itself the seeds of its own destruction.

The price of Partition was high, not only in terms of human suffering and the legacy of bitterness between the two successor states, but also in terms of the stated objectives of British policy. Among these were avoidance of loss of life and of dislocation as far as possible, protection of the minorities and preservation of unity to the maximum extent. On all three counts the Partition registered a failure.

*   *   *   *

Almost a year after the Partition, Nehru remarked: 'I do not know now, if I had the same choice, how I would decide.'[1] But did Nehru really have a choice or was Partition, like Indepen-dence, inevitable? And if so, when did it become irrevocable? Most persons are convinced that the outcome was in doubt as late as the middle of 1946. The event most frequently cited as decisive was the collapse of the Cabinet Mission. Some stressed Nehru's speech in July 1946 when he proclaimed the sovereignty of the Constituent Assembly; others, the paralysis of the Interim Government in the following autumn and winter; a few pointed to Attlee's statement of 20 February 1947. Nehru himself reflected

[1] *The Hindu* (Madras), 26 July 1948.

some years later: 'The partition of India became inevitable, I should say, less than a year before it occurred. I think now, looking back, that partition could have been avoided if the British Government's policy had been different, about a year or eighteen months before.'[1]

Nehru's crucial role in the great decision is beyond question: it was he and Patel who carried the Congress in favour of Partition. In a sense Nehru was the decisive member of the triangle of Congress leaders, for Patel could never have won a majority in support of the Mountbatten Plan had Nehru stood by Gandhi.

The Mahatma was heartbroken by the decision. However, he did not attempt to challenge his disciples. Apparently he favoured a final resort to civil disobedience but Nehru and Patel were firmly opposed. What, then, impelled Nehru to accept Partition.

With typical candour he laid bare his innermost thoughts on this vital issue. Seven closely related factors emerge from his speeches at the time. Perhaps the most compelling was fear—fear that civil war would ravage the sub-continent unless the deadlock were broken swiftly. Along with this concern was the belief that acceptance of the League demand would ensure security for the minorities. Moreover, partition seemed to him the only solution to the daily conflicts within the Cabinet. The League policy of obstruction reaped rich rewards.

Nehru also had grave doubts about the wisdom of an artificial and enforced unity. 'If they [the League] are forced to stay in the Union,' he said, 'no progress and planning will be possible.'[2] Nor would it be in accordance with democratic procedure or desirable in India's long-run interests. Further, he was besieged by Hindus and Sikhs in the Punjab and Bengal to accept Partition of these provinces in order to safeguard them against permanent discrimination in a Muslim-majority Pakistan. Finally, the thought that Indian freedom itself might be jeopardized or at least delayed weighed heavily in his decision. The Mountbatten Plan seemed to provide a way out of the tangled web of chaos and frustration; it seemed honourable and effective. Partition was for him the lesser of two evils.

These is a striking consistency in Nehru's views on the Partition. Nine years later he remarked to the author: 'Well, I suppose it

---

[1] To the author in New Delhi on 6 June 1956.
[2] Bose, D. R., op. cit., p. 163.

was the compulsion of events and the feeling that we couldn't get out of that deadlock by pursuing the way we had done; it became worse and worse. Further, a feeling that even if we got freedom for India, with that background, it would be a very weak India, that is, a federal India with far too much power in the federating units. A larger India would have constant disintegrating pulls. And also the fact that we saw no other way of getting our freedom —in the near future, I mean. And so we accepted and said, let us build up a strong India. And if others do not want to be in it, well, how can we and why should we force them to be in it?'[1]

In the atmosphere of tension which pervaded India throughout 1947, there was a widespread belief that Partition would be short-lived, that Pakistan was not a viable state and would be compelled by force of circumstances to return to the fold. Nor was this appraisal confined to the Congress. Another unstated consideration in Nehru's dilemma was the fear that if the Congress rejected the Mountbatten Plan the British Government would impose an even more disadvantageous award.

A more positive inducement was the imminent acquisition of power after a long struggle. For those who have been in opposition most of their political life, the prize of power is tempting. The Congress leaders had already tasted its fruits and were reluctant to part with it at the moment of triumph. This applies to Nehru as well as to his colleagues, for he is not averse to the benefits it confers. Their attitude to Gandhi's alternative policy was embarrassment coupled with the belief that it was unworkable in the conditions of 1947. They refused to take the plunge lest Gandhi should have miscalculated and the country be overrun by uncontrollable civil war. It is ironic that in this situation Gandhi, the great compromiser, acted as the pure revolutionary, while Nehru, the acknowledged revolutionary in the Congress, accepted a compromise solution.

It is easy to speculate on what might have been. But in terms of their oft-stated goal of a united India would it not have been wiser for Nehru and his colleagues to reject the Mountbatten Plan which, in any case, was on the verge of collapse? By so doing they would probably have won independence—and unity. Having waited thirty years, should they not have waited a little longer, as Gandhi suggested?

[1] To the author in New Delhi on 6 June 1956.

Despite this breach over Partition, the relations between Nehru and Gandhi remained basically unchanged during the last few months of the Mahatma's life. He continued to fulfil the role of guide, elder statesman and father-figure—but was not a super-Prime Minister. He did not interfere with the daily routine of government. Nor did he hamper Nehru's political leadership or determine policy, except when he felt that a strong ethical issue was involved. In such instances Nehru and the Cabinet submitted to his wishes. But these were few in number.

In the twilight of Gandhi's life Nehru was drawn closer than ever to his *guru*. Indeed, there emerged an almost compulsive attachment. To many, this seemed an abnormal relationship for a man of Nehru's stature and age—he was then fifty-eight. In reality it was the logical by-product of a pattern which had developed during the preceding thirty years—Gandhi the father, Nehru the son.

Gandhi's position was unique among the great public figures of this century. He was father as well as leader, a genuine patriarch, a philosopher-king. Almost all the outstanding personalities of the Indian nationalist movement were moulded by the Mahatma after 1920. They sought his advice, in both personal and political matters, and usually abided by his will. Indeed, there was an ingrained habit of leaving all major decisions to him. Nehru expressed this in a letter to Gandhi early in 1947: 'I know that we must learn to rely upon ourselves and not run to you for help on every occasion. But we have got into this bad habit and we do often feel that if you had been easier of access our difficulties would have been less.'[1] As the world seemed to crumble beneath him, it was natural for Nehru to turn to the person who had exerted the most profound influence on his life.

Gandhi returned to Delhi early in September 1947. Refugees from West Pakistan were pouring into the capital. Riots broke out afresh. The Cabinet itself was rent by dissension over the treatment of minorities and economic policy. Nehru persisted in his determination to build a secular state. Patel was less inclined to treat Indian Muslims with impartiality when Hindus were being maltreated in Pakistan. Nehru remained firm and Gandhi supported him unreservedly.

The disagreement widened over economic policy, Gandhi in

On 30 January 1947. Quoted in Pyarelal, Mahatma Gandhi, The Last Phase, p. 568.

this case siding with Patel and the business community: the Government yielded to the pressure for decontrol of prices on essential commodities. Smouldering discontent within the Congress burst forth at the same time with the resignation of Kripalani from the presidency because his colleagues in the Government did not take him into their confidence.

In the midst of all these strains open warfare broke out in Kashmir. Pathan tribesmen invaded the former princely State with the connivance and material support of high Pakistani officials. The Maharaja of Kashmir, whose procrastination contributed immeasurably to the dispute, finally sought Indian military aid and offered to accede to the Dominion of India. The offer was accepted and troops were flown into Srinagar to stem the tide of the advancing tribesmen. The city was saved and most of the Vale of Kashmir was cleared of the invaders. In time fighting gave way to military stalemate, political recriminations and, later, total deadlock, which continues to poison Indo-Pakistani relations.[1] Gandhi supported Nehru's dispatch of troops to the Vale, on the grounds that India had a moral obligation to aid victims of aggression. As one crisis followed another Nehru turned to his mentor for advice. During these anxious months he paid a daily visit to Gandhi. Invariably he returned invigorated.

As the new year dawned, communal tension reared its head once more. Gandhi responded with vigour and announced that he would fast until Muslims could move about freely in the streets. Nehru started a sympathetic fast but abandoned it in deference to the Mahatma's request. As always in the past Gandhi's threat of self-sacrifice had the desired effect. All communities promised to abandon violence, and peace returned to the city.

Before the fast began, however, a new crisis arose: the Indian Government decided to postpone the payment to Pakistan of 550 million rupees, its unpaid share of the cash balances under the Partition Agreements. Gandhi was stunned by what he considered to be an indefensible and immoral act. He was determined to have a showdown with Patel.

Gandhi heard about the decision in the middle of his fast over communal tension and let it be known that he would fast until death. A four-man Cabinet delegation was sent to explain the rationale directly to him. First Nehru, then Patel, tried to justify

[1] See the author's *The Struggle for Kashmir* (1953).

the decision. Gandhi lay flat on his back, weak and silent. There was no response. Then Patel began again. After a few minutes Gandhi raised himself slowly, with tears streaming down his cheeks. Turning to Patel, he said in a barely audible whisper: 'You are not the Sardar I once knew,' and then fell back. The visit ended abruptly. All were stunned and filed out. The following morning it was announced that the funds would be transferred immediately.

This episode showed Gandhi's great influence when he was aroused. It is, too, a classic example of his ethical approach to politics. Pakistan had a moral right to the funds, for a solemn agreement had been reached. Similarly, Kashmir had a moral claim to Indian aid because of aggression; therefore, troops should be sent. The fact that they were not in political harmony was of no consequence. Moral considerations dictated both decisions.

The climax to the year of decision was approaching. Gandhi's habit was to convey his thoughts at a daily prayer meeting, where hundreds gathered to have a *darshan* of (to enter into communion with) the master. In the winter of 1948 these were held on the lawns of the palatial residence of G. D. Birla, a prominent Indian industrialist. On 20 January the serenity of his prayer meeting was ominously disturbed by the explosion of a crude bomb in the vicinity. Nehru and Patel pleaded with Gandhi to accept police protection, but in vain. If he had to die by an assassin's hand, he said, he must do so without anger or fear. He was in the hands of God. Ten days later the Mahatma was dead.

On the afternoon of 30 January Patel was closeted with Gandhi who asked him for a solemn pledge that he would never forsake Nehru nor cause an open split. It was a heart-to-heart talk and many have speculated that they quarrelled. Nehru and Azad were to see Gandhi in the evening but this was not to be.

Like Nehru, Gandhi was punctual in his appointments. The prayer meeting always began at 5 p.m. On that day he was late. As he strolled towards the meeting, a young man stepped forward from the crowd and greeted Gandhi in the traditional *namaste* salutation, joining his hands palm to palm and bowing slightly. Gandhi reciprocated. At that point the youth pulled out a revolver and fired three shots. Two entered the Mahatma's chest, the third his abdomen. Gandhi fell, with the words *Hé Ram* (Oh God) on his lips. Within a few minutes he was dead.

The news travelled through the city, the country and the world like wildfire. Nehru rushed from his home, overwhelmed with grief. His face was like a white mask and his eyes revealed anguish as he approached the body of his beloved *Bapu* (Father). He knelt beside it for a moment and wept uncontrollably. All around him people milled about, too stunned to do anything but to moan and wail at the calamity that had befallen them.

Mountbatten, too, rushed to the scene. As he made his way through the vast throng which had gathered from all over Delhi, someone asked him who did it, a Hindu or a Muslim? Although he himself did not know, the Governor-General had the presence of mind to reply, 'a Hindu'. It was fortunate that he was correct. Had a Muslim been responsible for Gandhi's death a terrible bloodbath might have ensued.

Mountbatten performed another important function. With his flair for the dramatic, he approached Nehru and Patel and related Gandhi's expressed wish for a complete reconciliation. The two men looked at Gandhi's body and then embraced each other.

After the initial shock Nehru went out to inform the crowd. 'Mahatmaji is gone,' he said, in a voice choked with emotion. Later in the evening he addressed the nation. There was no time to prepare his speech but there was no need. Under the stress of this personal loss he rose to the occasion with an eloquent tribute to Gandhi.

Friends and comrades, the light has gone out of our lives and there is darkness everywhere. . . . Our beloved leader, Bapu as we called him, the Father of the Nation, is no more. Perhaps I am wrong to say that. Nevertheless, we will not see him again as we have seen him for these many years. We will not run to him for advice and seek solace from him, and that is a terrible blow, not to me only, but to millions and millions in this country. . . .

The light has gone out, I said, and yet I was wrong. For the light that shone in this country was no ordinary light. The light that has illumined this country for these many many years will illumine this country for many more years, and a thousand years later, that light will still be seen in this country and the world will see it and it will give solace to innumerable hearts. For that light represented something more than the immediate present, it represented the living, the eternal truths, reminding us of the right path, drawing us from error, taking this ancient country to freedom.[1]

[1] The text is in *Independence and After*, pp. 17–18.

The following day all India mourned the passing of its greatest son since the Buddha. From Birla House to the Jumna River, a distance of six miles, the funeral cortège passed while thousands lined the streets, dumbfounded and sad as they said farewell to the Mahatma. Over half a million were at the river-bank awaiting the cremation ceremony. In accordance with tradition Nehru paid his last homage by kissing the feet of his *guru*. Gandhi was no more.

Another tribute was paid to Gandhi in the Constituent Assembly by his forlorn successor. '. . . I have a sense of utter shame both as an individual and as the head of the Government of India that we should have failed to protect the greatest treasure that we possessed', began the eulogy.

How shall we praise him and how shall we measure him, because he was not of the common clay that all of us are made of? . . . A glory has departed and the sun that warmed and brightened our lives has set and we shiver in the cold and dark. . . . We mourn him; we shall always mourn him, because we are human and cannot forget our beloved Master. But . . . he would chide us if we merely mourn. . . . Let us be worthy of him.[1]

Others honoured the passing of a giant. The U.N. General Assembly interrupted its session as a mark of respect. Within India, too, many offered glowing praise. But Nehru's speeches were the best expression of the nation's sorrow. More than a man had passed. An era had come to an end. And Nehru was alone.

[1] *Independence and After*, pp. 20–23.

CHAPTER X

THE DUUMVIRATE

Two men ruled India during the transition period from 1947 to 1950—Jawaharlal Nehru and Vallabhbhai Patel, or 'Panditji' and the Sardar as they were known to friends and foes alike. It was a strange alliance in many ways. Indeed, no two leaders of any Asian nationalist movement in the twentieth century differed more than the duumvirs of the new India—in background, education, temperament, ideology, sources of power, and qualities and defects of leadership.

Nehru is an aristocrat who came under the influence of European culture, habits and manners at an early age. Patel's origins were plebeian and orthodox, a peasant family from Gujarat which was deeply attached to Hinduism. Like Gandhi he spent his formative years in an Indian milieu, though his family was sufficiently comfortable to allow the Sardar to complete his studies for the Bar.

Fortune was also kind to Nehru in his early political career: his rise to prominence in the nationalist movement was assisted by both Gandhi and his father. By contrast, Patel was a relatively unknown lawyer in his early forties without support from an elder statesman of the party.

There were other differences which set them apart. Nehru is a man of great charm, generous to a fault, sensitive and aesthetically inclined, impulsive and emotional. Patel was generally dour and ruthless, unimaginative and practical, blunt in speech and action, cool and calculating. Nehru disliked political intrigue; he was a lonely and solitary leader, above group loyalties. Patel was a master of machine politics. Nehru was the voice of the Congress, Patel its organizer (and Gandhi its inspiration).

To the world at large Nehru was, with Gandhi, the symbol of India's struggle for freedom. Patel never attained this stature, not even within India. Nor did he ever capture the imagination of the peasantry as a revolutionary leader, whereas both Gandhi and Nehru did. Nehru is a master of words and used this technique brilliantly to carry the message of independence and socialism to the far corners of the country. Patel had undisguised contempt for speech-making. He rarely toured the countryside. And except in his native Gujarat he never established a *rapport* with the masses, partly because of his disdain for 'the crowd'. The only elements in the countryside who looked to the Sardar for leadership were the landlords and the orthodox Hindus.

In the cities, too, they commanded the loyalty of different groups—Nehru the radicals and Patel the conservatives. Nehru appealed to the working class, the bulk of the Westernized intelligentsia, the young men and the minorities. Patel drew his support from the business community, orthodox Hindus, senior civil servants and most of the party functionaries. Nehru was (and still is) the outstanding idealist of the Congress and its leading exponent of socialism, a broad international outlook, a secular state and a modern approach. Patel was the realist *par excellence*, a staunch defender of capitalism, 'national interests', Hindu primacy and traditionalism. Both subscribed to the principles of parliamentary government.

On the communal problem, too, the duumvirs were temperamentally and intellectually at opposite poles. Nehru is an agnostic and a humanist, a firm believer in equal rights for all religious communities. Patel never really trusted the Muslims and shared the extremist Hindu Mahasabha view on the 'natural' right of the Hindus to rule India. For him there was only one true nationalist Muslim—Jawaharlal! During the riots of 1947, Patel openly questioned the loyalty of the Muslims who had remained in India, and Nehru, along with Gandhi, came to their defence. No wonder, then, that the Muslims turned to Nehru for support during the dark days after Partition.

'Jawahar is a thinker, Sardar is a doer.' There is a large element of truth in this remark by Gandhi.[1] Yet, like all neat formulas for describing the highly complicated, it is misleading. Compared with Patel and, indeed, most political leaders, Nehru must certainly be classified as a 'thinker'. But Nehru has always been a

---

[1] To G. D. Birla a few days before Gandhi's death. *Nehru Abhinandan Granth: A Birthday Book*, pp. 177–8.

man of action for whom thought is primarily the key to *right action*. While this quality leads to indecision it gives him a breadth of outlook which Patel never possessed.

Nor does Gandhi's comment do justice to Nehru's talent as a politician in the technical sense. Patel could command the Right wing only. Nehru was the indispensable link between Left and Right. It was he, more than anyone else, who rallied the trade unions and peasant leagues to the Congress. It was he who played the leading role in rebuilding the mass membership of the party from 1936 onwards. And with the passing of Patel, Nehru was to demonstrate considerable skill as a party tactician.

The coming of Independence found Nehru in the prime of life. He was fifty-seven then, but his youthful appearance and boundless energy belied his age. Patel was seventy-two when the duumvirate came into being. He was short and robust, slow of movement, yet dignified in his ample *dhòti*. His large, oval face generally wore a grave expression. He was impassive, cold, stern, and seemingly aloof and unresponsive. He rarely revealed his emotions, unlike the mercurial Jawaharlal.

Patel's mental prowess and his political acumen were no less formidable than in his earlier years. But he never possessed Nehru's capacity for work or his physical health. And now the ills of old age were upon him. Yet Patel's contributions during the 'time of trouble' following Independence were to mark him as one of modern India's men of destiny. The duumvirs had helped Gandhi to make a revolution. Now they had to rescue India from the dangers of internal chaos.

The duumvirate was the decisive fact of Indian politics from the Partition until the end of 1950. Though the procedures of Cabinet government were followed, Nehru and Patel dominated the proceedings. It was the same in Parliament, the Congress and the country at large.

What is far from obvious, however, is the nature of the duumvirate. Were Nehru and Patel co-equals? Was the division of power and function clearly defined? Could either have ousted the other? Did the duumvirs function as a team? Most of these questions are difficult to answer with certainty.

The 'Patelist' view may be paraphrased as follows: Patel was the senior partner in terms of sheer power, for he controlled the States, the police, propaganda and, most important, the party

machine. On any issue requiring party sanction Nehru was compelled to seek Patel's approval. Nehru was allowed to strut the
international stage, his control being limited to foreign policy and
Kashmir. The two men did not get on well together and the
rivalry was genuine. Nehru often felt that Patel was trying to
usurp his power; Patel was jealous of Nehru's prestige and
popularity. Patel could have ousted Nehru from the Prime
Ministership; the party would have backed him. But a severe
heart attack in March 1948 ended the possibility of change. It was,
then, an uneasy alliance, made necessary by the course of events.

'Nehruites' contend that this view is a figment of imagination:
no doubt it was a duumvirate in a sense, but Nehru was the
dominant figure throughout. He merely delegated authority to
Patel in certain fields. And the Sardar realized the limits of his
power. While he was supreme in party and organizational
matters, he had to concede to Nehru on such issues as Cabinet
appointments, foreign policy, the constitution, a secular state, and
Indo-Pakistani relations. Friction was common and the rivalry
deep, but at no time was Nehru's position in jeopardy. Patel was a
brilliant tactician but he lacked Nehru's touch with the people.
Nehru kept him in the Cabinet despite their disagreements because he needed the Sardar's administrative talent. But Nehru
would have emerged triumphant had a struggle for power ensued.

Neither interpretation does justice to a subtle, complex relationship at the pyramid of Indian political power. Both are rigid,
static and highly simplified formulae, whereas the relationship
was flexible, dynamic and extremely complicated. There were
many aspects of domestic politics over which neither Nehru nor
Patel had direct supervision, notably economic policy and the
constitution. Further, the Sardar never acted on a major policy
decision without the agreement or at least acquiescence of Nehru.
The two men were administratively 'sovereign' in different spheres
but policy matters were a joint prerogative, except in foreign
affairs where Nehru's word was rarely, if ever, challenged. To
assert that Nehru was 'allowed' free rein in foreign affairs is
merely wishful thinking. Patel himself knew better. Similarly, to
claim that the Sardar acted as the agent of the all-powerful Nehru
is a distortion of reality.

Such conjecture obscures a basic truth about the duumvirate.
Neither Nehru nor Patel derived his power from the other. Both

owed their position to the Mahatma and, indirectly, to the social forces they represented. In life Gandhi was the accepted arbiter of all the disputes which arose between 'Panditji' and the Sardar. And in death he forged a bond of unity which made an open split between them most unlikely. Only a fortnight after the Mahatma's assassination Nehru denied the rumours of an impending break: 'Of course, there have been for many years past differences between us. . . . But these have been overshadowed by fundamental agreements about the most important aspects of our public life. . . . Is it likely that at this crisis in our national destiny either of us should be petty-minded and think of anything but the national good?'[1] The following month Patel suffered a severe heart attack and almost died.

Rivalry between them was undoubtedly genuine, but it was highly exaggerated by cliques of civil servants and politicians devoted to one or the other leader. In the broadest sense they were equals, with Patel possessing substantial power to compensate for Nehru's greater prestige and popularity. Patel controlled a greater aggregate of power through the party and the key ministries of government, but Nehru commanded the country at large. Nehru could have carried the country alone through this period of turmoil, though the attainment of stability would have been delayed. His leadership was of a higher order.

The Sardar knew that his strength was ebbing and that 'Panditji' was the 'chosen son'. These facts, combined with his pledge to Gandhi, his relatively free hand in domestic affairs and a genuine sense of patriotism probably made the duumvirate acceptable to Patel. What of Nehru? Why was he prepared to share power? For one thing, he held the position of Prime Minister. Moreover, the fact of national crisis influenced his attitude. But there were other considerations, Gandhi had brought them together often and his memory now kept them together. Further, there was mutual confidence in each other's integrity and a firm belief that neither desired power *per se*. Perhaps most important was Nehru's deep loyalty to political comrades: 'When you have been working with a man twenty-eight years, you know all about him and forgive a lot.'[2] On the whole the two men adjusted reasonably well to the many stresses which beset the relationship,

[1] *Independence and After*, pp. 31–32.
[2] To Edgar Snow. *Nehru Abhinandan Granth: A Birthday Book*, p. 91.

though towards the end sharp conflict came to the fore over policy towards Pakistan and social change.

*   *   *   *

The Partition had released torrential forces of disorder: communal riots and mass migration; war in Kashmir; the danger of territorial fragmentation; and economic dislocation. That chaos was avoided was due primarily to the leadership of Nehru and Patel.

The gravest danger to Indian unity was Balkanization, the dispersion of power among 600 princely States scattered over the sub-continent. They ranged in size and population from Hyderabad, about as large as France with 16,000,000 people, to tiny estates of a few acres with less than a thousand people All had one thing in common which differentiated them from 'British India', a constitutional link with England embodied in the doctrine of Paramountcy. In essence the British Government was responsible for their defence, foreign relations and communications, while they retained internal autonomy.

As long as the British held sway, this distinction was insignificant. But with the impending transfer of power the question arose —to whom will the Princes owe allegiance once the British have departed, to the Government of India or the Government of Pakistan as the successor authorities, or to no one? The challenge was met with vision and statesmanship, and within a year of Independence the problem of the princely States had vanished into history. Apart from Kashmir and Hyderabad, there was no loss of life. It was a bloodless revolution comparable with the unification of Germany and Italy by Bismarck and Cavour. The directing genius was Sardar Patel. The brilliant technician who conducted the bulk of the negotiations was V. P. Menon, one of modern India's most gifted civil servants.

The campaign fell into three stages, accession, democratization and integration. As a result of a combination of persuasion, cajolery, bribery and the lack of sufficient military power on the part of the Princes, all but three acceded to the new India before the formal transfer of power. The exceptions were Kashmir, Junagadh and Hyderabad.

Junagadh was a tiny State in western India. Ruled by a Muslim, with a Hindu-majority population of 86 per cent., it became a pawn in the struggle over Kashmir. Briefly, the Ruler acceded to Pakistan, despite its predominately Hindu population. Delhi objected vehemently. After a brief period of charge and counter-charge, the Indian Army moved into Junagadh and held a plebiscite. With a declared result of 90 per cent. in favour of India, the State's accession to Pakistan was nullified. Pakistan has never accepted the verdict, but the issue is no longer a serious bone of contention, except in so far as it gives Karachi a debating point over Kashmir.[1]

The case of Hyderabad is much more complex. Like Junagadh the majority of the population was Hindu (90 per cent.), the ruler Muslim. (In Kashmir the position was reversed.) Moreover, Hyderabad had a special status; the Nizam was His Exalted Highness and Faithful Ally of the British Crown. It was large enough to be a viable independent state. And its Muslim aristocracy was determined not to give up its enriched position without a struggle. Hyderabad also had a substantial fighting force, about 50,000 regulars and an irregular army of about 200,000. With Delhi's energy concentrated in Kashmir, the Nizam hoped that a special arrangement could be made, at least to safeguard his internal autonomy.

The negotiations were long and tedious. Hyderabad held out against accession; New Delhi was adamant. Finally, on the grounds of atrocities against Hyderabadi Hindus, the imprisonment of 10,000 Congressmen in the State, border incidents and alarming evidence of an alliance between the fanatical Razakars and the Communists, the Government of India moved, in what has been called a 'police action'. Four days later all resistance collapsed. The Indian Army remained in direct control for a year and was then replaced by a civil administration. After the first general elections a popular ministry took over the reins of government.

Accession was followed by the introduction of democracy. The pace varied, for some states like Mysore had made rapid strides towards responsible government under enlightened Rulers while others like Hyderabad were almost complete autocracies. Civil servants on loan from Delhi assisted the change-over. By the time

[1] For a detailed account of the Kashmir story, see the author's *The Struggle for Kashmir*.

the new Indian Constitution came into effect (1950), most of the States had representative institutions similar to those of the provinces, though they did not function nearly as well.

Almost immediately after accession was completed, Delhi proceeded to the more advanced stage of integration. Various techniques were used to reduce the large number of principalities to a dozen viable units. The magnitude of the operation is brought into bold relief by the vital statistics: within a year an area of almost half a million square miles, with a population of almost ninety million, was incorporated into the Dominion (later the Union) of India. Nehru paid tribute to the achievement: 'The historian who looks back will no doubt consider this . . . one of the dominant phases of India's history.'[1]

Nehru's role in the execution of the greatest triumph of the duumvirate was negligible. Yet it would be wrong to disregard his contribution to the *policy* decisions. His writings and speeches had stressed the archaic character of the 'relics of medievalism', as he was fond of terming the princely States. During the tense days before Partition it was he who tenaciously opposed the official British interpretation of the meaning of the lapse of Paramountcy. And as Prime Minister, he delegated responsibility to Mountbatten to 'negotiate' with the Princes, especially with the Nizam of Hyderabad. Moreover, Patel never acted on major issues affecting the States without securing Nehru's approval. The integration of the States was Patel's master achievement. Nehru's role was secondary but none the less important. He set the objectives in general terms. Patel achieved them with consummate skill.

As the destruction of the princely order drew to a close, the last British Governor-General of India set out for home. A century of pomp and pageantry had come to an end. Lord Mountbatten's tenure as Viceroy was the shortest in the history of the *Raj* but no other representative of the Crown had acquired such popularity with the Indian people. The basic reason must be sought in the peculiar psychological atmosphere of India at the time. The struggle for freedom had been long and arduous. When at last Independence came, Mouhtbatten was its carrier, the symbol of a promise fulfilled. He was likened to a prince in Hindu folklore.

His appearance and manner seemed to give visible expression

[1] Quoted in Menon, *The Story of the Integration of the Indian States*, p. 489.

to this portrait. An exceptionally handsome man in his late forties, Mountbatten of Burma was one of the most striking figures in public life anywhere in the world. He was tall and erect, with an impressive, well-proportioned physique and strong, masculine features. His bearing and movement carried the imprint of a lifetime naval career and the pride of a man born to the highest rank of the aristocracy. He was polished, urbane, imperious and completely self-controlled. He could be stern or light-hearted, attentive or indifferent, conciliatory or adamant. To some his gestures were calculated to achieve the maximum effect. To others they were natural and intensely human. All agree, however, that there was a magnetic quality about 'the Admiral'.

In his immaculate white naval uniform Mountbatten looked every inch the born leader of men. He was a man of many talents —military commander, administrator, statesman. He was, too, a superb showman on the public stage, highly articulate and gifted with a sense of timing. His personality was forceful and dynamic, his energy irrepressible, his capacity for work enormous. Perhaps his greatest asset—and liability—was his habit of making important decisions swiftly, in the opinion of many, too swiftly. Of his capacity for leadership, a former colleague remarked: 'No man could get us out of a mess more quickly, or into one, than Mountbatten.'

He approached the problem of Indian independence as if it were a military campaign. Most revealing in this connexion was a calendar hanging on the wall behind his desk; inscribed in large, black print were numbers and below each, 'Days Left to Prepare for the Transfer of Power.' When D-Day arrived the surgical operation was performed.

Mountbatten was acutely conscious of his own place in history and acted his role with supreme self-confidence. He had a shrewd insight into men and affairs and possessed formidable powers of persuasion. His mind was quick and he was able to remember all manner of detail. In the darkest days he remained calm, immovable in a raging storm.

Unlike most of his predecessors, he was gifted with a common touch. He mingled freely with Indians at all levels, showed a keen interest in their problems and sympathy with their aspirations. And was he not, after all, a prince in fact, cousin to the King. It was this unusual combination of qualities that endeared him to many Indians. By all accounts he was an arresting figure, a man of irresistible charm.

Mountbatten's most notable personal triumph in India was an intimate bond of friendship with Nehru. This was the product of various factors, some of them highly intangible. First and foremost was a powerful mutual attraction between very similar personalities. Both men were proud, cultivated, worldly and conscious aristocrats; both possessed great charm and a human touch; both were men of action and masters of the art of public relations; both were vain. Nehru was far more sensitive and constantly beset by doubt. Mountbatten was more self-assured. Nehru had a mercurial temperament. Mountbatten was always serene. In the large, Nehru was the more noble man, more human personality, whose vision was broader and sense of morality more pronounced. Where they differed they supplemented each other well.

There was, too, a marked affinity of ideas. Nehru's stress on science, secularism, industrialization and a welfare state found a more sympathetic response in Mountbatten than in most of his colleagues. It was easy to talk to Mountbatten, for their way of thought was similar, two aristocrats who had forsaken the ideologies of their class. Moreover, Mountbatten was the first Viceroy to treat him as an equal, to abandon the rigid code of 'ruler' and 'subject'. Mountbatten's sympathy for Indian freedom undoubtedly strengthened the friendship. So too did his behaviour during the fifteen months he served as Viceroy and Governor-General, particularly his role during the Delhi riots in the autumn of 1947.

As for Lady Mountbatten, it can only be surmised that she helped to fill a void in Nehru's life. He had always suffered from a sense of loneliness. His wife's death at an early age had accentuated this feeling. Especially during the Partition days, when he was more prone to moods of despair, Lady Mountbatten's sympathy was a source of comfort. She, too, was a cultivated Westerner, and a woman of great charm who could understand him as most Indian women whom he knew could not.

In the years that followed, his friendship with the Mountbattens was sustained by personal reunions. During his frequent visits to England, Nehru invariably spent a week-end at their country estate at Romsey. At the Delhi end there were annual visits by Lady Mountbatten as part of her tour of the East for various welfare agencies; and Lord Mountbatten paid a brief official visit in 1956. Although friendship cannot be measured precisely, Nehru probably feels closer to the Mountbattens than to anyone in India, except for his daughter and, perhaps, Krishna Menon.

The political consequences of the Nehru-Mountbatten friendship are also noteworthy. The Mountbattens' persuasive powers undoubtedly helped to ease Nehru's acceptance of partition. They also succeeded in dispelling his distrust of British motives. And Nehru was probably influenced by them in deciding to remain in the Commonwealth. India paid an exorbitant price for Mountbatten's military approach to the transfer of power. But in terms of British interests it was a brilliant achievement.

* * * *

When Nehru accepted Dominion status many people were startled. And when India agreed to remain in the Commonwealth, Nehru was accused of violating solemn pledges undertaken during the struggle for freedom. But he had always made a sharp distinction between Britain as the ruling power in India and Britain as an equal. Once British control ended, he said over and over again, friendship was possible.

The road to India's membership in the Commonwealth as an independent republic is an illuminating example of Nehru's dominant role in the shaping of India's foreign policy. Many hands helped to pave the way, notably Mountbatten, Krishna Menon and Attlee. There were tortuous legal barriers in the final stage. Its completion was a triumph of fortitude.

The formal arrangement was concluded at the Commonwealth Prime Ministers, Conference in April 1949 and was embodied in the Declaration of London. It was a very brief document indeed, only four paragraphs. The first noted the existing position, referred to the *British* Commonwealth of Nations and the common *allegiance* to the *Crown*. The second indicated that India had informed the participants of its decision to establish a sovereign independent republic, of its desire to retain full membership in the Commonwealth, and of its willingness to accept the *King* as *symbol* of the free association of members and as such as *Head* of *the*

Commonwealth. The participants accepted India on these terms and affirmed their status as free and equal members.

Despite its simplicity, the Declaration of London had many hurdles to overcome. The core issue was the Crown. The Australians wanted the King to be designated King of the Commonwealth, but South Africa, Canada and India refused. There was a proposal to have the President of India formally appointed by the King, but India was opposed. Mountbatten suggested the inclusion of the Crown in the Indian flag; this, too, was rejected. Finally, they devised the formula, 'Head of the Commonwealth.' Absolutely no pressure was exerted by the British though they wanted India to remain in the Commonwealth.

Within India opposition was confined to the Left and sections of the right wing Hindu Mahasabha. The main themes of the critics were that it violated previous pledges; committed India to the West; represented a loss of independence; and was immoral because of racial discrimination in South Africa. In defence of his policy Nehru noted that India's independence was unimpaired; that it was in India's self-interest, and that it helped to promote international stability.

Various factors influenced Nehru's decision. The most important was the realization that India could not remain isolated in a world of tension and that the Commonwealth link was the most advantageous. The bulk of India's trade was with the Commonwealth; its foreign exchange reserves were tied up in the Sterling Area; its armed forces depended on British-made weapons. Moreover, membership of the Commonwealth would enable India to render greater assistance to the large communities of Indian settlers in South Africa, Malaya, British Guiana and other parts of the Empire. Viewed in the perspective of the duumvirate, it was an act of high statesmanship, for it was the first real stabilizing act in India's relations with the outside world.

In the midst of his negotiations with the Commonwealth, Nehru made his formal début on the world stage as Prime Minister of India. His address to the U.N. General Assembly in Paris in November 1948 marked him as the voice of new Asia.

He praised the principles of the Charter but stressed the priority of means over ends. In fact, this speech was an exposition of Gandhian non-violence. But it was more. While paying tribute to European cultures, he noted that the world was no longer synonymous with Europe. He pleaded for the end of colonialism and racial inequality. Economic problems were more vital than the political, he said, in criticism of the U.N.'s preoccupation with the latter. The great plague of the age was fear. And all states shared in the guilt for the vicious circle which had led to re-armament and constant preparation for war. His audience was visibly moved, especially by his eloquent appeal for understanding of the Asian revolution.

A year later Nehru made his first 'voyage of discovery' to America. For three weeks he toured the United States. He sought food—2,000,000 tons of wheat—and capital to help India break out of economic stagnation. The food came—eighteen months later—after thousands had died awaiting an act of mercy. The American Congress sought concessions from India. Nehru re-fused. More than that, he developed a thinly disguised contempt for American 'materialism'.

This attitude was traceable in part to his English public-school education in the Edwardian age when Americans were looked upon as *nouveaux riches* who lacked both social graces and a dis-tinctive culture. Yet he was fully aware of America's great tech-nical achievements, its enormous power and its strong democratic roots, all of which he admired. During World War Two he saw in America a friend of the colonial peoples, as indeed it was. By 1949, however, he had become disillusioned with American policy in Asia. The rebuff to his request for aid without strings deepened his disenchantment.

Nor was he impressed by the boastfulness of some Americans. 'You know, Mr. Prime Minister, around this table are seated leaders of corporations worth twenty billion dollars', he was told by a prominent businessman at a dinner in his honour. To a sensitive socialist from a poverty-stricken land, these words must have seemed graceless. By any standards this first visit to America was a failure. Nehru came away empty-handed. American leaders were not over-impressed with him, primarily because of his refusal to 'stand up and be counted'. And he was decidedly unhappy at his experience.

Nehru's visit to America coincided with another milestone in the story of the duumvirate, the completion of India's new consti-tution. The drafting process had lasted almost three years. From the deliberations emerged the longest written constitution in the world. It is, indeed, a forbidding document, with 395 articles and 8 schedules. The main reason for its inordinate length is that the drafters included many details normally left to the growth of convention.

One of the striking features of India's 'new' constitution is the continuity with British-Indian practice. Approximately 250 articles were taken either verbatim or with minor changes in phraseology from the 1935 Government of India Act. Another is the absence of distinctively Indian ideas. The Constitution of India is a purely Western charter. The influence of Great Britain is paramount, as expressed through the 1935 Act and the adoption of the parliamentary form of government. The federal idea owes much to the United States and Australia. From the Irish Free State came the inspiration for the Directive Principles of State Policy. From the United States was derived the idea of a detailed list of fundamental rights.

Many criticisms were levelled at the Constitution. Some persons decried the lack of originality and the absence of Indian influence; some even suggested that it should have been based on the traditional village *panchayats* (councils). Others argued that the fundamental rights were circumscribed by too many exceptions. Still others criticized the fact that the Directive Principles of State Policy had no legal force. Proponents of States' rights opposed the high degree of centralization. Finally, it was claimed that the amendment process was too difficult. The only organized group opposition came from the Communists and Socialists.

The chief architect of the Constitution was the Untouchable leader, Dr. B. R. Ambedkar. As Chairman of the Drafting Committee of the Constituent Assembly, Ambedkar held the spotlight, steering the draft through the oft-stormy debates. But it is very doubtful whether he shaped policy on controversial questions. Decisions were taken in the Congress party caucus and were then translated into constitutional language by the Drafting Committee.

Nehru was not actively involved in the debates, but his role was far from unimportant. He dominated the early proceedings with his Objectives Resolution, which defined the principles underlying the Constitution. Moreover, he was Chairman of three important committees from the reports of which the draft was prepared by Ambedkar and his colleagues. (Patel was Chairman of the remaining three vital committees—another reflection of the duumvirate.) While neither held the centre of the stage in the Assembly, both were involved in all basic decisions in the party caucus.

Nehru spoke infrequently in the Assembly but he did make a few noteworthy comments. He categorically rejected to introduce the principle of proportional representation. He also made it clear that he was strongly in favour of a powerful central government. And on the question of language he was the voice of moderation, the defender of English and regional Indian languages against the Hindi fanatics. Largely at his insistence the fifteen-year interim arrangement regarding the use of English was inserted in the draft.

The new Constitution marks the end of the initial challenge to stability and unity. The duumvirate continued for another year, but it was a year in which the relations between Nehru and Patel deteriorated sharply.

*   *   *   *

The catalytic agent was an outburst of communal tension in Bengal, partly because of economic warfare and partly because the East Bengalis desired to expel the Hindu professional and com-mercial classes. Extremist newspapers in Calcutta fanned the flames with exaggerated reports of atrocities, and a reverse flow of Muslims from West Bengal (India) was set in motion. By March 1950 the stream of refugees had become a flood. More than a million persons fled across the borders.

To many persons in India this seemed an ideal opportunity to 'avenge the wrong' of 1947. Patel himself advocated the policy of 'ten eyes for an eye', that is to say, the expulsion of ten Muslims from India for every Hindu driven out of East Bengal. Nehru stood fast against this tough retaliatory line which would have destroyed the new India's secularism and would almost certainly have led to war with Pakistan. The Sardar's approach had much popular backing. But Nehru remained firmly committed to principle.

The upshot was an agreement between Nehru and Liaquat Ali Khan, the Prime Minister of Pakistan, in April 1950, a reasoned attempt to stem the tide of two-way migration. In essence it pro-vided for the right of refugees to return to their place of residence and their protection in transit; the right to transfer all movable property and to dispose of immovable property as desired; the recovery of looted property and abducted women; the non-recognition of all forced conversions during the period of disturbances, and a renewed pledge of equal rights for minorities in both countries. Within a few months the flood of refugees subsided and many returned to their homes. The danger of war receded.

As Nehru and Patel went so went the Congress. An open split was avoided, but the rivalry was now no longer concealed. The contest took place in the public view: the occasion was the Congress presidential election in September 1950.

Patel's hand-picked candidate was Purshottamdas Tandon, a bearded, venerable orthodox Hindu from the United Provinces who admirably represented the extreme communalist wing of the party. In appearance he resembled the patriarch of old. Given the opportunity, he would have turned the clock of history back a few thousand years. Yet he was highly respected, for he was free from the taint of corruption, then as later a very live issue in Indian politics. His election rival was Acharya J. B. Kripalani, a devoted follower of Gandhi since 1917 and a member of the Congress High Command since the mid-'thirties. For twelve years he had served as General Secretary and, in the crucial year of Partition, as Congress President. By comparison with Tandon he was a revolutionary. Despite his control of the machine, the Sardar's candidate won a bare majority. As if in the nature of compensation, Nehru's policies were reaffirmed in the party resolutions on foreign affairs, Indo-Pakistani relations, the secular state and economic reform.

Before the year was out the duumvirate came to an end: at the age of seventy-five Sardar Patel was dead. The struggle for mastery of the party entered a new phase, but the contest no longer posed a grave threat to Nehru's leadership. The Right had lost its most brilliant tactician and was unable to find an adequate replacement. After months of friction, Tandon tendered his own resignation to the All-India Congress Committee and Nehru was asked to take over the presidency. The triumph was now complete.

In his assertion of supreme power within the party Nehru re-enacted the drama which had been played out in 1939 when Subhas Bose was forced to resign the presidency by Gandhi. The technique was identical: he established himself as super-President of the party by insisting that the members of the Working Committee be selected with his approval; the argument of his supporters was also the same—indispensability. The only difference was that Nehru himself took over the position. He had learned well from his mentor. Since 1951 he has retained this extraordinary status in Congress. He was President until 1954 and personally chose his successor, U. N. Dhebar.

The consequences of the party crisis were far-reaching. Nehru's assumption of leadership rescued the Congress from a possible catastrophe at the polls. Moreover, the ouster of Tandon eased the path to social reform, notably the enactment of the Hindu Code Bill. Thirdly, it affirmed the supremacy of the parliamentary wing over the party apparatus. Finally, the crisis marks a turning-point in Nehru's political life. The Congress was now for the first time his instrument; and from that date Nehru's decisiveness increased, though not to the degree that many would have welcomed. Powerful interest groups remained in opposition to some of his policies but they lacked a formidable leader. He was now master in his own household.

Nehru's triumph occurred on the eve of free India's first general elections based upon universal adult suffrage. The nation-wide election of 1951–2 was an historic experiment in constitutional democracy. It was the first to be held in a newly freed Asian state. Moreover, it was the first to be conducted by a wholly Indian government which had only recently tasted the fruits of power. The electorate was the largest in the world, 173 million people (compared with about 30 million in the 1937 elections). Over 80 per cent. of the electorate were illiterate and most of them completely unfamiliar with the ballot. All Asia—and the superpowers—watched the experiment of 'government by the people' in the largest 'uncommitted' state in the world.

The sheer magnitude commanded attention. More than 3,800 seats had to be filled. There were more than 17,000 candidates, representing 59 parties; many thousands ran as Independents. The technical aspects alone merited the term 'gigantic'—over $2\frac{1}{2}$ million ballot boxes, 600 million ballot papers, 133,000 polling stations and 196,000 polling booths. Because of the preponderant rate of illiteracy each party was allotted a symbol, a visible means of identification for the electors. To the credit of the Congress

Government the Election Commission was given a free hand; virtually no evidence of political interference was reported. Nehru himself took great pains to ensure the Commission's autonomy.

The Congress campaign was a one-man affair—Nehru, Nehru and more Nehru. He was chief of staff, field commander, spokesman and foot-soldier at one and the same time. It was he who drafted the party's election manifesto. It was he who set the tone of the party's appeal—selfless service, devotion to basic principles and faith in the Indian people. Nehru the incorruptible, Nehru, the favourite son of the Mahatma, had taken charge of the Congress.

He tried to determine the criteria for selection of Congress candidates, but in vain. Nehru could lay down policy objectives and act as the party's voice, but the machine remained in the hands of the professionals who were solely interested in winning elections and reaping the fruits of power. He was being used by the party but not followed.

If the party politicians were not prepared to heed his call, the masses were, and they showed their devotion in the tumultuous receptions given him everywhere. Nehru's election tour in 1951 was a prodigious feat of endurance, a re-enactment of the 1937 campaign. He travelled by almost every conceivable means of transport—plane, train, boat, automobile, horse, and even on foot. Official estimates place the number of persons who heard him at 30,000,000. According to one person who accompanied him during his campaign, they covered over 30,000 miles in forty-three days. Often Nehru delivered as many as nine speeches a day, besides brief roadside talks. Despite this blistering pace, with an average of five hours' rest a day, he seemed tireless. (He was sixty-two at the time.)

As in 1937 he fought the campaign on broad issues, a wise strategy in view of the disillusionment with local Congress officials. He hammered on the historic role of the Congress as the bearer of Indian freedom and on the unfinished character of the national revolution. He exhorted his people to grow more food (India was then in the throes of a critical food shortage); called for renewed efforts at unity; pledged himself to a ceaseless war on poverty; attacked unprincipled alliances of opposition parties; and defended his government's record at home and abroad. But he did not deny mistakes or weaknesses in the Congress record. Thus, to a crowd of 100,000 in the capital of Orissa he admitted that corruption still existed in the Government of India.

Among the rival contenders for power he singled out the communal parties for special attack. Theirs was an evil philosophy, he declared over and over again, the gravest threat to Indian unity, progress and stability. With the parties of the Left he was much more moderate. In fact he showed positive sympathy for the Socialists. But these concessions did not appreciably mar the effect of his campaign. People came in droves to hear and to see him. They listened and many of them believed.

Despite the large number of political groups and independent candidates, the contest centred on five parties of all-India stature: the Congress, the K.M.P.P., moderate Left Congress dissidents, the Socialist Party, the Communist Party and the Jan Sangh, the most powerful of three Hindu communalist parties. Stripped of the mass of words which poured forth day by day, the campaign focused on one question only—for or against the Congress. The primary objective of the opposition was to whittle down the Congress majorities and to establish themselves as contenders for future power. How did the parties fare?

The Congress won an overwhelming majority of *seats* in Parliament (362 of 489) and a working majority in all States except Madras, Orissa, PEPSU and Travancore-Cochin (Kerala), and in these four it had the largest single bloc of seats. However, in terms of *votes* the Congress was a minority government, with 45 per cent. of the total at the Centre and 42 per cent. of the total in the States.

The Socialists were the second largest party in terms of votes (10 per cent.) but they secured only twelve seats in Parliament. By contrast, the Communists showed surprising strength in the southern part of the country. Although they received only 3·3 per cent of the votes at the Centre and 4·4 per cent in the States, they returned the largest bloc of opposition Members of Parliament (sixteen) and formed the opposition in four State Assemblies. The reason for the discrepancy in Socialist and Communist seats and votes is that the Socialists ran many candidates while the Communists concentrated on those areas where they had considerable strength. The K.M.P.P. showed surprising strength, 6 per cent. of the votes and nine seats in Parliament. The Jan Sangh won 3 per cent of the votes and three seats in Parliament, and its ideological allies fared even worse—largely due to Nehru's merciless attack on communalism. Apart from the five main parties, forty other groups secured representation in Parliament or in a State Assembly. Moreover, approximately 30 per cent. of all votes for the State Assemblies went to Independents, most of whom were well known only in their own constituency.

Perhaps the most encouraging feature was the response of the electorate. More than 105,000,000 persons or 60 per cent of the voters cast their ballot, a figure which compares favourably with many democracies in the West. No less important was the lively interest shown by the electorate. Many observers, this writer among them, were struck by the eagerness with which illiterate peasants listened to the army of speakers who scoured the country-side in search for support at the polls. The deeply rooted belief in the West that democratic processes are suitable only to highly literate societies was seriously questioned by the Indian elections in 1951–2.

That the Congress won less than half the total votes was partly due to the crisis of 1950–1 and the defection of the Kripalani group. Beyond this was an inevitable reaction against the govern-ing party because of the glaring gap between promise and fulfil-ment. The transition period strained the resources of the Govern-ment to the breaking-point. Indeed, material conditions were probably worse in 1951 than on the eve of the second world war. The Government was not entirely responsible, but in the eyes of the Indian people it was accountable. Moreover, India in 1951 was in the grip of near-famine conditions. Nor did the Congress implement its long-standing pledge of sweeping land reform. Its positive record seemed to many woefully short of that which nationalists had been led to expect. Hence the large vote of pro-test.

That the Congress succeeded in returning to power was due to three factors. Firstly, it alone had established roots in the country-side, a powerful machine extending to most villages. Secondly none of the opposition parties offered an impressive alternative programme. Nor could they invoke the hallowed name of the Mahatma, so long associated with the Congress. But the decisive reason was Nehru's matchless popularity with India's millions. For many, a vote for the Congress was an expression of faith in one man. As some voters put it, 'We want Nehru's box.'

Nehru himself was disturbed by the implications of the vote. 'Where we have won, this was not always due to the Congress organization,' he wrote. 'Indeed, the Congress organization, as a whole, rather failed in this test.' But 'the important thing . . . was the almost utter lack of discipline, both among Congress candidates and among Congressmen. . . . Let us not find excuses and blame others. The fault is ours.' Turning to the future, the great problem was 'how to bring in the youth of the country'. The Congress, warned Nehru, must eschew all factions.[1] This criticism was wholly justified by the election verdict. But the advice was ignored, with the result that the Congress has become steadily weaker in recent years. The rot continues to take its toll.

[1] Letter to Presidents of the P.C.C.'s, in *Congress Bulletin*, No. 1, January–February 1952, pp. 11–16. An almost identical letter was sent to al lCongress candidates. Ibid., pp. 19–26.

CHAPTER XI

DEMOCRACY AT WORK

The general election of 1951–2 was the first major test of political democracy in the new Republic. India passed that test with high honours. But how has democracy fared since? And what role has Nehru played in this crucial experiment which will influence the course of events all over Asia? It is to these and related questions that this chapter is directed: to the central Cabinet and decision-making; Parliament in practice; election experience; States Reorganization; the language controversy; the Congress's decline and Nehru's efforts to resign from office.

In form, functions and powers, the Indian Cabinet follows the established British model. The executive power of the Union of India is vested in the President who is 'aided and advised' by a Council of Ministers (Cabinet) headed by a Prime Minister. The President appoints the Prime Minister—by convention, the leader of that party which commands a majority in the Lower House of Parliament—and, upon his advice, all other members of the Cabinet. The Cabinet is responsible to the Lower House. It is expected to function on the principle of joint responsibility and remains in office as long as it maintains the 'confidence' of the Lower House. If defeated on a major issue, it must either give way to another or must dissolve the legislature and call for new elections. As in Cabinet systems of government elsewhere, the Indian Cabinet drafts and presents the government's legislative programme and conducts the business of the Union.

There have been four Indian Cabinets since 1947, all headed by Nehru and all composed largely of Congressmen. At no time has the Government been in danger from a vote of 'no confidence', for the Congress has had an overwhelming majority in Parliament thus far. Hence the Cabinet system in India has known a high degree of stability. This has been one of its distinguishing features. Another has been Nehru's pre-eminence.

India is a federal state, in theory at least. It is also a nation of many creeds, castes and languages. On the whole, the Cabinet has reflected this diversity. However, from the outset a disproportionate share of senior ministerial posts (50 per cent.) has gone to two States—Uttar Pradesh (the former United Provinces or U.P.) and Bombay. In 1957 there were twenty-three Hindu members of the Cabinet, two Muslims, a Sikh and a Jain. Among the Hindus, Brahmins predominated with twelve. The majority were from well-to-do families. The educational level was extremely high; almost 90 per cent. received a university or college education. Many were trained for the law. Perhaps the most noteworthy fact is that sixteen of the twenty-seven (proudly) claim imprisonment under the British *Raj*! The average age was fifty-eight. One curious feature was the inclusion of Independents and even representatives of other parties, despite the large Congress majority in Parliament. Only by 1958 was the senior level of the Council of Ministers exclusively Congress.

Which persons left a mark on the experiment in Cabinet government? Until 1950 Nehru and Patel made all the decisions of substance. The only other person whose counsel was regularly sought, was Maulana Azad, the dean of India's nationalist Muslims. During the next four years the Prime Minister relied heavily on three colleagues: Azad, Ayyangar, and Kidwai. In financial matters Deshmukh had a relatively free hand. By 1954 Ayyangar and Kidwai were dead. Two years later Deshmukh resigned. By that time the inner Cabinet circle comprised Pant, Desai and Azad in domestic affairs, and Menon in foreign policy. The Maulana's death in 1958 left the domestic field to Pant and Desai.

It is impossible for an outsider to know with certainty how decisions are reached in any Cabinet. Nevertheless, there is evidence that the Indian Cabinet has not always functioned smoothly —there have been eight resignations over policy matters since Independence. Four concerned economic issues, in whole or in part; two arose from Indo-Pakistani relations; one from States Reorganization, and one from the Mundhra Affair, India's 'scandal of the decade'. Only one person was a Congressman of long standing.

The most dramatic resignation and one which provides the greatest insight into the workings of the Indian Cabinet was that of C. D. Deshmukh, the Finance Minister from 1950 to 1956. The only former civil servant in the Cabinet he had frequently come into conflict with his Congress colleagues. But the issue which led to his resignation was the highly charged struggle for control of Bombay City, in the nation-wide Reorganization of States.

Deshmukh spelled out the charge against Nehru's actions and the role of the Cabinet in a momentous speech to Parliament: 'There was no consideration of the proposal (regarding Bombay) in the Cabinet or even by circulation. There was no individual consultation with members of the Cabinet known to be specially interested, as for instance, myself. There is no record even of a meeting of a committee of the Cabinet, and to this day no authoritative text of the so-called decision is available to the members of the Cabinet. . . . This instance is typical of the cavalier and unconstitutional manner in which decisions have been taken and announced on behalf of the Cabinet by certain unauthorized members of the Cabinet, including the Prime Minister, in matters concerning the reorganisation of the states. [Even] the separation of Andhra from Tamil Nad [Madras State in 1953] was decided upon and announced by the Prime Minister without reference to the Cabinet.'[1]

A few days later Deshmukh repeated the basic charge. Nehru's initial reply had been moderate. This time he was blunt. 'I do not know where he got his facts from. I have consulted my papers, my Cabinet papers . . . and I say the two decisions . . . were made absolutely and repeatedly after consultations with every colleague of the Cabinet and with the full consent of the Cabinet. I have no doubt about it. And I say . . . this Bill itself was placed before the Cabinet . . . and the Cabinet adopted the Bill before it came before this House. . . . There was more consultation on this than on any other subject we have had since I have been Prime Minister.' Then he took Deshmukh to task on the constitutional issue. 'I know something of what the Prime Minister's duties are and that in the Constitution the Prime Minister is the linchpin of Government. To say that the Prime Minister cannot make a statement is a monstrous statement itself.'[2]

Deshmukh was succeeded by T. T. Krishnamachari who later became the centre of India's *cause célèbre*. It began at the end of

[1] *The Statesman* (Calcutta), 26 July 1956.
[2] *Times of India* (New Delhi), 31 July 1956.

1957, when Feroze Gandhi, journalist, M.P. and Nehru's son-in-law, brought to the public view a strange transaction involving a nationalized corporation. More than a year before, the State-controlled Life Insurance Corporation had purchased 15 million rupees (approximately $3.2 million) worth of poor-risk stock in six corporations controlled by Haridas Mundhra, a young industrialist-financier residing in Calcutta. Gandhi asked pointed questions of the Finance Minister, suggesting that there was either a grave error of judgement—or something worse. Krishnamachari tended to minimize its importance, but in the face of a parliamentary uproar he promised an inquiry. To leave no doubt of impartiality Nehru appointed a one-man commission, the Chief Justice of Bombay, M. C. Chagla, one of the most highly respected jurists in India.

There was a parade of star witnesses and much conflicting testimony. The Finance Minister denied having issued instructions to purchase the shares. The Principal Finance Secretary stated that the decision had been approved by the Finance Minister. The Governor of the Reserve Bank was equivocal on this and other aspects of the transaction. The Chairman and Managing Director of the Life Insurance Corporation were no more certain about what had happened. Moreover, the Finance Minister justified the investment on the grounds that it was necessary to stabilize the Calcutta stock market. In Parliament a few months earlier, however, he said that this was not the purpose. Mundhra himself was revealed as a speculator and manipulator whom a public corporation would not normally be likely to support.

Justice Chagla questioned the value of the shares and viewed the transaction as an attempt to save the crumbling Mundhra financial empire. Krishnamachari was found responsible, in so far as the Life Insurance Corporation was under the jurisdiction of his ministry, and was severely criticized for bad judgement in the use of public funds, though not for corrupt practice. The political outcome was inescapable; the Finance Minister left the Cabinet. Mundhra himself was arrested on a charge of forging share certificates. So ended this unsavoury affair.

Nehru is the outstanding figure in the Cabinet, as befits his office, and even more, his status in the governing party and the country at large. Each minister is expected to take an active part in discussion of items under his jurisdiction. A few venture beyond.

And Nehru's range of interests extends to all questions that come up at Cabinet meetings. The Prime Minister has great skill in winning his colleagues to his viewpoint by persuasion.

Where there is disagreement the outcome depends on how strongly Nehru feels about the issue. If he is firm his colleagues give way. However, Nehru does not feel strongly on all questions. There appears to be a gradation with corresponding reactions: first and foremost the need for social change, the attack on caste discrimination and the strengthening of secularism; secondly, socialism, regarding which he is willing to compromise only on marginal points; thirdly, foreign policy, the sphere in which only Menon and, occasionally, Pant and Azad, have questioned his proposals. On something like prohibition, however, he will concede to the rigidly held views of Morarji Desai and others, for he considers this secondary and has no desire to alienate his colleagues.

Since 1957 there appears to be an informal understanding among the 'Big Three' of the Indian Cabinet—Nehru, Pant and Desai—as to the permissible limits of disagreement. By and large they accommodate each other, with Nehru's pre-eminent position readily acknowledged. Where either of his colleagues presents a case forcefully he will make concessions in the interests of harmony —provided they do not undermine what he considers to be the pillars of his programme. The cardinal fact remains, however, that all major Cabinet decisions require Nehru's approval or at least acquiescence.

An analysis of the Cabinet suggests that Nehru is surrounded by persons who do not share his ideology. Few may be considered Nehruites in any meaningful sense. Why then does he retain his conservative senior colleagues? First, the heterogeneous character of the party must be reflected in a Congress Government. Moreover, Nehru may be trying to emulate Gandhi, who converted his opponents by example and brought them into his inner circle. Thirdly, he prefers to keep the potential sources of opposition in the Cabinet, where their activities are less harmful to his programme. There is, too, the need for 'strong administrators' like Pant and Desai. But most important is a sense of loyalty to old colleagues, persons who fought side by side for Independence.

*   *   *   *

The Indian Parliament has been described as 'the one institution of the kind [in Asia] which is working in an exemplary way.
. . . Pericles said that Athens was the school of Hellas. Mr. Nehru
without boasting may say that Delhi is the school of Asia.'[1] Others
have termed it a twentieth-century version of a *darbar*, and still
others a façade behind which the Congress and Nehru wield
absolute power.

What does the record suggest? At first glance the parliamentary
process'seems artificial because one party has had a preponderant
majority since 1947 and could push through any legislation with
ease. It is also true that Parliament is not the centre of power and
decision-making in India. This function is performed by the
Congress caucus and ultimately by Nehru and the party's High
Command. And yet it would be misleading to dismiss Parliament
as of no consequence.

Despite the Congress majority, debate is often vigorous, as
illustrated in the cases of States Reorganization and the Hindu
Code Bill. Questions raised by members are often forthright and
even embarrassing. And the Opposition, though small and fragmented, is keen, able and vociferous.

Gradually precedents are being established and conventions are being
recognized. The main difficulty is that the House has too much to do with
the result that there are stringent limits on the time available for debate.
The committees do not yet function efficiently, partly because of their
size and partly because of their lopsided composition. Yet they do provide
ample opportunity for opposition views to be heard. Another drawback is
that many Congress M.P.'s have little knowledge of the immense range of
parliamentary business. An encouraging feature is the attitude of the
Prime Minister and his senior colleagues, who are consciously trying to
raise the status of Parliament.

The most authoritative study of the Indian Parliament in its
first decade provides an even more sanguine assessment.[2] Professor
Morris-Jones notes ample opportunity for the ventilation of
grievances—spirited Question Periods, adjournment Motions,
Half-an-Hour Discussions, and debates on Demands for Grants.
The discussion of Bills is usually sufficient to bring out the main
issues and to give the Opposition an opportunity to express their

[1] *Manchester Guardian*, 5 June 1954.
[2] Morris-Jones, W. H., *Parliament in India* (1957). The quotation is from
p. 332.

views. Although Parliament cannot provide an effective restraint on the Executive because of the Congress majority, the Congress Parliamentary Party is, in reality, a miniature Parliament. The response of the public is evident by the attendance at parliamentary debates and the press coverage. Professor Morris-Jones notes various weaknesses. In the main, however, 'the "experiment" is working and parliamentary institutions are more firmly established in the way of life of the Indian people than they are in that of many a country in Europe'.

This achievement must be credited largely to Nehru. He has frequently declared his faith in the democratic process. He is present in the House every day during the session. He is consulted by the Minister for Parliamentary Affairs before the Business of the Day is decided. And he is active in debate. He is tolerant and usually courteous to the Opposition, and he encourages them, for he is genuinely trying to build up conventions of Parliament. He is remarkably attentive to M.P.s' inquiries and often responds within a few hours. Moreover, he has given instructions to civil servants that requests from M.P.s are to have top priority.

That he dominates its proceedings when he is in Parliament is beyond question. His pre-eminence can only be compared with that of Churchill at Westminster during the second world war. His gestures and moods cover a wide range. Sometimes he will sit hunched over, a pensive expression on his face. At other times he will scowl or crease his brow as he listens to a sharp attack from the Opposition. Frequently he will nudge one of his colleagues into silence or leap up to rescue a minister who is feebly answering questions. Often he will rise in anger when he feels an insult has been directed at the Government. And at still other times he will make moving and solemn speeches.

In the broadest sense Parliament in India is a symbol of the method of government which Nehru is trying to establish and an instrument to educate those who will wield power in the future. It is also a unifying force, representing different regions, castes, creeds, social and economic groups. Given time, Nehru may fashion the habit of looking to Parliament to solve disputes and to reduce the divisions in Indian society. Parliament will be respected only as long as it can assist the process of radical social and economic change. Should it fail to do so after a trial period it will be swept away or drastically modified—in India, as elsewhere in

Asia. For the crucial fact is that democratic processes are not yet rooted in Asian soil.

In the first decade of Independence Indian democracy underwent five tests at the polls: two general elections and three State-wide contests—Travancore-Cochin (later Kerala) in 1954, Patiala and the East Punjab States Union (PEPSU, later integrated with the Punjab) in 1954, and Andhra in 1955. What light do they throw on Indian politics during this transition period? The general election of 1957 provides a revealing case study.

The largest democratic poll in history, there were 193 million electors, 20 million more than in 1952, and some 3,400 seats at stake. This time, however, the number of 'national parties' was reduced to four as a result of a ruling by the Election Commission: the Indian National Congress; the Praja-Socialist Party; the Bharatiya Jana Sangh; and the Communist Party of India. Seven other groups were designated 'state parties', such as the Hindu Mahasabha, the Scheduled Castes (Untouchables) Federation and the Forward Bloc. This time, too, the technical aspects were conducted with greater efficiency. Except for a few remote constituencies the poll was completed in three weeks, instead of two months as in 1952. Perhaps the most encouraging feature was that over 60 per cent. of the electorate actually voted—this in a population of which more than 80 per cent. are illiterate.

The Congress sought a return to power on its record since Independence, with special emphasis on the Five-Year Plans and Community Development, India's status in the world, and the goal of a Socialist Co-operative Commonwealth. The Praja-Socialists placed before the voters a modified version of Narayan's 'fourteen-point' programme of drastic social, economic and political change. The Jan Sangh pledged all things to all people; in general, the creation of a Hindu *Raj*. The Communists concentrated on economic affairs. While praising the objectives of the second plan, they stressed the need for heavy industry—in the 'public sector'—and criticized the Government's 'soft' attitude to foreign capital.

What was the overall picture of voter preference? The Congress won a very large majority of seats at the Centre and was returned to power in all but one of the thirteen State Assemblies. The Praja-Socialists did better than expected but were ousted by the Communists as the leading opposition party; their popular vote declined at the Centre and in every State Assembly. The Jan Sangh showed some strength among Hindu middle-class voters in the towns of north-central India but did not justify its claim to all-India stature. The Communists won a major prestige victory in Kerala, doubled their popular vote and secured a foothold in every State.

On the surface the Congress victory was impressive. Its popular vote increased from 42 to 45 per cent. in the States and from 45 to 47 per cent. at the Centre. Moreover, it won 75 per cent. of the seats in Parliament and 65 per cent. of all seats in the State Assemblies. The reasons were essentially the same as in 1952: the diminishing but still potent aura of the 'party of independence'; the association with Gandhi; a nation-wide political machine rooted in the village; ample campaign funds; disunity among the opposition parties; and the magic name of Nehru. Its successes seemed all the more striking because of Nehru's inactive role in the campaign. Either because of age or because he wished to see how the party would fare without his leadership, or both, the Prime Minister confined his direct participation to tours of crucial areas.

Despite its assets, the Congress suffered some noteworthy losses. In Bombay, Orissa, Bihar, the Punjab, and the United Provinces its majority and popular vote were reduced. And then there was the dramatic defeat in Kerala, due to over-population, unemployment, maladministration by earlier Congress ministries, a powerful Communist trade-union movement and disgruntled educated young men in the towns.

The real 'defeat' of the Congress lay in the spectacular gains of the Communist Party. Not only did it obtain power in Kerala. Its popular vote was doubled at the Centre (5 to 10 per cent.) and increased even more in the States. Over 12,000,000 Indians cast their ballots for the C.P.I. in a free election, making it the largest opposition party in Parliament and a very close third to the Praja-Socialists in the State Assemblies as a whole. What accounts for this swing to the far Left? More effective organization and leadership; the gap between promise and fulfilment and the lengthy tenure of power by the Congress; electoral alliances; and India's friendly relations with the Soviet Union.

Among the major parties the real loser was the P.S.P., whose popular vote declined from about 15 to 10 per cent. Its poor showing was due to the lack of popular leadership; the absence of a clear-cut ideology; the defection of its Left wing, led by Lohia;

and the Congress's adoption of a socialist creed which, along with the Communist stress on socialism, robbed it of a distinctive character.

The bonds which tied religious minorities to the Congress loosened somewhat in the second general election. The pull of language was very powerful. Feudal loyalties asserted themselves in select areas. The most persistent and one of the most important forces in Indian electoral behaviour—caste—was evident everywhere, and at all levels of the electoral process. In the widest sense the election of 1957 revealed two fundamental trends: the polarization of Indian politics around the Congress and the Communist Party; and the decline of the Congress, symbolized by the Communist victory in Kerala.

*   *   *   *

A year after the general election Nehru surmised that the Congress had lost 100 seats in the State Assemblies because of resentment arising from the reorganization of States. The roots of this administrative revolution lie deep in the growth of Indian society and in the history of British rule. Over the centuries there emerged distinctive regional cultures and languages which came to embrace millions of people. Among them may be mentioned Bengali, Telugu, Tamil, Punjabi, Marathi and Gujarati. By the time the British arrived there were some fourteen such cultures, but the advance of British power cut across these units. In fact, segments of one cultural group were often scattered in different provinces of British India and/or princely States.

The desire for reorganization of boundaries along linguistic lines was already evident in the nineteenth century. And the Congress had pledged itself to this goal from 1920 onwards. After Partition, however, many Indian leaders had second thoughts about the wisdom of a nation-wide administrative revolution.

The first step was to integrate British and princely India. As noted earlier, this was accomplished in 1948–9. But even during that grave transition period the clamour for linguistic states was heard. The Linguistic Provinces (Dar) Commission of 1948 strongly opposed any change. The Congress Party's Linguistic Provinces Committee echoed this view the following year. But the demand persisted.

The first to wage a spirited campaign was the Telugu-speaking community of Madras. Using the time-honoured technique of Gandhi, one of their leaders went on a fast unto death—and he died in the Andhra cause. This act broke the back of Delhi's resistance. The new State was formally inaugurated in October 1953, in Nehru's presence. The Andhra episode was to be re-enacted on an all-India scale.

The next stage in the drama was the appointment of a three-man States Reorganization Commission (SRC) at the end of 1953. The Commission was instructed to bear in mind the need to preserve and enhance Indian unity; financial and administrative viability of the units; the welfare of the people of each proposed unit, including protection for linguistic minorities, and national security. The appointment of the Commission provided a respite, but no more. Special interest groups prepared for battle.

The Commission reported in the autumn of 1955. Almost at once the voices of discontent could be heard. With them came agitation, despite Nehru's plea to the nation. There were two major areas of discord—Bombay and the Punjab.

More than any other linguistic group in India, the Maharashtrians accused the Commission of discrimination. Why should everyone else (except the Sikhs) get a linguistic state while they remained in a bilingual Bombay? And why were the Marathi-speaking districts of Madhya Pradesh placed in a separate State of Vidarbha? The anger crossed party lines and found expression in the *Maharashtra Samyukta Samiti* (Organization for Greater Maharashtra). Leading Congressmen joined the chorus of dissent. Tension mounted.

The storm broke in January 1956, when riots enveloped Bombay City; eighty persons were killed and 450 wounded. The Gujarati-controlled Government of Bombay had resorted to large-scale police firing. In the face of pressure the central Government announced that Bombay City would be administered as a separate state. The agitation continued. Delhi retreated to the original formula of a bilingual state including the city. In March another change was made: two separate States of Gujarat and Maharashtra, with Bombay City as a centrally administered territory. The Maharashtrians remained dissatisfied. Then came Nehru's statement that after five years the fate of Bombay could be decided by the people of the City. By that time sentiment had shifted rapidly in Parliament to the bilingual state formula including Bombay City. The Government was relieved and acceded to the request.

Now it was the turn of the Gujaratis to vent their anger. Riots broke out in Ahmedabad, the proposed capital of a separate Gujarat and the site of Gandhi's *ashram*. Morarji Desai rushed to the City and went on a fast. He threatened to continue until calm was restored. Ultimately the bilingual formula, the original proposal of the Commission, was accepted. But bitter feelings remained and the Congress was severely trounced at the polls in the area as a whole.

The other prolonged battle over SRC, in the Punjab, arose from Sikh disappointment at not being given a separate state. Led by the tempestuous Master Tara Singh, they demanded *Punjabi Subha*, a Punjabi-speaking state in which the Sikhs would comprise 54 per cent. of the population. The Hindus created the Maha (Great) Punjab Front to ensure Hindu and Hindi predominance.

On a bright, cool north Indian winter morning the contending groups massed their forces in a show of strength, especially for the benefit of the Congress High Command which was camped close by. First came the Sikhs in the most impressive demonstration I have ever seen. Hour after hour and mile after mile they marched, eight abreast, down the main street of Amritsar, a hallowed name in Indian nationalism because of the shootings of 1919. Old and young, men and women, they came in an endless stream, most with an expression of determination and sadness in their eyes, many still remembering the ghastly days of 1947. What strength there was in the appearance of the older men who, with their flowing beards, looked like the Hebrew prophets of old! Many carried their traditional sword, the *korpan*, and many wore blue turbans, symbol of militancy. (The dyers in the city did a handsome business that week.) Almost without exception they marched in orderly file, portraying their unity of purpose. At intervals came the resounding cry, 'Punjabi Suba Zindabad' ('Long live a Punjabi State') and 'Master Tara Singh Zindabad', with intermittent music to enliven the proceedings. On they came, for five hours. By conservative estimate they numbered over 100,000. To this observer it seemed more like double that figure. The Maha Punjab Front display was very much smaller, perhaps 50,000. But this was far larger than anticipated.

Disputed territory under international consideration

CHINA

NEPAL
Katmandu
Panakha
BHUTAN
SIKKIM
Gangtok
Lucknow
Ghaghra
(Gogra)
Gandak
ASSAM
Brahmaputra
Ganges
Shillong
Patna
Benares
Son
BIHAR
E.
PAKISTAN
Agartala
Dacca
TRIPURA
MANIPUR
Imphal
W.
BENGAL
Chandernagore
Calcutta
Mahanadi
BURMA
ORISSA
Cuttack
ADESH
Yanam

R.W.FORD

The two demonstrations revealed something more than intense feelings on the reorganization of the Punjab. They showed the strength of communalism, both Hindi and Sikh, a grave threat to democracy and a barrier to social change. They also explained Nehru's continuous onslaught on communalism. This virus is far from being exterminated. It lurks beneath the surface and, in times of stress, rears its head. And it waits for a suitable opportunity to strike for power and Hindu *Raj*. A compromise was eventually found in the Punjab. But neither Sikhs nor Hindus were satisfied, and friction continues.

The States Reorganization Bill underwent various changes until it was passed by Parliament at the end of 1956. Ultimately, the sixteen States and three Territories proposed by the Commission were altered to fourteen States and seven Territories, the present administrative structure of India. The Bill, along with the necessary Constitution (Seventh Amendment) Act, was passed in time to be implemented before the 1957 election.

The pledge of States Reorganization along linguistic lines had been honoured in the main. There was comparatively little violence. But communal passions and regional loyalties had been aroused as by no other act since Independence. For its indecision the Congress paid dearly at the polls.

The indecision was largely that of the Prime Minister. Indeed, the story of SRC is one of the most striking examples of Nehru's vacillation in public affairs. The factual record supports this view. There were five different decisions on Bombay City alone. And the handling of Hyderabad suggested confusion. The difficulty lay in Nehru's attempt to carry everyone with him, a patent impossibility. The ceaseless quest for consent demonstrated Nehru's devotion to democracy. But it also illustrated ineffectual leadership. Had Nehru taken a firm stand from the beginning much of the friction would probably have been avoided. Nehru was badly jolted by the violence and bitterness accompanying States Reorganization. It is also clear that his reputation was not enhanced by the episode. The price of indecision was high.

Even before the dust had settled over SRC, another closely related source of discord came to the surface. The issue was language, one of the most divisive forces in Indian society. Since the coming of the Aryans 3,500 years ago the sub-continent has known many languages. With time they were crystallized into two distinct groups, apart from hundreds of tribal tongues and dialects: Sanskrit-derived languages, some of the more noteworthy being Hindi, Bengali, Gujarati, and Marathi; and Dravidian languages, four in number—Tamil, Telugu, Kannada and Malayalam. The division was north–south, the Dravidian languages being spoken in the southern states. The addition of English in the eighteenth century complicated the situation but it provided a common language for the Indian intelligentsia.

Until the arrival of Gandhi, English was the accepted language of the Congress, as of all political parties. Attempts were made to create a substitute *lingua franca*, Hindustani, which was essentially a merger of Hindi and Urdu. But at best this could serve north India only. Language friction aggravated Hindu–Muslim tension. But even after Partition the basic division between north and south Indian languages remains.

In the new constitution a compromise formula was approved: all major Indian languages (fourteen) were given equal status as 'national languages'; Hindi was made the 'official language' for all-India purposes; and English was to continue as an 'official language' for fifteen years from the date the Constitution took effect; the change-over to Hindi was to occur in 1965. The compromise was satisfactory for the moment. South Indians were mollified by the fifteen-year delay and the continued use of English, as were non-Hindi speakers generally.

Interest was aroused once more in 1955 by the appointment of the Official Language Commission to recommend a time-table and methods for the change-over to Hindi. When the report finally appeared in the autumn of 1957 the long-smouldering discontent of non-Hindi speakers burst forth. Of the Commission's twenty members only two expressed serious misgivings about the wisdom of replacing English by Hindi. The crucial question remained unanswered, namely, the time limit for the use of English for official purposes.

The stage was now set for a re-enactment of the SRC affair. Fortunately some lessons had been learned and the conflict was resolved in a peaceful manner. Nehru took the lead in a settlement. Unlike SRC there were only two protagonists. The most vociferous critics were south Indians, who argued that Indian unity would be undermined by an imposition of Hindi throughout the country and that a too rapid change-over would discriminate against south Indians in the Services. The governing party itself was in danger of a serious split over the issue.

Nehru brought the full weight of his prestige to bear on the side of compromise. At the Gauhati annual session in 1958 he stressed the need for a flexible approach and reprimanded the Hindi enthusiasts for trying to impose a language by decree. At the same time he noted the need for gradualism. He indicated, too, that he favoured the continued use of English after 1965.

Here lay the essence of the compromise resolution. South Indian Congressmen reconciled themselves to the *formal* introduction of Hindi by 1965 while the Hindi group, at Nehru's prodding, agreed that the change-over would be gradual and would be effected with the support of non-Hindi sections of the population; further, that English might be used as an 'official language' after 1965. The breach in Congress ranks was healed and, on the surface at least, the hostile factions seemed satisfied.

*   *   *   *

The reorganization of States and the general election indicated that all was not well with India's governing party. Nehru summed up the prevalent mood at the beginning of 1958: '. . . there can be no doubt that the Congress organization is suffering from a deep malaise.' As for the reasons, 'have we become too stale, too complacent, not having enough touch with realities?'[1]

Immediately after the first general election he had written with even greater candour about the ills besetting the party. Other leaders had occasionally indulged in self-criticism. And there was ample evidence of shortcomings. By 1958 the party's membership had been halved (in four years) and its active workers reduced to 54,000. Most of the 365 Congress M.P.s were content to leave the burden of work to a small group of ministers.

There were other symptoms of decline. The whole party seemed to depend on the health, vigour, popularity and leadership of one man—Nehru. Moreover, Congress ministers aped their British predecessors in their lavish display of the perquisites of authority: large, luxurious bungalows; limousines; private coaches on the railways; clerks and servants in splendid uniforms; and aloofness from the people. This set a bad example to local officials. Nehru

[1] 'A Deep Malaise' in the *Times of India* (New Delhi), 15 January 1958.

himself was largely responsible for the retreat from simplicity; soon after he became Prime Minister he gave up his modest home for the sumptuous estate of British Commanders-in-Chief. It would have been too much to expect his colleagues to do otherwise. Moreover, his towering position in the party hindered the emergence of younger leaders.

Beyond that was the lack of a clear-cut ideology and a disciplined organization. The Congress remained a nationalist movement, a 'mélange of interest groups, from feudal to radical socialist. Factional strife was endemic in the States. In 1957, for example, the contest in Bihar was so fierce that the ballot boxes for the election of the President of the Provincial Congress Committee had to be sent to Delhi to ensure a fair count! In a wider sense party squabbles in the States concerned the proper relationship of the ministry to the P.C.C. Nehru himself had written at length on this problem in 1937; he proposed a division of function, with the P.C.C. framing policy and the ministry having control over administration. His advice was not heeded then. It was also ignored later.

Added to factionalism are two other ills: nepotism and corruption on an alarming scale; and disregard of policy decisions of the party's High Command. Whether on land reform or on the need to eradicate untouchability and a caste mentality, or on fair treatment of the minorities, or on the importance of eliminating corruption, or on the economic plan, the state ministries have often gone their own way. In large part this is due to lack of adequate organizational control and the amorphous character of the Congress creed and programme. Like Hinduism they are all things to all people. Only in those states where a decisive figure was at the helm, like Bombay (Morarji Desai) and West Bengal (Dr. B. C. Roy), has the party been free from constant turmoil.

After a decade in power the Congress is in decline. The party controls all governments except one but its organizational base is withering away. And it shows no sign of remedying the rot that has set in. The prevalent attitude seems to be 'après nous le déluge'. The election results of 1957 jolted the Congress out of its apathy—for a while. But when the time came for action, the call for reform was stilled in the scramble for power. Of thirteen 'new' State Chief Ministers five were over sixty-five, three were over seventy and one was seventy-seven. Nehru himself failed to set a proper example; in the 'new' central Cabinet there was only one major change.

Many persons were disillusioned. A few expressed concern. 'The Congress was once a good cause,' wrote a young and talented journalist. 'Now it sometimes looks like degenerating into a bad habit.' He then spelled out the challenge: 'The Congress has been given a reprieve for five years. If it cannot rescue itself from itself in good time, it will be swept out of power.'[1]

Perhaps the most striking evidence of the party's decline is the pathetic response to its annual session in recent years. The 1956 gathering was witnessed by this writer who jotted down impressions of people and things. Some extracts follow.

Amritsar, holy city of the Sikhs, is a typical provincial Indian town, with scattered bungalows for district officials and the local gentry and endless rows of hovels that pass for homes in this part of the world. Its fame rests on two shrines, one religious and one national—the great Sikh temple surrounded on three sides by a pool of water, attracting the faithful and tourists alike, and *Jallianwalla Bagh*, site of the 1919 tragedy which sparked the first civil disobedience campaign. The Congress camp, some five miles from town, is a veritable city in itself, with shops, offices, hastily-constructed corrugated tin-shacks for delegates, pressmen and 'distinguished guests', and a huge *pandal* [enclosed stadium] to seat 200,000 people. . . .

At the first meeting of the Subjects Committee Nehru proclaimed war against the proponents of violence. With reference to the Bombay riots, he declared, 'If they think they can gain their objectives in the streets, let me make it clear that we will meet the challenge in the streets.'

The following day the pace quickened. The moods shifted from struggle to acquiescence and back again. . . . Crucial problems came up, notably economic policy and SRC, the burning issue of the session. Many harsh words were uttered, attempts were made to smooth over troubled waters, but those who felt strongly spoke their minds. . . . First the party brought up its heavy artillery. Then N. V. Gadgil, the highly-respected Maharashtrian leader, made an impassioned plea for the inclusion of Bombay City in a separate Maharashtra. After further stormy debate the SRC resolution was passed without amendment. For some strange reason the High Command refused to accept amendments. The A.I.C.C. is nothing but a rubber stamp these days. . . .

The open session was an anti-climax. The battles had been fought in the Subjects Committee. It remained only to repeat the spectacle for the crowd—minus the friction and strong words. The most striking feature was the small crowd gathered to hear the leaders. The *pandal* was less than a quarter full. On the last day even the nominal entrance fee was dropped,

[1] Verghese, B. G.: 'The Elections and After: II. Reprieve for Congress' in the *Times of India* (New Delhi), 2 May 1957.

but it remained much more than half empty. And many of those present left after Nehru had spoken at length.

Indifference was also evident at the Indore session in 1957 which was dominated by the scramble for seats on the party's ticket. Would-be candidates rushed to and fro in a feverish effort to prove their loyalty and merit. The story of Gauhati in 1958 is even more dismal. Senior Congress leaders termed it the most dispirited session in living memory. The audience was estimated at between 5,000 and 10,000; and on the last day there were only 300—including delegates. One disquieting feature was the extraordinarily active role played by Nehru. He delivered ten lengthy speeches, drafted every resolution and dominated the pallid proceedings as on no other occasion since Independence. It was a spectacle of one man trying vainly to reinvigorate a disunited and sluggish organization. His colleagues and the rank and file listened with due respect to 'Panditji's' words but remained unmoved. They had heard these 'pep-talks' more often than they cared to remember.

A few months after the Gauhati session Nehru expressed the *desire* to relinquish the post of Prime Minister. The place was the great Central Hall of Parliament where M.P.s normally gather during the session to exchange ideas and gossip. The audience was the Congress Parliamentary Party. The time was early evening, a warm, dry Delhi spring evening.

Many times had Nehru addressed his colleagues in Central Hall, usually in an informal schoolmasterish manner. On this occasion, however, he looked more sombre and dejected than usual. He was humble in addressing them. And he had a prepared statement. 'I feel now that I must have a period when I can free myself from this daily burden and can think of myself as an individual citizen of India and not as Prime Minister. . . . I am anxious to fit myself for the great tasks ahead and I feel that it might help me to do so if I am away from the centre of activity and responsibility.' 'Sir, it is an atom bomb to us,' cried one forlorn parliamentarian. 'Panditji, you are leaving us orphans,' bewailed another. Nehru calmed his followers and asked them to consider his request.[1]

Emergency meetings of the party, hurried conferences among the High Command and the Left wing—together they succeeded

[1] *The Hindu Weekly Review* (Madras), 5 May 1958.

in persuading him to yield. Those who observed him during that episode saw a disappointed and lonely man, sad at the thought that he had failed to make the break which he felt was necessary. And few, if any, doubted his sincerity.

What prompted Nehru's dramatic move at that time? He was tired and needed a rest. He was disturbed by the trend of events at home and abroad. Beyond that, however, he did not spell out the reasons for his despair. There were many. A shock was necessary to galvanize the Congress into awareness of its growing plight; the analogy of Gandhi's fasting technique comes to mind. Secondly, the controversies over SRC and the language issue revealed deep fissures in Indian society and the alarming growth of 'a certain coarseness, a certain vulgarity' in public life. Third was the increasingly audible concern about 'after Nehru who'. And the goals of the second Five Year Plan had just been pruned. Everything seemed to be going awry.

Why then did he not follow through? Partly because Nehru has always yielded to pressure, and the pressure in this case was intense; and partly because he was not sure of the wisdom of this act. Perhaps his direct leadership was more necessary now, in the face of these many problems. Hence he turned to his colleagues for advice. It was inevitable that they would beseech him to remain. Their only concession was to 'permit' him a month's vacation. He went off to the hills leaving his colleagues and his people somewhat bewildered by what had taken place.

This was not the first time Nehru had tried to resign. In the autumn of 1954, he had also expressed a *desire* to leave office. The striking feature of that episode was its similarity—in almost every respect—to the subsequent drama. As in 1958 he yielded—and the party made one concession; he was relieved of the Congress Presidency, and his hand-picked successor, U. N. Dhebar, was elected. His China tour served as a tonic, as well as a challenge, and Nehru plunged back into his myriad jobs strengthened and more determined than ever. The only difference in 1958 was his deeper 'urge' to give the country a new lead outside the Government.

Nehru had flirted with the idea of resigning on two other occasions: in 1951, in the midst of the struggle for control of the party; and in 1957, soon after the general election. In the light of these episodes and his awareness that the majority of his colleagues do not share his basic ideas, why did Nehru not leave the Congress and form a new party? For one thing, he was convinced that the Congress had not completed its mission and was still his most effective political instrument. For another it would have required much time and energy which would have delayed the initiation of social and economic reform. The basic reason, however, was Nehru's deep emotional attachment to the Congress. His whole public life has been bound up with this party, and after forty years he could not wrench himself away. Nehru himself remarked: 'I have grown up with the Congress and shared in its wide fold the comradeship of innumerable persons. What I owe to the Congress, I can never repay, for the Congress has made me what I am.'[1]

It was primarily due to this association that the Congress retained political power eleven years after Independence. But the age of Congress supremacy appears to be gradually coming to an end. A combination of pressures is at work—the challenge of the Communist Party, the rot in the Congress, the economic problems besetting India, and Nehru's advancing age. Its monopoly of power was broken in 1957. The challenges will grow stronger in the years to come.

[1] *Express* (Bombay), 17 January 1955.

CHAPTER XII

PLANNING AND WELFARE

With the partition of India an integrated economy was abruptly torn asunder. The raw jute of eastern Bengal now lay in Pakistan while the jute factories remained in Calcutta, capital of India's West Bengal. The main area of cotton-growing fell to Pakistan whereas the textile centres of Bombay and Ahmedabad were in India. The wheat granary of the sub-continent, the western part of Punjab, went to Pakistan, causing a grave food deficit across the border. Then came the refugees who had to be fed, clothed and housed without delay. The structural dislocation alone was sufficient to produce a major economic crisis. To it was added human folly and selfishness.

The coming of Independence brought to the fore sectional economic interests which pressed their special claims with little thought for the consequences. The principal offender was the business community. Backed by Patel it launched a full-scale attack on the system of price controls over food and other essentials. The battle raged throughout the autumn of 1947. Wisdom decreed their retention until the serious shortage of commodities was overcome. But greed decreed otherwise. Ironically it was Gandhi who tipped the scales in favour of decontrol. Only after a tremendous spiral of inflation were controls reimposed.

During that period production declined and capital moved into ventures which assured a quick profit. Businessmen were not alone in this display of selfishness. Congress officials indulged in corruption and nepotism, especially in the states. Trade unions joined in the fray with wildcat strikes.

Nehru attempted to stem the tide with words—blunt words, passionate words, angry words. His most scathing remarks were directed to Capital. 'I hope no one will challenge me when I say that during this last war a certain section of the employer class . . .

behaved exceedingly badly . . . We have to find some means and machinery to prevent this kind of shameful traffic in human beings and profiting at the expense of the nation.'[1] A measure of relief came early in 1948, with a three-year truce in industrial warfare. The real problem, however, was a crisis in business confidence, a fear of impending socialism now that Nehru was Prime Minister. Insecurity led to a 'strike of capital' pending the announcement of the Government's industrial policy.

When it came, in April 1948, Nehru's admirers and critics alike were surprised. Here was no programme of revolutionary change. Indeed, there was little resemblance to socialism. Public owner- ship was confined to three industries—munitions, atomic energy and railways. In six others the Government reserved to itself the exclusive right to start *new* ventures—coal, iron and steel, aircraft manufacturing, shipbuilding, telegraphic and telephonic materials, and minerals. *Existing* concerns in these industries were to remain free from government control; nationalization was postponed for at least ten years. And the rest of the industrial field would nor- mally be left open to private enterprise.

The business community was jubilant, but radicals were crest- fallen at the 'retreat from socialism'. What impelled Nehru to make these sweeping concessions to private enterprise? For one thing, Patel used his influence to prevent any move to the Left. For another, the crisis of production had reached alarming pro- portions and had to be surmounted at all costs. Beyond these specific reasons was the shock of the communal riots which dic- tated a policy of caution. As Nehru told the Constituent Assembly, 'There has been destruction and injury enough, and certainly I confess to this House that I am not brave and gallant enough to go about destroying any more.'[2] His approach was Fabian. It has remained so ever since.

Caution led Nehru to propound a novel variation of socialist economic planning. For want of a better phrase it may be termed 'socialization of the vacuum', that is to say, the concentration of public investment in those areas of the economy which are totally free from private interests. The line of argument developed in his speeches at the time may be summarized as follows: India is an underdeveloped country with limited capital and skills, both pub- lic and private; a steady increase in production is the prime

---

[1] *Independence and After*, p. 149.　　　　[2] Ibid., p. 173.

requisite if the basic goal of a higher standard of living for the masses is to be achieved; both public and private capital have important roles to play; to use public funds for nationalization of existing industry is both short-sighted and foolhardy; it is a waste of resources, for it does not increase the gross national product and diverts capital from much-needed growth in key sectors of the economy; moreover, there are certain fields of development which private capital will not enter because the profit margin is low and the gestation period very long; yet it is precisely in those fields that capital is desperately needed, such as power, irrigation, transport, and agricultural improvement; to nationalize the bulk of private industry is a rigid, formula approach to socialism; it may be appropriate to the highly developed economies of the West but it is singularly unrealistic in India where the key problem is growth, not control over large concentrations of economic power; furthermore, control is possible without nationalization; flourishing private enterprise contributes to the nation's welfare, and the government can impose necessary controls to avoid its evils; the primary function of the state in Indian conditions at this time is to add appreciably to production, not to effect a change in ownership; nationalization is not to be abandoned but it should be applied only in very special circumstances—where it facilitates growth. In essence, Nehru was subscribing to the principles of a mixed economy, with emphasis on the historic task of the State to fill the vacuum viewed in realistic economic terms.

The idea of economic planning was not unknown in India before Independence. Nehru has preached its virtues since the late 1920's. The Congress Socialists had embraced it wholeheartedly. And the party's National Planning Committee, under Nehru's inspiration, had paved the way for its acceptance. During the second world war a spate of plans appeared. The Government of India's Planning Department did valuable preparatory work in the final years of the *Raj*. Nevertheless, as late as 1949 planning had not yet made a serious dent in the thinking of the Indian Government.

The inducement to action was the steadily deteriorating economic situation. Everything pointed to a deepening long-term crisis: chronic unemployment and under-employment in the village; rising unemployment in the city; the reluctance of private capital to invest in productive enterprise—this despite the moderate Industrial Policy Resolution of 1948; growing inflation; the spread of black-marketeering and corruption; stagnant agriculture; inefficiency in industrial plants, along with shortages of experienced personnel, raw materials and spare parts; and pressure on resources arising from the growth of population. Discontent was widespread, especially among the intelligentsia, and lethargy was everywhere.

The problems confronting India's economic planners can only be described as gargantuan. There is, firstly, the sheer size and diversity of the country and its people, some 360 million (in 1950) inhabiting a sub-continent. Topographical features range from the world's highest mountains to the world's largest alluvial plain and include large tracts of desert along with areas receiving the world's most concentrated rainfall. United in many respects, India's millions are also divided by language, culture, creed and caste. There is, secondly, the novelty of the idea of planning in a predominantly peasant society which does not take easily to change. Apart from lethargy and distrust there is the immobility of the vast majority of Indians, both physical and social. Approximately three out of every four are dependent on the land for their livelihood.

Another powerful hindrance to planned development is the overriding importance of status in Indian society. Inequality is the hallmark of the caste system and caste consciousness continues to pervade Hindu life. Moreover, respect for age and tradition is deeply rooted and neither is conducive to change.

These obstacles would be formidable in any country. In India their effects are increased many-fold by the grim poverty which stalks the land, poverty of such dimensions that its impact can only be partly conveyed by words and statistics. Hundreds of thousands make their 'homes' on the streets of India's overcrowded cities. Calcutta can lay claim to the dubious distinction of having the foulest slums in the world. Other Indian cities are not far behind. Millions suffer from malnutrition; whereas 2,200 calories per day are the minimum required for health, the average caloric intake in India was less than 1,700 in 1956. The average *per capita* annual income in 1951 was about $53 or 14½ c. a day; and this must cover all expenses—food, clothing, shelter, medicines, education. The 50 million Untouchables and the 40-odd million landless labourers have, perhaps, half that income.

If life in the city is a perpetual struggle for survival, life in the village is devoid of material comfort for all but a few. The typical peasant home is a windowless mud hut with a few cooking utensils and a string cot. It is almost always dark; less than 1 per cent. of India's 500,000 villages had electricity in 1951. At the beginning of the First Plan few village streets were paved and sewage disposal was rare. India in general, and village India in particular, is a land of collective filth and individual cleanliness. Hinduism enjoins personal cleanliness on its followers and most Hindus bathe daily, but most are compelled to wear the same clothes for they lack more than one *dhoti*. Sanitation in the village is abominable. More than half a million die every year from tuberculosis. Famine takes its toll periodically; and malnutrition saps the strength of the majority of Indians. Most Indians eat only twice a day. Few get meat, fish, eggs or fruit, certainly not in sufficient quantities. The result is a very high death rate and the lowest life expectancy anywhere in the world—twenty-seven years in 1947, raised to thirty-two years in the last decade.

Despite the high death rate, India's population in 1951 increased by 4 to 5 million a year. In every plan period this means an additional 20 to 25 million mouths to feed. At the beginning of the First Plan period there were at least 2 million unemployed in the cities and perhaps 15 million in the villages—this apart from millions who are idle more than half the year. In 1958 it was estimated by the Deputy Chairman of the Planning Commission that 50 million peasant *families* were without work eight months a year, a colossal waste of human energy. This is perhaps the gravest problem of Indian economic development. As one senior planner put it to the writer, 'we are engaged in a deadly race between economic development, especially industrialization, and the growing pressure on land. Even assuming the achievement of targets set in the first *five* plans this problem cannot be easily solved.'

Another obstacle to development is the dire shortage of trained personnel and, more generally, the evil of illiteracy. About 83 per cent. of all Indians in 1951 were unable to read and write. School facilities were available for less than half of the primary school-age children. Over 90 per cent. do not attend high school; and less than 1 per cent. proceed to the university.

Perhaps the most striking economic paradox is that India is a rich country with poor people. Side by side with poverty, illiteracy and disease are bountiful resources for development: the largest known deposits of high-grade iron ore in the world and adequate reserves of coal for the expansion of the steel industry—which produced less than 2 million tons in 1951; the third-largest reserve of manganese; four-fifths of the world's supply of mica; adequate deposits of bauxite, gypsum, chrome, lime, gold, clay, salt and feldspar. India lacks zinc, copper, tin and lead, but future surveys may unearth some of these minerals. India has always been dependent on the Middle East for oil, but recent discoveries in Assam may well ensure a high degree of self-sufficiency in this vital commodity. Power for electricity is abundant, notably hydro-electric power to be harnessed from India's mighty rivers. The recent discovery of large deposits of thorium provides a basis for atomic power.

Thus the material needs for industrialization are present. There is, too, an almost unlimited supply of labour. But grinding poverty has hindered their utilization thus far. The fundamental problem is that of inadequate capital and know-how. At the same time India is engaged in a perennial struggle to feed its mounting population.

The machinery and method of Indian planning have changed little over the years. The principal agency is the six-member Planning Commission created in 1950. Of its original members only two retained membership in 1958—Nehru, the Commission's Chairman since its inception, and G. L. Nanda. Broad policy decisions are made by the Cabinet, to which the Commission is responsible. Its primary functions are research and the drafting of an all-India programme of development. Apart from Nehru, each member is responsible for certain areas of planning. Within the Commission are various specialized divisions, economic, financial, employment, agricultural, progress, statistical and the like.

At first the Commission exerted wide-ranging influence. Since 1954, however, the National Development Council and its Standing Committee have relegated it to the status of a research arm. Expert advice to the Commission and the Development Council is provided by the Economists Panel. Each State has its own planning agency which feeds the Commission proposals for local projects and constantly lobbies for a 'just' share of appropriations. Once the overall plan is approved, they administer specific programmes within their territory and provide the Commission with progress reports. The Commission itself sends out agents to report on local projects and to stir up interest.

Indian planning is the product of democratic ways of discussion and decision. The period of time allotted to deliberations, the widespread participation of persons at the State and local levels, the constant search to reconcile different conceptions and goals, the free play given to interest groups—all testify to a democratic planning process. Drafts of the first two plans were subjected to searching scrutiny by the press, political parties, industry and labour, the intelligentsia and Parliament; the effect is evident in the basic revisions. As one senior planner remarked, 'the Plan is a product of group thinking and decisions. It represents agreement among a large number of interest groups, local, regional and national.' Even after the plan is approved dissent is not stifled.

Nehru's role in the planning process is crucial, despite the fact that he lacks expert knowledge of economics and finance. Indeed, his influence extends from the drafting stage to implementation. Firstly, he stands at the centre of the decision-making structure by virtue of his positions as Prime Minister, Chairman of the Planning Commission and Chairman of the National Development Council —and because he is Jawaharlal Nehru. He is the link between the planning agencies and the Government and is brought into any matter requiring Cabinet approval, notably broad decisions concerning targets, aims and priorities. Secondly, he is the central object of attention for all pressure groups—the Commission itself and individual members, Cabinet Ministers, State Ministers, Congressmen anxious to please their constituents, trade unions and employer associations and special interest groups or individuals like Vinoba Bhave and the *Bhoodan* (land gift) Movement, co-operative associations, community development officials, etc. He is, therefore, the pivot around which discussion and decision revolve. A constant stream of letters and verbal representations seek his intervention and approval.

During the early years Nehru was inclined to depend on the Commission and not to busy himself with its deliberations. Since the autumn of 1954, however, he has devoted much of his time to planning problems. He attends and addresses all meetings of the National Development Council and its Standing Committee and expresses his views forcefully. Moreover, there is no doubt that these influence the planners and find expression in the Final Draft, notably his stress on heavy industry and on the proper relationship between the public and private sectors. 'Policy is made by the Prime Minister's public statements,' according to one senior official. Not the least important is his role as liaison between the planners and the people. Nehru is the most effective salesman of planning in the country as a whole. This may well be his most important contribution, spreading the gospel that planning is the key to welfare.

* * * *

India's First Five-Year Plan (1951–6) was modest in scope and cautious in approach. Indeed, it was not really a plan in the accepted meaning of the term. It was, rather, an amalgam of specific projects drafted by the pre-Independence Planning Department and its successor, the Advisory Board on Planning. Many of them had already been introduced. The Five-Year Plan merely integrated these into a rational framework, established priorities, allocated additional funds where necessary, and provided further guidance for their speedy implementation. Planned expenditure of public funds underwent various revisions, but at no time was it ambitious or risky. The total was just short of $5 billion.

Its most striking feature was the stress on agriculture (close on one-third of the total expenditure). Until food production could be substantially increased and made less dependent on the uncertain monsoon by enlarging the area under irrigation, the static barrier could not be broken; foreign exchange would be 'wasted' on consumer goods; and plans for industrialization would be seriously retarded. The large expenditure for transport and communications (23 per cent.) was also geared in part to the need for meeting local food shortages. Industry was given a nominal sum in the expectation that India could proceed to large-scale industrialization in the Second Plan period.

Approximately 83 per cent. of the anticipated public outlay was invested. Nevertheless, the Plan was a success. National income rose by 18 per cent. over the five years whereas the population increased by 6 per cent. Food production reached a new high, some 5,000,000 tons above the target, freeing India of the spectre of famine in the short run and eliminating the costly drain on foreign exchange. *Per capita* annual income rose from $53.34 to $59.01, not spectacular but a step forward. Production of capital goods rose by 70 per cent., consumer goods and industrial raw materials by 34 per cent. Some 16 million acres of land were brought under some form of irrigation. Electric power increased almost 70 per cent., as did cement production. The planners had reason to be satisfied, even though the increase in food production was due in part to three favourable monsoons in succession.

Perhaps the main achievement was to maintain the 'hope level' and to make planning more attractive by providing concrete evidence of its material benefits. Nevertheless, India was still desperately poor, unemployment was increasing and agricultural prices were falling. The time had come for a bolder, more ambitious programme.

Nehru took the lead. On the basic issue he came out clearly for a 'socialistic picture of society' though not 'in a dogmatic sense at all'. 'There is plenty of room for private enterprise, provided the main aim is kept clear.'[1] In the Second Plan, he added, the emphasis must be shifted from agriculture to industry. And so it was. Both Gandhians and 'Westernizers' could derive comfort from his view that heavy industries and cottage industries should be developed simultaneously. Throughout the great debate on economic policy he was moderate in tone. He criticized Marxism as outdated and reaffirmed the 'middle way'. Nationalization of existing industry was not contemplated. The approach, he told Parliament, would be pragmatic, and India would follow the peaceful, democratic, non-violent way.

Ideologically, the shift was given concrete expression at the Avadi session of the Congress in 1955. The road to socialism was charted, though what form it would take no one bothered to define: 'planning should take place with a view to the establishment of a socialistic pattern of society. . .' The State would have to initiate large-scale power and transport projects, have overall control of resources, maintain strategic controls, prevent the development of cartels and the like.[2]

[1] Nehru, *Planning and Development*, pp. 15–20.
[2] The text is in Fisher, Margaret W., and Bondurant, Joan V., *Indian Approaches to a Socialist Society*, Appendix II.

Indian reaction to the Avadi Resolution was mixed. All agreed that it was a logical outgrowth of Nehru's speeches during the preceding few months. But as to the meaning of 'socialist pattern' there was a wide range of views.

In response to a question about the possible link between his China tour a few months earlier and the Avadi Resolution, Nehru said to the author with some vehemence, 'absolutely nothing to do with it'. Further, 'we had talked about socialism throughout [the struggle for independence] and as long as twenty-five years ago the Congress said that the chief industries should be owned and controlled by the State [the Karachi Resolution of 1931]. After the coming of Independence it developed gradually and ultimately came out. Nothing special happened last year.'

Be that as it may, Nehru was deeply moved by what he saw in China. He was impressed by the energy and discipline of Chinese workers, in contrast to Indians, particularly under the direction of an efficient centralized government which gave China 'terrifying strength'. He admired the effective use of China's huge labour force in large-scale construction projects such as dams and hoped to emulate this in India—without the coercive mobilization of labour. He was comforted by the belief that India was more economically advanced *at present* (in 1954) but must have been disturbed by the fact that China's *rate* of progress was faster. Upon his return he commented critically on the lack of free speech in China and extolled the virtues of democracy and parliamentary government. It may well be that subconsciously he was driven to the Left upon his return by the concern that China was winning the crucial contest with India for ideologically uncommitted Asia.

Whatever the motive force, Nehru's speeches in the autumn of 1954 ushered in a new phase in Indian economic policy. First came the Avadi Resolution on a 'socialist pattern of society'. Then came the budget for 1955–6, termed by some (incorrectly) 'the first socialist budget'. Soon after, the Taxation Inquiry Commission recommended a statutory ceiling on incomes. In the spring of 1955 Nehru secured parliamentary approval of a constitutional amendment which gave to the legislatures the authority to determine the amount of compensation for expropriated property, a right formerly held by the Courts, and authorized the legislatures to acquire any property deemed in the public interest. Then came the first major act of nationalization since Independence. The Imperial Bank of India, which had the largest network of branches in the country, was converted to the State Bank of India. The primary intention was to enable the Government to assist small-scale industry in town and village by easing loan conditions and stimulating economic expansion. This was followed by the Indian Companies Amendment Act aimed at weakening the managing agency system, a unique Indian method of corporate management introduced by the British which created huge concentrations of economic power by means of inter-locking management.

These developments alarmed the business community. Nehru tried to smooth the troubled waters by clarifying the intent and means of achieving the 'socialist pattern'. 'We shall do so in our own way, and that is a peaceful way, a co-operative way and a way which always tries to carry the people with us, *including those who may be apprehensive or even hostile to begin with*.'[1]

Three years later, in 1958, Nehru expressed his considered thoughts on Socialism.

I do not want State socialism of that extreme kind in which the State is all powerful and governs practically all activities. The State is very powerful politically. . . . I should, therefore, like decentralization of economic power. We cannot, of course, decentralize iron and steel and locomotives and such other big industries, but you can have small units of industries as far as possible on a co-operative basis with State control in a general way. I am not at all dogmatic about it. We have to learn from practical experience and proceed in our own way. . . .

My idea of socialism is that every individual in the State should have equal opportunity for progress.[2]

India's Second Five-Year Plan (1956–61) is designed to place the country on the path of rapid progress. Broadly it aims at the creation of a Welfare State. Four specific objectives are set out by the drafters: 'a sizeable increase in national income; rapid industrialization with particular emphasis on basic and heavy industries; a large expansion of employment opportunities; and reduction of inequalities in income and wealth and a more even distribution of economic power.'[3]

[1] Letter to the Presidents of the Provincial Congress Committees. *Towards a Socialistic Order*, p. 31. (Emphasis added.)

[2] Speech to the All-India Congress Committee. *The Hindu Weekly Review* (Madras), 26 May 1958.

[3] *Second Five Year Plan*, p. 24.

The main features of the Second Plan may be summarized briefly. The total planned expenditure of public funds is Rs. 4,800 crores (approximately $10 billion), more than double the outlay in the First Plan. Private enterprise is expected to invest an additional Rs. 2,400 crores (approximately $5 billion). The national income target is an increase of 25 per cent. in the five years, compared with a target of 11 per cent. in the First Plan. The goal for *per capita* income is an increase of 18 per cent., from $58.80 to $69.30 *per year*. The plan also aims at 10 million more jobs—which barely covers the expected increase in the labour force during the five years.

In agriculture, the main targets are a 25 per cent. rise in food production and an increase of 21 million acres under irrigation. The goals for industry and mining are even more impressive: a 64 per cent. increase in net industrial production; a 150 per cent. increase in capital goods alone; a 63 per cent. increase in coal, 108 per cent. in cement and 231 per cent. in steel, from 1·3 to 4·3 million tons per year. Railways are to be modernized and extended—and India already possesses the fourth-largest railway system in the world. Enlarged transport and communications include the modernization of India's principal ports—Calcutta, Madras, Bombay and Vizagapatnam. Primary-school facilities are to be provided for 8 million more children, an increase of 23 per cent. The number of doctors is to be raised by 12,500, and there are to be some 3,000 new rural clinics. To achieve these goals the planners anticipate an investment of 11 per cent. of national income in the final year, compared with 7 per cent. in the last year of the First Plan period.

The Second Plan is modest in relation to India's needs but over-ambitious in terms of financial resources. Indeed, the original estimates indicate a willingness to gamble. Only 25 per cent. of the total planned outlay is covered by assured revenue—existing taxes, new taxation, railway profits, pension funds, etc. Another 25 per cent. falls in the category of loans and small savings. The third category, deficit financing in the proper sense, accounts for an additional 25 per cent. The remaining 25 per cent. is dependent on foreign aid and then unknown domestic resources. Realistically viewed, half the total public outlay depended on precarious or unreliable sources. But the planners felt that boldness was imperative if the 'hope level' was to be maintained. As Nehru remarked to Parliament, 'in the final analysis any effort is an act of faith. . . . I have faith in the capacity of our people.'[1]

Before the Second Plan was formally inaugurated, the Indian Government announced a new industrial policy to reflect the emphasis on an enlarged public sector. The Resolution of 1956 retained the form of three categories, but increased the scope of State enterprise. The list of reserved industries, the future development of which will be the exclusive responsibility of the State, was increased from six to seventeen and included all 'of basic and strategic importance, or in the nature of public utility services . . . and other industries which are essential. . . .' Moreover, in the concurrent list the State's dominant responsibility was clearly enunciated. And even in the third category, privately controlled industries, the State was not excluded. However, existing private industrial concerns would not be nationalized, and the division into categories was not intended to be rigid. In fact, the door was left open for joint State-private undertakings.

The business community has the added assurance that the road to a 'socialist pattern' is likely to be very long. On the eve of the Second Plan State-owned *industry* comprised no more than 5 per cent. of the total; the bulk of publicly owned capital assets lies in railways, ports and irrigation works. Moreover, all land is privately owned. If the budget on the eve of the Second Plan were any test, the 'socialist pattern' did not seriously encroach on private enterprise. On the contrary, the bulk of new taxes was levied on consumer goods.

India entered the Second Plan period with high hopes. Within a year, however, it was faced with the gravest economic crisis since Independence. Nature dealt the first blow, in the form of widespread floods, hailstorms and drought during the autumn and winter of 1956–7. It was a cruel blow causing human misery in many parts of the country. Food reserves which had been laboriously built up during the 'good years' of the First Plan were rapidly depleted. And still the threat of creeping famine remained.

The increase in food production during 1956–7 was only half the target; in 1957–8 there was a decline of 2 million tons. One effect was a substantial rise in food prices. Another was to narrow the permissible limit of deficit financing for industrial development; the fear of runaway inflation necessitated extreme caution.

[1] *Times of India* (New Delhi), 8 September 1956.

A third effect was to reduce the real value of Second Plan projects. A fourth has been increased pressure on India's foreign exchange reserves; in fact, the food crisis coincided with and aggravated a serious drain on foreign exchange.

The programme of industrialization required the import of costly equipment, the products of which will not be forthcoming for some years. At the same time inflation weakened India's trading position. Thus during the first year of the plan India's foreign exchange (mostly sterling) reserves declined to just over $1 billion, precariously close to the prescribed minimum of $840 million for currency backing. Moreover, the completion of industrial projects required a continued drawing on foreign exchange. As the Finance Minister remarked, 'we are riding the tiger of industrialization and can't get off'.[1]

Delhi's first response to this financial crisis was a draconian budget for 1957–8, designed to curb inflation and to increase domestic funds for development. No section of the community was spared. The very poor had the burden of higher customs duties on consumer goods; the middle class was affected by the lower income tax exemptions; and the well-to-do by new, special taxes on wealth and expenditure. The primary aim was to save the Plan, but the total expected yield from these new and increased levies was only $195 million.

More drastic action was necessary, for the drain on foreign exchange continued unabated. Capital goods imports requiring foreign exchange were banned unless sellers agreed to deferred payment. The Soviet bloc agreed at once, and at a low rate of interest, stealing a march on its ideological competitors. But this barely touched the problem. Then a drastic reduction in the import of consumer goods was announced; the expected saving was $210 million. However, the foreign exchange gap was $1·4 billion for the remainder of the Plan, even after certain cutbacks in industrialization. An approach to London was unsuccessful. West Germany was more helpful, easing the burden of payment on imported machinery for one of the new steel plants. And the United States responded with a loan of $225 million.

In mid-1958 the Second Five-Year Plan was in serious trouble. Hence the long-delayed 'pruning' of the Plan took place. The 'core' remains: agricultural production; power projects; and the

[1] *New York Times*, 9 May 1957.

three steel plants designed to treble India's finished steel output, one being built with the aid of Russian capital and technicians, another with British, and the third with German assistance. Yet the enormous foreign exchange gap remains—$1,200 million by the end of the Second Plan period—this to achieve the reduced targets of the plan. In the autumn of 1958 relief came in the form of multilateral aid agreement. The United States, the United Kingdom, West Germany, Japan, Canada and the World Bank made available $350 million in loans to ease the foreign exchange burden. The future now seemed more optimistic.

Perhaps the most notable casualty of the economic crisis in 1958 was the Community Development Programme. Nehru has often spoken with pride about this aspect of planning. Typical is the following: 'I think nothing has happened in any country in the world during the last few years so big in content and so revolutionary in design as the Community Projects in India. They are changing the face of rural India.'[1]

There is an aura of faith about this novel programme. It began in 1952 on the anniversary of Gandhi's birthday, and was partly inspired by the Mahatma's aim of bringing dignity and progress to the village through active participation of the common man. The other major goal was a large increase in agricultural production, income and employment. By the end of the First Plan it embraced almost a fourth of rural India. The Second Plan target was the entire rural population, 325 million people living in almost 600,000 villages. But the foreign exchange crisis intervened and the programme's completion will be delayed.

The basic unit is the Development Block of about 100 villages and 60,000 to 70,000 people. To each is assigned a group of specialists, for agriculture, animal husbandry, education, health, housing and the like, operating under the supervision of a Block Development Officer. All are specially trained for rural extension work. Direction from above takes place on two levels—the District Officer and the Development Commissioner of each State who works in co-operation with interested State ministries and administers broad policy laid down by the Ministry of Community Development in Delhi. Day-to-day operation of the programme is in the hands of the extension worker who is responsible for about ten villages and lives in one of them.

[1] Nehru, *On Community Development*, p. 36.

The essence of the programme is self-help, democracy at the grass roots. Field workers attempt to persuade the villager of the material benefits of new methods of cultivation, a health clinic, a new road, and of pooling their efforts in co-operatives. But decisions rest with the village acting through a local Council which the programme has tried to foster. The Block and extension workers cannot impose a set of projects; they advise and guide and stimulate interest in change. In fact, no project is undertaken without active participation of the village. In this way it is hoped that the long-dormant peasantry will be moved to purposeful activity. In this way, too, a new sense of personal dignity may come to the peasant, and the 'dung-heap' in which he has lived for millennia may be slowly changed into a self-respecting community. But this takes time. It also requires an army of well-trained and devoted rural workers.

The material record thus far shows limited progress: 15,000 new schools in the First Plan period; 1,000 health centres; 2 million acres brought under irrigation by local effort; 34,000 village councils formed; 250,000 acres reclaimed, etc. Somewhat disappointing is the fact that average food production in Community Development areas is only 11 per cent. higher than in the rest of the country. General education has lagged. Rural employment has not noticeably increased. The administration tends to be top-heavy and extension workers frequently lack skills. The gravest shortcoming, perhaps, is that the concept of self-help has not yet penetrated the mind of the Indian peasantry.

Nevertheless the villager has taken to the programme. He wants change; his wife and children get better care; his land is more productive; new seed and more assured water have helped. Not all are pleased. Some are indifferent; others are still suspicious of townsmen and officials; still others find the pace too quick and the pressures too severe. On the whole, however, the impression is one of progress. It is, potentially, a welfare achievement which could also strengthen the roots of democracy in India.

In the closely related sphere of land reform the record leaves much to be desired. The Congress had long pledged basic reform to remove the worst evils of the system. It was also committed to non-violent change and to fair compensation for expropriated property. The first step had to be the abolition of intermediaries, notably the *Zamindari* (tax farming) system which covered nearly half of India. By the end of the First Plan period this parasitical system had been eliminated, with minor exceptions. It was the most impressive aspect of Indian land reform, indeed, the only real measure of change.

Even this was not accomplished without strong opposition. Finally, in 1951, Nehru forced through a constitutional amendment which had the effect of placing the Zamindari abolition acts beyond the purview of the courts and of giving them retroactive validity. Yet this did not automatically ensure 'land to the tiller'; the tenant could purchase his land, in theory, but the cost is exorbitant, and the rent (land tax) now paid to the State is usually too high to leave any margin for the acquisition of owner-ship rights. Despite pressure by the Centre on the States, rents remain high, ranging from one-sixth to one-half of total crop value. Protection against eviction of tenants has been improved, but cases crop up very frequently.

The record is no more impressive in the positive aspects of agrarian reform—consolidation of holdings, co-operative farming, improved credit facilities, and the like. There is ample evidence that Nehru, along with many others, is dissatisfied with the pace and scope of reform. In 1955 he pushed through another consti-tutional amendment which included the right of the State to fix a ceiling on land holdings and to distribute excess lands. Most important, it removed from the courts the authority to determine the amount of compensation. Nevertheless, land reform lags. And Nehru must bear much of the responsibility, even though it falls under State law.

India's land problem is seriously aggravated by a rapid and steady rise in population. This absorbs much of the annual in-crease in gross national product—more than a third of the 3·5 per cent. increase during the First Plan period. In 1956 India's popu-lation stood at 384 million. At present rates of expansion it will reach 408 million at the end of the Second Plan period and 500 million in 1976, at the end of the Fifth Plan period. While national income may be expected to rise at an ever-faster rate, this upward trend of population poses a serious problem. Yet Nehru is still not as population-conscious as some economists believe necessary. In 1956 the Prime Minister remarked to the author:

I should like to limit the population of India or, if I may say so, to pre-vent it from growing too much. However, the question of limiting the family is not the primary question. We have to make economic progress much more rapidly and we cannot wait for family planning to bring results. Also the rate of population growth in India is not high. India can support a larger population given economic growth.

The fact remains, however, that the population increase is a heavy drag on economic progress. The efforts to curb it thus far are puny compared with the need.

Having said all this, it remains to be emphasized that India's progress is impressive, measured both against its own previous conditions and against the record of any other under-developed country which has chosen the *democratic* way to social and economic change. No less vital is the point that whatever progress has been achieved is primarily due to the efforts of Nehru. Indeed, he is the heart and soul and mind of India's heroic struggle to raise its living standards. He has been the prime mover in India's planning effort. He has striven valiantly, almost single-handed, to establish firm foundations for a secular order of society. And he has set in motion a reformation of Hindu society through the Hindu Code Bills. By the same token, the shortcomings of these programmes, especially in the fields of land reform, population and the public sector, reflect in large measure the weaknesses of Nehru's policies and his frequent reluctance to act resolutely when forcefulness is necessary.

CHAPTER XIII

INDIA AND THE WORLD

Indian views on international affairs may be traced to many sources, some traditional, others contemporary. Almost two centuries of foreign rule produced an instinctive antagonism to any form of Western domination over Asian and African peoples. Closely related to this feeling is an intense hostility to racial discrimination. Indeed, the twin experiences of colonialism and racialism have played an important part in moulding the attitudes of Indian statesmen.

Their impact on Indian foreign policy is amply illustrated by recent events. The extreme sensitivity of Nehru and others to SEATO (1954) and the Baghdad Pact (1955) was largely due to the belief that these alliances represented an indirect return of Western power to former colonial areas. Moreover, Nehru's ambivalent response to the Hungarian revolt and the Anglo-French invasion of Egypt in 1956 revealed two subconscious emotions: first, a continuing mistrust of Western actions, because of the lengthy history of Anglo-French colonialism, and a willingness to give the Soviet case a fair hearing, because of the absence of direct Russian control in Asia; secondly, a belief that while violence is bad white violence against non-whites is worse. The Korean War also revealed the depth of these emotions, particularly when the U.S. disregarded India's advice about crossing the 38th Parallel and bombed the Yalu power plants.

Napoleon once declared that the foreign policy of a state flows from its geographic position. No Indian statesman can ignore the compelling fact that the two Great Powers of the Communist world stand at the gates of the Indian sub-continent; indeed, that China rings a substantial part of its northern and eastern frontiers; the Chinese occupation of Tibet in 1950 (and parts of Ladakh in 1959) shows that the Himalayan mountain barrier is not impregnable. Nor can Nehru and his colleagues forget that the Soviet-Chinese bloc has vastly superior power to India. Powerful neighbours must not be provoked or alienated, though vital interests must be protected, as in the case of the tiny border states—Nepal, Sikkim and Bhutan. Geographic position also dictates a policy of friendship with Burma, lest a powerful enemy stand at the gates of eastern India with consequences even greater than the Japanese thrust in the early 1940's. Moreover, India's location at the head of the Indian Ocean and its dependence on sea routes for the flow of goods and services give it an important stake in the rivalries of the region.

Closely linked with the geographic pressures on Indian foreign policy are those stemming from the structure of India's economy and the plans for development. A low standard of living, a high rate of population growth, stagnant agriculture, the lack of heavy industry worthy of the name, an inadequate supply of capital—these were the cardinal features of the Indian economy at the time of Independence. Partition seriously aggravated the problem. The first few years had to be devoted to the formidable task of achieving internal stability. When, in 1950, serious planning got under way, dependence on the outside world for capital and machinery assumed great importance.

India's economic weakness and the basic goal of development provide powerful inducements to the policy of non-alignment. The doors must be kept open to all possible sources of aid, Western and Soviet, if the desired economic targets are to be achieved. For these reasons, too, global peace is of paramount importance; the outbreak of war between the super-Powers would wreck the ambitious Indian economic programme. Indeed, all other factors which shape India's world-view are subordinate to this consideration, as Nehru has candidly stated on many occasions.

These geo-political and economic factors derive added significance from the character of world politics at the present time. Three courses of action were open to Nehru's India: formal association with the Western or Communist bloc, or non-alignment. Some of the reasons for the choice of the last alternative have already been noted. Non-alignment is considered essential to the fulfilment of India's economic revolution, and avoids alienation of India's two powerful neighbours, China and Russia. Beyond that is the conviction that it contributes to the maintenance of peace and the relaxation of tension. Indeed, the possibility of total destruction and the international balance of power impose a moral as well as a practical obligation on India to remain 'uncommitted'.

The argument advanced by Nehru and others is essentially simple. If India allied itself openly with one of the two blocs the danger of world war would be increased. Moreover, an uncommitted India can perform, and has performed in some measure, the necessary task of building a bridge between the two blocs. In doing so, it is serving not only Indian vital interests, but also the real vital interest of all states. And India is happily situated to fulfil this role—as an Asian state, having no legacy of conflict with Russia, friendly to the West, and following a 'middle way' in economic and social matters. The wider the 'area of peace', that is to say, the area of non-alignment, the less the likelihood of war among the super-powers. Such is Nehru's oft-stated rationale for India's foreign policy.

Non-alignment has the added merit of satisfying a deep urge for recognition, a natural result of colonial subjection. And it enables a relatively weak, newly independent India to play a major role on the world stage. There is, finally, a psychological barrier to joining any bloc. Like the American 'founding fathers', Indian leaders are intent on guarding their recently won freedom from all possible encroachments. Membership of a bloc is equated with loss of freedom of action in foreign affairs.

The legacy of India's traditions also merits attention. More so than any other religion, Hinduism breeds tolerance. The roads to truth and to an understanding of Brahma are infinite. No system of thought and belief is capable of comprehending the complete truth. Every approach to communion with God, from primitive animism to the most sophisticated metaphysics, represents but a different form of man's quest for the Good. On the road to truth some may advance more than others. But there is not one correct path. The rigidity and intolerance of some Western religions is alien to Hinduism. Indeed, it is possible to be a Christian, Muslim, Jew, Buddhist or member of any other faith, and still be a Hindu. Thus it was that Gandhi constantly invoked the teachings of other religions and paid tribute to their moral principles.

Tolerance is not always practised by the followers of Hinduism, as revealed in the tragic history of communal riots. Nevertheless, it is a part of the Hindu (and, therefore, Indian) way of thought. This influences India's attitude to the ideological war of the mid-twentieth century. There is no messianic mission to convert the peoples of the world to one political or religious faith. There is, in fact, hostility to the ideological crusades being waged by Communism and the West throughout the 'uncommitted' world.

Another legacy of India's ancient tradition is the principle of *ahimsa* or non-violence. In the land where Buddhism originated non-violence as a method of social action is deeply rooted. More recently, in the hands of Gandhi, it became the creed of Indian nationalism and left an indelible mark on the generation which now rules the State. The Mahatma's conception of *ahimsa* has been termed impracticable by Nehru and his colleagues, and violence has been used, notably in Hyderabad (1948) and Kashmir (1947–8). Nevertheless, the principle has been accepted as a worthy ideal to be applied wherever possible.

There is, too, a conviction that non-violence can serve to lessen world tensions. Perhaps the most striking example is Nehru's restraint on the problem of Goa. A show of force would end the conflict within a few hours; there is no physical barrier to invasion and annexation. Yet Nehru has consistently rejected this course of action, partly because of a desire not to alienate Western goodwill, but also because of the strictures imposed by the principle of non-violence.

No survey of the formative influences on Indian policy-makers would be complete without reference to Indo-Pakistani relations. A Cold War, sometimes not so cold, has raged incessantly. Suffice it to note in this context that neither Delhi nor Karachi can escape from the imperatives posed by this tragic situation. What is more, neither can judge other, wholly distinct, aspects of foreign relations without being conscious of the implications for their relations with one another.

These, then, are some of the factors that shape India's world-view. That in turn moulds India's foreign policy. The *pillars* may be summed up as follows: *anti-colonialism* or, in more positive terms, active support for the right to self-determination of all peoples in Asia and Africa; anti-racialism, i.e., a demand for *full equality among all races*; *non-alignment* with power blocs, not in the negative sense of neutralism, but an active, dynamic, positive assertion of independent judgement on all issues, taking each on its merits, but maintaining freedom of action in international politics; *the recognition of Asia* as a new, vital force in the world and the right of Asian states to decide the issues of direct concern to them; *mediation* with a view to relaxing international tensions; the creation of a no-war area in the 'uncommitted' part of the world, *a third force* under India's leadership, which would reduce the possibility of world war; and *non-violence* as the preferred means of settling international disputes. *All other features of Indian foreign policy are mere refinements of these elements.*

*   *   *   *

The most articulate expression of Indian foreign policy is to be found in the speeches of Nehru. In Parliament and party caucus, within India and abroad, he has hammered on these themes with remarkable consistency. The emphasis may have shifted but never the pillars of policy.

The influence of a Foreign Minister varies widely from one state to another. Nowhere does one man dominate foreign policy as does Nehru in India. Indeed, Nehru is the philosopher, the architect, the engineer and the voice of his country's policy towards the outside world. This does not mean that he is entirely a free agent. It does mean, however, that he has impressed his personality and his views with such effect that foreign policy may properly be termed a private monopoly.

Nehru prepared for this role long before the coming of independence. From the mid-'thirties onward he was the acknowledged Congress spokesman on international affairs. Since 1947, it was he who carried the philosophy and practice of non-alignment to the world at large. And throughout this period he has dominated the policy-making process. No one in the Congress or the Government, not even Sardar Patel, ever challenged his control in this sphere.

The decision to remain in the Commonwealth was, in the last analysis, Nehru's. India's Asian policy and the initiative for the Asian Relations Conferences in Delhi in 1947 and 1949 derive entirely from Nehru. So do the doctrine of peaceful coexistence (the *Panch Shila*) and India's policy towards China and the Soviet Union. It was Nehru, too, who intervened with an offer of mediation in both Korea and Indo-China. Even in the execution of policy his role has been decisive—through his widespread travels which have taken him to China (1954), Russia (1955), the United States (1949 and 1956), South-east Asia (1950 and 1955), Japan (1957), many countries in Europe, and Great Britain (almost annually since 1948, usually for the Commonwealth Prime Ministers' Conference). He is, then, Minister, chief policy planner and roving Ambassador, a combination of roles which has no parallel anywhere, with the possible exception of the United States in its Dulles period.

Nehru's approach to foreign policy was cogently stated in the following comment: 'A policy must be in keeping with the traditional background and temper of the country. It should be idealistic . . . and . . . realistic. If it is not idealistic, it becomes one of sheer opportunism; if it is not realistic, then it is likely to be adventurist and wholly ineffective.'[1] On the question of motives in foreign policy he told the author: 'Ideological urges obviously play some part . . . especially in a democracy because . . . no policy can go very far if it is quite divorced from the people's thinking. However, *in the final analysis, all foreign policy concerns itself chiefly with the national interest of the country concerned.*' As for India's view, he remarked: 'apart from our desire for peace is our feeling that peace is absolutely essential for our progress and our growth. And with the coming of nuclear weapons, war seems to us—and seems to most people everywhere—as extreme folly, that is, it has ceased to promise what you want.' Furthermore, 'I would say that non-alignment is a policy which is nationally profitable for any country. But in some cases there is danger—because of the smallness of the country or because of its geographical position— that, whether it is aligned or non-aligned, it may suffer from the war.'

The content and conduct of any state's foreign policy are subject to various pressures operating on the government of the day. In India's case most of these have been of little importance. The Cabinet may be dealt with first. Since Independence Nehru has held the External Affairs portfolio as well as the Prime Ministership. No Minister other than Krishna Menon has concerned himself with the political aspects of foreign affairs, except in very special instances—Maulana Azad on Pakistan and the Middle East, and Azad and Pandit Pant on Hungary in 1956. In general

[1] *Congress Bulletin*, No. 5, June–July 1954, p. 246.

Nehru's word was and still is final in Cabinet discussions on foreign policy. This is equally true of the Congress Party.

In Parliament, the overwhelming Congress majority (365 of 489 in the 1957 elections) assures approval for Nehru's policies. Criticism comes from the Opposition benches—e.g. from Socialists on the Hungarian uprising in 1956 (and the Tibet revolt in 1959) and from the communalists on Kashmir. Parliamentary approval, however, is never in doubt.

In the press, too, there is widespread support for Nehru's policies, aside from purely party journals and a few national dailies like the *Indian Express* and the *Times of India*. A few prominent commentators, like A. D. Gorwala ('Vivek'), call for a fundamental revision of Indian foreign policy. But these are voices in the wilderness.

There has always been dissatisfaction among some industrialists, notably over the strained relations with America, but they have been unable to exert any significant influence on policy. Neither have the career diplomats, on the whole. During the first five years of independence, Sir G. S. Bajpai, Secretary-General of the Ministry, exerted a major influence on the *conduct* of policy. He was Nehru's technician and a valued counsellor. His successor, N. R. Pillai, controls the day-to-day operations of the Ministry. Moreover, since 1956 his views appear to carry considerable weight with the Prime Minister. But the Foreign Office has not deflected Nehru from the basic goals he laid down many years ago.

Nehru's role on the world stage has always had the backing of the vast majority of politically conscious Indians. For one thing his policies have brought great prestige to India, providing compensation for past colonial rule and present economic ills. For another, there is a mass faith in Nehru's leadership which extends to large sections of the intelligentsia. But most important is his ability to express the moods and goals of his people. Non-alignment, anti-colonialism and anti-racialism admirably reflect these emotions and objectives.

Nehru has wielded supreme power over Indian foreign policy since 1947. However, he has not relied entirely on his own personal judgement. At different periods and for different issues the advice of a few people has weighed heavily in his decisions: the Mountbattens, whose principal role has been to strengthen India's ties with the Commonwealth; Madame Pandit, Nehru's sister, whose influence was primarily directed to friendship with the West; Dr. Radhakrishnan, India's philosopher-Vice-President and former Ambassador to Moscow; Maulana Azad, a Muslim divine, who provided a cultural and religious link with the Arabs; Sardar Panikkar, the first Indian Ambassador to Peking (1950-3), who laid the foundations for cordiality and trust between these two great Asian powers; and V. K. Krishna Menon, Nehru's right hand in foreign affairs.

Menon's rise to prominence was meteoric. After a lengthy period as head of the India League in London, he was appointed the first High Commissioner of (free) India to the United Kingdom. Since 1953 he has led India's delegation to the annual sessions of the United Nations General Assembly and has served as Nehru's personal ambassador to many international conferences. In 1956, he became Minister of Defence.

There is no doubt that Menon has been Nehru's chief foreign policy adviser for some years, almost an Adjunct Minister of External Affairs. The basis of his influence is a personal relationship with the Prime Minister—which dates to the early 'thirties. Menon accompanied Nehru on his European tour in 1938 and the friendship blossomed. He also edited some of Nehru's books for publication in the West. But the reason for his influence is more than friendship. Menon has shown an ability to grasp Nehru's thoughts and objectives and to convey them forcefully to the outside world. He has been the carrier of Nehru's views the world over. In this sense he performs a function identical to that of Harry Hopkins for President Roosevelt. He is, however, more than roving ambassador.

Menon is consulted on all issues of foreign policy by the Prime Minister—and his views carry considerable weight. To what extent he shapes policy is difficult to know. Yet a broad distinction can and should be made between strategic and tactical decisions, and between general policy goals and the details of negotiation.

The core objectives and guiding principles of India's foreign policy are Nehru's contribution. Long before Menon arrived on the scene, the policies of non-alignment, anti-colonialism, racial equality, non-violent methods, and a third force were formulated by Nehru. And these have remained unchanged. Similarly, the strategic decisions regarding Kashmir and Indo-Pakistani relations, China, Russia, the Commonwealth and Asian co-operation were made by Nehru. Menon has not altered these policies. He has, rather, acted upon them to achieve specific goals.

It has been in the capacity of 'trouble-shooter' that Menon has performed his distinctive role. Outstanding examples include the Korean armistice, the Geneva Conference on Indo-China in 1954 and the Suez crisis from 1955 to 1957. He has also relieved Nehru of the heavy burden of day-to-day decisions in many spheres. Constant discussion results in a fusion of ideas and, very often, in Menon's suggestions being taken up by Nehru and unconsciously adopted as his own.

It would be a grave error, however, to exaggerate Menon's influence on the fundamental character and direction of Indian foreign policy. Nor does the evidence suggest that Menon would steer Indian policy into another course even if he had the authority to do so. Indeed, he has been among the staunchest Indian advocates of close ties with Great Britain. As for his frequent denunciation of American policies and his more sympathetic tone to those of the Soviet Union, part of the explanation lies in his past political radicalism and the emotional legacy of the 'thirties.

*   *   *   *

A detailed account of Indian foreign policy since 1947 does not lie within the scope of this book. However, certain key areas merit general discussion here. A distinction can be drawn between Indo-Pakistani relations and those with the rest of the world though, of course, they are very closely related.

The story of the tragic enmity between India and Pakistan is too well known to require a lengthy exposition.[1] Suffice it to note that they have been engaged in undeclared war, with varying degrees of intensity, throughout their brief history as independent states. A host of problems arose from the Partition, some political or economic, some technical, but all charged with violent emotion. Many minor disputes have been eliminated. The critical ones, however, remain unresolved, namely Kashmir, the division of the Indus Valley canal waters and compensation for properties left behind by the ten million refugees.

[1] See the author's *The Struggle for Kashmir* (1953) and Sisir Gupta, *India's Relations with Pakistan 1954–1957* (I.P.R. 1957).

The price of discord has already been exorbitant. The constant threat of renewed war over Kashmir has resulted in a very high 'defence' expenditure—an annual average of approximately 80 per cent. for Pakistan and 50 per cent. for India. This, in turn, has had grave economic repercussions, notably the slowing-down of much-needed development programmes in both countries. Tension has also reduced the flow of goods and services, for some time eliminating it almost completely. Propaganda war has been endemic, heightening the sense of insecurity among minorities, and stimulating a continuous migration.

The strategic consequences have also been severe. The sub-continent is a natural military unit whose security depends on joint defence policies and co-ordination of their armed forces. The historic threat to the area came from the north-west, and any future invasion of Pakistan would inevitably affect India. Instead of military co-operation, however, the two states have been forced to prepare for a possible war with each other—a war which could destroy the stability of both and cause incalculable harm for the 500 million people of the area.

What makes the picture especially distressing is that no one seems capable of finding a way out of the impasse. Kashmir is the crux because it symbolizes the root of the conflict between India and Pakistan. Here is the final test of the validity of the two-nation theory, the basis of Pakistan which rent the sub-continent asunder in 1947. Indian leaders still reject the theory, though they accepted partition on grounds of self-determination.

India's continuing struggle for Kashmir is largely due to the belief that its secular state and security for its 40 million Muslims are at stake. The wounds of Partition are still deep. The secession of Kashmir and its inclusion in Pakistan would, in the opinion of Nehru and others, lead to a strengthening of Hindu communal forces, increasing distrust of the Muslim minority, and a clamour for war with Pakistan. It is this which deters them from carrying out their pledge to hold a U.N.-supervised plebiscite—though most Indians remain convinced of Pakistan's aggression, of the U.N.'s dereliction of duty, and of their legal and moral claim to Kashmir.

For Pakistan, the fate of Kashmir is no less vital. The two-nation theory goes to the very heart of the state. The actual danger of communal discord is little, but so much attention has been focused on Kashmir that it has become *the* internal political issue. No Pakistini government could remain in office if it conceded India's claim, and the internal repercussions would be grave. For both states the element of prestige now looms large.

Given these circumstances, it is natural that Indian foreign policy should be influenced by the struggle for Kashmir. On various occasions since 1948 Indo-British relations have been strained as a result of London's support for the Pakistani claim. When India opposed the 1956 proposal to hold a U.N.-controlled election in Hungary, it was clear that Delhi wanted to avoid a precedent for Kashmir. The outstanding example is Indo-U.S. relations. Nothing has done more harm to friendship between Delhi and Washington than American arms aid to Pakistan since 1954. India considers this an indirect threat because it augments Pakistan's war potential. And Pakistan continues to proclaim its intention of 'liberating' Kashmir, by force if necessary. Moreover, American assistance to Pakistan deepened Indian mistrust of U.S. motives in creating military blocs in the Asian rimland.

The prospects for a friendly solution seem no brighter now than at any time in the past. It is pointless at this stage to apportion blame for the dispute. One thing is certain: the wrangling has accomplished nothing thus far; and in the absence of a bold new approach, the future of India and Pakistan will continue to be plagued by the impasse over Kashmir.

*   *   *   *

India's decision to remain in the Commonwealth occasioned much surprise both at home and abroad. Some years after the event Nehru remarked to the author: 'We decided that there was absolutely no reason why we should break an association which didn't come in our way at all, legally, constitutionally, practically, in any sense, and which merely helped us to co-operate in a measure, consult each other and maybe influence others and maybe to be influenced ourselves. . . . We are freer than two countries tied by an alliance.' It was, in short, Independence plus, not Independence minus.

There were, however, more positive reasons for the decision as noted earlier. India could not risk total isolation immediately after

Independence, especially in an era of Cold War. Moreover, Commonwealth membership widened the stage on which India could play an important international role—without committing it to a bloc. Most important were strong material bonds which could be severed only at great cost: India's foreign exchange reserves and, therefore, its industrial development were tied up with the sterling area, as was a major part of its trade; and India's armed forces were equipped with British-made weapons.

It is doubtful whether the decision was received enthusiastically, even by those who recognized the force of these arguments. In accepting it they were merely expressing faith in Nehru's leadership. To this day there is no genuine attachment to the Crown, however symbolic, or indeed to the Commonwealth as such. The link is tolerated because it serves India's interests. Its tenuous nature is illustrated by the frequent demands for withdrawal—whenever Great Britain's actions offend Indian sensibilities. This has happened over the Kashmir issue frequently. The greatest crisis came over the Anglo-French invasion of Egypt in 1956. A tremendous outcry followed, even amongst normally pro-Commonwealth groups. Only Nehru's firm refusal to countenance such a step prevented a break.

As long as Nehru is at the helm of affairs it seems certain that India will remain in the Commonwealth. Thereafter it is an open question. The Communists are openly committed to withdrawal. So are many Socialists, as well as a substantial number of Congressmen who have remained silent thus far, in deference to Nehru's strong feelings on the matter.

India's foreign policy has borne out Nehru's thesis that Commonwealth membership does not restrict its freedom of action. Nevertheless the connexion has exercised a subtle influence on Delhi's judgement of certain issues. There is firstly a more restrained criticism of British colonial policies than of the French, Dutch and Portuguese variety, amply revealed by Nehru's words and deeds on Malaya, Kenya and British Guiana on the one hand, and Indo-China, Indonesia and Goa on the other. The distinction may be intangible, but its existence is undeniable. Secondly, India's criticisms of the West have been directed more to the United States, though Britain is no less devoted to the alliance. Thirdly, with the qualified exception of the Suez War, India is inclined to be more favourably disposed to the British case where it would normally be staunchly anti-West. An excellent illustration is the involved negotiations over the seizure of the Anglo-Iranian oil properties in the early 'fifties. In general the evidence suggests that India's attitude to many international problems has been affected by the Commonwealth tie. The reverse is also true, the outstanding example being Nehru's plea for Commonwealth pressure to moderate American attitudes on the Chinese 'off-shore islands' crisis in 1955.

*   *   *   *

The record of Indo-American relations from 1947 to 1958 reveals a wide gulf between the two largest democratic states in the world. Notable examples of friction on international problems are the recognition of Communist China; the Japanese Peace Treaty; disarmament and nuclear tests; Kashmir; the type and conditions of foreign aid; and the value of military blocs. Even where their policies were in substantial agreement, it was qualified as in Korea (1950), Hungary (1956) and the Middle East (1956–7).

This divergence of policies was partly due to individuals—the lack of personal sympathy, understanding or trust between Nehru and Dulles. However, it stems from a more fundamental difference in world-view and in ideas about the tasks facing statesmen in the mid-twentieth century.

Nehru rejects the premises and, therefore, the policy proposals of the Dulles black and white, good and evil, argument. To divide the world into rigid moral categories, he says, is to indulge in fanciful self-righteousness. No state or way of life has a monopoly of truth or virtue. None is an absolute threat to peace and freedom. On the contrary, both East and West are guilty of provocative deeds and words. But both are firmly established and can only be eradicated by war. Since global war now means total annihilation, it is the absolute immoral act of our time. Indeed, the moral imperative is to rule out war and to search unceasingly for a negotiated settlement between the two blocs. The greater the area of the bloc system, the greater the likelihood of war. Hence non-alignment is vital to peace, an ethical and practical necessity. As long as India and the 'uncommitted' countries persist in this policy, they help to delay a catastrophe. And they perform the vital role of maintaining a link between the hostile blocs. Nehru also believes that the elimination of Colonialism and racialism are the most compelling immediate goals. The tasks of statesmanship, therefore, are to moderate the conflict between Communism and the West, to press for national self-determination and to struggle for racial equality.

Given this cleavage in basic outlook, disagreement on foreign policy questions is inevitable. Yet India and the United States are akin in many respects. They share a belief in the dignity of the individual and the rights of man. Their political institutions derive from the same roots. They reject the theory and practice of Communism. And in so far as modern India has been influenced by non-Asian ideas and institutions, that influence has been overwhelmingly of the democratic West. Thus, to term India pro-Soviet is to mistake appearance for reality.

It is true that India has criticized the United States more frequently than the Soviet Union. The reasons are many and complex. The hangover of emotional hostility to the West because of colonialism affects even a convinced rationalist like Nehru. With the departure of the British this feeling was transferred to the U.S., the assumed successor to British interests in many parts of Asia. Moreover, all politically conscious Indians are sensitive to racial discrimination. The image of America held by many includes the inferior position of the Negro. The Soviet Union, by contrast, is believed to be a land of racial equality. Another reason for India's softer tone towards Moscow is its acceptance of India's non-alignment without qualms. Moreover, the Soviet Union, alone of the Great Powers, has supported India's claim to Kashmir, a crucial test of friendship in Indian eyes. The failure of the United States to match Russia's denunciation of South Africa's policy of *apartheid* has a similar effect. Furthermore, Indian leaders are acutely conscious of their geographic position. In their view it is wise to tread lightly when confronted with powerful neighbours.

There were also certain factors which antedate the Cold War. First was the powerful attraction of Marxism for the Indian intelligentsia in the 'thirties. This created an initial climate of opinion favourable to the Soviet experiment. Intimately related was the admiration for the far-reaching changes brought about by the Soviet revolution, particularly because they concerned problems which were similar to those of India: illiteracy, land, industrialization and nationalities. This does not mean that Indian leaders were enamoured of Soviet methods. Nehru himself was profoundly troubled by the regimentation, the intolerance and the ruthlessness, and made known his reservations from the outset. With the passage of time his hostility to Communist methods became more outspoken. So too did his critique of Marxism. Finally, there is the practical consideration of Soviet economic aid. India is anxious to keep the door open to both worlds in order to expedite economic development.

Indo-American relations have not been consistently strained, nor have Indo-Soviet relations been consistently friendly. During the first two years of independence Delhi was more favourably disposed towards Washington, and the Soviets dubbed India an 'Anglo-American satellite'. Relations with the United States cooled after Nehru's unsuccessful bid for large-scale American aid without strings in the autumn of 1949. The period of greatest stress was 1953–4 when American arms aid to Pakistan seemed like a dagger pointed at India. Delhi began to see more virtue in Soviet policy, and Moscow reciprocated by hailing India's neutralism. But the friction with Washington eased considerably towards the end of 1956 as a result of America's pro-Egyptian stand during the Suez crisis, at the expense of its chief allies. At the same time Indian trust in the Soviets received a rude shock with the brutal suppression of the Hungarian revolt. From that point onwards the scales were more evenly balanced in the mind of Nehru and others.

*   *   *   *

India's outstanding achievement in foreign policy has been to provide leadership in the political awakening of Asia after centuries of colonial rule. The Indian National Congress served as a model for the intelligentsia of South-east Asia and to a lesser extent of the Middle East. India's freedom in 1947 was the major break in European control of the Asian rimland and hastened the coming of independence throughout the area—Ceylon and Burma in 1948, Indonesia in 1949 and Malaya in 1957. The withdrawal of British power from the sub-continent also influenced the course of events in the Middle East, for with the loss of its imperial bastion England could no longer retain its paramount influence in the Arab world. There were, of course, other factors responsible for the steady decline of colonialism—the devastating effects of the Japanese sweep through East Asia in the early 1940's, the rise of America to world power and the intervention of both the United States and the Soviet Union in the area as a whole. But it was India's attainment of political freedom which set the process in motion.

Nehru had often proclaimed the goal of closer relations with all Asian states. Although he has persistently denied any claim to Asian leadership, he is acutely conscious of a 'special position' which makes India pre-eminently fitted to play this role. 'India is the central point of the Asian picture,' he remarked in 1949. 'India's role of leadership may not be so welcome to others although it may satisfy our vanity. But it is something which we cannot escape. We cannot escape the various responsibilities that arise out of our geography and history.'[1]

On the eve of Independence he summoned the peoples of Asia to the first Asian Relations Conference in modern history. Two years later this was followed by an emergency Conference of Asian states in Delhi to bring pressure upon the Dutch and the U.N. in order to facilitate Indonesian independence. From 1950 onwards India has co-operated with its immediate neighbours in a loose grouping known as the Colombo Powers. And in 1955 Nehru's efforts culminated in the historic Afro-Asian Conference at Bandung, a gathering of twenty-nine non-Western states, most of whom had only recently emerged from a lengthy period of colonial rule.

It would be wrong to exaggerate the importance of Bandung in *contemporary* world politics, for little emerged of a practical value. The divisive forces—ideological, economic and other—were sharp. No permanent organization was created. A third bloc did not ensue. None the less, the mere fact that these states gathered together symbolized Asia's reawakening.

The principal contribution to the 'Bandung spirit' was undoubtedly made by Nehru during the preceding decade.[2] However, he has failed to forge the kind of non-aligned Asian group which he considers necessary for world peace. Only Burma and

[1] To the Overseas Press Club in New York. Nehru, *Inside America*, pp. 54-55.
[2] For an account of the Bandung Conference see Kahin, G. Mct., *The Asian-African Conference* (1956).

Indonesia adhere to the policy of non-alignment. Ceylon is sympathetic, and Cambodia follows India's lead in so far as its freedom of action permits. But Asia is largely fragmented into blocs which are controlled from outside the area: Japan, South Korea, South Viet Nam, Formosa, the Philippines, Thailand, Malaya and Pakistan are closely tied to the Western bloc; China, North Viet Nam and North Korea are part of the Communist bloc. In West Asia, India's 'middle way' has found more adherents, but the states of the area are weak and generally unstable. In the formal sense, then, Nehru has not succeeded in creating a materially significant third force.

And yet, the notion of an 'area of peace' has assumed increasing importance in world affairs, as the balance of power between the West and Communism approaches equality. Regardless of what the smaller Asian states do, India's deeds and words are treated with respect. For in the last analysis the future of Asia rests primarily on the course of events in India and China. China has already made its choice. India remains 'uncommitted'. Barring some unforeseen shift in internal Indian politics, it will continue to plough this lonely furrow, certainly as long as Nehru dominates the national political scene. It will do so because of the firm conviction that in this way it will contribute to the basic objectives of Indian foreign policy—the preservation of independence and economic development—and to the goal of world peace.

CHAPTER XIV

PORTRAIT OF A LEADER

Few statesmen in the twentieth century have reached the stature of Jawaharlal Nehru. As the pre-eminent figure in India's era of transition he bears comparison with Roosevelt and Churchill, Lenin and Mao, men who guided their people through a period of national crisis. Only Gandhi inspired greater faith and adoration among the masses. Only Stalin, perhaps, had greater power. Like these outstanding men of the age he has also imposed his personality on a wider canvas. He is for many a symbol of Asia's political awakening. His name conjures up a host of associations—resolute fighter for national freedom, Gandhi's devoted aide, the Mediator, the neutral in a struggle between good and evil, the self-appointed guardian of morality in international affairs. Yet friends and foes alike recognize him as a leading actor on the stage of contemporary history.

What enabled Nehru to achieve this illustrious position? What are the sources of his power and popularity? The key to his extraordinary appeal is a host of personal qualities which have long attracted people in India and in far-off lands. His courage is renowned. So are his integrity and selflessness, his sincerity of purpose and his devotion to Indian freedom and world peace. Some have been drawn by his generosity and loyalty to colleagues, others by his honesty and apparent purity of motive. Few have failed to succumb to his inordinate charm. Many respect his detachment and intellectual tolerance, his idealism and abnegation of absolute power. For others still he is the romantic hero in politics, the impulsive, youthful and daring leader of men, intensely human, fearless, and champion of the oppressed. In words attributed to Sir Winston Churchill, an outspoken foe of Indian Independence, 'here is a man without malice and without fear'.[1]

[1] Quoted in Rao, B. Shiva, 'Jawaharlal Nehru, Crusader for Freedom' in *The Hindu Weekly Review* (Madras), 18 November 1957.

Most Westernized Indian intellectuals viewed Nehru in this light during the past thirty years, for he was the ideal expression of their class. Indian by birth yet Western by education, modern in outlook yet influenced by the heritage of his native land, a staunch patriot with international vision, he was the symbol of a new society—liberal, humanist and equalitarian.

The rare appeal of Jawaharlal Nehru arose from his combination of contradictory elements. As one of his admirers remarked in the mid-1940's, he is explosive in speech, disciplined in action, impulsive in gestures, deliberate in judgement, revolutionary in aim, conservative in loyalty, reckless of personal safety, cautious about matters affecting Indian welfare. The same writer, Krishna Kripalani, observed: 'An aristocrat in love with the masses, a nationalist who represents the culture of the foreigner, an intellectual caught up in the maelstrom of an emotional upheaval—the very paradox of his personality has surrounded it with a halo.'[1]

Nehru drew the intelligentsia to the Congress as Gandhi mesmerized the peasantry. Yet he appealed to the rural masses as well, in time acquiring a popularity only slightly less than that of the Mahatma. Nehru, with his constant broadsides on the injustice of the land system and his pledge for a new order in the countryside, was their hope for the future.

For many years he was Gandhi's acknowledged heir. This alone endowed him with enormous prestige. He had, too, the halo of a modern prince who had sacrificed wealth and leisure in the struggle for independence. And he benefited from the tradition of hero-worship. No one was more suited to the role. This, indeed, has been one of the pillars of his support since 1947. Moreover, as the co-architect of independence, Nehru is the continuing symbol of the freedom struggle. The only two conceivable rivals have long since passed from the scene—Subhas Bose in 1945 and Sardar Patel in 1950. Since that time he has been the last remaining hero of the Indian revolution.

In the broadest sense Nehru's influence derives from his role as the strategic link among diverse groups in Indian society. The older politicians in the Congress value his loyalty, the younger ones look to him for inspiration; the Right wing finds him indispensable, the Left wing has always considered him amenable; he

Gandhi, Tagore and Nehru, p. 73.

was and is reasonable enough for capitalists, radical enough for most socialists; and many peasants view him as their main hope for land reform. Intellectuals see him as the bridge between tradition and the modern world. This unique role is strengthened by Nehru's political philosophy.

In the realm of thought Nehru has always been a lonely traveller seeking answers that seem to elude his grasp. Almost all the ideological currents of the past half-century appealed to his keen and receptive mind: first in time was classical liberalism with its emphasis on individual rights; then, at Cambridge, he was drawn to Fabian Socialism; thereafter, he was influenced by the Gandhian stress on the purity of means and the message of non-violence; and in the late 'twenties and 'thirties by Marxist theory and the gospel of a classless society. He was also attracted to the ethical norms of Western humanism, and later, during his long war-time imprisonment, to the precepts of the *Vedanta*, the ancient system of Hindu philosophy, but stripped of its purely meta-physical and religious beliefs. Underlying all was a passionate devotion to the ideas of nationalism and racial equality. None of these dominated his outlook; all of them influenced his thought. Indeed, the key to his thinking is scepticism about all claims to absolute truth and virtue.

Scattered throughout his voluminous writings are fragments of a world outlook. Nowhere is there a systematic personal and political philosophy—for Nehru is an eclectic in intellectual matters. Nevertheless, he did set down his mature reflections in *The Discovery of India*. Many years after they were penned, Nehru told the author these were his most considered thoughts on 'Life's Philosophy'.

As in all his writings there are moving passages. There are, too, candour and humility, intellectual tolerance and gnawing doubt about the right path. 'What was my philosophy of life [in the late 'thirties]?' he asked at the outset. 'I did not know. . . . The ideals and objectives of yesterday were still the ideals of today but they had lost some of their lustre. . . . Evil triumphed often enough, but what was far worse was the coarsening and distortion of what had seemed so right.'

His constant dilemma over means and ends received this expression: 'What then was one to do? Not to act was a complete confession of failure and a submission to evil; to act meant often enough a compromise with some form of that evil, with all the untoward consequences that such compromises result in.'

Despite this uncertainty and occasional lapses into pessimism, faith in the future and in science emerge from this self-analysis. There emerges, too, a portrait of a humanist with a passionate interest in the welfare of men: 'The real problems for me', he affirmed, 'remain problems of individual and social life . . . of the ceaseless adventure of man. In the solution of these problems the way of observation and precise knowledge and deliberate reasoning, according to the method of science, must be followed. . . . A living philosophy must answer the problems of today.'

Partly because of his preoccupation with material problems, he was indifferent to religion as a guide to action. In fact, orthodox religion as practised in the modern world repelled him while mysticism irritated him. Here, as elsewhere, he boldly proclaimed his agnosticism. But he felt strongly attracted to an 'ethical approach to life' and acknowledged the profound influence of Gandhi. His intellectual debt to Marxism was also acknowledged. However, 'it did not satisfy me completely [because] life is too complicated and, as far as we can understand it in our present state of knowledge, too illogical for it to be confined within the four corners of a fixed doctrine.'

Perhaps because of the difficulty in resolving the many philosophical dilemmas, his attitude was to concentrate on the immediate, urgent and concrete problems of life. This is, indeed, the essence of Nehru's approach, to merge thought and action in the achievement of social goals. 'The call of action has long been with me,' he wrote in 1944, 'not action divorced from thought, but rather flowing from it in one continuous sequence. And when, rarely, there has been full harmony between the two . . . then I have sensed a certain fullness of life and a vivid intensity in that moment of existence. . . . I am not enamoured of death, though I do not think it frightens me. . . . I have loved life and it attracts me still. . . . Without that passion and urge [to action], there is a gradual oozing out of hope and vitality, a settling down on lower levels of existence, a slow merging into non-existence.' The discourse ends on a typically ambivalent note: 'Whatever gods there be there is something godlike in man, as there is also something of the devil in him.'

The world has changed since Nehru reflected upon his philosophy of life. But the essentials of his outlook remain unchanged. The central fact is that he does not possess a systematic world-view. He does not cling to ideas as such but views them in a social setting.

The principal strand in his thinking is Western liberalism as expressed in his firm devotion to political democracy and individual freedom. Socialism is also rooted in his thought, providing the stimulus to planning and the stress on social and economic equality. Gandhism provides the basic approach to social, economic and political change, i.e., the method of morally sanctioned non-violent change—though many find his attitude to Kashmir a striking deviation from this attitude. And nationalism is the vital force behind India's claim to recognition, as well as the right to independence for all colonial peoples.

In this practical sense the four main strands in Nehru's social and political philosophy have been reconciled. At different times one or another will predominate in accordance with the needs of India in transition. But they remain the broad guides to policy. Flexible on tactics, he is rigid on goals: democratic socialism, achieved by planning, secularism or, more correctly, equal rights for all communities in the Indian family, rising standards of living for the masses, and the preservation of individual rights. These may be termed his fixed objectives.

Nehru is a convinced socialist but he is not a Communist. The record of word and deed is clear on this point. He drank deeply of Marxist literature in the 'thirties but he *never* became intoxicated. Indeed, at the very height of his attraction to Communism he remained the sceptic, impressed by certain Soviet achievements but repelled by their methods, influenced by the Marxist interpretation of history but unalterably opposed to its dogma, enamoured of Communist ideals but distressed by Communist practice.

The second world war proved to be the turning-point as far as his attitude to *Indian* Communists was concerned. Their 'betrayal of the nationalist movement'—their co-operation with the Government after the 'August Revolt' and the imprisonment of the Congress leaders in 1942—rankled deeply. In 1945 he served on a special party committee which recommended the expulsion of all Communists from the Congress. Since that time Nehru has been increasingly critical of the C.P.I. In one of his sharpest attacks he declared: 'They have no moorings in the land of their birth, but always look to outside countries for inspiration and guidance. They are of the opinion that internecine trouble, violence and bloodshed are the main things to be pursued.' And he denounced them for maligning their country while abroad.[1]

Nehru's most scathing indictment of Communism as an idea and a system was written in 1958: 'Its contempt for what might be called the moral and spiritual side of life . . . deprives human behaviour of standards and values. Its unfortunate association with violence encourages a certain evil tendency in human beings. . . . Its language is of violence, its thought is violent [and it seeks change] by coercion and, indeed, by destruction and extermination.'[2]

Nehru's attitude to Marxism, Communism and the Indian Communist Party could not have been otherwise, given his temperament, values and philosophy of life. He has always been unable to identify himself wholeheartedly with a rigid body of doctrine. He was and is too much the nationalist to be a doctrinaire socialist and too much the aristocrat to be dominated by a proletarian party.

Where then shall we place him? He is a liberal and a democrat, a socialist and an individualist. Most of all, he is a humanist in the best tradition of East and West. His creed is best defined as democratic socialism and refined and humane materialism.

One change in his outlook since the mid-1950's is a growing attraction to Buddhism. The explanation seems to be that he is drawn to its stress on free will, its contempt for superstition, and its message of non-violence. Nehru's admiration for Buddhism was expressed during an unusual incident when the Soviet leaders visited India at the end of 1955. A proud and enthusiastic Nikita Khruschev greeted him one day with the news that Soviet scientists had just perfected a terrifying weapon of mass destruction. The Indian Prime Minister listened politely to the bubbling and boastful tale and then reportedly responded in the following manner. 'You know, Mr. Khruschev, more than two thousand years ago a great warrior ruled over India. His name was Emperor Ashoka. Through frequent wars he extended his

---

[1] *The Hindu* (Madras), 29 November 1954.
[2] 'Nehru on "The Tragic Paradox of Our Age"' in the *New York Times Magazine*, 7 September 1958, pp. 13 and 110.

dominion throughout the land. His generals were victorious every-where, and after every battle they would report thousands killed and many taken as slaves. Ashoka became troubled by this slaughter, and in time was converted to Buddhism. One day, after a victorious campaign, a general informed him that many more thousands had perished and untold destruction had been visited on his enemies. The Emperor could stand it no longer. Getting up from his throne, he removed his sword from its scabbard, broke it in two, and thundered, "Enough violence and carnage. There shall be no more. Peace will reign over the land." ' Khruschev listened attentively, but as far as is known he made no comment.

The true measure of Nehru's humanism, his tolerance and his liberalism, is perhaps best revealed in the following extempora-neous remarks to the author on 'what constitutes a good society and the good life?'

Broadly speaking, apart from the material things that are necessary, obviously, a certain individual growth in the society. For I do believe that ultimately it is the individual that counts. I can't say that I believe in it because I have no proof, but the idea appeals to me without belief, the old Hindu idea that if there is any divine essence in the world every individual possesses a bit of it . . . and he can develop it. Therefore, no individual is trivial. Every individual has an importance and he should be given full opportunities to develop—material opportunities naturally, food, clothing, education, housing, health, etc. They should be common to everybody. I do believe in certain standards. Call them moral stan-dards, call them what you like, spiritual standards. They are important in any individual and in any social group. And if they fade away, I think that all the material advancement you may have will lead to nothing worthwhile. How to maintain them I don't know; I mean to say, there is the religious approach. It seems to me rather a narrow approach with its forms and all kinds of ceremonials. And yet, I am not prepared to deny that approach. If a person feels comforted by that, it is not for me to remove that sense of comfort. I don't mind—I think it's silly for a man to worship a stone but if a man is comforted by worshipping a stone why should I come in his way. If it raises him above his normal level it is good for him. Whatever raises a person above his normal level is good, how-ever he approaches that—provided he does not sit on somebody and force him to do it. That is a different matter. So while I attach very considerable value to moral and spiritual standards, apart from religion as such, I don't quite know how one maintains them in modern life. It's a prob-lem.

*   *   *   *

Individualist though he may be, Nehru does not live in a self-contained universe. The magnitude of his responsibilities compels him to rely on others. Who, then, are the persons who share(d) his confidence? Whose judgement does he respect? For the period before Independence one is on reasonably sure ground. One man, Mahatma Gandhi, held Nehru's complete trust and confidence. A rare meeting of minds and hearts had developed over the years. Disagreements there were, of course, but never so keen as to affect the bonds that linked them in indissoluble friendship. Since the Mahatma's death in 1948 Nehru has not shown complete trust in any man. He seems to rely on different persons for different purposes. Moreover, the élite groups around the Prime Minister have changed through time in response to diverse pressures.

During the early years Nehru's confidant for internal politics and administration was Rajagopalacharia, the south Indian elder statesman. However, growing friction on sundry issues led to Rajaji's resignation towards the end of 1951. His successor in this role was Gopalaswami Ayyangar, the much-criticized U.N. spokesman for India in the early stages of the Kashmir dispute. The gap created by Ayyangar's death in 1953 was filled by Rafi Ahmad Kidwai, the second-ranking nationalist Muslim in India. A superb administrator, Kidwai was a nimble and shrewd political tactician with a brilliant sense of timing. As a close personal and family friend he had ready access to the Prime Minister; he spoke his mind fearlessly, and Nehru listened. His death in 1954 was a grievous personal and political blow and a great loss for the Congress. Since the beginning of 1955 the position of key adviser on internal politics has been held by Pandit Pant, the Home Minister.

If there was one man whose position approximated to Gandhi's as the recipient of Nehru's complete confidence it was Maulana Azad, leader of India's Muslims. For thirty-five years they were intimately associated in the Congress. Moreover, they were intellectually akin, even though one was a Western-type agnostic and the other a Muslim divine. At the basis of their relationship was genuine affection and mutual respect which ripened into a mature friendship. Of all the Congress leaders, Azad was the most detached after Independence, free of the struggle for power and prestige. As a result Nehru used to consult him frequently about all manner of decisions. With Azad he could open his heart to an old comrade. The Maulana had the unique distinction of being a member of all but one of the Prime Minister's élite groups: in the party's High Command, on internal Indian politics, in foreign affairs, and in the private sphere. When he died in 1958, Nehru reportedly wept as he delivered a moving eulogy. Like Gandhi and Patel he was a giant of the nationalist movement.

The wielders of influence on Nehru's foreign policy have already been noted. Overshadowing all since 1954 has been Krishna Menon. The Congress élite has changed little since the death of Patel in 1950. The key group is the Working Committee of about twenty members. But of these only a half-dozen were and are involved in making important decisions. Other than Nehru and Azad, the dominant figures have been Pant, Morarji Desai and Dr. B. C. Roy. Approaching the inner group is Lal Bahadur Shastri of the U.P. In the central Cabinet, as already noted, it is much the same group. Following the Prime Minister, the unofficial ranking is Pant, Morarji Desai and Shastri, with Krishna Menon occupying a special status in foreign affairs.

The position of economic adviser to the Prime Minister has been occupied by a succession of persons with widely diverging views. An important formative influence was Professor K. T. Shah, a professional economist of leftist convictions who directed the Congress's National Planning Committee from 1938 to 1946. In the aftermath of Partition the conservative ideas of Shanmukham Chetty and Dr. John Matthai, the first two Finance Ministers, tended to hold sway. Throughout the period of the First Plan Nehru gave *carte blanche* to Finance Minister C. D. Deshmukh. Within the Planning Commission the Vice-Chairman, V. T. Krishnamachari, provided wise counsel and administrative guidance.

One other person, Professor P. C. Mahalanobis, must be noted in this connexion. A brilliant statistician who was honoured with membership of the British Royal Society in 1945, Mahalanobis later achieved further renown as Director of the Indian Statistical Institute in Calcutta. From that vantage point he became involved in high-level economic planning. The Left wing has applauded his role, for Mahalanobis is the most articulate spokesman for radical state planning using the lessons of Soviet and Chinese experience—though he is not averse to Western technical and capital aid. The business community and conservatives generally consider him the grey eminence who is steering the Prime Minister into dangerous waters. Mahalanobis holds no official position, but his title, Honorary Statistical Adviser to the Government of India, does not represent a true measure of his influence. He is a key figure in Nehru's economic entourage with ready access to the Prime Minister, whose interest in science redounds to Mahalanobis's advantage.

One person dominates the scene in the Prime Minister's Residence—which many Indians consider a modern version of the Moghul Court: Mrs. Indira Gandhi, Nehru's charming daughter. She lives in her father's home and is constantly by his side.

Mrs. Gandhi is devoted to the care of her father, a widower for more than twenty years. By all accounts, she is an indispensable companion. Her functions are many and varied: official hostess at the Residence; Mistress of the Household; guardian of her father's health—in so far as his temperament permits—and travelling companion on almost all tours within India and abroad. Long overshadowed by her father, rather shy and retiring, and never in robust health, she has only recently emerged as a public figure in her own right. During the past few years she has been actively associated with many social welfare and women's agencies. In politics, too, she has become influential—a member of the Congress Working Committee since 1955 and of the powerful Central Election Committee of the party. (In 1959 she was president of the Congress.)

Her views on public issues are to the moderate Left. One significant index is her support for the Congress 'Ginger Group'. Her direct influence on the Prime Minister cannot be gauged precisely but must be considerable. She is, perhaps, the only person with whom Nehru can discuss most matters at ease, and the sheer amount of time which she spends in his company gives her a strategic position. She has also taken the burden of responsibility from her father in various secondary matters.

Mrs. Gandhi (and earlier, M. O. Mathais, a controversial 'special Assistant' to the Prime Minister) is the key figure in the 'court circle', but she is not alone. Mme Pandit has ready access to her brother and lives at the Residence during her infrequent visits to the capital. So too does her younger sister, Mrs. Hutheesingh, though she has no influence on public affairs. Another member of the select group is Gopi Handoo, sometime personal bodyguard of the Prime Minister and a senior security officer of the Indian Government. A special position is held by India's distinguished philosopher—Vice-President Dr. Radhakrishnan, whose wise counsel is often sought by Nehru.

At the time of writing, the influential people around Nehru would seem to be as follows: Pandit Pant for internal politics and administration; Krishna Menon for foreign policy; Pant, Morarji Desai, B. C. Roy and Shastri for party affairs; Mahalanobis for economic matters; Mrs. Gandhi in the private sphere; and Radhakrishnan as an elder statesman.

*   *   *   *

Nehru's public life thus far has spanned a period of forty years. What does the record reveal? What were his contributions to the nationalist movement? What are his achievements—and failures —as India's Prime Minister? What are his strengths and weaknesses as a political leader? And what is the likely legacy of his stewardship since 1947? Finally, what appear to be the prospects for India after Nehru?

We are on relatively sure ground with the nationalist phase of his career. We know that he was Gandhi's principal aide in the non-violent war for independence. We know, too, that he was beloved by the masses. We know of his writings and of his years in prison. Indeed, we are now in a position to assess his contributions to Indian nationalism.

Perhaps his most distinctive service was to prevent the movement from becoming narrowly nationalistic. In fact, he alone fashioned a Congress 'foreign policy'. Other members of the High Command were indifferent to this aspect of the struggle. Yet his relentless campaign penetrated their thought and widened their horizon. Nehru's second major contribution was to add a social and economic content to the meaning of *swaraj*. Independence, he argued, was the immediate goal but must be viewed as a prelude to the transformation of Indian society; and even during the political struggle a far-reaching reform programme should be enunciated. He hammered on this theme in his presidential addresses to the Congress in 1929, 1936, 1937 and 1946, in his writings and in innumerable speeches throughout the country.

Nehru was not alone in this view, but his influence gave it special weight in the party.

The twin vision of Jawaharlal Nehru made him the voice of Indian youth. This was another contribution, to enlist their active support for the nationalist cause. In performing this role Nehru made another, indirect, contribution: he offered the militant and radical youth a satisfying alternative to Communism. Because of his pledge of land reform and his magnetic personality he also attracted the rural masses to the Congress, supplementing the traditionalist appeal of Gandhi.

Not only did Nehru make the Congress conscious of the outside world. He also made the world aware of India and the struggle for independence. His autobiography in particular became the authentic voice of Indian nationalism, and Nehru became the symbol of a people in revolt. To a large extent it moulded the attitude of the North American intelligentsia to India in the early 'forties. And in England it provided ammunition for those elements who favoured early British withdrawal. Even among Tories it evoked a sympathetic response and raised doubts about the morality of continued British rule.

Within India, Nehru provided still another link—between the Congress and the All-India States People's Conference, which espoused the nationalist ideal in the princely States. Nehru was not responsible for its creation but he played an increasingly active role in strengthening the bonds between the two groups. To the militant popular leaders in the States, like Sheikh Abdullah of Kashmir, it was Nehru who provided the main source of inspiration. In the Congress proper Nehru rendered other services. Along with Subhas Bose he placed the issue of complete independence in the forefront of the party's deliberations as early as 1928. Moreover, he made the Congress plan-conscious, another seed which bore fruit after independence.

On the organizational side of party affairs Nehru's role has been deprecated in the face of Sardar Patel's administrative genius. Yet he was, with Gandhi, the party's voice to the Indian masses and the Congress's prize vote-getter. He was also intimately involved in the shaping of its programme and shared with Gandhi the role of principal draftsman of resolutions and manifestos. There remains one final contribution. Nehru's political, moral and personal integrity set an inspiring example and served as a bastion in a movement which, like all movements, was affected by different motives and impulses. Taken together, these contributions form an impressive record, perhaps without peer among political revolutionaries of this century. Gandhi's role in the attainment of Indian independence was greater, but Gandhi lacked Nehru's vision, both international and social.

How shall we judge Nehru's record of leadership since independence? Perhaps the best test is the extent to which he has translated his ideas into reality. Nehru has long considered himself a revolutionary; he denies the necessity of violence and stresses the elements of consent, gradualism and mass participation.

That India is in the midst of a revolution is beyond doubt. That Nehru has been its philosopher and guide, its voice, indeed, its very spirit, is also unquestionable. That it has been non-violent, gradual, democratic and, in the main, supported by the bulk of the Indian people can be easily demonstrated. The price, however, is severe: the pace and scope of the revolution do not measure up to Nehru's own expectations and are not adequate to the needs of India at this critical point in its history.

Along with his role as the symbol of Indian unity, Nehru has four major achievements in domestic affairs since 1947: political stability and democracy; the Plans; a secular state; and social change. Together they represent substantial progress.

The Constitution was drafted largely by Ambedkar, but Nehru provided its basic philosophy and goals in the Objectives Resolution. Moreover, his decision to hold elections as soon as the crises of the Partition were over helped to create the beginnings of a pattern of political democracy. Within a decade of Independence a democratic constitution has been enacted, two nation-wide elections have been held, and a parliamentary system of government has been established. The test of its durability, however, is still to come, but its growth has been encouraging. The final accomplishment in this sphere has been a strong, stable government.

Against this must be set inefficiency, maladministration and corruption. Nehru himself has frequently criticized the central bureaucracy as 'an administrative jungle'. The blame for this state of affairs rests largely with him. The problem is not that Nehru does not discharge his responsibilities; he over-discharges them.

The fact is that Nehru is an inept administrator. Decisions are concentrated in his hands to an incredible degree. He lacks both the talent and temperament to co-ordinate the work of the various ministries. Nor has he ever shown a capacity or inclination to delegate authority. The result has been the 'administrative jungle' which he bemoans. When Nehru is out of the country decision-making comes to a virtual halt. And even while he is in Delhi the bureaucracy functions only as rapidly as he can handle the vast amount of paper that crosses his desk. The long-term implications are no less disturbing. The habit of dependence on Nehru, a disease of Indian administration, has hindered the growth of self-reliance among those who will have to carry the burden of decision when 'Panditji' is no longer present.

The second area of achievement—and failure—has been economic affairs. The First Plan, modest in scope, was successful. The Second Plan ran into stormy weather in 1957–8, but the core remains. Nehru is also primarily responsible for the Community Development Programme. Psychological gains have been disappointing, but material progress thus far has been not inconsiderable.

Against these achievements must be set the inadequate land reform programme. Nehru himself has criticized its pace and scope .On occasion he has fought for more radical agrarian reform, and when he fought he was successful. By and large, however, he has not given it the importance it deserves. Indeed, the slow progress in land reform is the most striking failure in the economic sphere. More generally, social and economic change since 1947 have been less than that pledged, less than required, and less than possible.

This shortcoming points up one of Nehru's weaknesses as a political leader: the gap between words and deeds is often wide. Over the years he has denounced many features of Indian public life, but the matter frequently rested there. He has attacked nepotism and corruption in the civil service but has never acted against them. He has deplored the cesspools of disease and degradation that are the slums of Delhi and other major cities, but they remain. He has castigated black-marketeering and other nefarious aspects of Indian business life; in the earlier days, he even threatened to shoot or whip the guilty. But these practices continue. Of course, Nehru alone cannot solve all the problems of

Indian society. But rhetoric alone will not improve the situation. By his constant verbal attacks on things which offend his sensitivity, often without doing anything about them, he has tended to 'cheapen the coinage'. The gap between words and deeds suggests something else. In some instances it is not the lack of time or the inability to change institutions overnight; rather, it is a tendency to shrink from radical deeds. Nehru is a social reformer; he is not a social revolutionary.

Perhaps his most notable accomplishment is the creation of a secular state. Immediately after Partition, Hindu-Muslim tension was so great that only courage and resolution could safeguard the security of India's largest minority. Nehru achieved this—against strong opposition, even within his own party. He did so largely by force of personality but also by a clear indication that he would act decisively against communal violence. Communal harmony has not yet been fully realized, but the wounds of 1947 are gradually being healed. To Indian Muslims Nehru is a rock and a shield. Wherever possible he has bent over backwards to give them special consideration. It is no mere accident that the Foreign Office has the highest proportion of Muslim senior officers, except for the Education Ministry which was headed by a Muslim, Maulana Azad. Nehru's contribution has been to ease the transition to greater mutual trust between Hindus and Muslims and to embody the secular ideal in the Indian Constitution. He has also maintained a continuous onslaught on the ideas of communalism. With each passing year of Nehru's tenure as Prime Minister the forces of communalism are weakened. The secular state is likely to be Nehru's most enduring contribution to India, and it is the one of which he is most proud.

In the field of social reform proper the most noteworthy developments are the abolition of untouchability and the enactment of the Hindu Code Bills. Strong pressures were brought to bear on the reform of the ancient Hindu code; opponents could look to President Prasad and others for support. Nehru finally forced the issue and secured their passage through Parliament after four years, though he was compelled to make various concessions.

The record of Nehru's foreign policy has already been dealt with. It is sufficient to note an intangible contribution here. For almost two centuries before Independence India's voice was inaudible. In less than a decade, however, Nehru has raised his country's prestige and his people's national pride as no Indian but Gandhi has done in centuries. He has not resolved all disputes, particularly with his neighbours. But these pale into insignificance when set against India's and Nehru's stature in the world at large.

*   *   *   *

Some years ago Nehru set down his thoughts on the proper role of a leader: 'If he is a leader, he must lead and not merely follow the dictates of the crowd. . . . If he acts singly, according to his own lights, he cuts himself off from the very persons whom he is trying to lead. If he brings himself down to the same level of understanding as others, then he has lowered himself, been untrue to his own ideal, and compromised that truth. And once such compromises begin, there is no end to them and the path is slippery. What then is he to do? . . . He must succeed in making others perceive [this truth] also.'[1]

How does Nehru measure up to his own conception of a leader? Some of his weaknesses have already been noted. There are others. Perhaps his gravest defect is indecision. Moreover, he is completely lacking in ruthlessness. But there are times in the affairs of a nation when ruthlessness is desirable. It may well be that Nehru is an excessively pure democrat. Not only does he refuse to impose his will on the country—an admirable quality in a burgeoning democracy—but he seems to have a compulsion for universal consent. Partly this is due to his stress on mass participation; but in part it is due to an instinctive playing to the gallery, a desire to please the crowd, the ultimate basis of his political power. He tries to please everyone and so arrives at decisions slowly. In extreme cases, too, he will displease many.

Closely related to these defects is the tendency to yield to pressure. This was true in the years before Independence when Nehru frequently gave way to Gandhi and the Right wing of the Congress. It has also been true since Independence. A notable example was the concession to the demand for a separate state of Andhra in 1952.

According to many who know him well, Nehru is a bad judge of character. He is also blinded by past loyalties and previous

[1] Foreword to Tendulkar, *Mahatma*, p. xiii.

service of colleagues whom he retains in high party or govern-mental positions after they no longer merit this trust and influence. His normal response to charges of corruption is to dismiss them as gossip or to question the accused directly and to accept his denial without further investigation. He has never openly forced the resignation of a colleague—though on occasion he has made it difficult for a person not to resign. Thus the highest echelons of party and government are filled with dead wood, old and tired men who have outlived their political usefulness to the country. They remain in power and prevent the training of younger men for the tasks of tomorrow. Finally during more than a decade in power Nehru has not trained a successor group who can assure continuity in policy after he retires or dies. To many Indians this is the most disquieting feature of his leadership, the seeming lack of concern about tomorrow.

At first glance this catalogue of failings seems formidable. But these weaknesses have to be viewed in perspective. For Nehru is a giant, both as man and statesman. If political greatness be measured by the capacity to direct events, to rise above the crest of the waves, to guide his people, and to serve as a catalyst of pro-gress, then Nehru surely qualifies for greatness. Almost single-handed he has endeavoured to lift his people into the twentieth century. He has provided a symbol of unity at a time of great stress. He has laid the foundations of a working parliamentary democracy. He has fashioned the machinery for planning. He provided the philosophy for India's new Constitution with its emphasis on individual rights and the ideal of a secular and equalitarian society. He has restored India's faith in itself as well as its place in the family of nations. And he has begun the task of social reform.

In a wider sense Nehru has set in motion forces for long-term social, economic and political change. The abolition of untouch-ability and the ceaseless attack on casteism are steps towards the undermining of the caste system, the hard core of the Hindu social order. The new Hindu Code may well serve as a liberating force for Hindu women who for millennia have occupied a subordinate status. The Five-Year Plans and the Community Development Projects are breathing fresh air into the village. Whether or not these forces will realize their potentialities depends on many factors. But Nehru has fashioned the elements out of which can emerge a new India. The revolution is still unfinished; indeed it has barely begun.

On the international stage Nehru speaks for a large part of the Afro-Asian world. For many Westerners he is one of the few voices of sanity as the world hovers on the brink of disaster. For many he is the genuine voice of peace. In nineteenth-century terms he may be compared to Cavour with an admixture of Garibaldi, i.e., a nation-builder with the dash of the romantic nationalist. To this might be added Wilson in the twentieth century, the spokesman for idealist internationalism. But all comparisons fail to convey the measure of any man. Nehru is Nehru, a man and a leader to be measured in the age in which he lives.

*   *   *   *

'After Nehru who? After Nehru what?' These two questions have disturbed Indians and foreigners alike since the early 1950's. As Nehru approached his seventieth year a sense of urgency about the future became apparent. The Prime Minister was ageing quickly. He sought a respite from the gruelling pace of work and the responsibility which he had carried since Independence; but in vain. So it had been in 1954 also. But what would happen the third time, or the fourth, or the fifth? Some day Nehru would no longer be on hand to guide his people. For many there is anxiety.

The problem of succession to the Prime Ministership is rarely acute in stable democracies. There, established institutions and conventions usually assure a smooth change-over. A Macmillan succeeds an Eden, a Diefenbaker follows a St. Laurent. Policies may change; so too may the character and effectiveness of leadership. But society as a whole continues essentially along the same path. In India, however, such continuity is far from certain. Nehru has been no ordinary Prime Minister. And India is in a stage of transition.

Some of Nehru's roles will pass with him. And the institutions he has created, the forces he has unleashed—what will happen to them?

Nehru himself *appears* to be indifferent to the succession problem. Thus, in reply to a question about the safeguards for the continuity of his basic policies he told the author:

It's difficult for me to answer except to say that the policies I have encouraged, advocated, sponsored, have not been just individual policies. There are many people, and important people . . . who believe in them. What is much more so is that they have, vaguely and broadly speaking, the backing of the masses in this country. And, as step by step we give effect to those policies, well, that is a step confirming a certain direction of growth. It is very difficult to go back from these things. . . . My chief business, in so far as the people are concerned, has been . . . to try to explain things to them in as simple a language as possible. . . . For the rest, well, really, *one does one's best and one doesn't worry too much about the future.*

It is difficult to believe that Nehru should be as unconcerned about the future as this comment suggests. Indeed, those who know him claim that he has many deep and anxious moments about the succession, not in the sense of who will become Prime Minister but what will be the fate of his policies. One can only speculate on his line of reasoning. The following may provide an explanation:

Nehru is genuinely concerned about the succession. The most logical method of ensuring continuity would be a moderately leftist Congress led by a group devoted to his policies. Either he is incapable of training such a group or he has tried and has failed. In any event, he may well have come to the conclusion that the Congress of the future will be a conservative force. There is ample evidence that most prominent Congressmen do not share his ideas and goals. They pay lip service to the 'socialist pattern of society', for example, because they know how strongly he feels about socialism and because it would be imprudent to show disloyalty. But in his absence there might well be a reorientation of policy. Nehru knows this, though it would be impolite to say so. There is, then, one feasible alternative to the conservative Congress leaders of the future. This is a compact with the Indian people at large, an appeal above the party to the masses, to compel his successors to follow the basic policies laid down by him, in their own self-interest, namely, the retention of power. Here lies the insurance of continuity, the general will, as directed and expressed by Nehru since 1947. Regardless of who assumes the Prime Ministership, the forces set in motion by Nehru and the ideas instilled in the people will act as a formidable restraint on his successors.

This hypothesis gains support from Nehru's continuous personal contact with the masses. On every possible occasion he stresses the essentials of his programme. Most important, Nehru himself told the author that he considers the masses the key to the succession: 'All this trains, educates people, makes them think in a particular way and drives all of them forward in a particular direction. Now, some of them [successors] may stop the pace, not going in that direction, or they may make it faster. *But I don't think it is possible in the future for the mass of the people to be taken away, far away, from their moorings.*'

If this is Nehru's approach to the succession it is a gamble fraught with grave possibilities. Nehru's compact with the masses may be creating demands and expectations which no democratic party will be able to satisfy in the future, thus paving the way for some kind of authoritarianism, either Communism or a form of Hindu Fascism. Moreover, the masses may provide insurance for continuity but they are no substitute for positive leadership by a group devoted to his ideals and goals.

The question of *who* will succeed Nehru is less important than *what* will follow his death. (Even if he relinquishes the Prime Ministership he will remain the dominant figure in Indian politics.) Furthermore, any speculation depends on *when* the change-over takes place. As of 1958 (and 1960), the line of succession within the Congress High Command is clear. First in order is Pandit Govind Ballabh Pant, the seventy-one-year-old able Minister of Home Affairs and Deputy Leader of the Congress Parliamentary Party. A long-time Chief Minister of the United Provinces, the most populous State of the Union, Pant is considerably to the Right of Nehru on economic and social matters. In foreign affairs he is more inclined to the West—though a believer in non-alignment as best suited to India's position in the world.

Second to Pant is Morarji Desai, the sixty-two-year-old former Chief Minister of Bombay who came to the Centre at the end of 1956. Partly because of Pant's advanced age, Desai is the leading contender for the succession. But there are other qualities that endear him to the Congress, especially to the Right wing and the traditionalists. Like his hero, Sardar Patel, he is considered an able administrator. His integrity is above reproach. He is firm in action. In outlook he is more conservative than Pant and much more rigid. A fanatic on prohibition, he more than anyone else has been responsible for its retention—in the face of a large economic burden. A staunch defender of private enterprise, he is also the most orthodox in social outlook among senior leaders of the party. He makes no secret of his pro-Western views, though it is doubtful that he would abandon non-alignment in principle. An ascetic, he is devoid of that magnetism which lies at the root of Nehru's power. Few people are enthusiastic about Desai, but many respect him. He is the unquestioned choice of the Right wing in the Congress and the business community, two important levers of power.

Nehru is very fit, however, and may well outlive both Pant and Desai—or the Congress may be defeated at the polls. Should Nehru remain active for another decade the question of succession assumes a different perspective. It is impossible to foresee who will emerge from obscurity. One person who stands in the wings of the party is Lal Bahadur Shastri who ranks fourth in the hierarchy, immediately after Desai. Highly respected for his administrative ability, a middle-of-the-roader ideologically, a native of the all-important United Provinces, like Nehru and Pant, and young compared to other senior leaders—he was born in 1904—he has a growing following among the rank and file.

Krishna Menon has little strength in the party as of 1958 (and much less in 1960). It is difficult to conceive of Menon being acceptable to powerful conservative leaders. He might be retained because of his skill in international affairs, but his political influence rests almost entirely on his personal friendship with Nehru. In the long-run, however, he looms as a possible successor because of his growing links with the armed forces and his strength on the far Left.

Among the non-Congress democratic leaders two persons stand out. The first is Jaya Prakash Narayan, 'J.P.', founder of the Congress Socialists in the early 'thirties and leader of the Socialist Party (later the Praja-Socialist Party) until his formal withdrawal from politics in 1956. Even before that year he had become the right-hand man of Vinoba Bhave in the *Bhoodan* (land gift) movement. Narayan is the only political figure other than Nehru who commands the affection of the Indian masses, and his reputation for devoted service to the cause of independence is second to none. Until the early 1950's he was considered by many to be Nehru's heir, even though he was no longer in the Congress. He is, perhaps, the only person in this select group who is ideologically akin to Nehru, though he has recently espoused more Gandhian ideas about how to solve India's problems. The fact that he has retired from formal politics does not exclude him from the succession. On the contrary, Narayan has followed the time-honoured Indian path of renunciation and is strengthening his attachment to the peasantry. As Vinoba Bhave's stature grows so too does his. Vinoba himself is inconceivable as Prime Minister, but a combination of Narayan and Bhave, like Nehru and Gandhi, heading a mass movement—such an eventuality cannot be ruled out.

A possible alternative to all of these is C. D. Deshmukh, Finance Minister from 1950 to 1956. His gravest liability is that he was not associated with the Congress during the struggle for independence. However, he is admired by the business community; is the acknowledged dean of India's civil servants; is respected by the Congress Centre and Left; and was somewhat of a hero in his native Maharashtra because of his struggle over Bombay City. After leaving the Govermnent he became Chairman of the Universities Grants Commission. But he is, at sixty-two, still young enough to have a future in Indian politics.

Whoever succeeds to the Prime Ministership, no one can succeed to Nehru's position in modern India. He has towered over his colleagues and the nation at large as no one can in the foreseeable future. He is, uniquely, the leader of the transition period. His successors will have to be men of a different stamp and stature. Where Nehru has inaugurated certain ventures, they will have to consolidate and expand them. While Nehru has stifled initiative they will have to foster it. While Nehru has ruled by force of personality, they will rule by more traditional political practices. The age of the heroic leader will give way to a period in which the administrator will govern.

What does the future hold for India's governing party? On the surface, disintegration seems possible, for Nehru has been its unifier. But his absence does not assure its doom. One must distinguish between the Congress at the Centre and in the States. The State branches are the core of the party and they are not likely to disintegrate after Nehru. The machine which Gandhi built and Patel consolidated has deep roots in the countryside and in certain cities. Moreover, the party will be able to capitalize on Nehru's lengthy leadership for some years. Nor need the struggle for the succession destroy the party as an effective political force. Greater decentralization seems inevitable, but the Congress

leaders are flexible. In the interests of power adjustment of conflicting views is likely, at least in the short-run. The real struggle
within the party will be between the (minority) Nehruite Left
wing and the more orthodox, more traditionalist, more conservative group led by Pant and Desai. Total disintegration is possible,
but not probable. Rather, the Left wing may bolt the party and
join forces with the Praja-Socialists to form a stronger left-wing
democratic party. The remaining members of the Congress would
then refashion their policies along more conservative lines, not
breaking with Nehru's programme, but slowing down the process
of change.

Whether or not the Congress proceeds along these lines, one
thing is certain. The party in 1958 (and in 1960) is in the throes of
a severe crisis. It is likely to be returned to power at the 1962
elections, especially if Nehru remains active in public life. Even
then, its majority will almost certainly be reduced. After that one
can only surmise. But it would not be a surprise if the Congress is
removed from power within a decade.

What of the longer-term prospects for Indian politics after
Nehru? To take *national unity* first. Among the positive elements
are the following: geographic integration; a strong constitutional
bias in favour of centralization and overriding powers for the
Centre to deal with any serious threat of secession; a common way
of thought and behaviour for the vast majority of Indians
(Hinduism); the Plan, which creates a sense of national unity; the
continuing influence of Gandhi and Nehru; and the ideal of
nationalism which, having triumphed so recently, is not likely to
be discarded easily. There are, however, serious sources of concern: the mentality of casteism which leads to parochial loyalties;
communalism, particularly among Hindus, which has only
retreated in the face of Nehru's personal attack; a persistent pull
to regional cultures, which may be strengthened by the reorganization of States; the closely related fact of linguistic diversity, the
absence of a real national language and the continuing friction
arising from the attempts to impose Hindi on the country as a
whole; and the still-sharp division between village and urban
attitudes, ways of life and standards of living. Nehru's passing will
certainly put a serious strain on Indian unity; but on balance the
forces for unity seem sufficiently strong to prevent a reversion to
the chaos which preceded the British *Raj*. The fundamental source

of unity is not Nehru; it is the fabric of Hindu society and the stability of the peasantry. The consequences of the death of Gandhi and Patel were negligible in this regard. Of course, Nehru was present at the time. But the continuing factors for unity, along with Nehru's own legacy, would seem to outweigh the sources of disunity.

The future of *parliamentary government* in its present form is less certain. There are many favourable features: the constitutional provisions for a parliamentary system, periodic elections, an independent judiciary and the standard democratic freedoms; a working parliamentary system since Independence; two free general elections; the acceptance of defeat at the polls by the governing party (Kerala in 1957); the existence and unhindered operation of opposition political parties; the tradition of civilian control over the military services; and a decade's experience of a President who has not attempted to use his wide-ranging formal powers. Against these must be set the corruption in the Congress and the Administration; the tendency of the Executive to assert its power over the Judiciary; the frequency of constitutional amendment; the tradition of authoritarianism in Hindu society and the lengthy experience of the British *Raj*; powerful opposition to the parliamentary system as unsuited to India's traditions and needs, notably by Vinoba Bhave and Narayan; and the weakness of other democratic parties like the Praja-Socialists.

Perhaps the gravest concern is the reliance on one man during the formative period of the experiment in parliamentary government. Nehru has made a conscious effort to foster the idea and practice of parliamentary decision, and this has strengthened the institution. But he has a dual role. His pre-eminent position has delayed its acceptance by the population as a whole. The basic problem is to substitute loyalty to institutions for loyalty to a man. This must await Nehru's departure from the scene.

The ultimate test of democratic government is its capacity 'to deliver the goods'. Democracy is not yet sufficiently rooted in Indian soil to ensure its acceptance indefinitely. Widespread unemployment, particularly among young university graduates, does not augur well for the future. If democracy is unable to press forward more rapidly with Nehru's programme of reform, many will turn to other creeds which offer hope of more rapid and far-reaching improvement in their way of life. And as the English language declines in importance, the nourishment for a Western-type parliamentary system is sapped.

The prospects of *Communism* have been implied throughout this discussion. Since 1951 the Communist Party of India has made inroads into the electorate and by 1957 it had become the second-largest organized political force. The gap in votes and legislative seats between the Congress and the C.P.I. is still very large. But whereas the Congress is in decline, the Communists are devoted, well organized and imbued with a mission. They had a beach-head in Kerala for two years. They benefit from the growing discontent with the Congress, particularly because of the weakness of the Praja-Socialists. They are helped, too, by the friendship and economic aid of the Soviet Union. And more recently in 1958, they adopted the cloak of purely peaceful methods of attaining power by changing their constitution. Nevertheless, the road to Communism will not be easy in India. Non-Communist and anti-Communist forces are still powerful, as represented by the Congress and orthodox Hinduism. Communism's success will be in direct proportion to the Congress's failure to mend its ways and its inability to continue the revolution which Nehru has set in motion.

In the short-run the danger to constitutional democracy is more from the extreme Right than from the Left, some form of Hindu authoritarianism rather than Communism. The Congress will probably retain power for some time at least; and if conservative forces are in control, they will certainly slow down the process of social and economic change. They will probably not be able to freeze it entirely. But even slowing the process may strengthen the challenge from the Communists. Unless a non-Congress democratic party can take over after Nehru, a conservative Congress may drift or move deliberately to an authoritarian régime, with the backing of Hindu orthodoxy and possibly the armed forces. Such a course would be fatal for Indian democracy; henceforth, the contest for political power in India would be between a form of Hindu Fascism and Communism; and Communism, with its pledge to complete the revolution initiated by Nehru, would be the likely victor.

For all of these reasons the next decade is crucial to the future of India—and therefore of Asia as a whole. If Nehru remains at the helm of affairs and the Second and Third Five-Year Plans fulfil their goals, then India will have broken through the static barrier and will be on the way to realizing the pledge of a better life for its people. At the same time, democracy would have the necessary time to demonstrate its effectiveness as an instrument of reform, not only in India but throughout Asia. Thus Nehru's continued leadership is indispensable for some years to come, whether as Prime Minister or as elder statesman.

Some years ago, in a pensive moment about the future, Nehru proposed the following epitaph for himself: '. . . if any people choose to think of me then, I should like them to say: "This was a man who, with all his mind and heart, loved India and the Indian people. And they, in turn, were indulgent to him and gave him of their love most abundantly and extravagantly." '[1] They will indeed say this of Nehru. And much more. And it will be deserved.

[1] *The Statesman* (Calcutta), 21 January 1954.

INDEX